MW00827633

The Algebra of Revolution

"This is a lively, well-informed, and accessible work on Marxism, which always stays in touch with the historical and social conditions in which theory developed. Rees demonstrates that philosophical issues constantly arise in the revolutionary struggle. In a word, Rees vindicates dialectic as truly as the algebra of revolution."

Chris Arthur, author of *The Dialectic of Labour*

"John Rees has produced a challenging and readable account of the elusive concept of the dialectic. In so doing, he does much to illuminate both the Marxist tradition and the contradictions of contemporary capitalism."

David McLellan, author of *Karl Marx* and *The Young Hegelians and Karl Marx*

"*The Algebra of Revolution* offers a fresh and superbly clarifying account of the major developments in classical Marxism. It presents this account in terms that a wide range of readers will be able to understand – but with a depth of analysis and reference that will make the book indispensable for advanced students and scholars as well."

William Keach, Brown University

"John Rees's . . . *The Algebra of Revolution* is . . . an answer to a prayer. Written from the standpoint of Lukacs's 'Hegelian Marxism', it provides a clear and accessible account of the dialectic which succeeds in offering the reader an easy way into the subject and at the same time treats difficult and controversial issues with the depth and rigour they require."

Alex Callinicos, University of York, author of *The Revolutionary Ideas of Marx*

John Rees is the Editor of *International Socialism* and a leading member of the Socialist Workers Party. He is the author of *The ABC of Socialism* and *In Defence of October*.

The Algebra
of Revolution

The Dialectic and the
Classical Marxist Tradition

JOHN REES

London and New York

First published 1998
by Routledge
2 Park Square, Milton Park, Abingdon, Oxon, OX14 4RN

Transferred to Digital Printing 2005

Simultaneously published in the USA and Canada
by Routledge
270 Madison Ave, New York NY 10016

© 1998 John William Rees

All rights reserved. No part of this book may be reprinted or
reproduced or utilized in any form or by any electronic,
mechanical, or other means, now known or hereafter
invented, including photocopying and recording, or in any
information storage or retrieval system, without permission in
writing from the publishers.

British Library Cataloguing in Publication Data
A catalogue record for this book is available from the British Library

Library of Congress Cataloguing in Publication Data
Rees, John. 1957–
The algebra of revolution: the dialectic and the classical
Marxist tradition / John Rees.
p. cm. – (Revolutionary studies)
Includes bibliographical references and index.
1. Dialectical materialism – History. 2. Dialectic – History.
I. Title. II. Series.
B809.8.R39 1998
335.4′1–dc21 97–24653

ISBN 0–415–19876–3 (hbk)
ISBN 0–415–19877–1 (pbk)

Contents

Acknowledgments

This introduction to the marxist dialectic has been a long time in the making. The chapters on Hegel and Trotsky are expanded and redrafted versions of articles that first appeared in *International Socialism*, issues 43 and 47, respectively. The debts that I have accumulated in the course of finishing the book are varied and numerous. Some years ago I was fortunate to be taught by a convinced Hegelian, Steve Bosworth. We did not agree, but, in the way of the dialectic, I learned a great deal. At Hull University, Bhikhu Parekh was a skilled interpreter of Marx's philosophy and considerate of the demands of political activism. The longest standing debt is to Maggie Backon who, from first germ to first draft, never failed to encourage the project's completion.

I am particularly thankful for the intellectual company and friendship of four people who commented on the finished draft: Alex Callinicos, Chris Harman, Tony Cliff, and John Molyneux. Gill Hubbard commented on the introduction and first chapter, and Jim Dixon provided vital technical assistence. I am grateful to them both. I owe my introduction to Paul Le Blanc at Humanities Press to my friends Ahmed Shawki and Sharon Smith. Paul Le Blanc was the editor for which every author wishes and without whom the book would be much poorer.

Judy Cox made it seem that I could do the impossible: write this book and edit *International Socialism* at the same time. It is only right to admit that this is an illusion sustained by her hard work.

Lindsey German read innumerable drafts and made many valuable criticisms, but that is only a small part of the great debt that I owe her. Finally, if the dialectic is understood in its original sense, as truth that emerges through discussion, then I learned it first from my parents. This book is, therefore, dedicated to Margaret Rees and to the memory of Edgar Rees.

Introduction:
Contradictions of
Contemporary Capitalism

The very possibility of human life is governed by contradictions. Consider this: In the last three decades, the average life span of a human being has lengthened by ten years or more. In the poorest parts of the world, it has grown from forty-eight years to sixty-three years. The causes are various, but any account would include the increased application of science to agriculture (the so-called green revolution), improvements in medical provision, and the consequent halving of the infant mortality rate. Progress, by any criterion.

But this is only half the story. Over a similar period, in the years *since* the Second World War, there have been 149 wars which have left more than 23 million dead—a population almost as large as Canada's today. On an average yearly basis, the numbers killed in wars during this period have been more than double the deaths in the nineteenth century and seven times greater than in the eighteenth century.[1] Were we to extend our survey to the entire twentieth century, and thus include two World Wars, our age would appear even more murderous. Regression, by any criterion. Yet it is the very same development of human productivity that gives rise both to the possibility of life and to its destruction.

The number of physicians in the world has grown from nearly 1.6 million in 1960 to nearly 5.7 million in 1990. A step forward certainly. But the numbers of the armed forces have grown from over 18 million to over 26 million in the same period. A step backward. In the same thirty years, education spending has grown worldwide from $486 to $1,048 per student. But military spending per soldier has risen from $18,140 to $26,536.[2] Just one item in that expenditure, the B2 Stealth bomber, costs $2.3 billion per plane, making it the most expensive combat plane in history. Each Stealth bomber is worth three times its own weight in gold.[3]

Everywhere we look another paradox appears. How can it be, for instance, that in the richest capitalist society in the world, the United States, real weekly incomes have fallen steadily since 1973?[4] One consequence is that the gap between the income of the wealthiest 20 percent and the poorest 20 percent is greater in the US than in Egypt, India, Argentina, and Indonesia.[5] How can it be that, in the same country, while the number of

1

people working in health care has doubled in the 1980s, the United States occupies last place among major industrialized countries in child mortality, life expectancy and visits to the doctor.[6] How is it that in Britain, where the economy, despite the ravages of recession, produces more than it has ever done, the British Society for the Advancement of Science can be told that a full quarter of the population live below the poverty line?[7]

The contradictions are no less striking if we shift our gaze from economics to politics. The introduction of the market into Russia and Eastern Europe was supposed to bring stability and prosperity but has actually produced the opposite. The end of the Cold War was supposed to usher in a peaceful New World Order. In fact, even if we exclude the Gulf War, the global number of conflicts rose to an all time record of twenty-nine major wars in 1992 with war deaths reaching a seventeen-year high.[8] On the fiftieth anniversary of the Second World War, fascist organizations reached their post-war peak of influence in several European countries. Yet at the same time, when the working-class movement in the advanced industrialized countries was regularly described by journalists and academics alike as a spent force, there were mass strikes during the 1990s in, for instance, Italy, Spain, Greece, Canada, and France.

Faced with such contraries, it might seem obvious, at least to those on the left, that it is necessary to return to the one political and intellectual tradition that has specifically developed a method of analyzing such situations. The classical marxist tradition has, after all, always insisted that capitalism was a contradictory system and that huge advances in the forces of production coexisted with forms of property ownership which would frustrate their deployment and further development. And was it not Marx who insisted that the result of such conflicts would inevitably be chronic political instability? His most famous statement of the case argues:

> At a certain stage of their development the material productive forces of society come into conflict with the existing relations of production, or—what is but a legal expression for the same thing—the property relations within which they have been at work hitherto.
> From forms of the development of the productive forces, these relations turn into their fetters. Then begins an epoch of social revolution.[9]

One does not have to be a particularly acute observer of social change to see this process at work in the modern world—in the collapse of the state capitalist economies, often at the hands of popular movements, in Eastern Europe and Russia, in the worldwide crisis of capitalist growth now in its third decade, in the explosive relations between international production and nation states, in the end and aftermath of South African apartheid, and in the developing crisis in China, among others.

Yet the dialectical method of which this kind of analysis is a fruit, and the classical marxist tradition that has nurtured it, have rarely been as unfashionable among the left-wing intelligensia as they are today. It is this dislocation between a world that cries out for dialectical analysis and the current paucity of theoretical response that provides the motivation for this book. It only remains to give a brief summary outline of the main elements of which the dialectic is composed, the full description of which is the subject of the rest of this book.

WHAT IS THE DIALECTIC?

The rise of capitalist society, from its beginnings in the sixteenth century, brought with it a division of labor that made the isolated individual appear to be the basic unit from which society was constructed. Wage workers took their chance on the labor market—the individual, in competition with other individuals, for an individual employer. Wages had to be spent in other markets where workers, as individual consumers, bought from individual sellers. Much later the political norm of capitalist society, even now honored more in the breach than the observance, became the individual secret ballot. Art, at first for a tiny elite and later more generally (although far from universally), came to reflect not, as previously, the collective experience of religious worship but the individual's desires—for love, sexual satisfaction, wealth, position, happiness. In short, for individual fulfillment, however measured. Many forms of art came to favor private consumption over public experience. Printing brought, first, individual Bible study, and, second, the novel in place of the public sermon; television predominates over cinema and theater; the CD or tape over the public performance. More importantly, access to art, whether privately or publically consumed, could only be gained by individual acts of purchase.

This compartmentalization of experience is even more extreme today than it was in earlier phases of capitalist development, both as social fact and as ideology. In the main, schools and universities still insist that arts and sciences be studied in isolation, that language and history, engineering and sociology, poetry and business studies are separate disciplines.

In newspapers and news bulletins, for instance, it is so routine as to pass without comment that the unemployment rate and the suicide statistics are "different stories." The poverty level is reported on page 4, the crime rate on page 6. Art criticism is in the arts supplement, art auctions on the business pages; films are reviewed on the arts programs, and studio mergers are reported on the financial news.

At a more abstract level, this understanding of the world has been developed into various scientific approaches known as empiricism, positivism,[10] or formal logic. These approaches stress that the facts of a situation are pretty much as they appear when we first observe them; that the compartments in which we find such facts are the inevitable and unalterable properties of the things themselves, not the product of historical development imposed on the world by our way of understanding it; that connections between these facts are less important than each fact taken in isolation; and that this complex of facts is more or less stable, or, if it develops, it does so in in an orderly manner entirely explicable in straightforward cause and effect terms.

Biologists Richard Levins and Richard Lewontin describe this method as Cartesian reductionism, after the philosopher Rene Descartes (1596–1650). They list four properties that define this approach:

1. There is a natural set of units or parts of which any whole system is made.

2. These units are homogenous within themselves. . . .

3. . . . the parts exist in isolation and come together to make wholes. The parts have intrinsic properties, which they possess in isolation and which they lend to the whole. . . .

4. Causes are separate from effects, causes being properties of subjects, and effects the properties of objects. While causes may respond to information coming from effects (so-called "feedback loops"), there is no ambiguity about which is causing subject and which is caused object.[11]

When this approach fails to account adequately for a truculently contradictory reality, there are two strategies that are frequently adopted by mainstream thinkers. One, rationalism, simply tries to reconstruct reality by insisting that only those aspects of the world which conform to preconceived canons of reason have any true substance; the rest is insubstantial illusion bound to be condemned to oblivion as rationality gains ground against error and superstition. The second, mysticism, simply abandons the struggle to understand the contradictions with which it is faced and retreats into supernatural speculation.

Moreover, because these approaches—positivism, rationalism, and mysticism—are all partial, one-sided methods of looking at the world, the failure of each often engenders the rise of the others, sometimes in rival schools, sometimes as unintegrated aspects of a single system. These were called the 'antinomies of bourgeois thought' by George Lukacs and the best critique of them appears in his *History and Class Consciousness*, discussed in chapter 5.

The modern dialectic arose as a response to these contradictions and the society from which they arose. These developments are sketched in chapter 1. That such a critique is still necessary can easily be seen in the frequency with which some or all of these claims are advanced by, particularly, analytical marxists, and, despite their pretentions to reject "Enlightenment rationality," postmodernists for whom rigid compartmentalization of image and reality is the starting point of deliberation. These issues are elaborated in the concluding chapter of this book.

The dialectical critique of this method involves, first and foremost, three principles: totality, change, and contradiction. Taken separately these principles *do not* constitute a dialectical approach. Only when they are taken together do they become dialectical. Nevertheless, we must examine, each in turn.

Totality refers to the insistence that the various seemingly separate elements of which the world is composed are in fact related to one another. Production is really a *collective* act—not merely the result of individual effort. The market is a *social* institution, not the natural result of individual behavior. Poverty and crime, unemployment and suicide, art and business, language and history, engineering and sociology cannot be understood in isolation, but only as part of a totality.

Moreover, when we bring these terms into relation with each other, their meaning is transformed. Once we understand the relationship between poverty and crime, it is impossible to look on either the criminal justice system or those who live in poverty as we did when they were taken to inhabit two separate realms. In empiricist systems, the part is seen as a pre-existing unit which, at best, collides with others. Thus they may effect each others' trajectory but not their fundamental nature. In a dialectical system, the entire nature of the part is determined by its relationships with the other parts and so with the whole. The part makes the whole, and the whole makes the parts.

In this analysis, it is not just the case that the whole is more than the sum of the parts but also that the parts become more than they are individually by being part of a whole:

> The fact is that the parts have properties that are characteristic of them only as they are parts of wholes; the properties come into existence in the interactions that makes the whole. A person cannot fly by flapping her arms, no matter how much she tries, nor can a groups of people fly by all flapping their arms simultaneously. But people do fly, as a consequence of the social organization that has created airplanes, pilots and fuel. It is not that society flies, however, but individuals in society, who have acquired a property they do not have outside society. The limitations of individual physical beings are negated by social interactions. The whole, thus, is not simply the object of interaction of the parts but is the subject of action on the parts.[12]

One important point to note about this approach is that it is, by its very nature, opposed to reductionism. It does not abolish the role of the individual in favor of the whole, the collective, or any other such abstraction. Neither does it abolish any notion of society by reducing it to the simple sum of the individual atoms said to constitute its basic units, as in establishment economics and analytical marxism. A dialectical approach shows the one-sided and partial nature of both approaches and replaces them with specific and concrete description of how the interaction of the two gives rise to a qualitatively new situation, both for the totality and for the parts of which it is composed.

Totality alone is not, however, a sufficient definition of the dialectic. Many undialectical views of society make use of the idea of totality. The Catholic Church has its own mystical view of the all-embracing nature of God's creation and a very practical view of the temporal hierarchy that goes with it. "The Taoist tradition in China shares with dialectics the emphasis on wholeness, the whole being maintained by the balance of opposites such as yin and yang."[13] Even the commonsense understanding of human nature sees all human life as shaped by a small number of general, underlying properties that manifest themselves in otherwise different individuals and in the most varied of circumstances.

What unites all these explanations is that they see the totality as static. Beneath all the superficial bustle of the world lies an enduring, eternal truth: the unchanging face of God, the ceaseless search for the balance between yin and yang, or the timeless shapes, for good or ill, of human values. What they all lack is any notion of a totality as a process of change. And even where such systems grant the possibility of instability and change, it is considered merely as the prelude to a restored equilibrium. Free market economics work on precisely these principles—supply and demand will naturally balance if left to its own devices (i.e., without interference from governments or trade unions). Instability will quickly be replaced by equilibrium, crises with stability, when such "obstacles" are removed.

Change, development, instability, on the other hand, are the very conditions for which a dialectical approach is designed to account. The "great merit" of the Hegelian system, wrote Engels, is that:

> For the first time the whole world, natural, historical, intellectual, is represented as a process, i.e., as in constant motion, change, transformation, development; and the attempt is made to trace out the internal connection that makes a continuous whole of all this movement and development. From this point of view the history of mankind no longer appeared as a wild whirl of senseless deeds of violence, all equally condemnable at the judgement seat of mature philosophic reason and which are best forgotten as quickly as possible, but as the process of evolution of man himself.[14]

But, even taken together, change and totality are not sufficient to define a dialectical system. In addition we have to provide some general indication of *how* such change originates. Most theories refer to a simple chain of cause and effect when they want to explain change. It is still common, for instance, to find accounts of the period between the wars that take the following form: the Second World War was caused by the crisis of the international system and the rise of the nazis in the 1930s. The rise of the Nazis was a result of the collapse of the Weimar Republic; the collapse of the Weimar Republic was a result of the Versailles settlement; the Versailles settlement was the result of the outcome of the First World War, and so on. This approach has even found a finished formulation in the historian A. L. Rowse's dictum that "in history, chronology is everything." Yet it should be obvious that, however sophisticated and detailed the account of the chain of events, we have here mere *description*, not *explanation*; the what, but not the how or the why.

Hegel described this kind of account as "bad infinity," because it postulates an endless series of causes and effects regressing to "who knows where?" The defect of all such approaches is that they leave the ultimate cause of events outside the events they describe. The cause is external to the system. A dialectical approach seeks to find the cause of change within the system. And if the explanation of change lies within the system, it cannot be conceived on the model of linear cause and effect, because this will simply reproduce the problem we are trying to solve. If change is internally generated, it must be a result of contradiction, of instability and development as inherent properties of the system itself.

Contradiction is, therefore, the *form* of the explanation of how one type of class society succeeds another, of how the conflict between the classes that compose the system leads to the negation of the system itself and the emergence of a new society. It is only the *form* of an explanation, because the explanation itself will depend on the concrete, empirical conditions that obtain in each society. The exact contradictions and the working out of those contradictions will vary accordingly.

This then is the general form of the dialectic: it is an internally contradictory totality in a constant process of change. The principle of contradiction is a barrier to reductionism, where linear notions of causality are not, because two elements that are in contradiction cannot be dissolved into one another but only overcome by the creation of a synthesis that is not reducible to either of its constituent elements.

Furthermore, a dialectical approach is radically opposed to any form of reductionism because it presupposes the parts and the whole are not reducible to each other. The parts and the whole mutually condition, or *mediate*, each other. And a mediated totality cannot form part of a reductionist philosophy because, by definition, reductionism collapses one element of a totality into another without taking account of its specific characteristics.

These terms—totality, change, contradiction and mediation—are the key terms of the dialectic. They are, in the marxist tradition, not simply intellectual tools but real material processes and so this is a *materialist* dialectic. The full extent to which Marx and Engels transformed the dialectic when they rooted it in natural and social development has often been underestimated, as chapters 1 and 2 make clear.

One consequence is that some adherents of "Hegelian" marxism reproduce Hegel's errors within their own theoretical framework. These "false friends" of the Hegelian dialectic fall into two broad camps which, for want of better terms, I call "right Hegelians" and "left Hegelians." The right Hegelian interpretation leans toward the deterministic and fatalistic aspect of Hegels's system: the dominant aspects of Plekhanov's Marxism came from this mold, as chapter 3 demonstrates. So did the Deborinite trend in Russia in the 1920s, discussed in chapter 4. Although it casts its formulations in dialectical language and although it is formally ranged against deterministic theories, this approach ends in reproducing all the problems of reductionism.

The left Hegelian approach seeks to hold fast to the critical, dynamic aspect of Hegels's system but fails to understand fully how such concepts are transformed in a materialist dialectic. Often such formulations remain, at best, abstract and, at worst, reproduce Hegel's idealism. The original Young Hegelians, discussed in chapter 2, and much of "Western critical theory," for instance, the work of Adorno and Benjamin, suffered this weakness. But so, too, despite much else that is valuable in their work, do some Marxist commentators: some of the work of Trotsky's former secretary Raya Dunayevskaya and of C. L. R. James is a case in point.

In both the right and left Hegelian cases, the crucial missing element is often a close involvement with, or theoretical understanding of, the centrality of working class self-activity to the marxist dialectic.[15] It is an appreciation of this question that leads toward the concrete, materialist application of the dialectic. Its underestimation, on the other hand, leads both to determinism and to abstraction.

Nowhere is this concrete application of the dialectic more necessary than in the one further aspect of the marxist method that needs to be addressed here: the so-called "three laws of the dialectic."

The "three laws" are: the unity of opposites, the transformation of quantity and into quality, and the negation of the negation. These are useful reminders of forms in which dialectical contradictions sometimes work themselves out. But, before we briefly go on to expound their meaning, a word of warning is necessary. The three laws are not, even in Hegel, the *only* way in which dialectical development can take place. They cannot be understood without the broader definition of the dialectic discussed above. They are not, as Marx and Engels were quick to insist, a substitute for the difficult, empirical task of tracing the development of real contradictions, not a suprahistorical master key whose only advantage is to turn up when no real historical knowledge is available. But, treated carefully, they are useful developments in dialectical understanding.

The unity of opposites is simply a way of describing contradiction. In Levins's and Lewontin's example, cited above, individual and society, the parts and the whole, are examined as a unity of opposites. The most obvious example from Marx is the relationship between capitalists and workers. They are, by definition, the opposite poles of one capitalist system—those who own and control the means of production and those who do not and are therefore obliged to work for a wage. The one could not exist without the other. The conflict between them is the internal contradiction that animates capitalist society.

The transformation of quantity into quality refers to the process by which gradual changes in the balance between opposed elements suddenly results in a rapid and complete change in the nature of the situation. Hegel used the example of a man who successively plucks single hairs from his head. At first no qualitative change takes place. But eventually the man becomes bald— quantative change has resulted in a qualitative change in his condition. Marx made the point that if workers in one workplace strike against their employer for a reduction in the working day, the strike has the quality of an economic dispute. If more workplaces join the strike, if it becomes a general strike, if the workers demand a change in the law governing the length of the working day, then a qualitatively different movement, a political movement, has arisen.

The negation of the negation points our attention to the way in which new and distinct situations arise from contradictory circumstances in such a way that aspects of the old circumstances appear, transformed, as part of the new conditions. It is an essential reminder that the future will always contain elements from the past, but only in ways quite distinct from their previous form. From a revolutionary conflict between workers and capitalists, Marx explains in *Capital*, we do not expect a simple reversion to precapitalist forms of society. We expect that a new form of society, quite different both to the society that preceded it and to the two classes that currently compose it, will emerge from the conflict. The new society, socialism, will result from the productive forces developed under capitalism and the class struggle waged by the classes that constitute capitalism—but socialism will be a qualitatively distinct society that further develops these forces on the basis of abolishing classes altogether. The negation of the negation refers to the process whereby existing conditions are both preserved in, and completely transformed by, the changes that result from their own internal contradictions.

Marx's theory of alienation is an equally important part of the dialectic, although it is not always seen in this context. Alienation is fundamental to the marxist dialectic because it involves an account of how a subject arises that is able to resolve consciously the contradictions thrown up by social development. As part of this account, the theory of alienation explains why in both science and working-class consciousness the world appears different from its real structure. The theory goes on to explain how and under what circumstances it is possible to move from the surface appearance of society to an appreciation of its underlying nature. Alienation is therefore bound to Marx's dialectic of subject and object and to his dialectic of essence and appearance. These themes are elaborated throughout the book, especially in chapters 2 and 5.

It only remains to conclude with this point: the dialectic operates blindly, beyond the understanding or control of human beings, so long as no class is able to become conscious of the nature of society and to exercise enough power to overcome the destructive contradictions encrypted in the capitalist system. Marx and Engels transformed the Hegelian dialectic at precisely the same time that they identified the working class as the force able to emancipate itself, and the rest of society, because it occupied just such a position. The materialist dialectic *is* Marx's theory of proletarian revolution.

Notes

1. R. Leger Sivard, *World Military and Social Expenditures 1993* (Washington: World Priorities, 1993). 42 and 20.
2. At the 1987 U.S. dollar rate. See ibid., 42.
3. Ibid., 56.
4. P Kennedy, *Preparing for the Twenty-first Century* (London: Harper Collins, 1993), 294. See also S. Smith, "Twilight of the American Dream," in *International Socialism* 54 (London, 1992), 15–17.
5. See P Rogers, and M. Dando, *A Violent Peace, Global Security after the Cold War* (London: Brasseys, 1992), 138. The figures are as follows: in the United States, the richest fifth have 59 percent of total income, the poorest fifth have 5 percent. In Egypt, the figures are 48 percent and 6 percent, respectively; in India, 50 and 7 percent; in Argentina, 50 and 4 percent; and in Indonesia, 50 and 7 percent.
6. See P. Kennedy, *Preparing for the Twenty-first Century*, 303.
7. In a report from Dr. Jane Millar of Bath University, based on government statistics. The poverty line for a single person was set at 59 pounds a week, at 1993 prices, after housing costs. For a couple with two children under the age of eleven, the figure was 148 pounds a week. Dr. Millar reported: "The figures are startling. In 1979, fewer than 1 in 10 people were estimated to be in pov-

erty. By 1990–91, the figure stood at 24 percent, one quarter of the population." See *The Independent*, 1 September 1993. Naturally, if we were to exclude the middle and upper classes from the sample and take the percentage from among those who are actually likely to experience poverty, the working class, the figure would be considerably higher than 25 percent.

8. R. Leger Sivard, *World Military and Social Expenditures 1993*, 20.

9. K. Marx, *Preface to a Contribution to the Critique of Political Economy*, (Peking: Foreign Languages Press, 1976), 3.

10. Positivism denotes "the rejection of value judgements in social science" and the belief that science should be "concerned . . . only with observable facts and relationships." I. McLean, *Oxford Concise Dictionary of Politics* (Oxford: Oxford University Press, 1996).

11. R. Levins, and R Lewontin, *The Dialectical Biologist* (Cambridge, MA: Harvard, 1985), 269.

12. Ibid., 273.

13. Ibid., 275.

14. F. Engels, *Socialism Utopian and Scientific*, in Marx and Engels, *Selected Works*, Vol. III (Moscow: Progress, 1970), 130.

15. In Dunayevskaya and James's cases, the appreciation of the self-activity of the working class is present, but in an idealized and abstract form, not in the concrete and historically specific form in which it always appears in the work of Lenin and Trotsky. This allows them to map the categories of Hegel's philosophy directly onto the history of capitalism in an unmediated and abstract manner. The combined effect is that the working class appears as the realization of the dialectic and the totality of society is never analyzed concretely enough to reveal its specific contradictions. Thus, despite its authors' best intentions, theory is no longer a guide to action.

1

Hegel's Algebra of Revolution

Hegel's name has often come to the lips of marxists during great crises in history or at crucial turning points in the development of marxism. When Marx and Engels first laid the foundations of historical materialism in the 1840s, they did so by developing a critique of Hegel's thought. As Marx labored on *Capital*, he found Hegel's *Logic* "of great service to me."[1]

When confronted with an unprecedented imperialist war and the collapse of the Second International, Lenin looked to Hegel to help refurbish his understanding of marxism. He concluded: "It is impossible completely to understand Marx's *Capital* . . . without having thoroughly studied and understood the *whole* of Hegel's *Logic*. Consequently, half a century later none of the Marxists understood Marx!!"[2]

Again, in the great revolutionary crisis that shook Europe between 1919 and 1923, George Lukacs made his way to marxism through a study of Hegel. The result, *History and Class Consciousness,* was the greatest work of Marxist philosophy since Marx himself. Between the invasion of Hungary in 1956 and the events of 1968, the Stalinist monolith began to crack, and a new generation of activists looked for the authentic voice of revolutionary marxism. They looked to the works in which the young Marx had engaged with Hegelianism, and they looked to the work of George Lukacs.

By contrast, Hegel's name has been missing from those periods when the fortunes of a genuine revolutionary marxism have been in decline. During the long night that stretched from the defeat of the 1848 revolutions to the Paris Commune, Marx himself noted how "ill humoured, arrogant and mediocre epigones . . . began to take pleasure in treating Hegel . . . as a 'dead dog.'"[3] Similarly, as the Second International slid into bureaucratic reformist practice and a vulgar materialist theory, it had little time for Hegel. Even where it mentioned Hegel, it focused on the dead formalism of his system, not the living dialectic at its core. Plekhanov was one of the best theoreticians of the Second International, yet Lenin noted, albeit with slight exaggeration, "Dialectics is the theory of knowledge of [Hegel and] Marxism . . . to which Plekhanov, not to speak of other Marxists, paid no attention."[4] When the revolutionary storms of the 1920s had passed and Stalinism's dead hand lay

13

over the movement, a similar deliberate neglect set in. Stalin's economic reductionism deliberately removed the negation of the negation from theory— and with it went any notion of how a radical break with the present can emerge from current conditions.

Hegel's philosophy has had such resonance in periods of crisis and revolution precisely because it was born of one such crisis—the French revolution. Hidden in its core is the last great attempt by a bourgeois philosopher to understand the dynamics of social change and social revolution. Hegel lived through the revolution and into the era of reaction that followed. He saw the death of the old society and looked fearfully at the shape of the new. This unique vantage point gave his philosophy the enduring value that Marx and Engels, Luxemburg, Lenin, Lukacs, and Trotsky all recognized. Marx and Engels founded historical materialism in opposition to Hegel's philosophy, but they never ceased to pay tribute to "the colossal old chap." Likewise, in renewing the marxist critique of Hegel, we must also avow ourselves the pupils of that mighty thinker.[5]

THE ENLIGHTENMENT

Before we can understand Hegel, we must understand his world. Hegel was deeply imbued with the values of the Enlightenment, the intellectual tradition of his times. He was one of its last great inheritors and, until Marx, its greatest critic. The Enlightenment was a broad intellectual movement that championed religious toleration against the tyranny of church and state, science against mysticism, education against ignorance, and favored humanism over superstition.

The origins of the Enlightenment lie in the scientific revolution of the seventeenth century, which, in turn, resulted from the growth, particularly in England, of trade and craft manufacture, accelerated by technological improvements in surveying, navigation, metallurgy, and dyestuffs. The increasing use of the compass in the West had already fostered exploration and trade. The development of the cannon promoted the study of ballistics and metallurgy. The earlier invention of printing allowed these new discoveries wider dissemination. This revolution in science both contributed to the intellectual environment that accompanied the English Revolution and received new impulse from the battles of the revolution and the settlement that followed. Such an atmosphere encouraged the empirical study of nature and the search for causal laws, rather than blind obedience to the dictates of the church.

We can usefully examine the intellectual and social background to Hegel's philosophy and the changes in the intellectual atmosphere that took place during the Enlightenment itself by briefly examining the work of some of the great scientific and philosophical figures of the epoch. The achievements of Francis Bacon (1561–1627), Isaac Newton (1642–1727), John Locke (1632–1704), David Hume (1711–76) and Jean-Jacques Rousseau (1712–78) will serve to give an impression of the age.

The work of Francis Bacon, lord chancellor under James I, was largely ignored by his own generation, but it became important for the civil war generation that followed him. His biography of Henry VII insisted on a causal explanation of history rather than a divine one. He claimed, "Men have been kept back . . . from progress in the sciences by reverence for antiquity, by the authority of men accounted great in philosophy, and then by general consent." His call for a new science was based on the belief that traditional learning, tied to Christian theology and the writings of the ancient Greeks, was "a wicked effort to curtail human power over nature and to produce a deliberate artificial despair. This despair . . . confounds the promptings of hope, cuts the springs and sinews of industry, and makes men unwilling to put anything to the hazard of trial."[6] This faith in human reason, scientific experiment, and progress made Bacon a true precursor of the Enlightenment.

Isaac Newton's theory of gravity was the high point of the scientific revolution. It bound together all movement of matter in the heavens and on the earth in one single mathematical law. It provided startling proof of Bacon's faith that human reason could, by careful observation and experiment, explain the workings of the natural world. Newton's own ideas, inevitably, were a mixture of the old world and the new. He believed in alchemy and insisted that although the universe operated according to mechanical laws, like the workings of a clock, God must first have set the clock running.[7] Newton's universe retained a role for God, but later Newtonians drew the logical conclusion and banished God to some distant original cause. In the here and now science triumphed. Pope caught the impact graphically:

> Nature and Nature's laws lay hid in night,
> God said "Let Newton be!" and all was light.

Newton's *Principia* was greeted by his colleague Halley with an ode that concluded:

> In reason's light, the clouds of ignorance
> Dispelled at last by science.[8]

These social, technical, and intellectual developments resulted in one very important philosophical foundation of the Enlightenment: mechanical materialism. Thomas Hobbes (1588–1679) was one of the most radical of the materialists. He saw society as an unremitting "war of all against all" in which self-preservation was the only guiding thread, the basis of ethics. In this picture, religion was mostly eliminated. This dark view found little echo in the first, more optimistic phase of the Enlightenment. It wasn't until the mood began to change in the latter half of the eighteenth century that Hobbes's influence began to grow.

In the meantime, it was John Locke who stood at the nexus of some key political and intellectual developments. He was involved in the Glorious Revolution of 1688 which, in overthrowing James II, finally ended claims for the Divine Right of Kings in England. His *Treatise on Civil Government* (1690) was a theoretical justification of the bourgeois settlement of 1688, arguing that the monarchy was simply a limited and revocable contract between ruler and ruled in which authority finally rested with "the will and determination of the majority." Marx summarized the conditions that gave Hobbes and Locke such an unparalleled intellectual sweep:

> Hobbes and Locke had before their eyes both the earlier development of the Dutch bourgeoisie (both of them had lived for some time in Holland) and the first political actions by which the English bourgeoisie emerged from local and provincial limitations, as well as the comparatively highly developed stage of manufacture, overseas trade and colonisation. This particularly applies to Locke, who wrote during the first period of English economy, the Bank of England and England's mastery of the seas. In their case, and particularly in that of Locke, the theory of exploitation was still directly connected with economic content.[9]

Locke's major philosophical work, the *Essay Concerning Human Understanding*, extended what he took to be the empirical method of the scientific revolution into the realm of human affairs. Locke's friendship with both Isaac Newton and the chemist Robert Boyle was based in part on a common, empirical, observational approach to science.

Locke rejected the idea, advanced by Descartes, that ideas were innate. Locke argued that our mind at birth is a "white paper" and that all our ideas are derived from experience. Our more complex ideas may be the result of reflection on the images that we gain from experience, but, nevertheless, all the raw material for knowledge is gained from the senses. Locke thus tied together an empirical approach to the origins of knowledge with a crucial role for human reasoning. Real knowledge is a product of reason working out the connections between the varied ideas we receive from experience.

In some cases, Locke believed, knowledge arose from comparing our ideas with the real things that they were meant to represent. The closer the correspondence, the nearer we were to the truth. This is the most empirical aspect of this thought.

But there are other ideas, according to Locke, whose truth depended solely on their internal consistency. Here reason was its own judge and did not depend on experience. Geometry, for instance, was a rational construction whose laws (for instance, that every equilateral triangle has three sides of equal length) were not given to us by experience. Morality was, likewise, not innate, nor given to us by experience, but the product of rational deliberation.

Locke, like Newton, kept within a Christian frame of reference, but the impact of his ideas led to secular, rationalist, and materialist social attitudes which underpinned much Enlightenment thought. Locke's argument against innate ideas, for instance, was taken as a blow against religion.

More generally, materialist arguments could be used to defend toleration of different beliefs, because these were the product of differing environments, not of heresy or demonic possession. The equality of man was at least a possibility, because social inequality was the product of environment, not of heredity and lineage. Rationality, education, and social reform were the key to progress. The stage was set for the spread of such ideas throughout Europe, for Diderot, Voltaire, and Rousseau.

During the eighteenth century such ideas came to dominate the thinking of many Europeans—at least those who had the time, leisure, and ability to read. If one project can summarize such a long and complex movement, it must be the *Encyclopedia*. This was the great collaborative dictionary compiled under the eye of Diderot to which nearly every major French thinker, including Voltaire, Montesquieu, and Rousseau, contributed. Charged with the belief that society should be organized along lines dictated by human reason, instead of the hierarchy of caste and privilege that marked aristocratic absolutism, the *Encyclopedia* set out to popularize the sum of human knowledge.

Such rationalist ideas invoked the authority not of God but of human reason verified by empirical science, even when the language in which they were expressed was designed to avoid the attention of the censor. Inevitably, they were a challenge to authority. As Diderot wrote elsewhere, using the form of a dialogue between father and son,

> "The point is, father, that in the last resort the wise man is subject to no law . . ."
> "Don't speak so loudly."
> "Since all laws are subject to exceptions, the wise man must judge for himself when to submit and when to free himself from them."
> "I should not be too worried if there were one or two people like you in town, but if they all thought that way I should go and live somewhere else."[10]

That such ideas could spread in Europe was proof that some of the same forces that had given them such a vigorous life in England were also at work in other countries. If we exclude England and certain Dutch cities, France was the most economically developed part of Europe. In the forty years before the revolution, the value of French trade quadrupled. France's cities were the largest on the continent. Factory-based production had small but impressive footholds.[11] Some provinces, encouraged by entrepreneurial aristocrats, the new school of Physiocrats (or economists), and the government's own Department of Agriculture (established in 1761) were also beginning to employ new scientific agricultural techniques.[12] The materialist ideas that were part of the intellectual armor of the rising bourgeoisie in England and that received their fullest expression after the old order had been broken by the revolution of the 1640s now took strongest root in France.

But it wasn't just emulation and common circumstances that encouraged the educated classes in France to adopt materialist ideas. England and France were not intellectual partners but commercial rivals. Where England led, others must follow. "Enlightened" monarchs throughout Europe were willing to promote mild reform, encourage their own bourgeoisie, and give cautious backing to the new science so long as the process did not go beyond their control. The French, and other monarchies, balanced between the old order, on which their whole political prestige depended, and the rising bourgeoisie, on which they increasingly depended financially. Such harmony could last only so long as the bourgeoisie could tolerate being the dominant force economically while also being the junior partner politically. As it grew in strength, the bourgeoisie became less tolerant, and the monarchy, encouraged by the most irreformable nobles, tried to halt the processes it had long half encouraged. George Rude summarizes this turning point:

> The great question was: should the way to reform be sought by enlarging the authority of an "enlightened" monarch at the expense of the estates; should aristocratic or other "intermediate bodies" be strengthened as a check to the power of the Crown; or should the power of both be balanced, or eclipsed, by vesting greater responsibility in the hands of the people themselves? . . . The answers given naturally varied from country to country and from class to class.[13]

Such developments gave the latter half of the eighteenth century a quite different tone. The harmony of the Enlightenment began to turn to discord. A more skeptical note began to sound, even in England. History might not inevitably be moving forward under the guidance of sweet reason. This note of skepticism sounds loudest in the work of the Scottish philosopher and historian David Hume, although it is perhaps significant that his *A Treatise of Human Nature* was written during the later half of the 1730s during his stay in the French town of La Fleche.

Hume was a far more radical empiricist than Locke. He saw the human mind divided between impressions ("sensations, passions and emotions") and ideas ("the faint images of these"). Complex ideas may be constructed out of simple ideas. These, however, can only be "copies of our impressions."

Hume was also certain that there was a far more limited field for the operation of human reason than Locke had allowed. He maintained, for instance, that reasoning by induction (i.e., the argument that because the sun has risen every morning it will do so again tomorrow morning) is not true knowledge but simply belief. It is insufficiently grounded in experience, because the mere fact that something has happened in the past is no guarantee that it will happen again in the future.

Hume does not deny that, in fact, one thing does follow another. Nor does he deny that this sequence gives us the impression, after repeatedly experiencing the same thing, that the first thing causes the second. But he says that "we are never able, in a single instance to discover . . . any necessary connection." We do not have a rational explanation, therefore, merely a belief based on "habit and custom."

Even more damning for the whole tradition represented by Newton and Locke was Hume's contention that our ideas represent, resemble, or are caused by external objects. This is a contention that we have no way of proving. We have no way of standing outside our perceptions, and so we are unable to carry out a comparison between them and the real object which they are supposed to represent. Hume drew back from the more extreme conclusions of his position—that all that exists are ephemeral images and ideas. But, though he asserted his belief in the exterior world, he admitted that he could not "pretend any arguments of philosophy to maintain its veracity."

Hume's skepticism was so all-embracing that, if accepted, the whole elaborated structure of the scientific revolution would dissolve into an unconnected welter of sense-impressions. Causal laws would be merely the result of habit and custom, and external reality itself would be merely a convenient fiction.

Hume was not the only one to assail the optimism of the early Enlightenment. Another sign of the change in the intellectual atmosphere was the dispute between Rousseau and Diderot. Rousseau had been one of the contributors to the *Encyclopedia*. In fact, he wrote so much that he recorded "I am worn out." Nevertheless, he persisted because "I want to get at the throats of people who have treated me badly, and bile gives me strength, even intelligence and knowledge."[14] One of the people who had treated Rousseau badly had been the Comte de Montaigu, ambassador in Venice. Rousseau had been the ambassador's secretary, but his employer constantly referred to him as a "servant." Rousseau suffered the frustration of a whole generation who felt the old order blocked their rise to the position that their talents merited.

It was this situation, this social impasse, of which Rousseau's individual circumstances were just one example, that reflected itself in his work. Rousseau began to break with the cheerful Baconian optimism of the Encyclopedists. In the preface to the *Encyclopedia*, Diderot had written that "our aim is to gather all knowledge, so that our descendants, being better instructed, may become at the same time happier and more virtuous."[15] Rousseau disagreed. Society was regressing, not advancing. "Civilization" only "cast garlands of flowers over the chains that men bore."[16] Without war, conspiracy, and tyranny, there would be no history. Rousseau's attitude to society was unremittingly bitter:

> The first man who fenced off a piece of land, took it upon himself to say "This belongs to me" and found people simple-minded enough to believe him, was the true founder of civil society.... Such was, or may have been, the origin of civil society and laws, which gave new fetters to the poor, and new powers to the rich ... and to benefit a few ambitious persons, subjected the whole of the human race thenceforth to labor, servitude and wretchedness.[17]

This note of class hatred and the notion of a decaying regressive social order was quite foreign to the *philosophes*. But the notion that men had purposively made society, even for the worse, began to break with mechanical determinism. Materialists such as D'Holbach had argued that the world operated according to "necessary and immutable laws" which "distributed good and evil" among men.[18] Helvetius denied the existence of free will: "All our thoughts and will must be the immediate effect or necessary consequence of impressions we have received."[19] But Rousseau argued that human beings could arrest the slide into tyranny. His solution, the Social Contract, might not be democratic in the modern sense, but it was certainly anti-feudal and republican.

This new subjective strand became increasingly insistent in its opposition to mechanical materialism in the years before the French Revolution. But it received its most pronounced expression in Germany, not France. It was this tradition from which, and in opposition to which, Hegel's thought developed.

German Conditions and German Idealism

Marx once observed that because German society was so economically backward the German bourgeoisie achieved in thought what other nations achieved in reality.[20] If we are to understand Hegel's philosophy, we need to examine this aphorism.

The Germany into which Hegel was born was not a unified nation state. Throughout the eighteenth century, it existed only as hundreds of small duchies, principalities, imperial free cities, petty kingdoms, bishoprics, margraviates, and landgraviates loosely held together under the imperial crown of the Habsburg dynasty.[21] The economic and social structure of even the largest states, such as Prussia, lagged far behind England and France. On the land the peasantry labored much as they had done from time immemorial.[22]

Nevertheless, some towns were growing, such as the trading centers of Hamburg and Hanover. The population of Berlin grew from 20,000 in 1688 to 70,000 by 1740. But even this was small compared with Paris (approximately 600,000) or London (nearer 800,000) in 1780.[23] And the mass of urban dwellers were house-owning master craftsmen "who grew up in the narrowest philistinism."[24] In 1800, there were still almost twice as many masters as journeymen.[25]

Despite these enormous obstacles, there were some small signs of capitalist development. Saxony, where the beginnings of capitalism dated from before the Reformation, had long been a stronghold of the mining industry. Leipzig fairs were the biggest trading markets in Eastern Europe, and Chemnitz became a "Saxon Manchester."[26] In Westphalia and the Rhineland, influenced by neighboring France, industry was even more developed and more diverse. Cotton, wool, and silk industries gave rise to bleaching, printing, and dyeing enterprises. The iron founding, mechanical engineering, mining, and arms industries employed a population of a density unheard of in other parts of Germany.[27]

These pinpoints of light in the feudal night were important, but they were puny compared with England and France.[28] The German bourgeoisie were marked by the backwardness from which they were emerging. Among the leading manufacturers of Berlin, there were many who could scarcely write their own name, according to Prussian Privy Councillor Kunth.[29] But if the commercial and industrial bourgeoisie were still weak, there was another sort of middle class that was more educated, more vociferous, and growing in size.

The patchwork of quarrelsome German states vied with each other socially and politically, as well as militarily and economically. In fact, because Prussia dominated the area militarily and the economy of other states hardly allowed them to keep up, the rivalry between them was often more political, cultural, and social than anything else.

To compete in these terms meant to follow France, the cultural and social leader of eighteenth century Europe. The entire European aristocracy followed French fashion and spoke French as their first language. Even in Vienna, where German was spoken, it was peppered with imported French phrases. "I am a great prince and have adopted the forms of government which befit a great prince, like others of my kind," said Eberhard Louis, duke of Wurttemberg, who ruled over a population no bigger than that of Paris.[30] In the tiny court of Weimar, there were two hundred officials, many of whom must have felt, like Rousseau, superior to those they served— especially since the German nobility were often no better-off than British tenant farmers. Universities and court orchestras were important status symbols. Saxony maintained three universities, as many as England, despite having a total population of only 2 million. There were 37 universities in the Holy Roman Empire and another 5 in the German-speaking areas beyond. In the Saxon court of 1716, the Elector boasted an orchestra of 65, a French choir of 20, a French ballet of 60, and a theater company of 27. Some of the Elector's ministers had orchestras of their own. In Prussia, the streamlined state structure, inherited from "enlightened monarch" Frederick the Great, helped create a layer of educated officials.

With this mass of officials, clerks, lawyers, academics, and artists came a boom in intellectual argument and debate. In the 1780s alone, 1,225 periodicals were launched in Germany. Even though they were often quickly suppressed or censored, they outstripped the numbers in France. Among this intelligensia were many who felt deeply alienated from their aristocratic overlords. The universities produced "highly qualified graduates for whom there was no work," and "thousands of would-be writers [who] had no one to write for" because the aristocracy preferred French to German.[31] Contempt for German culture was little diminished since the time when Frederick the Great had refused to pay a salary of 2,000 thalers to his librarian on the grounds that "one thousand is enough for a German."[32] This was "a situation which left a whole class of young Germans thumb-twiddling and broody, staring out of windows, waiting."[33]

It was from this combustible material of "craftsmen and petty officials in church, school and state, and not from the big and medium bourgeoisie"[34] that successive waves of intellectual protest were to burst. Although the Sturm und Drang (storm and stress) movement in art and Idealism in philosophy stood on the shoulders of the Enlightenment thinkers, the unreconstructed nature of German society made it impossible for them to accept the happy optimism of English, and to a lesser extent French, materialism. English materialism remained "an esoteric doctrine, a secret of the top ten thousand,"[35] because the English bourgeoisie had already gained a measure of political power and had no wish to use its science to dispel the mists of religion among the lower orders. Classical economy, typified by Adam Smith, was appropriate to a class that already wielded considerable economic power and was confident that its growing strength would deliver increased political power. German idealism developed among a middle class that held ideas that it had neither the political nor economic power to realize. Consequently, it stressed the one thing left to it—the power of thought. Where Adam Smith saw the "hidden hand" of the free market, Hegel was to see the "cunning of Reason." But before Hegel there was Kant.

Immanuel Kant (1724–1804) was a philosophy professor in Koenigsberg. It was said that the citizens of Koenigsberg set their watches by the professor's appearance for his daily afternoon walk. He only failed them on two occasions. The first was the publication of Rousseau's *Emile*. The second was the fall of the Bastille.[36] Rousseau's portrait was the only one in his study. Kant said that he was woken from his "dogmatic slumber" by Hume's challenge to the Newtonian view of the universe. He set out to provide a renewed intellectual defense of the essential role of reason, intellect, and mind in composing our picture of the world, denying that this picture was simply the result of passively registering information received by our senses.

The problem that Hume bequeathed to Kant, "the central problem of classical empiricism," was set by "the assumption that experience offers us nothing but separate and fleeting sense-impressions, images and feelings; and the problem was to show how ... we could supply rational justification of our ordinary picture of the world as containing continuously and independently existing and interacting material things and persons."[37]

The *Critique of Pure Reason* (1781) agreed with the empiricists that all knowledge *begins* with experience. But this only provides the *material* for thought. It does not provide the means and methods by which these materials, these raw sensations, are ordered, classified, and related to one another. As Marcuse says, "If it could be shown that these principles of organization were the genuine possession of the human mind and did not arise from experience, then the independence and freedom of reason would be saved."[38]

Thus Kant is in no doubt that there is an objective world, and, therefore, he starts from a more "materialist" proposition than Hume. But Kant also "rejected the basic empiricist dogma which Hume never questioned" by insisting that the "minimal empiricist conception of experience was incoherent in isolation." What was required was the use of rational concepts to interpret the data supplied by our senses. Without such concepts, sense data were simply a mass of chaotic images. Kant's philosophy is devoted to explaining how it is possible to imagine concepts that are *not* drawn from experience.[39]

Kant argued that space, time, and causation, for instance, are not characteristics of objective reality but the inevitable and unavoidable mental concepts with which we look at the world. They are not drawn from experience of the world, they are the *precondition* of being able to experience the world intelligibly. They are not "facts" but necessary concepts which we must entertain *before the fact*. If we did not have an idea of space or time, we could not interpret the data supplied by our senses and it would appear simply as a meaningless whirl of unstable images. Therefore, notions of space and time must *precede* any knowledge we might gain from the senses. They must be attributes of the human mind, even before it has any contact with the objective world.

Similarly, Kant argued, with the concept of cause. Plekhanov's summary accurately catches Kant's meaning:

> It is quite possible that we are mistaken when we say that phenomena A is the cause of phenomena B. But we are not mistaken when we say in general that a causal connection between phenomena exists. Abolish the concept of cause and you will have nothing left but a chaos of phenomena of which you will understand nothing at all. But the point is precisely that it is *impossible* to abolish this concept. It is obligatory for us, it is *one of our forms of thinking.*[40]

So it was that Kant regained from the empiricists an active role for thought in the construction of our image of the world. But it was a victory gained at enormous cost. Certainly Kant had proved that our thoughts can be rationally ordered, but he had also proved that all we know about the world is our thought. There might be an objective reality that produced the sensations which we understand by the deployment of concepts such as space, time, and causation—but the nature of this reality, other than bare fact that it is "out there," remains hidden behind the veil of appearances with which we are presented by our sense impressions. We can never be sure, even after these impressions have been interpreted by reason, that they actually correspond to reality. There is, therefore, an unbridgeable gap between the way things appear to us and what Kant called "the thing-in-itself," the reality that exists independently of our senses and reason.

Our senses are the never-to-be-removed spectacles through which we see the world. It may be that the color we see as red actually is red and would be seen as such even if we could see it in some other way than through our senses. But this is just what we cannot do, and so we can never know the red thing-in-itself or any other such objective reality. As Kant put it: "Once we abstract from the subjective conditions of perception it is nothing at all and cannot be attributed to the things in themselves."[41]

Thus Kant's initial agreement with the materialistic premises of the empiricists remains purely formal: There is an objective reality from which the senses derive their data, but we can know nothing of it. Consequently, the logic of Kant's system, quite contrary to his intentions, carries him to the outer reaches of idealism. As P. F. Strawson's standard commentary on Kant notes:

> What really emerges here is that aspect of [Kant's] transcendental idealism which finally denies to the natural world any existence independent of

our "representations" or perceptions, an aspect in which . . . Kant is closer to Berkeley than he acknowledges.[42]

Consequently, "the doctrine is not merely that we can have no knowledge of a supersensible reality. The doctrine is that reality is supersensible and that we can have no knowledge of it."[43]

Moreover, Kant's theory rested on a fundamental contradiction. Kant claims that our sense impressions are *caused* by the action of objective reality, the thing in itself, on us. This position obviously attributes causation, at least in this one respect, to the thing in itself. Yet Kant also claims that the principle of causality is limited to our consciousness and is *not* a property of the objective world at all.

There are only two possible paths by which we can escape from this dilemma. We could continue to insist that causation is not a property of the thing in itself and so also reject the idea that it is the action of the objective world on us that produces our sensations. In this case, "we are taking the direct road to *subjective idealism*, because, if the thing in itself does *not* act on us, we know nothing of its existence and the very idea must be declared unnecessary." Or we could admit that our sensations are caused by the objective world. In this case, we are admitting knowledge of the objective properties of the thing in itself, properties that have their counterpart in our mental make-up. In this case we are on the path of materialism.[44] Thus Kant's philosophy ends in a paradox.

This impasse in philosophy was only broken by the intellectual consequences of the eruption of the French Revolution. That unparalleled intervention of the masses into the course of history redefined the terms in which philosophers thought of the relationship between the active subject and the objective material world. Fichte, Kant's successor as Germany's leading philosopher, tried to solve the problem of dualism by taking the path of subjective idealism—everything is the emanation of thought. The real world was simply a projection of our minds. This "idealism with a vengeance" fitted the first enthusiasm with which many European intellectuals reacted to the French Revolution. Fichte's system, like the German middle class, thought actively and critically about the world, hoping that this would be sufficient to bring about real change in the real world.

But Fichte's philosophy never survived the reverses and complexities of the revolution. It was Hegel who really expressed the experience of the French Revolution in a philosophical system, despite the fact that he was less politically radical than Fichte. Before we turn to Hegel's theoretical revolution and how it evolved in opposition to Kant, we must first chart his attitude to the revolution in society.

THE MASTER THEME OF THE EPOCH

For Hegel the French Revolution was, in Shelley's phrase, the master theme of the epoch. His early republican ideas, his attitude to the Jacobins and the Terror, his joy at Napoleon's successes and his despair at his defeat, his hopes and fears about capitalist society, all marked stages in his philosophical development.

In 1770, Georg Wilhelm Friedrich Hegel was born into precisely the class that we have seen to be the heart of the Enlightenment in Germany. His father was a civil servant in the finance ministry of the Duchy of Wurttemberg, and his brother became an army officer. He studied at the Stuttgart Gymnasium, or secondary school, graduating top of his class. Hegel's school studies imbued him with the ethos of the Enlightenment. In an essay on the religion of the Greeks and Romans, he wrote, "Only when a nation reaches a certain stage of education, can men of clear reason appear amongst it, and reach and communicate better concepts of divinity to others."[45]

In 1788, the year before the French Revolution, he graduated to the *Tubinger Stift*, a theology seminary attached to the State University of Tubingen, which prepared students for service in the government, teaching, or the church. Hegel studied philosophy and religion.

He shared rooms with, and became the close friend of, the poet Friedrich Holderlin and fellow philosopher Friedrich Schelling. Together they planted a "liberty tree" to celebrate the French Revolution and danced around it singing the *Marseillaise*, which Schelling was the first to translate into German. They are also said to have been involved in a secret club which read the writings of the revolution and which came under investigation by the authorities.[46] Hegel left Tubingen in 1793 to take up a post as a private teacher with a patrician family in Berne. The friends parted with the words *Reich Gottes!* ("To the coming of God's kingdom"), hoping French events would be repeated in Germany. In the same year, Holderlin wrote,

> I love the race of the coming centuries. . . . For this is my blessed hope, the faith which keeps me strong and active—our descendants will be better than ourselves, freedom must come at last, and virtue will thrive better in the holy warming light of freedom than under the ice-cold sky of despotism. We live in a period where everything is working for the better.[47]

Hegel undoubtedly shared his friend's sentiments, including the religious coloration added by German circumstances. Hegel saw the revolution implementing the rational order long predicted by Enlightenment thought. Now the rational mind could renovate an irrational world. Even in later life, when the first enthusiasm for the revolution had long faded, Hegel would maintain,

As long as the sun has stood in the heavens and the planets circled around it, we have never yet witnessed man placing himself on his head, that is, on thought, and building reality according to it . . . but now man has come for the first time to recognize that thought should rule spiritual reality. This was a magnificent dawn. All thinking beings joined in celebrating this epoch. A sublime feeling ruled that time, an enthusiasm of spirit thrilled through the world, as if we had now come to the real reconciliation of the divine with the world.[48]

At the time, life in Berne and a study of Kant and English political economy helped Hegel's thought move beyond the simple celebrations of the revolution that occupied him in Tubingen. Hegel said of Berne, "In no country that I know is there so much hanging, racking, beheading and burning as there is in the Canton of Berne."[49] He was appalled by the political corruption involved in the selection of the ruling council.[50]

During this period, Hegel saw himself as working, albeit critically, within the Kantian framework. He told Schelling, "From the Kantian system and its ultimate consummation I expect revolution in Germany."[51] But the impact of events in France was already equipping Hegel with an understanding of historical change that reached beyond Kant's abstract categories. In the same letter to Schelling, Hegel celebrated "the fact that mankind . . . is being treated with so much reverence," because it proves "that the halo which has surrounded the heads of the oppressors and the gods of the earth has disappeared." He then went on to explain how the revolution in philosophy and the revolution in society are related:

The philosophers demonstrate this dignity [of man]; the people will learn to feel it and will not merely demand their rights, which have been trampled in the dust, but will themselves take and appropriate them. Religion and politics have played the same game. The former has taught what despotism wanted to teach: contempt for humanity and its incapacity to reach goodness and achieve something through man's own efforts. With the spreading of the ideas about how things should be, there will disappear the indolence of those who always sit tight and take everything as it is. The vitalizing power of ideas even if they still have some limitation, like those of one's country, its constitution etc.—will raise the spirits.[52]

This is an early example of the great themes of Hegel's philosophy. The leading role of philosophy, the "vitalizing power of ideas," the keystone of idealism is here—it is not the limitations of one's country that shape thought, but thought that transforms the limitations of the society. But in this letter there is also a revolutionary conception of the way in which social movements and ideas interact to produce historical change. This is the enduring conquest that Hegel's philosophy won from the experience of the French Revolution.

During Hegel's time in Berne, the French revolution, under internal and external threat, saw Robespierre rise to power. To overcome the dual threat of counterrevolution, Robespierre and the Jacobins unleashed the Terror. This was the point at which many of the revolution's intellectual admirers, such as Tom Paine and Wordsworth, began to recoil from their early enthusiasm. In one sense, Hegel was no exception. He had little sympathy with the Jacobins and the sansculottes and even less with the Terror.

In 1794, he wrote to Schelling complaining of the Terror. In the *Phenomenology of Mind* (1806) he reiterated his criticisms, referring to the Terror as "absolute fear." The Terror was the demand for absolute freedom uncontrolled by any institutional limit. The Terror was "merely the fury of destruction." But once this fury has "completed the destruction of the actual organization of the world," it has no plan for how the world should be reconstructed, what a new, better society should be. Therefore the Terror "exists now just for itself . . . an object which no longer has any content." For this reason, "the sole work and deed of universal freedom is therefore *death*, a death which has no inner significance or filling . . . it is thus the coldest and meanest of all deaths, with no more significance than cutting off the head of a cabbage or swallowing a mouthful of water."[53]

The Jacobins' decrees and the Maximum on prices were surely what Hegel had in mind when he attacked the "supreme public authority" whose "pedantic craving to determine every little detail" means that "the appointment of every village schoolmaster, the expenditure of every penny for a pane of glass . . . the appointment of every toll-clerk . . . is the immediate emanation and effect of the highest authority."[54] The Jacobins were endangering the principle that "in the states of the modern period . . . all legislation hinges upon security of property."[55] But for all his abhorrence of the Jacobins, Hegel did not reject the gains of the revolution—he celebrated Bastille Day all his life—or even the necessity of the Terror.[56] He wrote that the tyranny (by which he meant Robespierre) "is *necessary* and just to the extent to which it *constitutes and maintains the state as a real individual entity*." Once the tyrant ceases to be necessary, he is overthrown.

> Tyranny is overthrown by the people because it is abhorrent and base, etc.: but in reality only because it is superfluous. *The memory of the tyrant is execrated*; but . . . he has acted as a god only in and for himself and expects the ingratitude of his people. If he were wise he would divest himself of his powers as they became superfluous; but as things are his divinity is only the divinity of the animal: blind necessity which deserves to be abominated as sheer evil. This was the case with Robespierre. His power abandoned him, because *necessity had abandoned him* and so he was violently overthrown. That which is necessary comes to pass, but each portion of necessity is normally assigned to individuals. One is counsel for

the prosecution and one for the defence, another is judge, a fourth executioner; but all are necessary.[57]

Here Hegel mirrored the attitude of the mainstream of the French bourgeoisie: Robespierre was a god only so long as he was necessary. While he was necessary, even the threat to private property was preferable to the success of the counterrevolution. But once the counterrevolution was beaten back, Robespierre was no longer tolerated.

The impact of the Jacobin dictatorship also had far more wide ranging consequences for Hegel's thought. It not only reinforced his commitment to democracy and his distrust of the "perfidious Robespierrists" but also his belief that the state is indispensable. This change did not take place immediately. As late as 1796, at the end of his time in Berne when his republican sentiments were at their height, Hegel could write, "We must . . . transcend the state. For every state is bound to treat free men as cogs in a machine . . . hence the state must perish."[58] But two years later on the basis of the Terror, Hegel had become convinced that, "Anarchy has become distinguished from freedom; the notion that a firm government is indispensable for freedom has become deeply engraved on men's minds." Order that guaranteed property was vital, albeit allied to "the notion that people must have a share in the making of laws."[59] This framework would enable Hegel to welcome the rise of Napoleon as the inheritor of the revolution, the guarantor of bourgeois stability, and the liberator of Germany from the feudal yoke.

There was a second change in Hegel's thought as a result of events in France. He began to think more critically about the legacy of the Enlightenment. The Jacobins generally, and Robespierre in particular, were the self-proclaimed followers of the Enlightenment thinkers. After all, was it not the Enlightenment belief that by altering men's environment we could improve their natures which stood behind Saint-Just's epigram, "It is for the legislator to make men into what he wants them to be"?[60] Wasn't Robespierre Rousseau's ardent pupil? Hegel now began to question whether the stark project of the Enlightenment—to confront a recalcitrant world with the rational schemes of man—doesn't lead to the guillotine.

Initially this may seem like a collapse into a straightforward conservative opposition to change, but it is not. It is the beginning of overcoming the contradictions that lay unresolved by Kant's philosophy. Hegel is beginning to see that the human mind cannot simply impose rationality on a chaotic reality, it must search out those elements in the real world which are tending toward rational change and ally itself with them. Freedom is not the attempt to frustrate the necessary structure of the world but the appreciation of that necessity. Freedom is to act in accordance with necessity. It was a point that Marx would bend to his own purposes in the debate with the utopian socialists, themselves descendants of the Enlightenment line.

Another major theme also began to surface during Hegel's time in Berne. The changes in his thought are only discernible in some important but esoteric studies of ancient Greece and of the origins of Christianity. Hegel puzzled over how the beautiful unity of Greek civilization, where each individual felt at one with the society in which he lived, degenerated to the modern situation in which individuals are pitted one against another and all against the state. He also examined how it was that Christianity developed from the heartfelt belief it once was to the formalistic, externally imposed code that he saw around him. The historical inaccuracy of these observations is not the point. Their importance lies in the fact that Hegel had begun to raise the question of alienation. How was it, he asked, that the institutions and ideologies that human beings created came to dominate their lives? How did they lose their vitality and become dry husks waiting to be blown away by the wind of historical change? While in Berne these ideas were only present in dim outline, but later they became central to Hegel's thought.

In 1797, Hegel gladly left Berne and accepted a teaching post that Holderlin had found for him in Frankfurt. Once back in Germany, Hegel began to think about how the gains of the French Revolution might help to sweep away the unreconstructed feudal states that surrounded him. Hegel was only in Frankfurt until 1801 when Schelling found him a lecturer's post at the University of Jena. Nevertheless, there are some fragmentary writings from the Frankfurt period which show us that Hegel was still thinking through how changes in history could leave old institutions stranded as anachronisms. They also show that, despite the Terror, Hegel was clear that a bourgeois revolution was still a necessity in Germany.

In *The German Constitution*, Hegel again wrestled to produce a historical understanding of the problems that confront society: we must understand that it is not "arbitrariness and chance that make it [society] what it is." Instead we should see "that it is as it ought to be."[61] This is a plea to understand how events and institutions emerge in the course of history, not a recipe for political quietism. This is made clear in *On the Recent Domestic Affairs of Wurttemberg* (originally called *That Magistrates Should be Elected by the Citizens*) where Hegel says, "How blind they are that hope that institutions, constitutions, laws which no longer correspond to human manners, needs and opinions, from which the spirit has flown, can subsist any longer." And he saw that:

> Calm satisfaction with the present, hopelessness, patient acquiescence . . .
> have changed into hope, expectation, and a resolution for something different.

The picture of better and juster times . . . has moved all hearts and set them at variance with the actuality of the present."[62]

Hegel came even closer to the heart of things when he moved to Jena. Although its bloom was fading by 1801, Jena had been a center of the Enlightenment and the *Sturm und Drang* movement. Schelling was there. So were Schiller and the Schlegal brothers. Fichte, Germany's leading philosopher, had just left. Hegel published some minor works, and, after he became an associate professor in 1805, he began work on the first major statement of his system, the *Phenomenology of Mind*. His work was rudely interrupted by the Battle of Jena. Napoleon's troops seized the city, burning down Hegel's lodgings in the process. He escaped, clutching the second half of the manuscript of the *Phenomenology*, completed the previous night, in his arms. The experience didn't undermine Hegel's full-hearted support for Napoleon which lasted until the emperor's defeat at Waterloo.

On the night before the Battle of Jena Hegel wrote, "This morning I saw the Emperor—this world soul—ride through the town . . . it is a marvelous feeling to see such a personality, concentrated in one point, dominating the entire world from horseback. . . . It is impossible not to admire him."[63] In a letter to a friend, he said, "All wish the French army luck." Hegel's mood reflected that of many bourgeois republicans throughout Europe, that is, the hope that Napoleon would free them from the old order, avoiding recourse to the methods of the revolution itself.

A new and decisive shift took place in Hegel's thought at about this time. Although the battles of Napoleon's armies were world-shattering events, it was not, Hegel argued, the bayonets and cannon that were the real the cause of social change. It was the changing spirit of the age, the collective consciousness, which determined that the world must change. This was the real motivating force. This spirit, often identified with philosophy, was the real first cause of events, simply using commanders and their cannon as a means to its end. Napoleon, like Robespierre before him, had become necessary, but he acted blindly. Only philosophy saw the pattern of events unfolding behind cannon smoke. Only philosophy had made the battles possible:

Philosophy is something lonely; it does not belong in the streets and the market place, yet it is not alien to man's actions . . . spirit intervenes in the way the world is ruled. This is the infinite tool—then there are bayonets, cannon, bodies. But . . . neither bayonets, nor money, nor this trick nor that, are the ruler. They are necessary like the cogs and the wheels of a clock, but their soul is time and spirit that subordinates matter to its laws.[64]

The role of philosophy in this "time of ferment, when spirit moves forward in a leap" is to "welcome its appearance and acknowledge it while others, who oppose it impotently, cling to the past," as Hegel announced in his end of term lecture of 1806.[65]

Hegel expected great things of Napoleon, and, in some senses, he was not disappointed. Even before the period of French occupation, the revolution had forced sweeping changes in Germany's ramshackle structure.[66] In 1801, Napoleon forced the German emperor to sign a treaty relinquishing his Rhine territories, just as the Prussians had already done. Some 1,150 square miles with a population of 4 million were lost to Germany. Even then the German princes proved incapable of reordering their society, so, in 1803 and in agreement with Russia, Napoleon forced the abolition of more than a third of the three hundred German states.

In 1805, England enticed Austria and Russia into war with France. The Prussians promised the tsar aid, but their emissary had not even arrived with the news before Napoleon had beaten Austria and Russia at Austerlitz. Prussia rushed back into Napoleon's arms. Austria was forced to cede 1,140 square miles and 800,000 inhabitants. These lands went primarily to German states. Napoleon kept his army in southern Germany and swept away countless more petty states. A population of 1.25 million, occupying 550 square miles, were divided between sixteen states that declared themselves independent of the German emperor. This was the Confederation of the Rhine, and it recognized Napoleon as its protector. The Prussians considered revolt, but the Battle of Jena put an end to that.

Some form of bourgeois reconstruction, often based on the Napoleonic legal code, followed in many of these states. But, to the extent that French occupation led to bourgeois rule, it began to forfeit the support of those who had been happy to see it deal blows to the old order. The bourgeoisie, always fearful of thoroughgoing transformation, would now be happy to take their deliverance from Napoleon's hands and bid him farewell. They got their chance in 1812 when war broke out between France and Russia. The wars of liberation now pitted Napoleon against a united Europe. He was deposed for the first time in 1814 and for a second and final time in 1815.

Waterloo was a victory for old Europe, but too much had changed for the old order ever to be the same again. There was no better proof than the fact that the Prussian aristocrats had driven their troops to war by promising a free and independent Germany. The king of Prussia even promised a constitution if his subjects would save his throne. Thus, the old order could only get its citizens to fight the inheritor of the bourgeois revolution if they were promised the fruits of bourgeois rule. Nevertheless, reaction followed. As Mehring says,

> If the people had overthrown a foreign despot, the princes had overthrown the heir of the bourgeois revolution, and if what followed was

not the reconstruction of old Europe, it was indeed a stale and desolate reaction.[67]

AFTER THE REVOLUTION

We left Hegel celebrating Napoleon's victory at Jena and forecasting the opening of a new epoch. How did the course of French occupation and its ultimate demise affect his philosophy? Throughout his time in Jena and later as a newspaper editor in Bamberg (1807–8) and as rector of the Gymnasium in Nuremberg (1808–16), Hegel was an unstinting supporter of Napoleon. He hoped "the great constitutional lawyer in Paris" would teach the German princes the lessons of the French Revolution. He was, however, worried that the state structure would be modernized without necessarily introducing the "most noble" aspect of the French experience, "the liberty of the people, its participation in elections and decisions." It was a well-founded fear.

During this period Hegel became even more firmly convinced that "theoretical work achieves more in the world than practical. Once the realm of ideas is revolutionized, actuality does not hold out."[68] With Napoleon's armies achieving the work that the indigenous bourgeoisie were too afraid to contemplate, the revolution in thought was an increasingly attractive option. This period of dramatic social change is the most productive period of Hegel's life. He wrote the great mature statement of his philosophy, the *Science of Logic*, and published it between 1808 and 1816. In 1816, he wrote the *Encyclopedia of the Philosophical Sciences*.

What Hegel achieved in these works was to condense the experience of the great social contradictions of his age, filtered through a debate with their previous philosophical expressions, into a theoretical system. Hegel had seen the massive conflicts of his age at first hand. He had seen great ideas come to power only to achieve the opposite of what their authors intended, seemingly impregnable states overthrown, great classes humbled, the religion of centuries discarded, and a new world emerge from the ruins.

Hegel, as we have seen, believed that philosophy played a pivotal role in all this. His mature system sought to fuse logical categories of analysis with the real course of historical change. The contradictions of thought *are* the contradictions of reality. The power of thought is the power to change reality. What is true of the methods of thought is simultaneously true of the history of the world. The history of the world is the rationality of the human mind working itself out in time. This is self-evidently an idealist method, but, equally self-evidently, it is also an historical method that seeks to explain the totality of social change by examining the conflicts and contradictions at its heart. It is, therefore, the real birth of the dialectic in its modern form.

Hegel felt this great conquest of the rational mind to be under threat as anti-French sentiment grew, endangering the gains made by Napoleon. Throughout this period, Hegel opposed the growth of the anti-French liberation movement, which he saw as consisting of "Cossacks, Bashkirs, Prussian patriots." In a letter, he wrote, "I am willing to fall down on my knees if I see one liberated person." Napoleon's defeat and first exile struck him low: "It is an immense spectacle to see an enormous genius destroy himself. This is the most tragic thing that exists. The whole mass of mediocrities presses incessantly with all the absolute iron of its gravity."[69] In his rectorial address of 1815, he said,

> We must oppose this mood which uselessly misses the past and yearns for it. That which is old is not to be deemed excellent just because it is old, and from the fact that it was useful and meaningful under different circumstances, it does not follow that its preservation is commendable under changed conditions—quite the contrary. . . . The world has given birth to a great epoch.[70]

When Napoleon returned from exile, Hegel said he would have put a rifle on his shoulder and joined the battle if there had been any hope of victory. But Hegel held out no hope. After Waterloo, a note of resignation became the leitmotif of Hegel's thought. Hegel never reconciled himself to a return of the old order. "The dead," he said, "cannot be revived." But he did reconcile himself to the partly reformed and modernized Prussian state of the 1820s and 1830s. In 1818, he took the chair in philosophy at Berlin, now the capital of one of the two superpowers of the German Confederation. From here Hegel dominated German intellectual life for two decades until his death in 1831.

Perhaps the best known words he ever wrote, beautiful as they are, contain his most profound pessimism:

> When philosophy paints its grey in grey, then has a shape of life grown old. By philosophy's grey in grey it cannot be rejuvenated but only understood. The owl of Minerva spreads its wings only with the coming of the dusk.[71]

Philosophy can no longer imbue the age with the urge for change, as Hegel once maintained. It can only understand a world that has already grown old. The owl of Minerva, the symbol of knowledge, takes flight only when the great events of the day are over. All that philosophy can teach us now is to find "the rose," the symbol of joy, "in the cross of the present." History has reached its culmination in the present state and the current philosophy. Hegel was wrong, of course, but Avineri shows why it is a mistake to be too dismissive.

The point . . . is that . . . the socio-political order has been completely transformed. The order Hegel is now beginning to defend is not the old order
he so radically attacked in 1801. It is not Hegel's views which have changed
in the crucial decade between 1805 and 1815, but the whole fabric of
German social and political life which has been transformed by the tremendous jolt it had received from the Napoleonic wars.[72]

Even in its most conservative form, Hegel's system continued to shock.
Hegel was afraid that his *Philosophy of Right* might be banned, and the Prussian state would certainly have had to undergo significant further reform
before it would match Hegel's vision of a constitutional monarchy. Indeed,
when the king heard that the *Philosophy of Right* contained the view that, in
a constitutional monarchy, the monarch's role should be reduced to formally
agreeing to legislation, he asked suspiciously, "What if I don't agree to dot
the i's and cross the t's?"[73]

But for all this, Hegel *had* become more conservative. Throughout the
1820s and 1830s, he taught that history had reached its end, and, for twenty
years, the stability of reaction seemed to bear him out. But in 1830, new
revolutions swept Europe, and Hegel railed against them. He even found
the English Reform Bill too much to stomach. Mehring claims his students
deserted him in favor of his pupil, Eduard Gans, who emphasized the revolutionary side of the master's teaching. "At the time it was said in Berlin
that the great thinker died of this painful experience, not of the cholera."[74]

Having looked at the intellectual and social circumstances into which Hegel
was born and traced the outline of his thought as it changed in reaction to
the events of the French revolution, it is now possible to examine some of
his major themes more closely.

LABOR AND ALIENATION

So far we have stressed the Enlightenment tradition and the French Revolution as the forces that shaped Hegel's thought. But Hegel's ideas were also
shaped by the Industrial Revolution. In fact much of the power of his thought
is a product of the fact that "Hegel does know bourgeois society, but his
estimation of it is very low."[75] Of course, only a little of this knowledge
could come from direct experience given the underdeveloped nature of German
society. Hegel depended on his reading about the most advanced industrial
society of his day, Britain. He had read the classical economists, including
Adam Smith, as early as his stay in Frankfurt. In strictly economic terms,
Hegel never progresses beyond the ground marked out by the British economists,
and his treatment lacks the kind of concrete analysis that they provide. But
Hegel does integrate political economy and the historical perspective he found

in writers such as Adam Smith into his wider understanding. This requires him to attempt to penetrate the appearance of economic relations and to spell out the contradictions at their heart.

Marx pointed out that "when Hegel adopts the standpoint of modern political economy" he sees "labour as the *essence*, the self-confirming essence, of man."[76] Hegel understood alienation as the lack of control over the work process, as forced, unfree labor. This was partly a reflection of the way he saw the lifeless institutions of the old order counterposed to the living vitality of the new classes that made the French Revolution. But there can be little doubt that Hegel also drew the abstract picture of alienation from the living reality of capitalism, as these passages from his 1805–6 lectures show:

> The abstraction of labour makes man more mechanical and dulls his mind and his senses. Mental vitality, a fully aware, fulfilled life degenerates into empty activity. . . . He can hand over some work to the machine; but his own life becomes correspondingly more formal. His dull labour limits him to a single point and work becomes more and more perfect as it becomes more and more one sided. . . . The individual . . . is subject to a web of chance which enmeshes the whole. Thus a vast number of people are condemned to utterly brutalising, unhealthy and unreliable labour in workshops, factories and mines, labour which narrows and reduces their skill. Whole branches of industry which maintain a large class of people can suddenly wither away at the dictates of fashion, or a fall in prices following a new *invention* in other countries, etc. And this entire class is thrown into the depths of poverty where it can no longer help itself. We see the emergence of great wealth and great poverty, poverty which finds itself unable to produce anything for itself.[77]

In the same lectures, Hegel defined his concept of objectification: "(a) In the course of work I make myself into a thing, to a form which *exists*. (b) I thus externalize this my existence, make it into *something alien* and *maintain* myself in it."[78] Hegel saw that man created his own world through his own efforts. He also saw that man lost control over his own creation. As Marx noted,

> The importance of Hegel's Phenomenology . . . lies in the fact that Hegel conceives the self creation of man as a process, objectification as loss of object, as alienation and suppression of this alienation; that he therefore grasps the nature of *labour* and conceives objective man—true, because real man—as a result of his *own labour*.[79]

Hegel had made a great discovery, but it is a great discovery that is also the root of Hegel's weakness. Alienation is not seen, as in Marx, as a social relationship whereby a class controlling the means of production alienates the workers' product from them. In Hegel, to produce *any real object* in the real world is an act of alienation. To work is to externalize yourself. Alienation is the inevitable outcome of all labor, not just of labor in a class society.

The only answer to such a condition is mentally to reconcile yourself to the world, to see that you have created the object, even if you no longer control it. This is possible for Hegel, because all labor is ultimately reducible to *mental* labor.

Such an active conception of man's self-creation and self-alienation could only come after Kant's break with the determinism of the Enlightenment materialists. But in developing the idea of alienation (or, more properly, objectification), Hegel had stepped beyond Kant. First, Hegel saw labor as "a process," something that takes place over time. This is to see labor as subject to change. It develops the historical sense that Hegel gained from the events of his era. "Hegel took history seriously. In contrast to Kant, who thought he could say on purely philosophical grounds what human nature is and always will be, Hegel accepted Schiller's suggestion that the very foundations of the human condition could change from one historical era to another."[80] Or as Engels put it:

> What distinguished Hegel's mode of thought from that of all other philosophers was the tremendous sense of the historical upon which it was based. Abstract and idealist though it was in form, yet the development of his thoughts always proceeded parallel with the development of world history and the latter is really meant to be only the test of the former.[81]

Second, in Hegel there is division, loss, alienation, and, therefore, conflict at the heart of this process of "self-creation." Finally, although historical contradictions are ultimately resolved in forms of thought, there is nevertheless a real world which thought can know. Hegel insists, against Kant, on the unity of subject and object.

We can see all these points more clearly if we examine a famous passage from the *Phenomenology* called the master-slave dialectic, sometimes referred to as the dialectic of lordship and bondage.

THE MASTER-SLAVE DIALECTIC

The master-slave dialectic is, according to Charles Taylor, "one of the most important in the *Phenomenology*, for the themes are not only essential to Hegel's philosophy but . . . the underlying idea, that servitude prepares the ultimate liberation of the slaves, and indeed general liberation, is recognizably preserved in Marxism. But the Marxist notion of the role of work is also foreshadowed here."[82] Hegel's theme is the way in which the primitive "war of all against all" emerges into a relationship of lordship and bondage. We should not imagine, however, that Hegel is trying to describe an actual historical event. Like Rousseau's state of nature, or the "Robinsonades" of the classical economists, this is intended as a parable about the nature of class society. Its content is, however, incomparably richer than Rousseau's vision of the emergence of "civilization."

We are first introduced to the bondsman as one who simply lives in "fear of the lord." Indeed, Hegel believed this fear to be "the beginning of wisdom," because society must start with rulers and the ruled to overcome primitive chaos. Consequently, lord and bondsman are two "unequal and opposed . . . shapes of consciousness." The lord is "the independent consciousness whose essential nature is to be for itself." The bondsman is "the dependent consciousness whose essential nature is to live . . . for another." The lord has power over "the object of desire," and the bondsman only exists to fulfill that desire.

The lord consumes, but he can only achieve "the sheer negation of the thing." And the lord can only gain his desires through the labor of the bondsman. It is the bondsman who actually prepares the products that the lord consumes. So, paradoxically, through his work the bondsman achieves something that the lord is unable to achieve—he affirms his independence from the world of things.

Whereas the lord's consumption of the fruit of someone else's labor is only a "fleeting" satisfaction, "work, on the other hand, is desire held in check, fleetingness staved off; in other words, work forms and shapes the thing." In his work, the bondsman comes to realize his own power and to develop his own consciousness:

> . . . in fashioning the thing, he becomes aware that . . . he himself exists essentially and actually in his own right. . . . It is in this way, therefore, that consciousness, qua worker, comes to see in the independent being of the object its own independence. . . . Through this rediscovery of himself by himself, the bondsman realizes that it is precisely in his work wherein he seemed to have only an alienated existence that he acquires a mind of his own.[83]

Thus, the tables have been turned. The lord now exists only through another, the bondsman. The lord only enjoys the world through another's labor and, even then, only "fleetingly." But the bondsman, who previously suffered an "alienated existence" in his work, has now escaped from the world of servitude by discovering a "mind of his own" through the work he performs, work that "acquires an element of permanence."

Three things should be noted here. First, this analysis allows Hegel to see that "the high road to human development, the humanization of man, the socialisation of nature can only be traversed through work" and that "the advance of consciousness goes through the mind of the servant not that of the master."[84]

Second, the terms of this relationship form the characteristic Hegelian triad of thesis, antithesis, and synthesis. The lord's dominance is the first term; the bondsman's labor on the object is the mediation between them; and the conflict between the two terms results in the emergence of a new consciousness in the bondsman. Or, to put the same point another way, the lord and the bondsman form a contradictory totality, a unity of opposites. The bondsman's fear of the lord remains "inward and mute" unless he is set to work in the lord's service. This service forms and disciplines the bondsman's fear so that it achieves work in the "real world of existence." From this process, emerges the new consciousness which overcomes the bondsman's alienation. The negation has been negated.

Third, the dialectic of lordship and bondage confirms the idealist nature of Hegel's analysis. Only the bondsman's *consciousness* has been transformed, not his real relation to the lord. There has been a revolution in thought but no revolution in social relations. The Hegelian dialectic starts with the dominant consciousness of the lord and the subservient consciousness of the bondsman and ends with the transformed consciousness of the bondsman. The "real world of existence" and work is necessary, but only features as the mediating middle term. By contrast, Marx would insist that the first term in the dialectic is material reality and the final term the human activity by which it is transformed; consciousness is then the mediating middle term.

It is this reconciliation with alienation that led Hegel to the belief that ownership of private property is the way to overcome objectification. We repossess our lost selves in bourgeois ownership. Not seeing the historically transitory nature of capitalism's war of all against all, Hegel reveres the state as the guardian which stands above the fray.

Hegel's inability to override his idealism is the great tragedy of his philosophy. It means that whenever he does have an insight into the nature of real capitalist contradictions, it appears either as a mere empirical adjunct to his philosophy, the proverbial fifth wheel, or as a conflict that must be resolved in thought. This is precisely the fate of his great analysis of alienation.

WORLD HISTORY — TRUTH FORMED IN THE WOMB OF TIME

Hegel's *Philosophy of History* spells out the key concepts of his dialectic more clearly than any of his other writings. Hegel began by explaining why non-philosophical methods of looking at history are inadequate. Hegel's critique not only helped to define his own approach but also still applies to some fashionable methods of studying history, and so it is worth taking a brief look at this discussion.

Least acceptable, to Hegel, is the view held by the ancient Greeks Herodotus and Thucydides. This is "for the most part limited to deeds, events, and states of society, which they had before their eyes. . . . They simply transferred what was passing in the world around them, to the realm of representative intellect."[85] Modern times have transformed this parochial history, because "our culture is essentially comprehensive, and immediately changes all events into historical representations."[86] Even so, such histories still contain much that is "anecdotal, narrow and trivial." Hegel had contempt for the kind of history that concentrates on the personal details of historical figures, an approach he disparagingly described as "the psychology of the valet."

Only a few writers manage to "take an extensive view—to see everything." To see the totality is out of the question for those who "from below merely get a glimpse of the great world through a miserable cranny."[87] Hegel aimed for a total history, which has a pattern and a meaning. One only has to think of various contemporary empiricist historians and local specialists to see that Hegel's views are more than historical curios.

Hegel was also dismissive of "didactic history," the sort that "Rulers, Statesmen, Nations, are wont to be emphatically commended to."[88] Hegel was not against understanding "the lessons of history," but he was against the kind of writer who simply "arranges and manipulates" history, so that he can "insist upon his own spirit as that of the age in question."[89] Much of what we now call historiography, what Hegel called the "History of History," suffers from a similar defect, because it merely picks other historians' work apart by "putting subjective fancies in the place of historical data."

Finally, Hegel was against the kind of approach that has become so entrenched in contemporary higher education and that has been given a fashionable gloss by poststructuralists. This divides history into history of art, history of law, history of religion, history of madness, history of sexuality, or whatever. This approach is useless if it simply studies these issues in isolation from the totality of historical development, in their "external relations." These studies can only overcome their "superficiality" if the "connection of the whole is exhibited."[90]

Thus, Hegel broke from many of the ahistorical traditions of study which marked the Enlightenment and which still persist today. He even said, "We must proceed historically—empirically. Among other precautions we must take care not to be misled by professed historians who . . . are chargeable with the very procedure of which they accuse the philosopher—in introducing *a priori* inventions of their own into the records of the past."[91] This was a promise that Hegel could not keep. Nevertheless, it is a testimony to the strong historical sense that informed his work.

Hegel, as we have seen, rejected the empiricist notion that history is just a succession of dates and events. Neither was he happy with a simple causal explanation where one event causes the next and so on in an infinite regression—the billiard ball theory of history. Hegel found, on one level at least, that societies are totalities in which change occurred because they developed internal contradictions, not simply because they were the last link in a chain which stretched back in history to "who knows where?" To God? Again, Hegel was ultimately unable to solve this dilemma, but he grappled with it for so long that his analysis provided crucial material for those who came after him.

The reason that Hegel was unable to solve this contradiction lies in his view of historical change. For Hegel the world worked according to a rational process, which could be understood by scientific laws. This, as in much Enlightenment thought, was true both of nature and of society. But for Hegel, as for Anaxagoras whom he cited favorably, there was also a difference:

> The movement of the solar system takes place according to unchangeable laws. These are Reason, implicit in the phenomena in question. But neither the sun nor the planets, which revolve around it according to these laws, can be said to have any consciousness of them.[92]

But human beings can become conscious of the rational principles that govern social development. In fact, for Hegel, the whole of human history is about the way in which the rational structure of society is revealed to the consciousness of human beings. At the dawn of human history, the rational structure of the world is hidden from consciousness, but, through the successive phases of historical development, this rationality becomes clear to human beings. At the start of the process, people are *implicitly* rational—they are rational, but they are not aware of the fact. At the end of the process, they are self-consciously rational—they know and understand that reason governs the world.

The historical process is therefore identical with the rational method of scientific investigation. History is a gigantic scientific investigation strung out in time. This conception is already a massive advance on most Enlightenment thought. Kant had left human knowledge inherently limited in its field of operation. Hegel contested this viewpoint in the *Phenomenology of Mind*. The very title tells us why. Mind, human rationality, is not confined to its own world, cut off from the thing in itself. It is connected to phenomena, to things as they appear in the real world. Indeed, the whole structure of the *Phenomenology* is designed to lead thought from its everyday methods of perception to the heights of philosophical reason. This process, Hegel argued, was both possible and necessary, because everyday commonsense thought was a mass of contradictions that could only be resolved by moving to progressively greater abstractions. The contradictions at each level powered the progress to the next level. Hegel proposed to show that history has the same sort of structure as mind.

For Hegel, history was reason coming to self-consciousness. He had a unique term for reason, the German word *Geist*. Although there is no exact English equivalent, *Geist* is most often translated as Spirit or Mind. But Hegel is not referring to the mind or spirit of any single individual. *Geist* is probably best understood as the sum content of human consciousness as it has developed throughout history. Today, when we talk about a common culture or ideology, or the worldview of a certain epoch, it captures something of what Hegel meant by *Geist*.[93]

Spirit develops through history because it never wastes the gains of previous epochs. These were preserved, albeit in a different form, in subsequent ages. At the end of the process, the entire achievements of the development of human thought are summarized in Spirit. In a similar way, the entire content of the *Phenomenology* was preserved in its last category, Absolute Knowledge, and the entire content of the *Science of Logic* is preserved in its last category, the Absolute Idea. It would not be good enough, however, simply to look at the last stage of development and believe that you have comprehended the whole. The truth is contained in *the process* of change, *not* in any one of its concepts, even the *last*, which summarizes this process.

These are path-breaking notions. The idea that everything is an interrelated whole and that this totality is in a constant process of change; the view that static concepts are inadequate and that what is needed is to see things as a process; to recognize that change is not the result of external impact but of internal contradiction, all this is completely to revolutionize the modes of thought that dominated the Enlightenment. Let us now examine the use to which Hegel put these ideas. As we have seen, Hegel began with the assertion that the world was rationally structured—"Reason is sovereign of the world."[94] But in a blow against Kant and Fichte, Hegel insisted,

> Reason is not so powerless as to be incapable of producing anything but a mere ideal, a mere intention, having its place outside reality, nobody knows where; something separate and abstract, in the heads of certain human beings.[95]

Kant had split the totality of human experience into mind and "outside reality." Hegel insisted on their unity, a unity of opposites. For most of history, reality was only implicitly rational, and men did not recognize this. Nevertheless, Reason or Spirit was at work in both the dumb rationality of the objective reality and the subjective reason of men. History shows how these two rationalities merge into one self-conscious rationality. Hegel insisted on the unity of subject and object.

This may become clearer if we can recognize here an echo of the master-slave dialectic in the *Phenomenology*. There, too, the slave only came to consciousness when he saw that the objective process of work was not the alienated existence, as he first thought, but the route to liberation. In history human beings generally overcame their alienation from the objective world when they recognized it as another aspect of the rationality that inhabits their own subjective mind. For Hegel, as for Marx, human history presented long stretches in which people were faced with a hostile environment over which they exercised little control—they are alienated. For both thinkers, in very different ways, human beings could only alter this situation through a series of revolutions in society, revolutions that stemmed from the internal contradictions of those societies. It was because progress could only come through conflict that Hegel said, "The history of the world is not the theatre of happiness. Periods of happiness are blank pages in it, for they are periods of harmony—periods when the antithesis is in abeyance."[96]

The contradiction (or antithesis) that Hegel refers to is very different from the social and economic contradictions examined by Marx. Hegel's contradiction, as we might expect, was between two forms of consciousness, as it was in the master-slave dialectic. In any given society, the institutions, laws, morals, and beliefs embody a certain stage in the development of reason. Hegel called this the "spirit of the age." The greater the appreciation of rationality, the more free a people had become.

Thus, in Oriental society only one man, the emperor, was free, and even he was not really free because he was a despot. In Greek society, only some men were free, because the localized nature of the Greek city states and the slavery on which they were based prevented the knowledge of freedom from becoming general. Only with the rise of individuality, the product of Christianity, and the modern representative state was an era of general freedom and rationality possible.

The transition from one form of society to another was a result of a contradiction that emerges in the spirit of the age. When nations or historical epochs are born, they are free of contradiction. The contradiction between the total potential rationality and freedom of mankind (Spirit) and the particular social structure is not in evidence. "Spirit" and "the spirit of the age" are at one. The people "are moral, virtuous and vigorous" while they pursue Spirit's "grand objects" and "defend its works."[97]

But when the "objective world, that exists and persists in a particular form of worship, customs, constitution and political laws" hardens and grows old, it ceases to represent the full potential for reason that has been developing among its citizens. Spirit leaves the people. Within society, some people begin to look at their own laws and institutions and question whether they really are rational or merely accidental, contingent, and irrational. Those who look beyond the age are now the true bearers of Spirit. Theirs is the "universal thought," reason reaching beyond its age:

> Universal thought . . . shows up the limitations with which it is fettered— partly suggesting reasons for renouncing old duties, partly itself *demanding reasons* and the connection of such requirements with universal thought, and not finding that connection seeking to impeach the authority of duty generally as destitute of sound foundations.[98]

At the same time as some are looking for a new rationality on which to build society, others are simply renting and tearing a social structure that no longer fits the needs of the age. The "isolation of individuals from each other and from the whole [i.e., society] makes its appearance." This process of decay means that "aggressive selfishness and vanity, personal advantage, corruption, unbounded passion, egoistic interests" advance "at the expense of the state."

This is an example of the "cunning of reason" that not only uses the positive search for a new rationality as its tool to destroy the old order but also makes use of the more base materials that lie to hand. Thus it is that the old order, created by reason, is swallowed up by reason once it has served its turn—"Zeus and his race are swallowed up, and by the very power that produced them."[99]

Yet as society moves on to a more self-consciously rational form, it does not leave its past behind. It takes with it all that was genuinely advantageous about the old order, preserving it in its new form.[100] A new social reality has emerged, but the real revolution was a revolution in thought: "We must remark how perception—the comprehension of being by thought—is the source and birthplace of the new and in fact higher form. . . . The particular form of Spirit not merely passes away in the world by natural causes in time, it is annulled in the automatic self-mirroring activity of consciousness."[101]

Here we can see how Hegel reflected the revolutionary changes of his own time in the categories of thought, surpassing all previous philosophies in the process. The picture of an old order grown sclerotic and crisis ridden, the emergence of contradictions, and the view of progress through a revolutionary change that preserved the gains of the old order are dramatic precursors of Marx. But again Hegel's idealism, inevitable given his social position and the development of the intellectual traditions of which he was a part, brought the revolutionary insights back into the quiet harbor of intellectual thought.

Once again the formal mechanism that achieved this was the negation of the negation in its idealist form. Just as labor was reduced to a middle term in the dialectic of lordship and bondage, so here "the realising *activity . . . is* the middle term." The movement began with rationality in its dumb objective form and ended with rationality in its conscious, articulate form. The two poles that it united were "the complex of external things—objective matter" and "the *Idea*, which reposes in the penetralia of Spirit."[102] This is a dialectic that has assumed its end before it begins, a dialectic in which the contradiction never really becomes a social conflict.

HEGEL'S DIALECTIC

Lenin wrote, "The quickest way of getting a headache," when he studied Hegel's *Science of Logic*, where the dialectic appears in its fullest form.[103] This difficulty is partly a result of the legendary complexity of Hegel's language. Hegel may have wished to "teach philosophy to speak German,"[104] but Germany was not able to listen. The Spirit spoke in mysterious words, because, after Napoleon's defeat, the words that could be understood were no longer permitted.[105] Philosophy had ceased to speak German, Marx said, because German had ceased to be the language of thought.

Hegel's idealism also partly ensured that his thought was genuinely mysterious. The Spirit was a substitute for a class that was incapable of making its own revolution. This mystical substitute was then projected back into history as its moving force.

But Hegel is also difficult for reasons that are not the result of character and circumstance. His theories use terms and concepts that are unfamiliar, because they go beyond the understanding of which everyday thought is capable. Ordinary language assumes that things and ideas are stable, that they are either "this" or "that." And, within strict limits, these are perfectly reasonable assumptions. Yet the fundamental discovery of Hegel's dialectic was that things and ideas do change—empires rise and fall, likewise religions and schools of philosophy. And they change because they embody conflicts which make them unstable. As Hegel explained: "Thus we say of sensible things, that they are changeable: that is, they *are*, but it is equally true that they are *not*." And of ideas and concepts, which we tend to regard as "absolutely firm and fast," Hegel said,

> We look on them as separated from each other by an infinite chasm, so that opposite categories can never get at each other. The battle of reason is the struggle to break up the rigidity to which the understanding has reduced everything.

It is to this end that Hegel *deliberately* chooses words that can embody dynamic processes: "The double usage of language, which gives to the same word a positive and a negative meaning, is not an accident, and gives no ground for reproaching language as a cause of confusion. We should rather recognize in it the speculative spirit of our language rising above the mere Either-or of understanding."[106] For instance, Hegel uses the term "moment" to indicate that aspect of reality which is both a temporary point of stability and part of a dynamic process. Similarly, "sublate" is used to indicate that process which both produces something new and at the same time preserves, in an altered form, the old elements from which it emerged. If we are to understand Hegel, then we must have a little patience with what Marx called "this harsh, grotesque melody."[107]

Hegel summarizes some of the key characteristics of the dialectic in his preface to the *Phenomenology*. The first task of the *Phenomenology* is to examine the contradictions in various ways of seeing the world. It goes on to show that these contradictions can only be resolved by adopting the dialectical approach defended by Hegel. Hegel's way of criticizing other philosophical approaches is itself dialectical. He does not wish to show that they are simply wrong but rather that they are one-sided. The partial truth that they contain can then be sublated within his own system:

> The more conventional opinion gets fixated on the antithesis of truth and falsity, the more it tends to expect a given philosophical opinion to be either accepted or rejected. . . . It does not comprehend the diversity of the philosophical systems as the progressive unfolding of the truth, but rather sees in it simple disagreements.[108]

Indeed, it is this process of criticism and absorption that *is* Hegel's dialectic. He goes on to give a striking metaphor for this progressive sublation of other systems, demonstrating the way in which he regards this process as giving access to the truth:

> The bud disappears in the bursting forth of the blossom, and one might say that the former is refuted by the latter; similarly, when the fruit appears, the blossom is shown in its turn as a false manifestation of the plant, and the fruit now emerges as the truth of it instead. These forms are not just distinguished from one another, they also supplant one another as mutually incompatible. Yet at the same time their fluid nature makes them moments of an organic unity in which not only do they not conflict, but in which each is as necessary as the other; and this mutual necessity alone constitutes the life of the whole.[109]

The great principles of Hegel's dialectic are clearly displayed in this passage. "The truth is the whole," not any separate part. But the whole is not just the end result, the whole is the *process of development* through which the parts come to constitute the whole and, in doing so, become different than they were in their preexisting form.[110] Moreover, this process of development is not the result of some external cause, but of the inherent, "mutually incompatible" structure of the organism itself. Only in this way can "truth be its own self-movement" rather than a "mode of cognition that remains external to its material."[111]

Hegel is insistent that no real knowledge can emerge from a system that makes a sharp separation between its method and the object that the method is supposed to analyse. "To consider a thing rationally means not to bring reason to bear on the object from the outside and so to tamper with it, but to find that the object is rational on its own account," as he put it in *The Philosophy of Right*.[112] It followed that "this dialectic is not an activity of subjective thinking applied to some matter externally, but is rather the matter's very soul putting forth its branches and fruit organically."

This notion puts Hegel at odds with Kant's assumption that we must know the instrument of thought before we can know what the instrument can, or cannot, tell us about reality. The disagreement is succinctly summarized by Hegel in the shorter *Logic*: "We ought, says Kant, to become acquainted with the instrument, before we undertake the work for which it is to be employed; for if the instrument be insufficient, all our trouble will be spent in vain."[113] Hegel objects to this approach partly because it turns thought "back upon itself." But, more fundamentally, Hegel thinks that Kant's approach is self-contradictory, because knowledge, unlike other tools, cannot be understood "in advance" but only through use:

> In the case of other instruments, we can try and criticize them in other ways than by setting about the special work for which they are destined. But the examination of knowledge can only be carried out by an act of knowledge. To examine this so-called instrument is the same thing as to know it. But to seek to know before we know is as absurd as the wise resolution of Scholasticus, not to venture into the water until he had learned to swim.[114]

Hegel did not reject the demand that our method of analysis should be open to scrutiny, he merely insisted that such work could only take place in the course of investigation of substantive objects and not as a preliminary to such investigation:

> ... what we want is to combine in our process of inquiry the action of the forms of thought with criticism of them. The forms of thought must be studied in their essential nature and complete development: they are the object of research and the action of that object. Hence they examine themselves: in their own action they must determine their limits, and point out their defects. This is that action of thought, which will hereafter be specially considered under the name of Dialectic.[115]

The test of such a procedure is whether the method and the substantive knowledge obtained by the method reinforce each other. "The manner of thinking and the product of thought must mutually justify each other, else the method fails or the result is meaningless," as Frederick Weiss's useful commentary puts it. Furthermore, "Hegel's central idea, that of the concrete, is precisely that point of synthesis in which the object and its explanation coincide, the so-called identity of opposites, of knowing and being."[116]

One consequence of this approach is that, if the object develops historically, as a process unfolding over time, the method used by the philosopher must be capable of expressing this dimension of reality. Kant is again at fault in not being able to handle this dimension of reality. Kant makes time a function of human consciousness and attributes to the thing in itself only the mere fact of existence (or being, as Hegel calls it). But, argues Hegel, "the main point is not, that [objects] are, but what they are.... It does no good to things to say merely that they have being. What has being, will also cease to be when time creeps over it."[117]

Those approaches which reject the dialectic remain mired in static, nondevelopmental methods. They cannot account for how things come into being and pass out of being over time. Hegel describes these approaches as "monochromatic formalism," because they have no way of "coping with that sheer unrest of life." They simply content themselves with categorizing the "paralysed form" of reality.

To avoid this fate, we have to be willing to follow both objects and forms of thought through their long process of development. "Impatience," says Hegel, "demands the impossible, to wit, the attainment of the end without the means. But the *length* of the path has to be endured, because ... each moment is necessary." And each moment contributes to the definition of the totality that emerges at the end of this process; equally it is only the totality that gives meaning to the parts of which it is composed. Thus, for knowledge to become science "it must travel a long way and work its passage."[118]

Even the dialectic, the "triadic form" as Hegel calls it, can be "reduced to a lifeless schema, a mere shadow ... when scientific organisation is degraded into a table of contents." This was Kant's error. "Kant rediscovered this triadic form by instinct, but in his work it was still lifeless and uncomprehended."[119] This, in Hegel's view, is bound to be that fate of any method, including those of both Kant and Fichte, which treats consciousness and reality, subject and object, as separate:

> What results from this method of labelling all that is in heaven and earth with a few determinations of the general schema, and pigeon-holing everything in this way, is nothing less than "a report as clear as noonday", on the universe as an organism, viz., a synoptic table like a skeleton with scraps of paper stuck all over it, or like rows of closed and labelled boxes

in a grocer's stall. It is as easy to read off as either of these; and just as all the flesh and blood has been stripped off this skeleton, and the no longer living "essence" has been packed away in the boxes, so in the report the living essence of the matter has been stripped away or boxed up dead.[120]

Every part of Hegel's system was consciously designed to avoid this fate. In the *Philosophy of History*, Hegel described how Spirit, the accumulated totality of human knowledge, unfolded over time as a result of contradictions in the various societies in which it was inadequately embodied. In the *Phenomenolgy*, Spirit emerged from the contradictions in inadequate forms of thought. The *Science of Logic* looks at this same process in terms of scientific method, the process of "thinking about thinking." Spirit now stands before us without historical dress or the garb of everyday thought.

The *Science of Logic* was Hegel's attempt to bring together all the different ways that we look at the world—empirical thought, art, religion, natural science—and to show how they are connected. The *Science of Logic* was itself, therefore, another example of one of Hegel's key concepts—totality. From the very elementary concepts at the start of the book, Hegel showed how each concept is connected to every other concept. This process continues until the final concept (the Absolute Idea) is shown to be the summation of all the previous ideas in the book. One concept gives birth to the next by a process of contradiction. Science, like history, is dialectical.

How this process works is shown in the famous first contradiction in the *Logic*. Trotsky, when he examined this passage, said that it "seemed at first glance a subtle but fruitless play of ideas. In fact, this game brilliantly exposes the failure of static thinking."[121]

The *Science of Logic* begins with the most abstract of all human ideas, Being. This is the bare notion of existence shorn of any color, size, shape, taste, or smell. This first concept is also, in its way, a totality. Although Being reveals no characteristics or distinguishing marks, it does, nevertheless, include everything. After all, everything must *exist* before it can take on any particular characteristics. Being is therefore a quality that is shared by everything that exists; it is the most common of human ideas. Every time we say, "This is ——," even before we say what it is, we acknowledge the idea of pure Being. Being is, therefore, only an "immediate" (or unmediated) totality. But Being also contains its opposite, Nothing. The reason is that Being has no qualities and no features that define it. If we try to think about pure Being, it simply disappears into thin air. So, if we try to say what Being is, we are forced to the opposite conclusion, Being equals Nothing.

But even Nothing is more than it seems. If we are asked to define Nothing, we are forced to admit that it has at least one property—the lack or absence of any qualities. This may be only a negative definition, nevertheless, it is a definition. This presents us with a strange dilemma: Being is Nothing, and yet Nothing is something. Hegel, however, is not so stupid as to think that there is no difference between Being and Nothing, even though this is what our logical enquiry seems to suggest. All that this contradiction means is that we must search for a new term that which can explain how Being and Nothing can be both equal and separate (or an "identity of opposites," in Hegel's jargon). Hegel's solution is the concept of Becoming.

In German, Becoming means both "coming to be" and "ceasing to be." By replacing two static concepts with one dynamic concept, by seeing a process of change instead of stable definitions, Hegel superseded the ideas of Being and Nothing with a third term that contained both these ideas and at the same time surpassed them. This third term, which both contains and surpasses the previous two, Hegel calls the negation of the negation.

This process reveals the characteristic stages in the Hegelian dialectic. First the "immediate totality" (Being) is broken down into its contradictory definitions or parts (Being as Nothing, and vice versa). This is the "first negation." Then these "moments" are shown to require that they be united in a new "concrete totality" (Becoming). This new totality negates the parts and is, therefore, the "negation of the negation." This new concrete totality is much richer and more varied, because it contains within it the parts by which it was "mediated."

Lenin seized the key point about all this in his notes on the *Science of Logic*: "Shrewd and clever! Hegel analyses concepts that usually appear dead and shows there is movement in them."[122] Contradictions produce movement—this is the decisive advance that is contained in Hegel's dialectic. Hegel's method not only sees the world as a totality in which each part is connected to all the other parts, it also sees that the relationships between the parts are contradictory. It is the search to resolve these contradictions that pushes thought past commonsense definitions which see only separate, stable entities.

Some of the most unambiguous passages in the *Science of Logic* insist on the vital role that the idea of contradiction plays in Hegel's system. "*Everything is inherently contradictory*," he writes, "in the sense that this law in contrast to the others expresses rather the truth and essential nature of things."[123] And again, "contradiction is the root of all movement and vitality; it is only in so far as something has a contradiction within it that it moves, has an urge and activity."[124]

Anything that is defined simply by reference to itself (in the jargon, according to the law of identity) can have no possibility of movement, unless it is struck by an external force.[125] But external force can only ever be a partial explanation because, if we ask where this external force came from, we have either to repeat the reply (that this was caused by another external force), or, we have to admit that self-movement produced by internal contradiction is a feature of the system at some level. As Hegel puts it,

> ... internal self-movement proper ... is nothing else but the fact that something is, in one and the same respect, *self-contained and* deficient, *the negative of itself*. ... Something is therefore only alive is so far as it contains contradiction within it, and moreover is this power to hold and endure the contradiction within it.[126]

The role that contradiction plays in Hegel's thought can also be seen in his criticism of a notion that many take to be a definition of the dialectic— reciprocal relations. Reciprocal relations, the idea that two factors mutually influence each other, may be an advance on linear notions of cause and effect, but it falls short of being a wholly satisfactory dialectical explanation of development, as Hegel explains in the shorter *Logic*. Thought takes refuge in the idea of reciprocity "when the conviction grows that things can no longer be studied satisfactorily from a causal point of view, on account of the infinite progress already spoken of." Hegel then gives an example:

> Thus in historical research the question may be raised in the first form, whether the character and manners of a nation are the cause of its constitution and laws, or if they are not rather the effect. Then, as a second step, the character and manners on one side and the constitution and laws on the other are conceived on the principle of reciprocity: and in that case the cause ... will at the same time be an effect, and vice versa.[127]

Hegel does not dismiss this relationship out of hand, granting that "reciprocity is undoubtedly the proximate truth of the relation of cause and effect, and stands, so to say, on the threshold of the notion." But he goes on to insist, "if we get no further than studying a given content under the point of view of reciprocity, we are taking up an attitude which leaves matters utterly incomprehensible." Or, as he put it in the *Phenomenology*, "In this sort of circle of reciprocity one never learns what the thing in itself is, nor what the one or the other is."[128]

Hegel's point is that simply to see things in terms of action and reaction tells us nothing about the origin of either term in the relationship, nor does it tell us how these can change or pass out of existence. Reciprocity, that is, tends to stress equilibrium, a constantly reproduced state in which the different sides of the relationship may influence each other, but no progress or fundamental change takes place. Thus Hegel argues "to understand the relation of action we must not let the two sides rest in their state of mere given facts, but recognize them, as ... factors of a third and higher, which is the notion and nothing else." Characteristically, Hegel calls for the contradiction between action and reaction to be solved by the development of a higher category, "the notion," rather than a real struggle between social forces.

> To make, for example, the manners of the Spartans the cause of their constitution and their constitution conversely the cause of their manners, may no doubt be in a way correct. But, as we have comprehended neither the manners nor the constitution of the nation, the result of such reflections can never be final and satisfactory. The satisfactory point will be reached only when these two, as well as all other, special aspects of Spartan life and Spartan history are seen to be founded in this notion.[129]

Again, the weakness of Hegel's solution—to found both sides of the contradiction in the notion, the "spirit of the age," which would then provide the basis for explaining how both Spartan manners and constitution came into being and passed away—is evident. Nevertheless, his criticism of reciprocity retains its force and can only be superceded by an explanation that roots the customs and laws of a society in social and economic development and the class struggles that it engenders.

Finally, Hegel did not, for all his criticisms of cause and effect theories, abandon empirical concepts. In fact, Hegel thought that the standard empirical procedure of breaking things down into their constituent parts, classifying them, and recording their properties was a vital part of the dialectic. This is the first stage of the process (where we tried to define Being). It is only through this process of trying to capture things with "static" terms that contradictions emerge which oblige us to define something by its relations with the totality, rather than simply by its inherent properties. To show their transitory nature, Hegel called these stable points in the process of change "moments." Hegel said that the whole was "mediated" by its parts. So empirical definitions were not irrelevant. But they were an inadequate way of looking at the world and so in need of a dialectical logic which could account for change.

HEGEL'S IDEALISM

Hegel described himself as an "absolute idealist." He meant that in his system the decisive factor was the development of human consciousness, rather than the consciousness of any particular individual. If we think back over the issues considered in this chapter, we can clearly see this aspect of his work. In his appreciation of the French Revolution, it was the role of philosophy, embodied in the spirit of the age, which lay behind the roar of the cannon and the smoke of battle. In his path-breaking analysis of alienation, it was consciousness, externalizing itself in the material world, that was the root of the matter. In the master-slave dialectic, it was the consciousness of the slave that was at issue. In the *Phenomenology*, the dialectic advanced by showing the contradictions that emerged in both everyday thought and other philosophies. And in the *Science of Logic*, it is the contradictions in concepts that give birth to a true scientific approach.

There is in Hegel a genuine recognition of the objective world and a real attempt to come to terms with its structure. But this understanding is won only by ultimately resolving all the contradictions of the real world into categories of thought. "The tendency of all man's endeavours is to understand the world, to appropriate and subdue it to himself; and to this end the positive reality of the world must be as it were crushed and pounded, in other words, idealized."[130] In this idealized realm, the contradictions of reality are ultimately annulled. Hegel's dialectic begins and ends with forms of consciousness. Reality is only a middle term, the antithesis, which the negation of the negation once again returns to the world of philosophical categories.

Thus both Hegel's logic and his philosophy of history conclude not just that thought can know the world but also that thought is the force which shapes the world. "In other words, although we set out merely to trace the path of mind as it comes to *know* reality, at the end of the road we find that we have been watching mind as it *constructs* reality."[131]

It is from this perspective that Hegel reprimands Kant for his "excessive tenderness towards things;" that is, Kant did not claim enough for the powers of thought. Yet, in trying to unify what Kant had rent asunder by sucking all reality through to the side of thought, Hegel failed to keep his promise to present subject and object, knowing and being, as a unity of opposites. The paradox that Hegel inherited from Kant ultimately lay unresolved.

If Kant's dualism and Hegel's absolute idealism had both been inadequate to this task, what strategy was left? Marx and Engels mark a new era because they pictured the evolution of consciousness as part of the natural world, as a historic conquest of mankind emerging as a distinct part of nature. They thus provided a natural, material basis on which it was possible to analyze subject and object as a unity of opposites. Only on this basis could they supercede both Kant's dualism and Hegel's vision of a unity predicated on assimilating the natural world to the world of consciousness. They superceded Kant by providing a natural basis on which the unity of knowing and being could be predicated. And they superceded Hegel by developing a dialectic that did not frustrate its own purpose by reneging on its promise of explaining the real interaction between consciousness and its material basis.

NOT BETTER THAN THE AGE, BUT
THE AGE AT ITS BEST

Hegel's dialectic surpassed all previous and, so far, all further developments in bourgeois philosophy, because he summarized the experience of the international bourgeoisie at the high point of its development as a revolutionary class. He was, as he aspired to be in a youthful poem, "not better than the age, but the age at its best."[132] Only a theoretical position based on a new revolutionary class was capable of incorporating and further developing his insights. Some of Marx's most penetrating critiques of Hegel were written at precisely the time when he recognized the working class as the new agent of social change.

Marx and Engels, having "settled accounts with our former philosophical consciences,"[133] moved on from philosophy to study the real economic contradictions of capitalist society. But philosophy has not turned its back on marxism. While capitalism exists, philosophy, like its supernatural relation, religion, will always be with us. The influence of bourgeois ideas, be they materialist, rationalist, or idealist, and the emergence of new problems constantly demand that we return to the fundamentals of theory to clarify, extend, and defend marxism.

Hegel's philosophy stands in the same relation to that task as the lessons of the Great French Revolution do to marxist politics as a whole. Today's generation cannot repeat the experience uncritically—it was the revolution of a very different class—but we can learn from it. Hegel marked a high point from which much subsequent mainstream philosophy has either fallen back into dualism or else contented itself with elaborations of ideas that can be found, in embryo, in his thought.

Hegel could not ultimately solve the problem of Kantian dualism, but his attempt contained some key revolutionary developments. Marx inherited these and transformed them into a materialist dialectic. "I should very much like to make intelligible to the ordinary human intelligence—in two or three printer's sheets—what is *rational* in the method which Hegel discovered,"[134] Marx wrote in a letter to Engels. He never did have the time, but we still have much to learn from Hegel. Despite his mysticism, Hegel remains the great founder of the algebra of revolution.[135]

Notes

1. Marx and Engels, *Selected Correspondence* (Moscow: Progress, 1955), 93.
2. Lenin, *Collected Works*, Vol. 38 (London: Lawrence and Wishart, 1961), 180.
3. Marx, *Capital*, Vol. I (London: Penguin, 1976), 102.
4. Lenin, *Collected Works*, 362.

5. The full phrase, "I am of course no longer a Hegelian, but I still have a great feeling of piety and devotion towards the colossal old chap," is Engels's. See *Selected Correspondence*, 162. The expression, "I therefore openly avowed myself the pupil of that mighty thinker" is from *Capital* Vol. I, 102–3.

6. Quoted in N. Hampson, *The Enlightenment, an Evaluation of Its Assumptions and Values* (London: Pelican, 1968), 36–37.

7. See, for instance, P. M. Harman, *The Scientific Revolution* (London: Methuen, 1983), 30–32.

8. Pope and Halley's verse is quoted in Hampson, *The Enlightenment*, 38.

9. Marx and Engels, *The German Ideology* (London: Lawrence and Wishart, 1970), 111.

10. *Entrehen d'un pere avec ses enfants* (1770), quoted by N. Hampson, in *The Enlightenment*, 190. As it happens, it is unlikely that more than one or two people in town did hold such ideas—at least not if they depended on the *Encyclopedia* to learn of them. Its four thousand copies may have been widely disseminated throughout France but at such a cost that it reached only the very well off. Its seventeen volumes of text and eleven plates, produced between 1751 and 1772, mark a convenient summary of Enlightenment ideas.

11. One French textile mill employed 12,000; the Anzin mining company 4,000; and in Paris, there were 50 "manufactories" employing between 100 and 800.

12. See G. Rude, *Revolutionary Europe 1783–1815* (London: Fontana, 1964), 11–12.

13. Ibid., 34–35.

14. Quoted in M. Cranston, Introduction to Rousseau, *The Social Contract* (London: Penguin, 1968), 14

15. Quoted ibid., 16.

16. Quoted ibid., 16.

17. Ibid., 21.

18. Quoted in Hampson, *The Enlightenment*, 94.

19. Ibid., 126.

20. Marx may have been extending Hegel's own observation that "among the Germans" the revolutionary spirit of the times "assumed no other form than that of tranquil theory; but the French wished to give it practical effect." *The Philosophy of History* (New York: Dover, 1956), 443.

21. A Landgrave is "a count having jurisdiction over a territory, and having under him several inferior counts": the Shorter *OED*. (Oxford, Third Edition, corrected 1970)

22. Some Junkers, that is, the Prussian aristocracy, wanted to make changes—but only to increase their hold over the peasants by replacing forced labor with wage labor. But "in their deeply rooted class selfishness the mass of the Junkers did not even understand this." Only the defeats they suffered in the Napoleonic Wars clarified their thinking. See F. Mehring, *Absolutism and Revolution in Germany 1525–1848* (London: New Park, 1975), 151.

23. Hampson, *The Enlightenment*, pp. 45 and 63.

24. The journeymen's associations, which had made attempts to break out of the guild system and create a free market, thus facilitating the rise of a bourgeoisie, had been crushed. The Prussian monarchy's Imperial Law of 1731 suppressed the last resistance, and the Statute of Handcrafts of 1733 threatened imprisonment and, eventually, death for those who resisted. The result was that tiny craft enterprises survived. See Mehring, *Absolutism and Revolution*, 154.

25. Ibid.

26. One calico mill employed 1,200, and another calico printing plant and cotton mill had over 3,000 workers.
27. For economic conditions in Germany, see Mehring, *Absolutism and Revolution*, 149–69.
28. For instance, English mills had two hundred Arkwright water frames by 1790, while France had eight. Germany did not get her first until 1794. See Hampson, *The Enlightenment*, 169.
29. Ibid.
30. Ibid., 60.
31. R. Christiansen, *Romantic Affinities— Portraits from an Age 1780–1830* (London: Sphere, 1989), 74–75.
32. See Hampson, *The Enlightenment*, 61.
33. Christiansen, *Romantic Affinities*, 75.
34. Mehring, *Absolutism and Revolution*, 169. The parallels with the social origin of the most determined sections of the French revolutionary leadership and with the leadership of "deflected permanent revolutions" in the twentieth century are interesting.
35. Ibid., 173.
36. See E. J. Hobsbawm, *The Age of Revolution 1789–1848* (London: Abacus, 1977), 82 and 304.
37. P. F. Strawson, *The Bounds of Sense, an Essay on Kant's Critique of Pure Reason* (London: Routledge, 1989), 18.
38. H. Marcuse, *Reason and Revolution* (London, Routledge and Kegan Paul, 1977), 21.
39. Strawson, *The Bounds of Sense*, 19.
40. G. Plekhanov, "Notes to the Russian Edition" of F. Engels, *Ludwig Feuerbach and the End of Classical German Philosophy* (Peking, 1976), 141.
41. I. Kant, *The Critique of Pure Reason*, quoted in S. Korner, *Kant* (London: Penguin, 1955), 38.
42. Strawson, *The Bounds of Sense*, 35. Kant's idealism was transcendent is the sense that his categories provide the preconditions of any possible experience. George Berkeley (1685–1753) was horrified at the skepticism that he saw implicit in Locke's contention that there is a gap between what we know and reality, because all our knowledge of the world is derived from our sense impressions. He attempted to solve the problem by simply denying the existence of matter. Certainty about experience was retained simply by asserting that there is no gap between matter and our sense impressions, because all that we have are our sense impressions, mere "collections of ideas."
43. Ibid., 38.
44. Plekhanov, "Notes to the Russian Edition," 142–43. In this connection, Strawson makes another valuable point which demonstrates the consequence of not treating space and time, as well as causality, as properties of the thing in itself: "The doctrine that we are aware of things only as they appear and not as they are in themselves because their appearances to us are the result our constitution being affected by objects, is a doctrine that we can understand just so long as the affecting is thought of as something that occurs in space and time; but when it is added that we are to understand space and time themselves as nothing but a capacity or liability of ours to be affected in a certain way by objects not themselves in space and time, then we can no longer understand the doctrine, for we no longer know what "affecting" means, or what we are to

understand by ourselves." Strawson, *The Bounds of Sense*, 41.

45. See S. Avineri, *Hegel's Theory of the Modern State* (Cambridge: Cambridge University Press, 1972), 2.
46. See ibid., 3, and G. Lukacs, *The Young Hegel* (London: Merlin, 1975), 10.
47. Quoted in Christiansen, *Romantic Affinities*, 84.
48. Quoted in C. Taylor, *Hegel* (Cambridge: Cambridge University Press, 1975), 424.
49. See Avineri, *Hegel's Theory of the Modern State*, 6.
50. In a letter to Schelling, he complains that: "All the intrigues in the princely courts . . . are nothing compared with the combinations that go on here. The father nominates the son or the groom that will bring in the heaviest dowry, and so on. In order to understand an aristocratic constitution, one has to spend one such winter here." See ibid., 3.
51. Ibid.
52. Ibid., 4.
53. G. W. F. Hegel, *Phenomenology of Spirit* (Oxford: Oxford University Press, 1977), 359–60.
54. Quoted in Avineri, *Hegel's Theory of the Modern State*, 48.
55. Ibid., 9.
56. See H. S. Harris, "Hegel's Intellectual Development to 1807," in F. C. Beiser, ed., *The Cambridge Companion to Hegel* (Cambridge: Cambridge University Press, 1993), 26.
57. Hegel, *Realphilosophie*, quoted in Lukacs, *The Young Hegel*, 310–11. In an otherwise valuable account, Jean Hyppolite's *Studies on Marx and Hegel* (London: Heinemann, 1969) quotes a sentence from this passage and assumes that Hegel is referring to Napoleon (see 58–59). But the fuller context makes it clear that Hegel has Robespierre in mind.
58. Hegel, *Erstes Systemprogramm des Deutschen Idealismus*, quoted in Marcuse, *Reason and Revolution*, 12.
59. Quoted in Lukacs, *The Young Hegel*, 308.
60. See Hampson, *The Enlightenment*, 281.
61. See Avineri, *Hegel's Theory of the Modern State*, 39.
62. Ibid., 37.
63. Ibid., 63.
64. Ibid., 64.
65. Ibid.
66. The supposedly mighty Prussian state had been forced to sue for peace in 1795, after which "it withdrew from great world affairs to carry on a semblance of life under the shield of cowardly neutrality, hated and scorned by all . . . it was utterly finished, intellectually and morally, financially and militarily." See Mehring, *Absolutism and Revolution*, 137.
67. Ibid., 148.
68. Quoted in Avineri, *Hegel's Theory of the Modern State*, 68.
69. Ibid., 70–71.
70. Ibid., 71.
71. Hegel, *Philosophy of Right* (Oxford: Oxford University Press, 1952), 13.
72. Avineri, *Hegel's Theory of the Modern State*, 70.
73. Mehring, *Absolutism and Revolution*, 183.
74. Ibid., 184.
75. Ibid., 182.

76. Marx, *Economic and Philosophical Manuscripts*, in *Early Writings* (London: Pelican, 1975), 386.
77. Quoted in Lukacs, *The Young Hegel*, 331.
78. Ibid., 334.
79. K. Marx, *Economic and Philosophical Manuscripts*, 385–86.
80. P. Singer, *Hegel* (Oxford, OUP, 1983), 9.
81. F. Engels, *Karl Marx, the Critique of Political Economy*, in *Selected Works*, Vol. I (Moscow: Progress, 1963), 512.
82. Taylor, *Hegel*, 154–55.
83. *Phenomenology*, 117–19.
84. Lukacs, *The Young Hegel*, 327.
85. Hegel, *Philosophy of History* (New York: Dover, 1956), 1.
86. Ibid., 3.
87. Ibid.
88. Ibid., 6.
89. Ibid., 7.
90. Ibid., 8.
91. Ibid., 10.
92. Ibid., 11.
93. Nevertheless, there remains a problem with seeing *Geist* in these terms. Because no one human being, class, or nation can ever rise above their own particular "spirit of the age," they can never embody the whole of *Geist*. This has led some to a religious interpretation that identifies *Geist* with God. In some passages, Hegel himself was not above this mysticism. Following Hegel's death division rent his followers. Right Hegelians tended to translate *Geist* as Spirit, to give Hegel a religious coloring, while Left Hegelians translated *Geist* as Mind, insisting on a secular interpretation.
      I have continued to translate *Geist* as Spirit for two reasons. Firstly, it is the most common translation. Secondly, a marxist understanding of Hegel does not primarily depend on rescuing him from religious interpretations as it does for liberal scholars. Hegel's thought did have a genuinely mystical dimension which stems from his idealism. See also M. George and A. Vincent's admirably clear introduction to G. W. F. Hegel, *The Philosophical Propaedeutic* (Oxford: Blackwell, 1986), xxiii.
94. *Philosophy of History*, 9.
95. Ibid.
96. Ibid., 26–27.
97. Ibid., 74.
98. Ibid., 76.
99. Ibid., 77.
100. "Spirit annuls the reality," but "it gains the essence of that which *it only was.*" Ibid.
101. Ibid.
102. Ibid., 27.
103. Marx suffered from a worse affliction on his first encounter with Hegel, complaining of "sleepless nights, isolation, illness." See M. Rubel, *Marx, Life and Works* (London: Macmillan, 1965), 2.
104. See Avineri, *Hegel's Theory of the Modern State*, 63.
105. See Mehring, *Absolutism and Revolution*, 172.
106. Hegel, shorter *Logic*, quoted in F. G. Weiss, *Hegel, the Essential Writings* (New York: Harper and Row, 1974), 11.

107. Quoted in Rubel, Marx, Life and Works, 2.
108. Hegel, *Phenomenology of Spirit*, 2.
109. Ibid.
110. Ibid., 11.
111. Ibid., 28.
112. G. W. F. Hegel, *The Philosophy of Right* (Oxford: Oxford University Press, 1952), 34–35.
113. G. W. F. Hegel, *Logic, Being Part One of The Encyclopedia of the Philosophical Sciences* (Oxford: Oxford University Press, 1975), 14.
114. Ibid.
115. Ibid., 66.
116. F. G. Weiss, "Introduction: The Philosophy of Hegel," in F. G. Weiss, *Hegel, the Essential Writings* (New York: Harper and Row, 1974), 13. See also Singer, *Hegel*, 51–52.
117. Hegel, *Logic*, 70.
118. *Phenomenology*, 15–17.
119. Ibid., 29.
120. Ibid., 31. Formal categories, putting things in labeled boxes, will always be an inadequate way of looking at change and development, argues Hegel, because a static definition cannot cope with the way in which a new content emerges from old conditions. This approach leads Hegel to see only a limited role for the law of identity, that way of looking at things which rejects the possibility of internal contradictions and which is signified by the notation A = A. Taken as an absolute principle, this law is the "undoing of all distinct, determinate entities (or rather the hurling of them into the abyss of vacuity without further development or any justification)." The final phrase, in brackets, tells us why Hegel is dissatisfied with the law of identity. It may tell us, in a limited way, what a thing is, but it cannot tell us why a thing is (its justification), or how it will develop. Consequently, "to pit this single insight, that everything . . . is the same [A = A], against the full body of articulated cognition [a dialectic approach], which at least seeks and demands such fulfillment, to palm off its Absolute as the night in which, as the saying goes, all cows are black—this is cognition naively reduced to vacuity." *Phenomenology*, 8–9. Also see the *Science of Logic*, 439.
   On Hegel's criticism of Kant, Paul Guyer's generally dismissive essay, "Thought and being: Hegel's critique of Kant's theoretical philosophy," in F. C. Beiser, ed., *The Cambridge Companion to Hegel*, (Cambridge: Cambridge University Press, 1993) nevertheless contains a useful summary. See especially the points on 190–91.
121. L. Trotsky, *Notebooks 1933–35: Writings on Dialectics and Evolution* (New York: Columbia University, 1986), 103.
122. Lenin, *Collected Works* Vol. 38, 110.
123. Hegel, *Science of Logic*, 439. Emphasis in the original.
124. Ibid.
125. See note 118 above for Hegel's discussion of the law of identity. Also see *Science of Logic*, 438–39.
126. Hegel, *Science of Logic*, 440.
127. Hegel, *Logic*, 218–19.
128. Hegel, *Phenomenology*, 29.
129. Hegel, *Logic*, 219.
130. Ibid., 69.

131. Singer, *Hegel*, 70.
132. Quoted in Lukacs, *The Young Hegel*, 105.
133. Preface to *A Contribution to the Critique of Political Economy*, in *Early Writings*, 427.
134. *Selected Correspondence*, 93.
135. The phrase was coined by Alexander Herzen (1812–70), a leading Russian democratic revolutionary.

2

The Dialectic in
Marx and Engels

Hegel died in 1831 and in the decade that followed his disciples argued over the meaning of his legacy. The Young Hegelian grouping attempted to develop a radical interpretation of Hegel's system in reply to the increasingly reactionary conclusions to which its original author subscribed in later life and which his influential, government-sponsored inheritors continued to support. Marx and Engels first formulated their views in the course of disputes among the Young Hegelian group, of which they were both members.[1]

The group arose "during the reconstruction period which followed the Napoleonic wars" when "liberal ideas acquired a new momentum," writes Sidney Hook. "They were imported into Germany from France by the enthusiastic members of the Young German and Young Hegelian schools. Although no overt political movement resulted from them, they caused a stir in intellectual and academic circles."[2] But by the early 1840s, the authorities were in full flight from their earlier infatuation with Hegelianism.

> The official spokesman of semi-feudal German society sought to find a more stable base for public morality and cultural authority. Hegel, they discovered, was too ambiguous in his positions. His reliance upon reason was a double edged weapon.[3]

The pro-Hegelian Altenstein was replaced by the well-known anti-Hegelian Eichhorn as minister of culture. Gans, one of the editors of Hegel's complete works, found his academic position given to the jurist Friedrich Julius Stahl, an unashamed supporter of the autocratic state. The Prussian state issued a secret decree forbidding Hegelians to lecture on any subject except aesthetics. In 1841, the philosopher Schelling, once Hegel's close friend but now bitter that Hegel's reputation had outstripped his own, was called to Berlin. His task was, in the King's words, to root out "the dragon seed of Hegelianism."[4] Looking back, one Young Hegelian sympathizer said of the *Hallische Jahrbucher*, one of the group's publications, that it marked "the fall of the Hegelian philosophy from divine grace, and its expulsion from the

61

paradise of Prussian government appointments."[5] Bruno Bauer, one of the leading Young Hegelians, was dismissed from his university post and the annual itself, renamed the *Deutsche Jahrbucher*, was closed by the government in 1843.[6]

Government suppression both accelerated the Young Hegelian's radicalization and intensified their arguments about philosophical issues and political strategy, two concerns that could hardly be disentangled in this situation. In March 1844, the editor of *Deutsch Jahrbucher*, Arnold Ruge, launched a sequel, *Deutsch-französische Jahrbucher*. His co-editor was Karl Marx. The paper published an article called "A Contribution to the Critique of Political Economy" in which Marx read the first great analysis of capitalist exploitation. The author of the article was Frederick Engels.

But most political developments in the Young Hegelian group were not following the same path as Marx, Engels, or, even, Ruge. Bruno Bauer and his brother Edgar, for instance, founded another journal, the *Allgemeine Literatur Zeitung*. It published for a year, beginning in late 1843. "Its main theme," writes David McLellan, "was that, since the public had accepted with indifference the suppression of the press and all the illiberal measures of the Prussian government, the radicals had been wrong to put their trust in the people, the "mass", and that in the future criticism should hold aloof from such deceptive alliances."[7] Bauer himself wrote:

> All great actions of previous history were failures from the start and had no effective success because the masses became interested in and enthusiastic over them—or, they were bound to come to a pitiful end because the idea underlying them was such that it had to be content with a superficial comprehension and therefore to rely on the approval of the masses.[8]

So it was that Marx and Engels not only were faced with a government crackdown and the overall degeneration of the Hegelian school but also with the particular crisis facing the Young Hegelians. In response, they forged a new way of looking at the world.

In the years 1843–47 they brought together what they had learned from the German philosophical tradition, from political economy as it had developed in Britain, and from the knowledge they had gained from their own experience and that of the socialist writers and activists in France and England. This provided a new basis for radicalism, the old Hegelian one having so clearly blown itself out in the kind of cynical elitism of which Bauer was the most extreme spokesman. In these years, Marx and Engels wrote two long polemics against the Young Hegelians: *The Holy Family, or Critique of Critical Criticism* (with its subtitle *Against Bruno Bauer and Company*) and *The German Ideology* (with its subtitle, *Critique of Modern German Philosophy According to Its Representatives Feuerbach, B. Bauer and Stirner, and of German*

Socialism According to Its Various Prophets). Marx also wrote the *Critique of Hegel's Doctrine of the State* and the *Introduction to a Contribution to Hegel's Philosophy of Right*, the *Economic and Philosophical Manuscripts*, the *Theses on Feuerbach*, and *The Poverty of Philosophy*. Engels wrote *The Condition of the English Working Class* and the first draft of the *Communist Manifesto* during the same period.

In all this, Marx and Engels never forgot how much they owed to the Hegelian dialectic—its notions of totality, contradiction, alienation, and its sense of historical change. But they were equally clear that, if what was useful in the Hegelian system was to be preserved, it would have to be reconstituted on an entirely different basis—different from both the original foundations which Hegel had provided and also different to the transformations which it had undergone at the hands of the Young Hegelians.

CRITIQUE OF HEGELIANISM

Hegel's fundamental error sprang from his appreciation of a real problem, namely, it is impossible simply to stare at the world as it immediately presents itself to our eyes and hope to understand it. To make sense of the world, we must bring to it a framework composed of elements of our past experience; what we have learned of others' experience, both in the present and in the past; and of our later reflections on and theories about this experience.

But from this valid insight, that concepts and theories are necessary to interpret the world, Hegel not only drew the mistaken conclusion that all real knowledge of the world is theoretical knowledge but also that the development of knowledge primarily depends on the further elaboration of concepts. We have seen, in chapter 1, how the *Science of Logic* begins with the most abstract category, Being, and seeks to derive ever more concrete concepts from one another until an account has been given of every meaningful aspect of the world. Marx gave a succinct summary of how Hegel arrived at this idea:

> Is it surprising that everything, in the final abstraction . . . presents itself as a logical category? Is it surprising that, if you let drop little by little all that constitutes the individuality of a house, leaving out first of all the materials of which it is composed, then the form that distinguishes it, you end up with nothing but a body; that, if you leave out of account the limits of this body, you soon have nothing but a space—that if, finally, you leave out of account the dimensions of this space, there is absolutely nothing left but pure quantity, the logical category. If we abstract thus from every subject all the alleged accidents, animate or inanimate, men or things, we are right in saying that is the final abstraction, the only substance left is the logical category.[9]

This procedure, Marx and Engels argued, put the cart before horse. Even the most abstract theoretical concept ultimately has its roots in real existence. If we are ever to refine our theoretical concepts—and Marx and Engels agreed with Hegel that such a procedure was essential to a proper understanding of the world—then we must begin with the real world from which these ideas arise, not with the ideas and then seek to find our way back to their real preconditions. In *The German Ideology*, Marx and Engels wrote:

> The production of ideas, of conceptions, of consciousness, is at first directly interwoven with the material activity and the material intercourse of men—the language of real life. Conceiving, thinking, the mental intercourse of men at this stage still appear as the direct efflux of their material behaviour. The same applies to mental production as expressed in the language of the politics, laws, morality, religion, metaphysics, etc., of a people. Men are the producers of their conceptions, ideas etc., that is real, active men, as they are conditioned by a definite development of their productive forces and of the intercourse corresponding to these, up to its furthest forms. Consciousness can never be anything else than conscious being, and the being of men is their conscious life process.[10]

This way of proceeding, argued Marx and Engels, is "in direct contrast to German philosophy which descends from heaven to earth," whereas for them, "it is a matter of ascending from earth to heaven":

> That is to say, not of setting out from what men say, imagine, conceive, nor from men as narrated, thought of, imagined, conceived, in order to arrive at men in the flesh; but setting out from real, active men, and in their real life process demonstrating the development of ideological reflexes and echoes of this life process . . . men, developing their material production and their material world, also their thinking and the products of their thinking.[11]

It was on this basis that Marx and Engels formulated their famous dictum: "It is not consciousness that determines life, but life that determines consciousness." This formulation has often been interpreted by Marx and Engels's critics as evidence of a return to the mechanical materialism of the Enlightenment, leaving no role for consciousness in the shaping of history. Yet it should be clear from these quotations alone that this is not the case. Marx and Engels do not, for example, talk of a direct and immediate correspondence between thought and reality, preferring the terms "reflexes" and "echoes." Moreover, they go on to describe the way in which men "alter . . . also their thinking" as they alter their world. But if this is not proof enough, then Marx and Engels's further development of their critique of Hegelianism makes the case against seeing them as reductionists even clearer.

It was an essential part of Marx and Engels's critique of Hegel that the basically idealist thrust of his philosophy did not simply result in the claim that ideas were the moving force in the world. Ironically, it also forced him into crude, deterministic assertions about the empirical world as well. *The Holy Family* contains a marvelous parody of the Hegelian method which highlights both the idealism and the crude materialism of its approach. Marx and Engels begin by describing the idealist construction of concepts:

> If from real apples, pears, strawberries and almonds I form the general idea "*Fruit*," if I go further and *imagine* that my abstract idea "*Fruit*," derived from real fruit, is an entity existing outside me, is indeed the *true* essence of the pear, the apple, etc., then—in the language of speculative philosophy—I am declaring . . . that to be a pear is not essential to the pear, that to be an apple is not essential to the apple; what is essential to these things is not their real existence, perceptible to the senses, but the essence that I have abstracted from them and then foisted on them, the essence of my idea—"*Fruit*."[12]

This approach necessarily obliterates all specific, empirical differences:

> By this method one attains no particular *wealth of definitions*. The mineralogist whose whole science was limited to the statement that all minerals are really "*the* Mineral" . . . is reduced to repeating this word as many times as there are real minerals.[13]

And so to avoid this barren and empty conclusion, idealism is obliged to try and re-create the real world from its own abstractions; "having reduced the different real fruits to the *one* fruit of abstraction—'*the* Fruit,' speculation must, in order to attain some semblance of real content, try somehow to find its way back from '*the* Fruit,' from *Substance* to the *diverse*, ordinary real fruits, the pear, the apple, the almond, etc."[14]

Moreover, because Hegel then has to explain *why* "the Fruit" manifests itself as apples, pears, and so on, he is obliged to argue that his abstraction is not a "dead, undifferentiated, motionless" concept, but "a living, self-differentiating, moving essence." Thus, the origin of change and development is located in the realm of concepts, not in material reality.

Marx and Engels's point was this: Although Hegel's method did not begin by trying to account for the forces that really shape the material world, he could not simply ignore them either. He, therefore, tried to demonstrate how really existing material relations were derived from abstract ideas. The result was that whatever existing reality was found at hand *had* to be baptized as the legitimate offspring of Hegel's abstract concepts.

"Hegel," Marx argues in the *Economic and Philosophical Manuscripts*, "commits a double error" because his work contains "uncritical positivism and equally uncritical idealism." This leads Hegel to "the philosophical dissolution and restoration of the empirical world."[15] First Hegel's idealism dissolves the world into abstract categories, but then, to account for the material world, he is forced into the uncritical restoration of the existing social structure unchanged. Marx makes a similar point in the *Critique of Hegel's Doctrine of the State*. Hegel defended the institution of monarchy as a necessary requirement of philosophical reason. Marx exposes the philosophical error that led to such conservative conclusions:

> Hegel's purpose is to narrate the life-history of abstract substance, of the Idea, and in such a history human activity etc. necessarily appears as the activity and product of something other than itself. . . . This leads him to convert the subjective into the objective and objective into the subjective with the inevitable result that an *empirical person* is *uncritically* enthroned as the real truth of the Idea. For as Hegel's task is not to discover the truth of empirical existence but to discover the empirical existence of the truth, it is very easy to fasten on what lies nearest to hand and prove that it is an *actual* moment of the Idea.[16]

"Hegel thus provides," argues Marx, "his logic with a political body; he does not provide us with a logic of the body politic."[17] This process of moving from uncritical idealism to uncritical empiricism is deeply encoded in the Hegelian dialectic. Marx describes how Hegel's dialectical conception of the negation of the negation begins with abstract thought, passes through its opposite, material reality, and then returns to abstract thought, leaving material reality unchanged:

> Hegel starts out from the estrangement of substance (in logical terms: from the infinite, the abstractly universal), from the absolute and fixed abstraction. . . .
> Secondly, he supersedes the infinite and posits the actual, the sensuous, the real, the finite, the particular. . . .
> Thirdly, he once more supersedes the positive, and restores the abstraction.[18]

Marx illustrates his point by reference to Hegel's attitude to religion. Marx's dialectic involves starting with the real social conditions and showing how these give rise to religious illusions. It then proceeds to launch a theoretical critique of these illusions and a practical movement aimed at abolishing the conditions that give rise to them. But Hegel,

> having superseded religion and recognised it as a product of self-alienation . . . still finds himself confirmed in *religion* as *religion*. Here *is* the root of Hegel's *false* positivism or of his merely *apparent* criticism.

It follows that,

In Hegel, therefore, the negation of the negation is not the confirmation of true being through the negation of apparent being. It is the confirmation of apparent being or self-estranged being in its negation, or the negation of this apparent being as an objective being residing outside man and independent of him and its transformation into the subject.[19]

The conservatism of Hegel's system is thus buried in his notion of contradiction. Contradictions in Hegel are merely intellectual contradictions to be resolved by merely intellectual methods. The real world exists only as a foil to intellectual development, the means by which intellectual thought is clarified to itself. Reality is just a phase through which thought passes on its journey to self-understanding. The dialectic is therefore only a pseudo-dialectic; its contradictions are never those of opposed material forces capable of doing real damage or of effecting real progress. It is, Marx says, simply "a divine dialectic . . . the pure products of the labor of thought living and moving within itself and never looking out into reality."[20] Consequently,

> thoughts are therefore fixed phantoms existing outside nature and man. In his *Logic* Hegel has locked up all these phantoms, conceiving each of them firstly as negation, i.e. as *alienation* of *human* thought, and secondly as negation of the negation, i.e. as supersession of this alienation, as a real expression of human thought. But since this negation is itself still trapped in estrangement, what this amounts to is in part the restoration of these fixed phantoms in their estrangement and in part a failure to move beyond the final stage, the stage of self-reference in alienation, which is the true existence of these phantoms.[21]

Marx's point is that, in Hegel's dialectic, forces in contradiction are always prevented from any real conflict, because, as soon as they are shown to be opposed, they are, just as quickly, shown to be simply different aspects of the underlying concept. The opposition is merely to show that the concept is more complex and all-embracing than was first thought. The "resolution" of the conflict is simply to demonstrate that two contradictory aspects of the concept can be reconciled in a more fully developed understanding, a more complex concept. No real antagonism is involved.

Thus Hegel's political philosophy sought to show that there was no real contradiction between the idea of civil society and the idea of monarchy, because both could be resolved (or mediated) by the idea of the legislature which stands between them. Marx replied:

> The *legislature*, the middle term, is a hotch-potch of the two extremes of the monarchical principle and civil society, of empirical individuality and empirical universality, of subject and predicate. And in general Hegel regards the *syllogism* as the middle term, as a hotch-potch. We may say that in his

exposition of this deductive process the whole transcendental and mystical dualism of his system becomes manifest. The middle term is a wooden sword, the concealed antithesis between the particular and the general.[22]

We have seen the same process at work in Hegel's account of the master-slave dialectic (see chapter 1). There, too, the middle term served to undercut the apparent contradiction between the master and the slave and to lead the slave back to reconciliation with the existing reality.[23] Marx continues:

> It is evident that the company as a whole like a fight but are too afraid of getting bruised to take things too far. So the two who wish to fight arrange matters so that the third man who intervenes bears the brunt of the blows. But then one of the original two becomes the third and altogether they are so cautious that they never reach a decision.[24]

Marx praised another member of the Young Hegelian group, Ludwig Feuerbach, not only for his materialist analysis of ideology but also, specifically, for having opposed the fatalistic twist in Hegel's notion of the negation of the negation. It was, as Marx wrote in the *Economic and Philosophical Manuscripts*, Feuerbach's "great achievement . . . to have opposed the negation of the negation."[25] Marx, however, did not reject the negation of the negation. And he later came to the conclusion that, although Feuerbach "was epoch-making *after* Hegel because he laid *stress* on certain points which were . . . important for the progress of criticism, points which Hegel had left in *clair-obscur* [semi-obscurity]," nevertheless, "compared with Hegel, Feuerbach is certainly poor."[26]

Marx was, however, obliged to transform completely the terms of the dialectic when he altered its starting point from abstract concepts to real material forces. Mediation is no longer a peaceful process of reconciliation but the elaboration of the different forms in which the central contradiction of the age is played out in every aspect of social development. Patrick Murray has captured the key distinction between Hegel and Marx:

> The crucial point at issue is how to conceive *mediation*. This should come as no surprise since reconciliation is the heart and soul of Hegel's philosophical synthesis. Mediation is called for in the face of conflicting extremes such as Hegel perceived in the dualisms of the Enlightenment. Mediation is likewise at the centre of Marx's concept of science. Finding the "ought" in the "is" involves mediation. Where Hegel finds reconciliation, Marx spots contradiction.[27]

Reaching back to Hegel's political philosophy, Marx argues, "With the Estate and the executive supplying the middle term between the sovereign and civil society we find for the first time all the prerequisites for an *antithesis* in which the two sides are not only drawn up ready for battle, but we have also reached the point of *irreconcilable conflict*." "Thus this '*middle term*' . . . far from accomplishing a mediation . . . is the embodiment of a contradiction," says Marx.[28]

The contradictions are no longer simply between concepts but between real, material forces. Hegel's chief error is that he regards "*contradiction in the phenomenal world as a unity in its essence, in the Idea*." But, says Marx, "There is however a profounder reality involved, namely an *essential contradiction*, e.g. in this case the contradiction in the legislature is itself only the self-contradiction of the political state, and hence of civil society."[29] The resolution of such contradictions is no longer merely a question of intellectual development, but a real clash of arms. "Clearly the weapon of criticism cannot replace the criticism of weapons, and material force must be overthrown with material force." This did not mean that theory was an irrelevance, merely that it must mesh with the real course of social development, then "theory also becomes a material force once it has gripped the masses."[30] Marx's point was simply that *theory alone* was inadequate.

This was precisely the opposite of Hegel's approach where "the act of superseding is the act of superseding an entity of thought." And "this supersession in thought . . . leaves its object in existence in reality" although it "thinks it has actually overcome it."[31] The link between idealism and the conservative form of the dialectic found in Hegel was made even more explicit when Marx and Engels turned their attention to the Young Hegelians:

> Since, according to their fantasy, the relations of men, all their doings, their fetters and their limitations are products of their consciousness, the Young Hegelians logically put to men the moral postulate of exchanging their present consciousness for human, critical or egoistic consciousness, and thus removing their limitations. This demand to change consciousness amounts to a demand to interpret the existing world in a different way, i.e., to recognise it by means of a different interpretation. The Young Hegelian ideologists, in spite of their allegedly "world shatering" phrases, are the staunchest conservatives.[32]

Marx's own conclusion was simply that any effective strategy must be embodied in practice:

> In order to supersede the *idea* of private property, the *idea* of communism is enough. In order to supersede private property as it actually exists, *real* communist activity is necessary.[33]

THE DIALECTIC OF HUMAN LABOR AND NATURE

Marx and Engels's elaboration of a materialist dialectic led them to conclude that, because society was shaped by contradictory material forces, a revolution in philosophical consciousness would not be enough to change it. "The philosophers have only *interpreted* the world, in various ways; the point is to *change* it," as Marx wrote in the famous final thesis on Feuerbach.[34] But Marx and Engels's view of practice had far deeper roots than the imperative to political action, vital though they considered that to be. Ultimately Marx and Engels's view of human beings' ability to shape society and to interact with the natural world was based on their view of human labor.

Marx and Engels regarded it as one of Hegel's great achievements to have recognized that human beings create their world through their own labor, even though Hegel only understood this as mental labor. But where Hegel saw the disembodied and timeless work of consciousness, Marx and Engels saw the material and historical work of human labor. Hegel began the *Science of Logic* with Being, the most abstract concept. Marx and Engels's analysis in *The German Ideology* begins with a parody of such concerns. But this parody also makes a serious point:

> Since we are dealing with Germans, who are devoid of premises, we must begin by stating the first premise of all human existence and, therefore, of all history, the premise, namely that men must be in a position to live in order to be able to "make history". But life involves before everything else eating and drinking, housing, clothing and various other things.[35]

Marx and Engels insist that "the first historical act is thus the production of the means to satisfy these needs." Not only is this "a fundamental condition of all history" but also one "which today, as thousands of years ago, must daily and hourly be fulfilled merely in order to sustain human life."[36] In fact, even those things which we take to be definitions of what it means to be human are the product of an historical evolution during which laboring to fulfill need was the motive force. In later works, written after Darwin published *The Origin of Species*, Marx and Engels elaborated their view that even the development of human capacities is a product of the labor necessary to survive. The operations of the human hand, for instance, are an historical achievement won through labor:

> The first operations for which our ancestors gradually learned to adapt their hands during the many thousands of years transition from ape to man could only have been very simple ones. . . . Before the first flint could be fashioned into a knife by human hands, a period of time probably elapsed in comparison with which the historical period known to us appears insignificant. But the decisive step had been taken, *the hand had become free*.

"Thus," concluded Engels, "the hand is not only the organ of labour, *it is also the product of labour*."[37] Even the development of consciousness is an historical act bound up with the process of labor. "Even from the outset" human consciousness "is not 'pure' consciousness," argue Marx and Engels,

> The "mind" is from the outset afflicted with the curse of being burdened with matter, which here makes its appearance in the form of agitated layers of air, sounds, in short, language. Language is as old as consciousness, language *is* practical, real consciousness that exists for other men as well, and only therefore does it also exist for me; language, like consciousness, only arises from the need, the necessity, of intercourse with other men.... Consciousness is, therefore, from the very beginning a social product, and remains so as long as men exist at all.[38]

Although it is itself an historical product, conscious labor, once it has arisen, is the defining characteristic of human beings and the original model for the dialectical integration of ideas and reality, theory, and practice. In Volume I of *Capital*, Marx rehearses the themes that he and Engels had first outlined in the early 1840s:

> Labour is, first of all, a process between man and nature, a process by which man, through his own actions, mediates, regulates and controls the metabolism between himself and the nature. He confronts the materials of nature as a force of nature. He sets in motion the natural forces which belong to his own body, his arms, his legs, head and hands, in order to appropriate the materials of nature in a form adapted to his own needs. Through this movement he acts upon external nature and changes it, and in this way he simultaneously changes his own nature.[39]

This unique ability to change oneself while changing circumstances is the key to differentiating human labor from the behavior of animals.

> We presuppose labour in a form in which it is an exclusively human characteristic. A spider conducts operations which resemble those of the weaver, and a bee would put many a human architect to shame by the construction of its honeycomb cells. But what distinguishes the worst architect from the best of bees is that the architect builds the cell in his mind before he constructs it in wax. At the end of every labour process, a result emerges which had already been conceived of by the worker at the beginning, hence already existed ideally.[40]

Marx is absolutely unambiguous on this point, even going so far as to argue, "man . . . realizes his own purpose . . . And this is a purpose he is conscious of, it determines the mode of his activity with the rigidity of a law, and he must subordinate his will to it."[41] But this does not mean to say that the products of labor are the free creation of consciousness. The aims of consciousness and the materials that make their realization possible are given by the natural and social circumstances in which human beings find themselves. Thus Marx argues:

> The simple elements of the labour process are (1) purposeful activity, that is work itself, (2) the object on which that work is performed, and (3) the instruments of that work.[42]

These are, of course, only the most abstract determinants, a consideration of "the labour process independently of any specific social formation." It is not, therefore, a level at which Marx was content to remain. Nevertheless, it is important to note that it is on labor at this fundamental level that Marx and Engels build their conception of the interaction between the conditions in which human beings find themselves and their ability consciously to transform those conditions. It is from this same framework that Marx drew his most famous formulation of the relationship between consciousness and its material limitations: "Men make their own history, but not of their own free will; not under circumstances they themselves have chosen but under given and inherited circumstances with which they are directly confronted."[43]

So it was that Marx and Engels developed a notion of the relationship between human beings and the natural world which neither reduced human beings to the level of animals—as various "naked ape" theorists do to this day—nor pretended that human beings and human consciousness were totally separate from the natural world. Instead, they insisted that both human beings and human consciousness developed from, and still depended on, interaction with the rest of the natural world. Labor was the pivot on which this relationship turned. Labor is the way in which human consciousness and the material world interact, transforming both.

This is a dialectical conception that can stand as a model for Marx and Engels's whole approach. It conceives of nature and human beings as a totality, but not one in which either side of the contradiction can simply be reduced to the other. Consciousness is not absolutely "free," as the Young Hegelians asserted, neither is it simply a natural reflex, as the mechanical materialists insisted. Rather both sides of the totality are mediated by conscious labor, an activity that in itself combines both the materiality of human physical attributes and the consciousness of the human brain.

Two important issues are raised by this approach. First, Marx and Engels's conception of a "differentiated unity" restores the role of mediation to a meaningful place in the dialectic. Hegel's idealism had reduced the middle term to a sham—a "wooden sword"—which merely became the means for suppressing real conflict and restoring the original relations from which contradiction arose in the first place. Here labor becomes the means of overcoming the contradiction between human beings and the natural world and opening up the possibility of real progress, real change in both conditions and consciousness.

Chris Arthur has rightly argued that Marx takes the category of mediation from Hegel and that "it is as central to his work as it is to Hegel's." Arthur goes on to explain that mediation "is to be contrasted with 'immediacy'" and that,

Someone who argues that man is nothing but a part of nature, a natural being subject to natural laws, is taking the position that man is in *immediate unity* with nature. By contrast, someone who takes a dualistic position, representing man as separate from the natural realm, developing himself spiritually, and struggling against the power of nature latent in himself as well as the influence of external determinants, is taking man to be *immediately opposed* to nature.[44]

The materialists of the Enlightenment and Feuerbach took the first view, the Young Hegelians took the second. Both thereby destroyed the possibility of a real dialectical relationship emerging between the two elements of the totality and, consequently, the mediation between them. Arthur concludes:

Marx's position was much more complex. On the one hand, he speaks of nature as "man's inorganic body" and says that "he must maintain a continuing dialogue with it if he is not to die . . . for man is part of nature." On the other hand, he says that "it is in his fashioning of the objective world that man really proves himself"; through such productive activity "nature appears as *his* work and his reality."[45]

Second, it is important that we fully understand what Marx and Engels mean by "labor" and, more broadly, by "practice." They *do not* mean that a conscious idea is "carried out" by laboring, or that a theoretical scheme is "implemented" by practice. Such notions simply reproduce the old dualism, albeit within a narrower compass. Marx and Engels mean that labor and practice *are* the unity of materiality and consciousness, the simultaneous human experience of physicality and its directing intelligence. Franz Jakubowski accurately captures Marx's meaning:

Consciousness no longer stands outside being and is no longer separated from its object. . . . Consciousness is determined by the transformations of being; but, as the consciousness of acting men, it in turn transforms this being. Consciousness is no longer consciousness *above* an object, the duplicated "reflection" of an individual object, but a constituent part of changing relations, which are what they are only in conjunction with the consciousness that corresponds to their material existence. Consciousness is the self-knowledge of reality, an expression and a part of the historical process of being, which knows itself at every stage of development.[46]

It is this understanding that informs Marx's *Theses on Feuerbach*, particularly the first thesis:

The chief defect of all hitherto existing materialism (that of Feuerbach included) is that the thing, reality, sensuousness, is conceived only in the form of the *object or of contemplation*, but not as *sensuous human activity, practice, not subjectively*. Hence in contradistinction to materialism, the *active* side was developed by idealism—which of course does not know real, sensuous activity as such. Feuerbach wants sensuous objects really distinct from thought objects, but he does not conceive human activity itself as *objective* activity. Hence . . . he regards the theoretical attitude as the only genuinely human attitude, while practice is conceived and fixed only in its dirty-judaical manifestation. Hence he does not grasp the significance of "revolutionary", of "practical-critical" activity.[47]

Marx's point is that in practice two things happen simultaneously: thought becomes an objective force and material reality becomes subjectively manipulable. This is because practice contains both consciousness and materiality. Feuerbach started out, in opposition to Hegel, with materialism. But just as Hegel's uncritical idealism led to uncritical positivism, so Feuerbach's uncritical materialism ended in restoring uncritical idealism. Feuerbach's mistake is to see practice simply as materiality and, therefore, to see no materiality in consciousness. As Sidney Hook notes:

Marx is criticizing him not so much for his inadequate materialism as for his vestigal idealism. It is one thing to overcome the idealistic hypostasis of different phases of temporal activity by demanding a return to the facts of experience. It is quite another to carry out the necessary reform and be faithful to one's own programme. Feuerbach, because of his unhistorical and abstract conception of man, needs, object, community and communism, sins against his own programme and relapses into idealism.[48]

Marx and Engels do not deny that there are forms of materiality which do not have consciousness (the inanimate world, for instance) nor that there are forms of consciousness that are abstracted from the real world (such as Hegelian philosophy). They simply assert that labor is a unique fusion of both these elements. Those theorists who are unable to see how labor becomes the subject-object of the historical process, the nodal point at which the lines of material determination and consciousness coincide, are deprived of the vantage point from which the development of the natural world, the development of society, and interaction between them, can be comprehended.

THE DIALECTIC OF NATURE

An important consequence of the approach outlined in the previous section is that Marx and Engels could hold that dialectical development was a feature of the natural world as well as the social world without needing to assert that the form of the dialectic was the same in both cases. Henri Lefebvre notes, "the sciences of nature and the social sciences are specifically creative, each having its own methods and objectives. However, the laws of human reality cannot be entirely diferent from the laws of Nature."[49] This approach prevented Marx and Engels from either pretending that economic laws worked with the same level of determinism as natural laws, or from being tempted to anthropomorphize the natural world by claiming that it reproduced the attributes of human consciousness.

There were times, even whole eras, where human beings could not or had not managed to exercise total control over society. In these conditions economic laws operated "with the necessity of a natural law." But these periods should not lead us to ignore the qualitative difference between nature and human society, their interdependence not withstanding. Even where the natural limits on conscious change are drawn very tightly, as in pre-capitalist societies, the process of conscious human labor still has a social effect quite different to the blind operation of nature even in the animal world, let alone at the inanimate level.

In the *Dialectics of Nature*, Engels sometimes uses metaphors and examples drawn from the natural world in inappropriate or unhelpful ways, allowing critics to assume that he did not understand the distinction between development in the natural world and social change. Yet it is precisely in *The Dialectics of Nature* that Engels makes this important distinction between the dialectic in human history and that in nature:

> In history, motion through opposites is most markedly exhibited in all critical epochs of the foremost peoples. At such moments a people has only the choice between two horns of a dilemma: "either-or!" and indeed the question is always put in a way quite different from that in which the philistines, who dabble in politics in every age, would have liked it put.[50]

And he goes on to give an example from the 1848 revolutions when "even the German philistine . . . found himself in 1849, suddenly, unexpectedly, and against his will confronted with the question: a return to the old reaction in an intensified form, or the continuation of the revolution." But, on the same page, Engels outlines a significantly different pattern of dialectical change in the natural world:

> *Hard and fast lines* are incompatible with the theory of evolution. . . . "Either-or" becomes more and more inadequate. . . . For a stage in the outlook on nature where all differences become merged in intermediate steps, and all opposites pass into one another through intermediate links, the old metaphysical method of thought no longer suffices. Dialectics, which likewise knows no *hard and fast lines*, no unconditional, universally valid "either-or" and bridges that fixed metaphysical differences, and besides "either-or"

recognises also in the right place "both this and that" and reconciles opposites, is the sole method of thought appropriate in the highest degree to this stage.[51]

Ferraro, quoting Engels, elaborates this point: While in nature, "a succession of phenomena which so far as our immediate observation is concerned, recur with fair regularity between wide limits," in human history repetitions are the exception, not the rule. Furthermore, "when such repetitions occur, they never arise under exactly the same conditions."[52]

In an important passage in *Ludwig Feuerbach and the End of Classical German Philosophy*, Engels wrote that although "dialectics was . . . the science of the general laws of motion, both of the external world and of human thought" and that although they were "two sets of laws which are identical in substance," they were necessarily "different in their expression insofar as the human mind can apply them consciously, while in nature . . . these laws assert themselves unconsciously, in the form of external necessity."[53] He also notes that human beings do not, in class society, have collective conscious control of their destiny and, as a result, "that which is willed happens but rarely." Consequently, social laws become analogous to those prevailing "in the realm of unconscious nature." Nevertheless, Engels insists:

> In one point, however, the history of the development of society proves to be essentially different from that of nature. In nature—insofar as we ignore man's reaction on nature—there are only blind, unconscious agencies acting on one another, out of whose interplay the general law comes into operation. Whatever happens . . . does not happen as a consciously desired aim. On the other hand, in the history of society the actors are all endowed with consciousness, are men acting with deliberation or passion, working towards definite goals; nothing happens without conscious purpose, without intended aim.[54]

The distinction between a dialectic where consciousness is present and one where it is absent, is not the only thing that distinguishes Engels's analysis from crude reductionism. Engels also insisted that *within* nature itself it was a mistake to reduce, say, biology to chemistry. Sean Sayers's excellent account of Engels's argument makes the point:

> For example, insulin is a biological product; it is a hormone which is secreted in the pancreas. The chemical composition of insulin is now known, and it can even be synthesized artificially. Some of its chemical effects in the body are understood. But this does not mean that the biology of insulin has been or can be reduced to chemistry. To describe and understand insulin in biological terms involves much more than a knowledge of its chemical composition and properties. It involves understanding its role as a hormone and its functions in the body as a whole. Chemistry can

provide an account of the mechanisms underlying this role, but this role itself can be comprehended only with a different level of concepts and principles which are constitutive of biology as a distinct science.[55]

For reductionists the whole is understood as the simple aggregation of its parts. But for dialectical materialists the whole is more than the simple sum of its parts. And this approach does not involve any form of mysticism:

> Of course, a living organism is composed of physical and chemical constituents, and nothing more. Nevertheless, it is not a mere collection of such constituents, nor even of anatomical and physiological parts. It is these parts unified, organized and acting as a whole. This unity and organization are not only features of our descriptions: they are properties of the thing itself; they are constitutive of it as a biological organism.[56]

Sayers recounts Engels's position with admirable clarity:

> These different levels are relatively autonomous: they are not only distinct but also united; there is continuity as well as difference between them. The clearest demonstration of this is provided for by the fact—and modern science takes it for a fact—that biological phenomena *emerge* from merely chemical and physical—i.e. non-biological—conditions, by purely natural processes.[57]

Two scientists, Richard Levins and Richard Lewontin, make a similar point in an excellent account of the contemporary applicability of Marx and Engels's approach. They, too, are clear that we must see human society as both part of, evolving from, and yet different to the rest of nature. They note that:

> Systems destroy the conditions that brought them about in the first place and create the possibilities of new transformations that did not previously exist. The law that all life arises from life was enacted only about a billion years ago. Life originally arose from inanimate matter, but that origination made its continued occurrence impossible, because living organisms consume the complex organic molecules needed to recreate life *de novo*.[58]

Nor is this idea of process in nature limited to biology. The emergence of higher and more complex forms from lower and more simple ones is general feature of material existence: "It is exhibited at simple level in the evolution of the universe as a whole—in the formation, development and ultimate death of galaxies, stars and planetary systems—described and explained by cosmology. Likewise, geology describes the development of material features of the planet."[59]

This idea, that nature has a history, that it changes and develops over time, rather than remaining fixed and frozen in the shape it first took at the beginning of time, is common today but was unknown in Hegel's day. Yet for all that we are now familiar with the idea of natural history, it still poses a problem for many contemporary philosophers and scientists that it would not have posed for Hegel, let alone Marx and Engels. Some simply relapse into the reductionism that Sayers criticizes. But, for those who are unhappy with this solution, the problem is this: If nature forms a totality, which it must unless we depart from materialism completely and become believers in the *super*natural, and if this totality develops, as evolutionary theory indicates, then are we not obliged to picture this as self-development powered by internal contradiction? It is on exactly this point that the theoretical core of Engels's argument in *The Dialectic of Nature* rested. And it is in having to confront precisely this kind of problem that has encouraged some scientists to develop a materialist, marxist-influenced, conception of change. Others, attempting to defend a more traditional vision of scientific method, often find themselves courting semi-mystical explanations of original cause.

   Those, like Levins and Lewontin, who are defending a dialectical notion of science, come to a remarkable agreement with Marx and Engels in maintaining that, because history gives rise to qualitatively new levels of development, "the laws of transformation themselves change." Unlike the mainstream view, which holds the objects to which laws apply change but the laws themselves do not, a dialectical view must insist that "the entities that are the objects of these laws of transformation become subjects that change these laws."[60] Consequently, it is not an abrogation of the dialectic that we find different forms of the dialectic in different aspects of reality but a confirmation of the usefulness of this approach and proof against accusations that marxism is a form of reductionism.

THE DIALECTIC OF HISTORY

To make sense of the human capacity to shape the world, we have to understand the constraints under which human beings exercise this capacity. Only when we know the exact natural, economic, social, and political conditions under which human beings find themselves will we be able to estimate what change is possible and by what means it can be effected. This is why Marx and Engels regarded even their own account of the relationship between human beings and nature as a meaningless generality unless it resulted in more concrete analyses of the various ways in which this relationship had developed historically.

   Marx and Engels's constant complaint against their political and theoretical opponents—whether they were Young Hegelians or the French socialist Proudhon, the German academic Duhring or the classical bourgeois economists—is that their theories are ahistorical and abstract. They assume that characteristics of one historical period are true of all history or that generalities which are true of all history can be made to account for the particularities of a certain period.

The very first point that Marx and Engels make is that the conception of human freedom, which is implicit in their own general notion of conscious labor, has actually been denied, or partially denied, by the conditions under which human beings have labored for most of their history.[61] Thus, throughout history,

> people won freedom for themselves each time to the extent that was dictated and permitted not by their ideal of man, but by the existing productive forces. All emancipation carried through hitherto has been based, however, on restricted productive forces.[62]

Here we are already moving in quite another direction from Hegel and his Young Hegelian successors. It is the circumstances in which human beings find themselves that requires a dialectical analysis, not just the ideas that people have about themselves. Moreover, Marx and Engels's notion of human labor directed their attention to the growing productive capacity that lay at the heart of human history.

> Each stage contains a material result, a sum of productive forces, a historically created relation to nature and of individuals to one another, which is handed down to each generation by its predecessor; a mass of productive forces which on the one hand is modified by the new generation, but on the other also prescribes for it its conditions of life and gives it a definite development, a special character. It shows that circumstances make men just as much as men make circumstances.[63]

And this capacity did not just circumscribe human history in some general way—it gave rise to quite specific forms of human interaction, class relations:

> The production which these productive forces could provide was insufficient for the whole of society and made development possible only if some persons satisfied their needs at the expense of others, and therefore some—the minority—obtained a monopoly of development, while others—the majority—owing to the constant struggle to satisfy their most essential needs, were for the time being (i.e. until the creation of new revolutionary productive forces) excluded from any development.

Human history as a whole is driven forward by the conflict at its heart: "Thus, society has hitherto always developed within the framework of a contradiction—in antiquity the contradiction between free men and slaves, in the Middle Ages that between nobility and serfs, in modern times between the bourgeoisie and the proletariat."[64] But in Marx and Engels the changing nature of society means that the dialectic can have quite different features in different historical periods.

Even at this still very general level, it is clear that Marx and Engels are developing dialectical concepts quite different to any that are to be found in Hegel. Hegel's idealism prevented him from allowing contradictions in material reality to show any real development. They were always simply the expression of thought in opposition to itself, soon to be reintegrated in a more rounded understanding of that same process of thought. Marx and Engels, in contrast, are obliged to develop further the actual processes by which economic contradictions work themselves out.

Thus not only does the level of the productive forces give rise to class contradictions in the most obvious sense, but, because labor also develops the productive forces over time, these forces change in a way that comes to conflict with the social and political institutions which originated on the earlier, less developed productive base.

Each generation inherits a new stock of tools and techniques from the previous generation, but it also inherits old institutions, class relations, and customs which have not necessarily changed as quickly. The antagonism between the new ways of producing and the old relations, which is simultaneously the antagonism between the producers and those who rule them, is the motive force behind social revolutions.

> In the social production of their existence, men inevitably enter into definite relations, which are independent of their will, namely relations of production appropriate to a given stage in the development of the material forces of production. The totality of these relations of production constitutes the economic structure of society, the real foundation, on which arises a legal and political superstructure and to which correspond definite forms of consciousness.... At a certain stage of development, the material productive forces of society come into conflict with the existing relations of production or—this merely expresses the same thing in legal terms— with the property relations within the framework of which they have operated hitherto. From forms of development of the productive forces these relations turn into their fetters. Then begins an era of social revolution.[65]

This famous "base and superstructure" formulation has often been taken to imply a deterministic attitude toward political institutions, parties, consciousness, and revolution. But it is clearly not Marx's intention to demonstrate the inevitability of revolution, merely that this material framework opens up the possibility of revolutionary transformation: "the productive forces developing within bourgeois society create . . . the material conditions for a solution of this antagonism."[66] But creating the possibility of a solution and actually achieving the solution are here, as in all walks of life, not necessarily the same thing. Actually resolving the contradictions of capitalism, and thereby being able to make use of the productive forces accumulated, depends on how the conflict between the classes is resolved. And a crucial part of a successful resolution is the "ideological forms in which men become conscious of this conflict and fight it out."[67]

This is why, if we put aside occasional rhetorical flourishes about the "inevitabilty" of this or that social development, whenever Marx and Engels directly confront the question of whether capitalism necessarily gives rise to socialism they insist that it does not. The *Communist Manifesto* explicitly insists that each time a class society enters a crisis the choice facing humanity is "a revolutionary reconstitution of society at large, or . . . the common ruin of the contending classes."[68] And in *Anti-Duhring*, Engels makes it clear that although revolutionary crises are inherent in the structure of capitalism, the outcome of such crises are not predetermined: the bourgeoisie's "own productive forces have grown beyond its control, and, as if necessitated by a law of nature, are driving the whole of bourgeois society toward ruin, or revolution."[69]

In precapitalist societies, the restricted basis of production not only determines the fact that society will be divided by class, it also limits the consciousness of those classes, even at the point where the old society is undergoing a revolutionary transformation. So, although Marx and Engels's general conception of labor describes the unique human capacity consciously to shape the world around them, this capacity cannot be fully exercised on a society-wide scale for long periods of human history.

Consequently, historical change often results from forces that have only a partially accurate reflection in the consciousness of the classes who make history. Even at decisive turning points in history, the glimpse of human freedom is necessarily only partial and, therefore, only partly understood even by the classes fighting for freedom. Ignorant of what the productive forces that they have created are capable of sustaining, they catch sight of the possibility of an increase in human freedom and fight on, only dimly sensing whether the new freedom will be for everyone or merely for a new minority.

In reply to Bruno Bauer's assertion, quoted above, that all great actions in history fail if the masses becomes interested in them, Marx and Engels write:

The *interest* of the bourgeoisie in the 1789 Revolution . . . was so powerful that it was victorious over the pen of Marat, the guillotine of the Terror and the sword of Napoleon as well as the crucifix and the blue blood of the Bourbons. The Revolution was a "failure" only for the mass . . . whose true life-principle did not coincide with the life-principle of the Revolution, the mass whose real conditions for emancipation were essentially different from the conditions within which the bourgeoisie could emancipate itself and society.[70]

Marx and Engels here wield a materialist analysis not to deny the role of consciousness in the revolution, but to analyze, on the basis of the development of society at the time of the French Revolution, which classes were conscious of what aims:

> If the revolution was a failure it was not because the mass was *"enthusiastic"* over it and *"interested"* in it, but because the most numerous part of the mass, the part distinct from the bourgeoisie, did not have its *real* interest in the principle of the Revolution, did not have a revolutionary principle of its *own*, but *only*, an *"idea"*, and hence only an object of momentary *enthusiasm*.[71]

Partly this enthusiasm is engendered because the bourgeoisie is obliged to present its interests as identical with those of all the other classes who are also confronting the old order:

> For each new class which puts itself in the place of one ruling class before it is compelled, merely in order to carry through its aim, to present its interest as the common interest of all members of society.... The class making a revolution comes forward from the very start, if only because it is opposed to a class, not as a class but as the representative of the whole society, as the whole mass of society confronting the one ruling class.[72]

But the sense of the masses that they have something in common with the bourgeoisie is not merely an illusion. The bourgeoisie can present itself in this way "because initially its interest really is as yet mostly connected with the common interest of all the other non-ruling classes, because under the pressure of hitherto existing conditions its interest has not yet been able to develop as the particular interest .of a particular class."[73]

So, in fact, the oppressed classes other than the bourgeoisie do, at first and in part, have interests in common with the bourgeoisie. Only in the course of the further development of the revolution do these interests become clearly separated and opposed. This process of class differentiation can be observed emerging during the course of all the great bourgeois revolutions: in Cromwell's relations, at first warm and later deadly, with the Levellers; in the fate of the Jacobins; in Lincoln's attitude to freeing the slaves; and the American bourgeoisie's battle against radical reconstruction. It is a process in which consciousness has a key role to play, even if it is very different to the role of consciousness in a workers' revolution. It is also a process that has the effect of deepening the contradictions in the social structure. The bourgeoisie may ultimately be victorious, and society may have progressed, but the class contradictions at its center have also been intensified:

> Every new class, therefore achieves domination only on a broader basis than that of the class ruling previously; on the other hand the opposition

of the non-ruling class to the new ruling class then develops all the more sharply and profoundly. Both these things determine the fact that the struggle to be waged against this ruling class, in its turn, has as its aim a more decisive and more radical negation of the previous conditions of society than all previous classes which sought to rule could have.[74]

Here we can see the broad outlines of the historical, materialist dialectic at work. In its formal aspect, this process has many similarities with the terms of the Hegelian dialectic. Society is taken to be in a process of constant change. Such change involves the totality of relations—economic, political, ideological, and cultural—of which the society is composed. This process of total change is a result of internal contradictions, manifested as class antagonism, which reconstitute society anew by both transforming and renewing the forces that first gave rise to the initial contradiction. Marx and Engels's own description of their approach highlighted precisely these points:

> This conception of history thus relies on . . . starting from the material production of life itself—and comprehending the form of intercourse connected with and created by this mode of production . . . explaining how all the different theoretical products and forms of consciousness, religion, philosophy, morality, etc., etc., arise from it . . . thus the whole thing can, of course, be presented as a totality (and, therefore, too, the reciprocal action of these various sides on one another).[75]

But, as this quotation also indicates, in its real operation Marx and Engels's dialectic is utterly different from Hegel's. It starts out from real, material, empirically verifiable contradictions. The forces involved are not merely ideas or even ideologies, though these are also present, but real economic and political institutions, classes, and parties.

> It has not, like the idealist view of history, to look for a category in every period, but remains constantly on the real *ground* of history . . . it comes to the conclusion that all forms and products of consciousness cannot be dissolved by mental criticism, by resolution into "self-consciousness" . . . but only by the practical overthrow of the actual social relations which gave rise to this idealistic humbug; that not criticism but revolution is the driving force of history, also of religion, of philosophy and all other kinds of theory.[76]

And if real circumstances change so must the strategies that people use to accomplish further change, and likewise the intellectual tools with which they seek to understand their circumstances. This is why the real transformation of society requires that the dialectical structure of change is itself altered by history. As Henri Lefebvre has written, "the unity of contradictions exists only in specific, concrete forms. There are different degrees of contradiction—and unity."[77]

So it is that when Marx and Engels come to describe the contradictions of capitalism and the possibility of socialist revolution, the process is significantly different from their description of bourgeois revolutions. The most obvious point is that a workers' revolution is the first revolution that has as its guiding principle the interests of the majority of the oppressed:

All previous historical movements were movements of minorities, or in the interests of minorities. The proletarian movement is the self-conscious, independent movement of the immense majority, in the interests of the immense majority.[78]

Consequently, clarity of consciousness is here an entirely different issue than it was in the bourgeois revolution. In the bourgeois revolution, a lack of clarity is not only unavoidable, given the level of social development, it is, in a certain sense, also necessary to mobilize the whole of society behind the aims of a minority, the bourgeoisie. But, for the workers' revolution to triumph, clarity of aims is necessary to unite a class that is itself already a majority in society. This is especially true because workers face a ruling class which has at its disposal ideological and practical weapons that are more sophisticated than those available to any previous ruling class.

Marx and Engels put the question of workers' revolution in no less dialectical terms than their description of the bourgeois revolution. They polemicize against the Young Hegelians for promising to look at wealth and poverty as part of a single totality but then contradicting themselves by going on to say that they are looking for the "preconditions" of this totality, that is, to look for something outside the totality to explain the totality. They do not see that if the totality depends on something outside itself, it is not a totality in the first place. "By investigating 'the whole as such' to find the preconditions for its existence," argue Marx and Engels, the Young Hegelians are "searching in the genuine theological manner *outside* the 'whole' for the preconditions for its existence."[79]

A properly dialectical analysis, by contrast, assumes that "the *whole antithesis* is nothing but the *movement of both its sides*, and the precondition for the existence of the whole lies in the very nature of the two sides." Marx and Engels show that the capitalist system is such a totality, a totality whose development is determined by the conflict between its two sides: "Proletariat and wealth are opposites; as such they form a single whole. They are both creations of the world of private property."[80]

But merely to show that capitalism is a totality and broadly to designate its contradictory sides may be enough to correct the Young Hegelians (who have fallen below the level attained by their master), but it is not specific enough to be of use in a materialist dialectic. For Hegel a transition from one state to another could be demonstrated simply by showing that two terms were in opposition, even in the weak sense that they defined each other or logically entailed each other, as Being and Nothing are said to do in the *Science of Logic*.

A materialist dialectic must do much more than this. Reciprocal action, where it means equal reaction, although a valuable subsidiary aspect of the dialectic, is often insufficient to show how a material contradiction gives rise to a process of change. Reciprocal action can give rise to new definitions at the level of abstract ideas, but at the level of real events, it can only show mutual interaction, not progress. It can show the relations between different aspects of a totality (say between ideology and class structure), but it cannot generate change. A different conception of dialectical contradiction is necessary for that. This is why Marx and Engels say of the contradiction between the proletariat and wealth, "It is not sufficient to declare them two sides of a single whole."[81] They go on to spell out their conception of the dialectical relationship:

> Private property . . . is compelled to maintain *itself*, and thereby its opposite, the proletariat, in *existence*. That is the positive side of the antithesis, self-satisfied private property.
>
> The proletariat, on the contrary, is compelled as proletariat to abolish itself and thereby its opposite, private property, which determines its existence, and which makes it proletariat. It is the *negative* side of the antithesis, its restlessness within its very self, dissolved and dissolving private property. . . .
>
> Within this antithesis the private property-owner is therefore the *conservative* side, the proletarian the *destructive* side. From the former arises the action of preserving the antithesis, from the latter the action annihilating it.[82]

This is a decisive change is our understanding of the dialectic, because, in the final paragraph of the quotation, Marx and Engels point to the side of the contradiction from which change, and consciousness of change, originates. Marx and Engels, like Hegel, are not content with the notion of reciprocity. But, unlike Hegel, they are able to provide a real scientific alternative. As Sidney Hook notes,

> The system which Marx was analysing was a *social* system in *movement*. The logic of *co-ordination* must be modified by the logic of *succession*. . . . The key to the development of the whole is to be found in the the specific character of its structural opposition. At any given moment the structural oppositions must be such that its mutually supporting elements are *not* of equal strength. The elements within the structure interact upon one another in way which threatens to upset the precariously established equilibrium. . . . In this tendency to disturb the equilibrium one can recognise incipient development.[83]

This "uneven" or "decentered" notion of contradiction not only underpins Marx's notion of the relationship between the development of the productive forces and the social relations that arise from them but also, simultaneously, points toward a crucial concern with the role of consciousness and organization in the course of the revolution. This is made explicit by Marx and Engels in the passage that follows the more formal description of the dialectic just examined:

> ... private property drives itself in its economic movement towards its own dissolution, but only through a development which does not depend on it, which is unconscious and which takes place against the will of private property by the very nature of things, only inasmuch as it produces the proletariat as proletariat, poverty which is conscious of its spiritual and physical poverty, dehumanisation which is conscious of its dehumanisation, and therefore self-abolishing.[84]

This consciousness is not the day-to-day consciousness of the working class, or only partly so. It is not the consciousness with which the working class begins the struggle:

> It is not a question of what this or that proletarian, or even the whole proletariat, at the moment regards as its aim. It is a question of *what the proletariat is*, and what, in accordance with its *being*, it will historically be compelled to do.[85]

That this is not the deterministic statement that critics of marxism often take it to be is clear from the context in which it is made. Immediately before Marx and Engels make this statement, they insist that workers' consciousness and their situation in capitalist society come into alignment through "the stern but steeling school of *labour*." Immediately following the argument that workers' position in society foreshadows their consciousness, they argue that "a large part of the English and French proletariat is already *conscious* of its historical task and is constantly working to develop that consciousness into complete clarity."[86] Indeed, so central was the issue of developing working-class consciousness that Marx and Engels insisted that it was a defining criterion of a successful revolution:

> Both for the production on a mass scale of this communist consciousness, and for the success of the cause itself, the alteration of men on a mass scale is necessary, an alteration which can only take place in a mass movement, a *revolution*; the revolution is necessary, therefore, not only because the *ruling* class cannot be overthrown in any other way, but also because the class *overthrowing* it can only in a revolution succeed in ridding itself of the muck of ages and become fitted to found society anew.[87]

And Engels insisted:

The time of surprise attacks, of revolutions carried through by small conscious minorities at the head of masses lacking consciousness is past. Where it is a question of the complete transformation of the social organization, the masses themselves must be in on it, must themselves already have grasped what is at stake, what they are fighting for, body and soul.[88]

Thus, the dialectic of human history finally opens up the possibility of achieving in the running of society what is implicit in humans' ability to labor: the conscious direction of their world.

ALIENATION, COMMODITY FETISHISM, AND CLASS CONSCIOUSNESS

Marx and Engels's theory of alienation is crucial to understanding their account of capitalist society and their critique both of Hegelian philosophy and of establishment economics. The theory explains how the most characteristic feature of human beings, their ability to transform consciously the world around them, is turned into its opposite, a system that escapes the control of those who live under it; and how the surface appearance of society is very different to its real, underlying workings. It, therefore, contains Marx's dialectic of appearance and essence.

The theory provides the basis for describing what kind of method is necessary to understand such a society and also the foundation for a critique of those theorists who mistake the surface appearance for the underlying reality. But before these methodological issues can be addressed, it is necessary to give an account of the theory itself, approaching it first through an examination of how class consciousness is formed.

Perhaps the most common explanation of working-class consciousness is the one based on Marx and Engels's observation that:

The ideas of the ruling class are in every epoch the ruling ideas: i.e., the class which is the ruling *material* force of society is at the same time its ruling *intellectual* force. The class which has the means of material production at its disposal, consequently also controls the means of mental production, so that the ideas of those who lack the means of mental production are on the whole subject to it.[89]

This is an indispensable starting point for any explanation of how class consciousness is shaped by capitalist society. It has the great advantage of insisting, against all those who claim that the media is balanced, that the state is neutral and that the education system is "value free," that the economic and political power of the ruling class inevitably has its counterpart in the ruling classes' control over the ideological levers in society.

But this is only the start of the problem. After all, it should be no surprise that Rupert Murdoch's printing presses produce papers that propagate ideas which tend to justify Rupert Murdoch's continued ownership of printing presses. But the real question is: Why should anyone who works for Rupert Murdoch, or, by extension for any other capitalist, believe a word that Murdoch's papers say? To complete Marx and Engels's account of ideology, we not only need to know why capitalists have the power to propagate pro-capitalist ideas but also what it is about the lives of workers in capitalist society that predisposes them to believe in the system.

One important argument often used by socialists to explain why workers adhere to procapitalist views is that they are misled by the leaders of the Labour Party and the trade unions. This argument notes, quite rightly, that the reformist leaders are a separate layer within the working-class move-ment, divorced from the rank and file by pay, lifestyle, and under no pres-sure from the daily exploitation of the production process. As importantly, trade union organization (by virtue of its function) and reformist parties (by virtue of political commitment) do not exist to challenge the system, but to bargain within it. They, therefore, mislead workers into accepting crumbs when they might have the cake.

All this is undoubtedly true, but it still begs the fundamental question: If the *interests* of workers and labor bureaucrats are different, why does this fact not register in the minds of the mass of workers? Why do workers often share the politics of the bureaucrats? Explaining the social position and function of labor leaders is enough to show why they will not countenance revolu-tionary politics, but it is not enough to explain why rank and file workers do not immediately break from them. This explanation is ultimately a variant of Marx and Engels's original formulation about the ruling ideas in society.

The difficulty with these and all similar explanations is that unless they are placed in the context of a wider social theory, they remain, ultimately, partial accounts of workers' consciousness. Taken in isolation, they assume that workers' heads are empty vessels that will hold any old pro-capitalist ideas which the media or the labor leaders care to pour into them. In con-trast, a dialectical explanation of workers' consciousness must try to see what it is about workers' daily experience of the capitalist system that predisposes them to accept bourgeois ideology. What is it about workers' lives that makes the ideas of the ruling class seem to fit, at least partially, their own experience? Unless we can provide a satisfactory answer to this question, we shall never be able to locate what it is that can break workers from ruling class ideas, never be able satisfactorily to account for those times when the old ideas break down and revolutionary consciousness seizes hold of the mass of workers.

Fortunately, Marx and Engels were not content to leave their analysis of class consciousness at the point where they insisted that the ruling ideas in every society are the ideas of the ruling class. The roots of Marx and Engels's broader views lie in their account of how class relations develop in capitalist society.

In Marx and Engels's model, capitalist society is characterized by two great cleavages. The first is between those who control the means of production and those, the working class, who do not and who must therefore sell their wage labor to survive. The second great division is between the different competing units of capital, be they corner shops or multinational corporations, state owned or privately controlled.

The nature of the first of these divisions, that is, between the classes, gives human labor in capitalist society a particular character that it has never previously exhibited. For the first time in human history, the mass of the laboring classes have completely lost control over the means of production and the products of their labor. The modern working class must go to the owners of the means of production in order to work; it must produce what it is told to produce, at the pace it is told to produce, in the time it is told to produce, by a capitalist class that has sole control over those means of production.

Feudal serfs were in a very different position. They had effective control over at least some land, they possessed their own plough and animals, and their home was a center of artisan production. Even in the ancient slave societies, the slaves themselves were, numerically, a minority of society and peasant agriculture of this kind was the predominant feature. Thus, although the peasants in precapitalist society might suffer from the vagaries of nature, and although they were subject to tithes and taxes that appropriated part of their product for the ruling class, within this tightly circumscribed world they nevertheless exercised a very real degree of control over the productive process through their control of part of the means of production.

The emergence of the working class at the dawn of capitalist society required a long and bloody civil war to turn peasants and artisans with some control over the means of production into a completely propertyless class with no control over the means of production—the enclosure of common land from the sixteenth century to the eighteenth century, the Highland clearances of the nineteenth century, the revolution of the 1640s, and the industrial revolution are only some of the most notable features of this process in the country where it happened first, Britain.

The paradox is that just as society developed a powerful enough productive engine to escape the misery, disease, and early death of feudalism, just as the wealth of society became great enough to provide for all, human beings' ability to control society was abolished by the very structure that produced the wealth.

Marx called this loss of control alienation. This alienation, this loss of control, is more severe under capitalism than in any previous human society and most extreme of all in the way that it effected the working class. In *The Economic and Philosophical Manuscripts* (1844), Marx describes four ways in which alienation works. The first two forms of alienation rest on the fact that workers do not own the means of production and are therefore forced to work for those who do: "The culmination of this slavery is that it is only as a *worker* that he can maintain himself as a *physical subject*"[90] This is forced labor, and no less forced because the means of compulsion are primarily economic rather than directly physical, and so it follows that workers have no control over the process of production or the fate of the products of their labor. Some of the most powerful passages in all Marx's work describe the effects of being deprived of control over the most fundamental of all human attributes, the ability consciously to control your own labor:

> ... labour is *external* to the worker, i.e. does not belong to his essential being; that he therefore does not confirm himself in his work, but denies himself, feels miserable and not happy, does not develop free mental and physical energy, but mortifies his flesh and ruins his mind. Hence the worker feels himself only when he is not working; when he is working he does not feel himself. He is at home when he is not working, and not at home when he is working. His labour is therefore not voluntary but forced, it is *forced labour*. It is therefore not the satisfaction of a need but a mere *means* to satisfy needs outside itself. Its alien character is clearly demonstrated by the fact that as soon as no physical or other compulsion exists it is shunned like the plague.[91]

It is already clear that Marx sees alienation as having an effect far beyond the immediate sphere of workplace relations. Alienation ruins the mental and emotional capacity of the worker:

> ... labour produces marvels for the rich, but it produces privation for the worker. It produces palaces, but hovels for the worker. It produces beauty, but deformity for the worker. It replaces labour by machines, but it casts some of the workers back into barbarous forms of labour and turns others into machines. It produces intelligence, but it produces idiocy and cretinism for the worker.[92]

And alienation establishes and then reinforces a rigid division of labor, first of all between domestic life and working life in a way unknown in precapitalist societies: "This relationship is the relationship of the worker to his own activity as something which is alien and does not belong to him... the worker's *own* physical and mental energy, his personal life... as an activity directed against himself, which is independent of him and does not belong to him."[93] The result is that the worker "feels that he is acting freely only in his animal functions—eating, drinking and procreating, or at most in his dwelling and adornment."[94]

This alienation is, literally, dehumanizing. For Marx the very definition of what it means to be a human being, rather than merely another animal, was bound up with the ability to perform conscious labor:

> It is true that animals also produce.... But ... they produce only when the immediate physical need compels them to do so, while man produces even when he is free from physical need and truly produces only in freedom from such need; they produce only themselves, while man reproduces the whole of nature; their products belong immediately to themselves, while man freely confronts his own product.[95]

Thus, alienation, by depriving human beings of their ability consciously to shape the world they inhabit, reduces them to the level of animals. This is the third form of alienation that Marx outlines—alienation from human nature (or "species being" as Marx calls it).[96]

Finally, Marx argues that if the workers are alienated from their product, their productive activity, and their very human nature, it is no surprise that they are also alienated from their fellow human beings. In the first instance, of course, they are alienated from those who do have some control over the labor process and its achievements, the capitalists: "If the product of labour does not belong to the worker, and if it confronts him as an alien power, this is only possible because it belongs to *a man other than the worker*.... The relation of the worker to labour creates the relation of the capitalist."[97] But alienation not only shapes the fundamental class conflict between capitalist and worker, it also shapes all other relations.

Thus, Marx sees "religion, the family, the state, law and morality, science, art, etc., are only *particular* modes of production and therefore come under its (private property's) general law." For instance, Marx sees "in the relationship with *woman* ... is expressed the infinite degradation in which man exists for himself, for the secret of this relationship has its *unambiguous*, decisive, *open*, and revealed expression in the relationship of *man* to *woman*." Hence, "it is possible to judge from this relationship the entire level of development of mankind." Thus, "the positive suppression of private property, as the appropriation of *human* life, is therefore the positive suppression of all estrangement, and the return of man from religion, the family, the state, etc., to his *human*, i.e. *social* existence."[98]

Marx is at his most passionate in his indictment of how commodities alienated from their creators return to haunt every human need. By turning these needs into an occasion for making a profit, capitalism debases the need itself:

> No eunuch flatters his despot more basely or uses more infamous means to revive his flagging pleasure, in order to win a surreptitious favour for himself, than does the eunuch of industry, the manufacturer, in order to sneak himself a silver penny or two or coax gold from the pocket of his

dearly beloved neighbour. Every product is a bait. . . . Every real or potential need is a weakness which will tempt the fly onto the lime-twig. . . . Just as each one of man's inadequacies is a bond with heaven, a way into his heart for the priest, so every need is an opportunity for stepping up to one's neighbour and saying to him: "Dear friend, I can give you what you want, but you know the terms. . . ." He places himself at the disposal of his neighbours most depraved fancies, panders to his needs, excites unhealthy appetites in him, and pounces on his every weakness, so that he can then demand money for his labour of love.[99]

This is the key factor linking the particular alienation in the process of production with alienation in the overall social structure: the generalized exchange of commodities characteristic of capitalism. Here the products of labor reappear before their creators as alien objects whose market movements shape all human life, not the reverse. And there is no commodity as powerful as the commodity that controls all commodities: money.

Money is the "inversion and confusion of all human and natural qualities, the bringing together of impossibilities . . . the alienated *capacity* of *mankind.*"[100] And so Marx argues, in a passage that reads like a description of our own times:

. . . the stronger the power of my money, the stronger I am. The properties of money are my, the possessor's, properties and powers. Therefore what I *am* and what I *can do* is by no means determined by my individuality. I *am* ugly, but I can buy the *most beautiful* woman. Which means to say that I am not *ugly,* for the effect of *ugliness,* its repelling power, is destroyed by my money. . . . I am a wicked, dishonest, unscrupulous and stupid individual, but money is respected and so is its owner. Moreover, money spares me the trouble of being dishonest, and therefore I am presumed to be honest. . . . It transforms loyalty into treason, love into hate, hate into love, virtue into vice, vice into virtue, servant into master, master into servant, nonsense into reason and reason into nonsense.[101]

So Marx's theory of alienation is already beginning to furnish us with some fundamental building blocks for a theory of class consciousness. The divorce of the workers from the means of production is revealed as much more than an economic condition. It also has immediate social, political, and ideological repercussions—producing passivity, division, a narrowing of horizons, and a set of values that are likely to predispose workers to accept the bourgeoisie's view of the world.

But the picture of class consciousness that arises from Marx's theory of alienation is very general. It also refers primarily to the ideological impact of class divisions at the point of production. This is a vital starting point which, in *The German Ideology* and *The Holy Family,* marks the beginnings of a more general theory of ideology based on the view that concepts which arise from direct interaction with the world cannot be false. But, once classes arise (and with them the separation of intellectuals, however conceived, from such direct interaction), the possibility of mistaken generalizations, false consciousness, and so on arises.

But the ideological impact of capitalist relations cannot be reduced to these general considerations. In his later works, particularly the *Grundrisse* and *Capital*, Marx not only repeats the themes of his theory of alienation, he also goes on to explain the ideological effects of the exchange and circulation of the products of alienated labor on the market. This is the process Marx calls commodity fetishism.

The starting point is necessarily the same whether we look at the process at the level of production or at the level of exchange—the separation of workers from the means of production:

> The worker's propertylessness, and the ownership of living labour by objectified labour, or the appropriation of alien labour by capital—both merely expressions of the same relation from opposite poles—are fundamental conditions of the bourgeois mode of production, and in no way accidents irrelevant to it.[102]

And because the products of labor are expropriated by capitalists, who are themselves divided by mutual competition, generalized commodity exchange, the market, becomes the only way in which society can organize the distribution of what it produces. In previous societies production was, for the most part, immediately related to human need. The majority of useful objects produced by labor were directly consumed. They did not have to become exchange values circulating by means of the market. This is the logical concomitant of the fact, discussed above, that in precapitalist societies the alienation of labor is not as complete as it is under capitalism. In medieval Europe, as Marx notes in *Capital*, human relations, even though they are still very much class relations of exploitation, are not the same as those between isolated individuals mediated through the market.

> Instead . . . we find everyone dependent—serfs and lords, vassals and suzerains, laymen and clerics. Personal dependence characterises the social relations of material production as much as it does the other spheres of life based on production. But precisely because relations of personal dependence form the given social foundation, there is no need for labour and its products to assume a fantastic form different to their reality. They take the shape, in the transactions of society, of services in kind and payments in kind. . . . Whatever we may think, then, of the different roles in which men confront each other in such a society, the social relations between individuals in the performance of their labour appear at all events as their own personal relations, and are not disguised as social relations between things, between the products of labour.[103]

Similarly, Marx argues, if we imagine a communist society where an "association of free men, working with the means of production held in common, and expending their many different forms of labour-power in full self-awareness as one single social labour force," then this, too, will be a society where "the social relations of the individual producers, both towards their labour and the products of labour, are here transparent in their simplicity, in production as well as in distribution."[104] So capitalism is quite unique, not because it is an exploitative class society—this was also true of feudalism— but because the social relations are *disguised* by the very mechanism of production and exchange. The basis on which this mechanism rests is the separation of the producers from each other:

> the producers do not come into contact until they exchange the products of their labour. . . . In other words, the labour of private individuals manifests itself . . . only through the relations which the act of exchange establishes between products, and, through their mediation between the producers.[105]

And so it is that "objects of utility become commodities only because they are the products of the labour of private individuals who work independently of each other."[106] Thus, the market interposes itself between the producers. What are actually human and class relations appear as relations between the inanimate products of labor: commodities. It is the success or failure of market transactions, over which not even the capitalists have control, that determines the fate of all who live in the society:

> What initially concerns producers . . . when they make an exchange is how much of some product they will get for their own. . . . These magnitudes vary continually, independently of the will, foreknowledge and actions of the exchangers. Their own movement within society has for them the appearance of a movement made by things, and these things, far from being under their control, in fact control them.[107]

Thus, argues Marx, although different producers pursue conscious aims through the market, the movement of the market as a whole is not under the conscious control of any individual, group of individuals, or institution. The market is driven by "the particular purposes of individuals," but its movements are "neither located in their consciousness, nor subsumed under them as a whole. Their own collisions with one another produce an *alien* social power standing above them, produce their mutual interaction as a process and power independent of them."[108]

And so to add to the sense of dehumanization, passivity, and division induced by alienation, commodity fetishism produces a very definite new element: the appearance that class exploitation is not a social product but the inevitable and unalterable result of the functioning of the market. Nowhere is this more true than in the fate of labor-power, the commodity that the worker must sell on the market:

> The *value* of the worker rises or falls in accordance with supply and demand, and even in the *physical* sense his *existence*, his *life*, was and is treated as a supply of a *commodity*, like any other commodity. . . . So as soon as it occurs to capital—whether from necessity or choice—not to exist any longer for the worker, he no longer exists for himself; he has *no* work, and hence *no* wages, and since he exists not *as a man* but *as a worker*, he might just as well have himself buried, starve to death etc. . . . The existence of capital is *his* existence, his *life*, for it determines the content of his life in a manner indifferent to him.[109]

And, precisely because there is a "labor market," unemployment and low wages appear as simply the impersonal dictates of a mechanism beyond control. Starvation in poor countries is as unavoidable as the weather. Cynicism or charity, fatalism or utopianism seem the only possible responses. And, however much one might prefer the latter to the former, they both leave the essential workings of the system untouched.

As well as making capitalism seem eternal, the workings of the market also tend to obliterate class distinctions:

> A worker who buys a loaf of bread and a millionaire who does the same appear in this act only as simple buyers, just as, in respect of them, the grocer appears only as a seller. All other aspects here are extinguished. The *content* of these purchases, like their *extent*, here appears irrelevant compared with the formal aspect.[110]

And so "if one grows impoverished and the other grows wealthier, then this is of their own free will and does not in any way arise from the economic relation."[111] Thus the workings of the market make capitalism appear as free, fair, and just—as well as inevitable and free of class distinction. These appearances, rooted in alienation during the productive process, reinforced and extended by commodity fetishism in the process of exchange, lay the basis for the political institutions and ideologies found in the rest of society:

> . . . exchange of exchange values [the market] is the productive, real basis of all *equality* and *freedom*. As pure ideas they are merely the idealised expressions of this basis; as developed in juridical, political, social relations, they are merely this basis to a higher power.[112]

Here Marx is approaching the point at which the material roots of class consciousness grow into the political and ideological foliage of law and custom, belief and religion that we see in the everyday consciousness of individuals in capitalist society.

Indeed, Marx and Engels saw the division into classes, from which the division of labor takes its form, as more than just a general loss of control over the productive process. The more the division of labor progresses, and the more the chaotic rule of the market becomes the governing principle of society, the more diverse become the political and ideological forms which this society produces.

Engels explains this process by looking at the ways in which state power can shape economic development. He argues that it can have one of three effects on economic progress. It can accelerate economic change, retard economic change, or it can alter the course of economic development and "prevent economic development from proceeding along certain lines, and prescribe other lines."[113] The state can gain this *relative* independence, because it is based on the development of the division of labor. Engels explains:

> Society gives rise to certain common functions which it cannot dispense with. The persons appointed for this purpose form a new branch of the division of labour *within society*. This gives them particular interests, distinct, too, from those of their mandator; they make themselves independent of the latter and the state is in being . . . the new independent power, while having in the main to follow the movement of production, reacts in turn, by virtue of its inherent relative independence—that is relative independence once transferred to it and gradually further developed— upon the course and conditions of production.[114]

And as each new area of political and social development opens up, there arise institutional structures and networks of social relations which, although ultimately related to the economic structure, develop a certain independent power of their own. Engels uses the example of the legal structure:

> As soon as the new division of labour which creates professional lawyers becomes necessary, another new and independent sphere is opened up which, for all its general dependence on production and trade, has also a specific capacity for reacting on these spheres.[115]

More than this, the very nature of the law means that it *cannot be a direct reflection of the economic conditions that gave rise to it.* This is for three reasons. First, the law, although fundamentally an expression of the ruling classes' control of property, cannot simply be a "blunt, unmitigated, unadulterated expression of the domination of a class," otherwise, it would fail to be effective as an arbiter of the class struggle. It must have, at least, the *appearance* of independence from the ruling class. Second, although based on a contradictory economic system, the law itself has to be seen to be internally coherent, to be rational in its judgments. But "in order to achieve this, the faithful reflection of economic conditions suffers increasingly."[116] Finally, and as a result of these two factors, "the jurist imagines he is operating with *a priori* propositions, whereas they are really only economic reflections; everything is therefore upside down."[117] So this *necessarily* independent sphere "influences the economic base and may, within certain limits, modify it." Indeed, Engels adds, laws like those governing inheritance can "exert a very considerable effect on the economic sphere, because they influence the distribution of property."[118]

None of this, however, was meant to deny the materialism of Marx and Engels's approach, merely to spell out that they were not *mechanical* materialists or economic *determinists*:

> It is the interaction of two unequal forces: on the one hand, the economic movement, on the other, the new political power, which strives for as much independence as possible, and which, having once been set up, is endowed with a movement of its own. On the whole, the economic movement prevails, but it has also to endure reactions from the political movement which it itself set up and endowed with relative independence, from the movement of state power, on the one hand, and of the opposition simultaneously engendered, on the other.[119]

Once again, the key elements of a dialectical analysis are in place: the whole of society is shown to be based on an economic contradiction that gives rise to a state structure which is related to, but distinct from, its economic base. The state thus mediates economic development. Either completely separating the economic and the political or completely dissolving one side into the other destroys the mediation and thus the real pattern of relations. Such relationships are, in dialectical terminology, contradictory totalities, a unity of opposites.

THE MARXIST METHOD AND THE THEORY OF ALIENATION

Marx's theory of alienation was one of the key vantage points from which he had launched his attack on Hegel's system. Hegel's idealism led him to equate objectification (the act of producing an imagined object in reality by means of labor) with alienation (the loss of control over both the act of production and the product). For Hegel the true reality of the world was to be found in concepts and so any material object must be a form of alienation—the passing of thought, the true essence of humanity, into its opposite, the alien realm of material objects. It followed that the natural world was thought outside itself. The completion of the dialectical process occurred when thought returned to itself, recognizing the material world as only a one-sided and inadequate expression of thought itself. Thus the overcoming of alienation was the work of thought, not a process of social transformation.

Hegel thus made alienation into an unalterable human condition (more uncritical positivism) that could only be "overcome" in the world of concepts (more uncritical idealism). The result was to leave the real social process of alienation unchanged (another conservative conclusion).

Marx's understanding of human labor led him to see objectification as a natural human attribute—an expression of the human capacity to shape the world. This process could only become alien under certain specific social circumstances—class society and, in its most extreme form, capitalism. And, because alienation is not an unalterable feature of human nature but the product of social circumstances, it could be ended by changing those circumstances.

Hegel's error, to imagine that alienation can only be overcome in thought, is only made possible because the appearance of capitalist society is so different to its underlying essence. Any theory that simply reproduces the surface appearance of capitalism without studying the underlying dynamics which reveal it as a historically transitory mode of production must end in viewing material alienation as eternal.

What is therefore necessary is the painstaking empirical and theoretical work of showing how the real nature of capitalist society results in appearances that are both the necessary product of, and very different from, the mechanism which gives rise to them.

It follows that Marx and Engels could not possibly have been supporters of a crude "reflection" or "copy" theory of knowledge in which the ideas in people's heads are said to be an immediate and direct translation of the material reality around them. When Marx and Engels talk about ideas "reflecting" material reality, they rarely do so without qualification and then only to indicate the most general correspondence between ideas and reality in opposition to the idealist assumption that human thought is somehow the free creation of consciousness uninhibited by material determinants.

When Marx and Engels come to talk more concretely, both about the formation of working-class consciousness and about the correct method of coming to a scientific understanding of society, they are clear that a *direct* reflection of reality can only lead to the mental reproduction of the most misleading appearances of capitalist society. This is precisely why independent theoretical effort is necessary to pierce the surface phenomena and trace the relationship to its very different roots.

> Vulgar economy actually does no more than interpret, systematise and defend in a doctrinaire fashion the conceptions of the agents of bourgeois production who are entrapped in bourgeois production relations. It should

not astonish us, then, that vulgar economy feels particularly at home in the estranged outward appearances of economic relations in which these *prima facie* absurd and perfect contradictions appear and that these relations seem all the more self-evident the more their internal relationships are concealed from it. . . . But science would be superfluous if the outward appearance and the essence of things directly coincided.[120]

This understanding of social reality and of the relationship between science and reality has a number of important consequences for Marx's understanding of the dialectic. It means, for instance, that the sham opposition between Hegel's notion of appearance and essence is replaced by a real process. Hegel had been the first to insist that appearance is no less real than essence, but his whole system undermined that claim. Appearance did not, in fact, have any independent reality—it was simply the thought essence in its otherness, manifesting itself briefly as nature before it was reabsorbed in thought.

For Marx the market is not a mere illusion but a real social institution that grows out of the relations of production while at the same time disguising its link with them. The market appearances are no less "real" than the internal structure of capitalist exploitation. Marx's project is to show how the one produces the other and in what ways they depend on each other. To do so, Marx has to highlight the links and interconnections between the two contradictory aspects of society. Thus, mediation is once again reinstated as an essential element in understanding the social totality. This is, in itself, an argument against those who accuse Marx of reductionism, because reductionism is, by definition, the forced and immediate insistence on a direct link between elements which are, in fact, only connected by a variety of mediating factors.

Further proof is provided by Marx's attitude to science. He and Engels are obviously some considerable distance from assuming that scientific thought can simply mirror empirical reality. Independent theoretical and conceptual work is the element that mediates this aspect of the totality. Theoretical concepts arise from and relate to the real world, but not in a direct and simplistic way. They are both parts of a single totality, but the relationship between them cannot be reduced to either one of the two terms.

THE LOGIC OF CAPITAL

There has been a long tradition of denying or underplaying both dialectical nature of, and the influence of Hegel on, Marx's mature economic writings, especially *Capital*. Perhaps the best-known postwar representative of this strand of thought is Louis Althusser, who insisted that Marx's later economic works were conducted in accordance with a strict scientific method utterly at variance with the philosophical concerns of his earlier work.[121] More recently, the analytical marxist school has either denied or sought to prove the baleful effects of the Hegelian influence on marxism.

The most obvious problem with these contentions is that they contradict Marx's own statements about the method that he employed in *Capital*. Marx wrote to Engels insisting that rereading Hegel's *Logic* had helped him overthrow "the whole doctrine of profit as it existed up to now." Indeed, he insisted, "When I have cast off the burden of political economy, I shall write a 'Dialectic.' The true laws of dialectics are already contained in Hegel, though in a mystical form. What is needed is to strip away this form."[122] In the course of *Capital*, Marx argues that "the Hegelian 'contradiction' . . . is the source of all dialectics."[123] And in the "Postface to the Second Edition" of *Capital*, Marx explicitly discusses his dialectical method and describes his relationship to Hegel in precisely the same terms that he uses in his early writings. Marx argues that, although he is a materialist and Hegel an idealist, when he found Hegel under attack from "ill-humoured, arrogant and mediocre epigones who now talk large in educated German circles," he "openly avowed" himself "a pupil of that mighty thinker, and even, here and there in the chapter on the theory of value, coquetted with the mode of expression peculiar to him."[124]

Remarkably, this last quotation is sometimes cited as evidence that Marx was not serious about his debt to Hegel, that he *only* or *merely* "coquetted" with Hegel's phraseology and did not really make any further use of the dialectic. That this interpretation is false should be obvious from this sentence alone. The meaning is clearly that Marx was so keen to identify with Hegel that he "even" went so far as to use the same terms as "that mighty thinker," not that he "only" used those terms. In any case, the remainder of the same paragraph makes the point absolutely clear:

> The mystification which the dialectic suffers in Hegel's hands by no means prevents him from being the first to present its general forms of motion in a comprehensive and conscious manner. With him it is standing on its head. It must be inverted, in order to discover the rational kernel within the mystical shell.[125]

In the paragraph that follows, Marx gives one of his most concise definitions of the dialectic:

> In its mystified form, the dialectic became the fashion in Germany, because it seemed to transfigure and glorify what exists. In its rational form it is a scandal and an abomination to the bourgeoisie and its doctrinaire spokesmen, because it includes in its positive understanding of what exists a simultaneous recognition of its negation, its inevitable destruction; because it regards every historically developed form as being in a fluid state,

in motion, and therefore grasps its transient aspect as well; and because it does not let itself be impressed by anything, being in its very essence critical and revolutionary.[126]

These are clearly not incidental remarks. Indeed, the "Preface to the First Edition" had ended on a similar note: "Society is no solid crystal, but an organism capable of change, and constantly engaged in a process of change."[127] And it was precisely this dialectical process of change that *Capital* set out to explain in detail. It could not help but be the case that this analysis would reproduce the key terms of the materialist dialectic. It is this fact that offers the most decisive rebuttal to those who wish to minimize or deny the dialectical structure of capital.

We have already seen Marx indicate that capitalist society is in process of constant change. This is the first fact requiring a concrete dialectical analysis:

> Modern industry never views or treats the existing form of a production process as the definitive one. Its technical basis is therefore revolutionary, whereas all earlier modes of production were essential conservative. By means of machinery, chemical processes and other methods, it is continually transforming not only the technical basis of production but also the functions of the worker and the social combinations of the labour process.[128]

Moreover, the process of change involves a contradiction:

> But on the other hand, in its capitalist form it reproduces the old division of labour with its ossified peculiarities. We have seen how this absolute contradiction does away with all repose, all fixity and all security as far as the workers' life situation is concerned. . . . We have seen, too, how this contradiction bursts forth without restraint in the ceaseless human sacrifices required from the working class, in the reckless squandering of labour-powers, and in the devastating effects of social anarchy.[129]

This, as Marx says, is "the negative side" of the contradiction. But just as capitalism "incessantly throws masses of capital from one branch of production to another," enforcing "variation of labour," and the constant learning of new skills, "with the blindly destructive action of a natural law," so it also raises the prospect that such variation in labor could be consciously planned to develop the all-round capacity of every individual in society. "Large scale industry, through its very catastrophes, makes the recognition of variation of labour and hence of the fitness of the worker for the maximum number of different kinds of labour into a question of life and death." Here it is possible to see how the "monstrosity of capitalist exploitation" prepares the way for "the totally developed individual, for whom the different social functions are different modes of activity he takes up in turn."[130]

But for the "negative side" of capitalism to be negated, thereby releasing the human potential which it creates but imprisons, the contradictions of the system must be exploded from within:

There is no doubt that those revolutionary ferments whose goal is the abolition of the old division of labour stand in diametrical contradiction with the capitalist form of production, and the economic condition of the workers which corresponds to that form. However, the development of the contradictions of a given historical form of production is the only historical way in which it can be dissolved and then reconstructed on a new basis.[131]

Here Marx presents capitalism as a totality whose process of change is governed by the nature of the contradiction at its heart. It is a society that contains the seeds of its own destruction and the embryo of a new society. Forces arise within capitalism that have the potential to negate it. But this can only happen as a result of observable and verifiable material and social processes and not as a result of society being required to manifest the patterns of some abstract philosophical scheme.

When Marx came to talk in the most general terms about the passage from feudalism to capitalism, involving the expropriation of peasant land, the rise of capitalist property, and the further development of capitalism to the point where its contradictory nature raises the possibility of capitalism itself being replaced by socialism, he explicitly refers to this process as the negation of the negation. Marx first describes how the rise of capitalism involved "the expropriation of the direct producers ... by means of the most merciless barbarism and under the stimulus of the most infamous, the most sordid, and most petty and the most odious of passions." This results in the ending of property based on the fusion of "the isolated, independent working individual with the conditions of his labour" and supplants it with "capitalist private property, which rests on the exploitation of alien, but formally free labour."

But no sooner is capitalism established than "the further socialisation of labour and the further transformation of the soil and other means of production into socially exploited and therefore communal means of production takes on a new form."[132] The means of production are now socially and collectively worked, in a more conscious and planned way than ever before, but they are still controlled by private, competing capitalist owners. Moreover, these capitalists become fewer in number and their capital becomes more concentrated as competition gives rise to monopoly. By the same token, the working class becomes more numerous and more concentrated:

Along with the constant decrease in the number of capitalist magnates, who usurp and monopolize all the advantages of this process of transformation, the mass of misery, oppression, slavery, degradation and exploitation grows; but with this there also grows the revolt of the working class, a class constantly increasing in numbers, and trained, united and organised by the very mechanism of capitalist production.

Marx is, once more, describing how the working class emerges as the antithesis of capitalist society. He goes on to explain how this process brings to a head the overall crisis that afflicts capitalism:

> The monopoly of capital becomes a fetter upon the mode of production which has flourished alongside and under it. The centralisation of the means of production and the socialisation of labour reach a point where they become incompatible with their capitalist integument. The integument is burst asunder. The knell of capitalist private property sounds. The expropriators are expropriated.[133]

And, just in case that final literary flourish were not sufficient to indicate that a dialectical process has reached its conclusion, Marx recapitulates the whole movement in unmistakable terms:

> The capitalist mode of appropriation, which springs from the capitalist mode of production, produces capitalist private property. This is the first negation of individual private property, as founded on the labour of its proprietor [feudalism]. But capitalist production begets, with the inexorability of a natural process, its own negation. This is the negation of the negation. It does not re-establish individual private property, but it does indeed establish individual property on the basis of the achievements of the capitalist era: namely co-operation and the possession in common of the land and the means of production produced by labour itself.[134]

This conception of the negation of the negation needs to be handled carefully, because it is one of the concepts that underwent a complete transformation in its passage from Hegel's system to Marx's. In Hegel, it was the mechanism for reconciling thought with existing reality, for restoring reality unchanged at the end of the dialectical process. This is why Marx is careful to insist that the negation of the negation that he describes "*does not re-establish private property.*" Marx's dialectic opens up the possibility of real material change, a real alteration in the mode of production. And although a crisis in society and the emergence of a class that can resolve it may arise "with the inexorability of a natural law," the successful resolution of that crisis is not predetermined. Precisely because real social progress is at stake, precisely because this involves real classes fighting for the leadership of society, the outcome is not a foregone conclusion, not an inevitability. Engels commented on exactly this passage from *Capital* in *Anti-Duhring*, arguing that the negation of the negation should not be seen as "a mere proof producing instrument." He was explicit in arguing that the process must be empirically grounded and that it did not involve a fatalistic attitude:

> Thus by characterising the process as a negation of the negation, Marx did not intend to prove the process was historically necessary. On the contrary: only after he has proved from history that in fact the process has partially already occurred, and partially must occur in the future, he in addition characterises it as a process which develops in accordance with a definite dialectical law. That is all.[135]

"It is therefore a pure distortion of the facts," Engels concludes, to declare "that the negation of the negation has to serve here as the midwife to deliver the future from the womb of the past."

Lefebvre makes the same point by drawing attention to the vital difference between Hegel's fatalistic conception of the negation of the negation and the openness of Marx and Engels's approach:

> In dialectical materialism . . . the third term, the triumphant outcome of the conflict, transforms the content of the contradiction by reassuming it; it lacks the conservative solemnity of the Hegelian synthesis. Only in this way can there be real movement, a dramatic history and action . . . man does not exist in advance, metaphysically. The game has not already been won; men may lose everything. The transcending is never inevitable.[136]

Neither did Marx and Engels simply assume that every aspect of society could simply and immediately be reduced to one central contradiction. Analyzing society as a totality does not mean, contrary to the accusations of various postmodern theorists, that the diversity of the social structure is eliminated. We have already seen, in Marx's understanding of the relationship between human beings and nature, that *immediate* unity obliterates differences, whereas dialectical unity, a unity of opposites, accounts both for their unity and their difference. Marx captures exactly this point in a passage from the *Grundrisse*: "The conclusion we reach is not that production, distribution, exchange, and consumption are identical, but that they all form the members of a totality, distinctions within a unity."[137]

Marx is again careful not to allow his conception of the relations between the different aspects of the totality to descend into mere reciprocal action:

> Production predominates not only over itself . . . but over the other moments as well. The process always returns to production anew. . . . A definite production thus determines a definite consumption, distribution, and exchange as well as *definite relations between these different moments.*[138]

This does not, however, reduce the real influence of these other moments to nothing. Marx continues:

Admittedly, however, *in its one-sided form*, production is itself determined by the other moments. For example, if the market, i.e. the sphere of exchange, expands, then production grows in quantity and divisions between its branches become deeper. . . . Mutual interaction takes place between the different moments. This is the case with every organic whole.[139]

And so to demonstrate that society is a totality and that it is animated by a central contradiction is not enough to present an adequate account of capitalism. We are dealing with real social processes and so the dialectic has to be able to show how the central contradiction of capitalist society is expressed, often in very different forms, in all the economic, cultural, political, ideological, and legal aspects of society. Once again, we are dealing with a differentiated totality in which the specific and particular mediations between the whole and the parts have to be empirically derived and then theoretically explained, not simply deduced from general characteristics.

It is, for instance, absolutely central to Marx's theory of crisis that the sphere of production and the spheres of exchange and circulation are seen as distinctions within a unity produced by very specific historical circumstances. Marx himself describes this crucial aspect of capitalism as unity of opposites. It is worth following his argument in some detail. Marx starts with the process of exploitation at the point of production:

> As soon as all the surplus-labour it was possible to squeeze out has been embodied in commodities, surplus-value has been produced. But this production of surplus-value completes but the first act of the capitalist process of production—the direct production process.[140]

But, Marx goes on, it is one thing to exploit workers at the point of production and so produce commodities, it is quite another to sell them.

> Now comes the second act of the process. The entire mass of commodities . . . must be sold. If this is not done, or done only in part, or only at prices below the prices of production, the labourer has been indeed exploited, but his exploitation is not realised as such for the capitalist, and this can be bound up with a total or partial failure to realise the surplus-value pressed out of him, indeed even with the partial or total loss of the capital.[141]

Consequently, argues Marx:

> The conditions of direct exploitation, and those of realising it, are not identical. They diverge not only in place and time, but also logically.[142]

This is not merely a distinction within a unity but an expression of the fundamental contradiction in capitalist society. The growth of the direct process of production is forced forward by "the general competitive struggle and the need to improve production and expand its scale merely as a means

of self-preservation and under penalty of ruin." But "the more productive-
ness develops the more it finds itself at variance with the narrow basis on
which consumption rests," because the very act of increasing surplus-value
tends to decrease the means available to the mass of the population to purchase what is produced. Thus says Marx:

> It is no contradiction at all on this self-contradictory basis that there should
> be an excess of capital simultaneously with a growing surplus of popula-
> tion. For while a combination of these two would, indeed, increase the
> mass of produced surplus-value, it would also at the same time intensify
> the contradiction between the conditions under which this surplus-value
> is produced and those under which it is realised.[143]

But because capitalist society is unable to bring together, say, unemployed
building workers and stockpiles of unsold bricks without undermining profit-
ability and thereby its own existence, it has to resolve this contradiction by
other means. This is achieved by uncontrolled economic crises that forcibly
realign the supply of commodities with demand by destroying all or part of
the value embodied in them—that is, by bankrupting sections of capital.

An important part of Marx's critique of the bourgeois economists—Say
and Mill, for instance—is based on the fact that they assume that everything
that is produced will be bought. They write as if capitalism were still a
simple barter economy where production and consumption are immediately
united. They see only a unity of supply and demand, when they should see
a unity of opposites, difference as well as unity. They would then understand that the unity between the two is brutally reasserted over their difference only in crises:

> Mill says purchase is sale etc., therefore demand is supply and supply demand.
> But they also fall apart and can become independent of each other. . . .
> If the relation of demand and supply is taken in a wider and more concrete
> sense, then it comprises the relation of *production* and *consumption* as well.
> Here again, the *unity* of these two phases, which does exist and which
> forcibly asserts itself during crises, must be seen as opposed to their *sepa-
> ration* and *antagonism* of these two phases, separation and antagonism which
> exist just as much, and are moreover typical of bourgeois production.[144]

In even more general terms, Marx argues:

> . . . purchase and sale . . . represent the unity of two processes, or rather
> the movement of one process through two opposite phases, and thus essentially
> the unity of the two phases, the movement is essentially ·just as much
> separation of these two phases, their becoming independent of each other.
> Since, however, they belong together the independence of the two corre-
> lated aspects can only *show itself*, forcibly, as a destructive process. It is just
> the *crisis* in which they assert their unity, the unity of different aspects.[145]

Mill sees the unity of capitalist society, but he doesn't see it as a unity of *opposites* and is therefore prone to reduce one aspect of the totality directly to another without the essential mediating links, the contradictions, being analyzed and explained. Marx's notion of the dialectic, by contrast, *necessarily* requires that he reject reductionist formulations and give full weight to the mediating contradictions between different elements of the totality.

Marx makes a similar point when he argues that Mill mistakenly tries to deduce the profit rate directly from the production of surplus value without taking account of the realization problem or the equalization of the rate of profit that takes place in the process. Thus, in Mill, "the contradiction between the general law and further developments in the concrete circumstances is to be resolved not by the discovery of the connecting links but by directly subordinating and immediately adapting the concrete to the abstract."[146]

The mistake is either to try to deduce directly particular events from general rules or to assume that general laws can be directly inferred from specific, empirical observations. In Mill, this fault is also directly bound up with his failure to see the contradictions inherent in the capitalist system:

Where the economic relation—and therefore the categories expressing it— includes contradictions, opposites, and likewise the unity of opposites, he emphasizes the aspect of the *unity* of the contradictions and denies the *contradictions*. He transforms the unity of opposites into the direct identity of opposites.[147]

Here the key terms of Marx's dialectic stand out in high relief—totality, contradiction, unity of opposites, mediation. Taken together with the discussion of the negation of the negation, they give a clear outline of Marx's vision of capitalism as a differentiated totality. He came to this understanding on the basis of a careful factual analysis of capitalist relations, not as a result of simply applying Hegel's categories indiscriminately to the world around him.

This is why Marx and Engels are at such pains to highlight the specific and peculiar dialectical structure of capitalism, a structure quite different to that which they uncovered in previous class societies. It is also why they are equally concerned to show that the dialectical structure of one part of the system, say that at the point of production, is not necessarily the same as that in another part of the system, say the realm of circulation and exchange. The two are, of course, related. But not so directly that no contradiction can emerge between them, or that the contradictions of one sphere simply mirror those of the other. The same unity in difference can also be seen in Marx and Engels's use of the dialectic as a method of analysis and the conclusions that they reached about the real structure of the world using that method.

THE METHOD OF *CAPITAL*

In reaction to those who deny the Hegelian influence on Marx and Engels's economic writings there have emerged commentators determined to assert the opposite—that Marx and Engels took over Hegels's dialectic with far fewer alterations than is often assumed. Bhikhu Parekh has summarized this approach:

> In their view Marx's materialism is basically an attempt to trace the genesis of what he himself called the "concept of capital." Marx's notion of capital has, it is argued, almost all the basic ontological properties of Hegel's *Geist* [Spirit], including the latter's ideal nature. After all, he himself insisted that capital is not a thing but a relation, and a relation is by definition an ideal and not a natural entity.[148]

Few writers would actually make a claim as bold as this, but there are elements of this approach to be found in a variety of commentators who have otherwise greatly contributed to the almost submerged tradition that has insisted on the dialectical nature of Marx's approach. Raya Dunayevskaya, once one of Trotsky's secretaries, produced a valuable and stimulating work in the Hegelian Marxist tradition, *Marxism and Freedom*, but thereafter increasingly tried to more or less directly apply Hegel's categories to the modern world. Her one-time co-thinker C. L. R. James attempted much the same thing. In both cases, a reproduction of Hegel's errors resulted: abstract generalization under which canopy a collection of empirical material was gathered with little connecting the two.[149]

A more recent writer, Tony Smith, has produced some valuable insights into the relationship between Hegel and Marx and into the structure of Marx's *Capital*.[150] Smith's argument starts from the perfectly reasonable point that Marx's analysis of capitalism required the development of a number of concepts and categories that have no direct empirical correlate—one cannot see, touch, hear, smell, or taste surplus value, for instance. Moreover, these categories are related to each other in a systematic way: use value to exchange value to surplus value and so on. Smith writes:

> The chain of thought goes as follows. If one wishes to grasp the basic intelligibility of the capitalist mode of production, this can only be done through categories. If one wishes to employ these categories reflectively, this can only be done by exhibiting their immanent connections. The immanent connections among the categories can only be brought out by ordering them in a systematic fashion.[151]

If all that were being argued here is that concepts are necessary and that any theory composed of concepts must be internally coherent, there would be little with which to argue. But Smith goes on to say that "categories define structures, and from these structures certain structural tendencies necessarily arise" which allow us to understand the nature of capitalism. But, in the example that follows, the analysis of structures (social relations) is conflated with the categories (mental concepts) that define them. So we are told, for instance, that,

> A simple category of unity (e.g. "money as a measure of value") necessarily involves structural tendencies that point to differences not explicitly taken into account by that category. This would justify moving to a category where the moment of difference was made explicit (e.g. "money as a means of circulation").[152]

This process involves risking the same fate that befell Hegel. Starting from the necessity of conceptual thought, Hegel ended with a system in which one category automatically produces another until a whole system results which, it is claimed, "must" be an adequate account of reality. Smith says that he is not trying to give the "impression that the positions of Marx and Hegel can simply be conflated," but it is hard to believe that he has not at least partly done so. This appears to be the case when, for instance, he writes:

> Categories articulate structures or moments of structures. If reasoning can establish a systematic connection between two categories, say "capital" and "exploitation," this is equivalent to showing that one sort of structure (that captured in the catagory "capital') is necessarily connected with another (that captured by the category "exploitation").[153]

This impression is bolstered when Smith seems to imply that the historical and empirical content of *Capital* is secondary to, or can only be understood as examples or embodiments of, its logical structure.[154]

There are a number of fundamental problems with this approach. First, Marx himself was insistent that his dialectical approach and his mastery of empirical material were aspects of one and the same method. He complained that one critic was "naive enough to say that I 'move with rare freedom' in empirical matter" without having "the slightest idea that this 'free movement in matter' is nothing but a paraphrase for the *method* of dealing with matter—that is, the *dialectical method*."[155]

Second, it seems to assume that because social relations are not reducible to empirical objects, they must therefore be merely mental constructs. But if we take this step, we are indeed beginning to pass over the bridge that leads to idealism, because we will quickly find that all sorts of key features of Marx's understanding of capitalism have no immediate natural existence.

There is, however, no need to take this step. There are many features of social reality that have no direct, empirical existence but that are still commonly and rightly regarded as part of the material world, broadly understood. Take "friendship," for example. It is obviously not a material object in the narrow sense: One can't define its existence with any of the five senses. The most one can do is to observe the visible effects of friendship— people spend time together, offer each other assistance and advice, share intimacies, exchange gifts, and so on. But even this essential empirical evidence is not conclusive because many people who are not friends do some or all of these things. Only the total context of two people's lives will allow us to decide whether or not they are friends. Then we will begin to see friendship as a social relation. It really does shape people's behavior. Without an understanding of friendship in this sense we would be unable to explain such behavior. Social relations are thus something more material than mere concepts. To reduce them to the status of concepts is to repeat Hegels's error.

Third, even if we allow that Smith does not intend to do this but merely wants, like Marx, to make an abstraction from the inessential and accidental features of reality to grasp more clearly its key features, there is still a difficulty with the way in which he suggests that this process takes place. He seems to mean that once we are sure we have made an accurate abstraction—once we are sure that our concept "capital" is a true reflection of the actual existing capital—then we can also be sure that any further categories that emerge as a result of contradictions which we find in our concept will necessarily be matched by contradictions in the real capitalist world. This, however, is only a safe assumption on the basis of constant empirical verification—which is precisely the reason why we cannot dispense with the historical and empirical material that Marx includes in *Capital*. We cannot treat the book as if it were simply a progression of self-generating categories.

The effect of suggesting that we can treat *Capital* in this way, whatever disclaimers are issued about treating "one aspect" of Marx's work, is to reduce *Capital* to the status of the *Science of Logic*, a dialectic of empty forms. Hegel asserted that the dialectic of form and content could not be separated, but in fact was forced by his idealism to violate his own injunction. Marx was able to develop a dialectic in which form and content were united, though distinct, and to specify the relation between the two, precisely because he *did not* take the step that Smith urges.

Fourth, real contradictions are in any case more diverse and complex, and change more rapidly, than the concepts that express them, even when these are dialectical concepts especially designed to capture complexity and change. Constant empirical work is therefore essential to renew both the concrete analyses and the dialectical concepts that are generalized from these analyses. Engels was clear on this issue:

> . . . the concept of a thing and its reality run side by side like two asymptotes, always approaching each other but never meeting. This differ-

ence between the two is the very difference which prevents the concept from being directly and immediately the reality and reality from being immediately its own concept. Because a concept ... does not therefore *prima facie* directly coincide with reality, from which it had to be abstracted in the first place, it is nevertheless more than a fiction, unless you declare that all the results of thought are fictions because reality corresponds to them only very circuitously, and even then approaching it only asymptotically.[156]

Here Engels manages both to preserve the distinction between, and the unity of, theory and reality. Smith sees a unity where he should make a distinction (i.e., between categories and reality) and makes a distinction where he should see a unity (i.e., between the empirical and the theoretical content of *Capital*).

Finally, the real world and the concepts with which human beings seek to understand it constantly meet on the ground of human labor and practice. Once concepts are said to reproduce reality by means of their own coherence, it is not at all clear what role is left for Marx's "practical-critical activity." It is not Smith's intention to diminish the status of such activity as both the origin and the ultimate test of consciousness, but the logic of his argument leads in this direction.

Engels has in fact given us a very different interpretation of the relationship between concepts and reality in Marx's economic writings. Engels starts by describing the choice that faced Marx when he began his critique of economics. Should he follow the historical development of capitalism, or should he examine the logic of the mature, functioning capitalist system? Should he proceed "historically or logically"? The historical form "apparently has the advantage of greater clarity, since it is the *actual* development that is followed" from its simplest origins to its current complexity, Engels observes.[157] But, in fact, he goes on, this would have been the wrong approach:

History often moves in leaps and zig-zags, and it would have to be followed up throughout, so that not only would much material of slight importance have to be included, but also the train of thought would frequently have to be interrupted; moreover, it would be impossible to write the history of economics without that of bourgeois society, and the task would thus become endless.[158]

Engels, therefore, concludes that "the logical method of treatment was therefore the only suitable one." Engels seems then to make the same point as those who argue that the development of categories can substitute for historical development: "As a matter of fact this [the logical method] is nothing but the historical method, only stripped of its historical form and its disturbing fortuities." But this is only half the story, as Engels then makes clear. Logical development might be abstracted from the historical process, but "the train of thought must begin at the same point as the beginning of history." More than this, "its further progress will be nothing but the reflection of the historical process in an abstract and theoretically consistent form; a corrected reflection *but corrected in accordance with laws yielded by the actual historical process itself*, since each factor can be examined at the point of development of its full maturity."[159] And Engels is absolutely adamant that this relationship to actual historical development is not confined to the initial process of abstraction, but a constant part of the elaboration of the logic of the system:

> One can see that with this method, the logical development need by no means be confined to the purely abstract sphere. On the contrary, it requires historical illustration and constant contact with reality. These proofs are therefore introduced in great variety, comprising references both to the actual course of history at various stages of social development and to the economic literature, in which the clear working out of the definitions of economic relations is pursued from the outset.[160]

And when Engels deals with simple commodity production, which is the simplest logical, and the earliest historical, relationship with which Marx begins his analysis of capitalism, he shows that the logic of development that stems from it cannot be conceived independently of historical practice:

> With this method we proceed from the first and simplest relation which is historically, factually available. . . . We analyse this relation. The fact that it is a *relation* already implies . . . reciprocal action. Contradictions will result which demand a solution. But as we are not considering an abstract mental process that takes place solely in our minds, but a real process which actually took place at some particular time or which is still taking place, these contradictions, too, will have developed in practice and will have probably found their solution. We shall trace the nature of this solution and find that it has been effected by the establishment of a new relation, whose opposite sides we shall now have to work out, and so on.[161]

On this account, it seems clear that Marx and Engels's method does not just rely on the abstraction of certain concepts said to represent the essential workings of the capitalist system and to claim further insight based on the development of contradictions in these categories. Instead, Marx and Engels rely on a constant interaction between the dialectic of categories, which does develop according to different principles from the dialectical development of society, but which takes the latter as their constant and unavoidable point of reference.

Marx's choice of the commodity as his starting point in *Capital* exemplifies this point. Simple commodity production is the historical point of origin for capitalist society and remains the most basic unit of analysis in the mature capitalist system. Marx and Engels were clear that the dialectic that describes the birth of capitalism from the womb of feudalism and the dialectic of the fully developed capitalist system were two different things, but in the commodity they identified an element that was present at the point of origin and that also remained essential to any understanding of the completed capitalist system.[162]

This is true even though, as commodity production becomes generalized, it integrates and transforms simple commodity production, so that the expanding net of relations which constitutes developed capitalism is quite different to those much simpler relations which obtained at an earlier period. As Lenin notes:

> In his *Capital* Marx first analyses the simplest, most ordinary and fundamental, most common and everyday *relation* of bourgeois (commodity) society, a relation encountered billions of times, viz. the exchange of commodities. In this very simple phenomena (in this "cell" of bourgeois society) analysis reveals *all* the contradictions (or the germs of *all* the contradictions of modern society. The subsequent exposition shows us the development (*both* growth *and* movement) of these contradictions and of this society in the summation of its individual parts, from its beginning to its end.[163]

The "subsequent analysis" of which Lenin speaks develops the pattern which he describes elsewhere as "a *double* analysis, deductive and inductive—logical and historical." This involves both "the history of capitalism and the analysis of the *concepts* summing it up." The two elements cannot, however, be separated: "Testing by facts or by practice respectively, is to be found in *each* step of the analysis."[164]

Roman Rosdolsky's majestic survey, *The Making of Marx's Capital*, makes the same point repeatedly. Rosdolsky warns that "to the reader who is not acquainted with Marx's theory this . . . might appear 'contrived'—an example of the empty 'dialectic of concepts', which endows economic categories with a life of their own, and, in the truly Hegelian fashion, lets them originate and pass over into one another." But, Rosdolsky continues, although Marx was interested in understanding the logic of the system, rather than simply reflecting its chronological development, and although he understood that this demanded the developments of specialized categories that could capture this logic, "the reader should not imagine that economic categories are anything other than the reflections of real relations, or that the logical derivation of these categories could proceed independently of their historical derivation." Rosdolsky concludes: "That this was Marx's method from the outset can be seen best of all in the numerous passages in the *Rough Draft* [the *Grundrisse*], in the *Contribution* [*to the Critique of Political*

Economy] and in *Capital* which provide—parallel to the logical derivation of value and money—a historical derivation of these same concepts, in which Marx confronts the results of his abstract analysis with actual historical development."[165]

Marx himself was at pains to show that although the laws of the developed capitalist system were different to its process of origination, these laws could never be divorced from their historical origins or the contemporary empirical evidence of the way in which the system works:

> In order to develop the laws of bourgeois economy, therefore, it is not necessary to write the real history of the relations of production. But the correct observation and deduction of these laws, as themselves having become in history, always leads to primary equations—like empirical numbers, e.g. in natural science—which point to the past lying behind the system. These indications, together with a correct grasp of the present, then also offer the key to the understanding of the past.[166]

Thus, Marx argues two points. On the one hand, independent conceptual effort is necessary to make sense of the system: "The totality as it appears in the head, as a totality of thoughts, is a product of the the thinking head, which appropriates the world in the only way it can." And the way in which the head does this is "a product . . . of the working-up of observation and conception in concepts." But, on the other hand, Marx insists that this method should not be confused with the kind of "philosophical consciousness" for which "the conceptual world is the only reality" and "the movement of categories appears as the real act of production—which only, unfortunately, recieves a jolt from the outside—whose product is the world." On the contrary, "the real subject retains its autonomous existence outside the head just as before; namely as long as the head's conduct is merely speculative, merely theoretical. Hence, in the theoretical method, too, the subject, society, must always be kept in mind as the presupposition."[167]

THE MARXIST METHOD

It is now time to recapitulate the essentials of the marxist dialectic. Marx and Engels took three central and interlinked notions from Hegel: 1) the world is in a constant process of change; 2) the world is a totality; and, 3) this totality is internally contradictory. This encouraged them to discard all partial explanation of change and to look at the fundamental structures of society in the search for the determinants of change. Similarly, it discouraged them from looking outside the system—to God, to abstract notions of human nature, to some animating first principle long buried in a mythical past—to find the causes of change. Instead it directed them to cleavages within the social structure, to contradictions between different aspects of the totality, as the force that drove the whole society forward.

Marx and Engels also acknowledge that "what distinguished Hegel's mode of thought from that of all other philosophers was the tremendous historical sense on which it was based." But even though "the material is everywhere handled historically, in a definite historical connection" in Hegel, this only happens "in an abstract distorted manner."[168] Consequently, the method became debased in the hands of Hegel's followers. For them, "Hegel's whole heritage was confined to a sheer pattern, by means of which any subject could be knocked into shape, and to a compilation of words and phrases whose only remaining purpose was to turn up as the right time whenever positive knowledge was lacking."[169]

Marx and Engels, themselves profoundly shaped by the political and economic struggles in Britain and Continental Europe and by the rise of political economy as a science, saw their task as reconstituting Hegel's dialectic on the basis of empirical and historical study. This was no minor modification. It involved the complete reconstruction of every single dialectical category on the basis of its systematic and verifiable relation with real social development. No element in Hegel's dialectic emerged unchanged; most were utterly transformed.

Hegel saw nature as the alienated opposite of human beings, whom he identified with their consciousness. Any objectification of thought was a form of alienation that would only be overcome when consciousness recognized itself in nature. Marx and Engels argued that human beings had developed from the natural world and were still dependent on it. The human ability to labor and to direct consciously that labour was a product of the natural process of evolution. Human beings were not alienated by producing objects but by *not* being able to produce objects *freely*. The possibility of doing this was only a recent historical conquest, based on the level of production attained by capitalist society.

Fundamental distinctions between the Hegelian and the marxist dialectic emerge at this point. In Marx, human beings are seen as part of nature, but a distinct and unique part of nature separated from their origins by the evolution of conscious labor. This is a unity of opposites. Human beings are both united with nature and opposed to it. In Hegel, we only have an identity of opposites—nature is thought, but alienated thought, thought opposed to itself. Consequently, for Marx and Engels, the dialectical pattern in the natural world and in the social world were different, but related. For Hegel, they were identical.

Similarly, Marx and Engels saw that the dialectic operated very differently in some societies than it did in others. The bourgeois revolution has a distinct pattern of development that does not simply reproduce itself in the workers' revolution. The dialectic between the subject of historical change and the objective structure of society is, for instance, very different in the cases of the bourgeoisie and the proletariat. In Hegel, the pattern of dialectical development may "manifest" itself in different periods, but this has nothing to do with their particular social structure and only to do with the specific aspect of the timeless Absolute Idea that appears in them.

Likewise, the structure of alienation is identical in all historical periods as far as Hegel is concerned. But for Marx and Engels, alienation under feudalism, insofar as it exists, is based to greater extent on the inability of the society to control or understand the forces of nature. Under capitalism, alienation is both more severe and almost entirely social in origin.

In other words, Marx and Engels made the dialectic socially relative, and its form is, therefore, subject to the very force that it was designed to analyze: historical change. And once the dialectic had to become concerned with real natural and social developments, not just their mental echoes, it had to be capable of dealing with all the complexity and unevenness that is part of real history. As Bhikhu Parekh notes:

> . . . since Hegel's dialectic is not empirically grounded it overlooks the diversity of forms, levels and degrees of dialectical development occurring in reality. Hegel's gaze is fixed on *Geist* [Spirit], and therefore on the major or principle dialectical development occurring in society. He does not notice how it actualises itself in, and conditions and is, in turn, conditioned by subsidiary dialectical developments operative in specific areas of social life, and nor does he appreciate the uneven development of contradictions in different areas of social life. Had Hegel not conceived society as a single *Subjekt* and had he investigated a concrete historical society carefully, he would have seen that every society is a complicated maze of interlocked patterns of dialectical interaction, and that no human society ever conforms to his image of a single monolithic pattern.[170]

This is precisely the task that Marx and Engels undertook, carefully drawing both the necessary distinctions and the vital connections between, for instance, means of production and relations of production, production and circulation, economics and politics, base and superstructure, social development and ideology. It also allowed them to develop a dialectical method that was related to, but not identical with, the real contradictions it was meant to analyze.

In such a differentiated totality, mediation obviously became central to Marx and Engels's dialectic. To trace the connections and the contradictions between the different elements of the whole clearly becomes a much more vital task when that whole is seen to have many different levels of development than it is if the whole can simply, immediately, and directly be reduced to one central contradiction. This element in Marx and Engels's method is worth emphasizing, because it helps us to avoid the danger to which Bertell Ollman rightly directs out attention:

> Dialectical thinkers . . . have a tendency to move too quickly to the bottom line, to push the germ of a development to its finished form. In general, this error results from not giving enough attention to the complex mediations, both in space and over time, that make up the joints of any social problem.[171]

And just as the notions of mediation and unity of opposites were transformed by Marx and Engels, so were the notions of the change of quantity into quality and the negation of the negation.[172] In Hegel, gradual, small changes which accumulate to the point where they give rise to separate, qualitatively distinct states necessarily had a quietest aspect. They were, after all, essentially changes of consciousness. The higher stages of consciousness always incorporated what was valuable, "the truth," of the preceding ideas now understood in their broader context. Historical changes of this kind are bound to be more violent. The police may only arrest a few more black suspects; it may be that a recent conviction by an all white jury is merely the latest in a long line—but it proves to be the incident that sparks a riot. The supervisor may have sacked or disciplined tens of workers before—but this last case is the one that leads to a strike. Engels expressed the same idea with his characteristic clarity:

> . . . we shall call one more witness for the transformation of quantity into quality, namely—Napoleon. He describes the combat between French cavalry, who were bad riders but disciplined, and the Mamelukes, who were undoubtedly the best horsemen of their time for single combat, but lacked discipline, as follows: "Two Mamelukes were undoubtedly more than a match for three Frenchmen; 100 Mamelukes were equal to 100 Frenchmen; 300 Frenchmen could generally beat 300 Mamelukes, and 1,000 Frenchmen invariably defeated 1,500 Mamelukes."[173]

Similarly, as we have seen, with the negation of the negation. To begin with one idea, develop its opposite, and then to negate that leaves the real social structure unchanged. In Hegel the negation of the negation is used to close the dialectical movement. It is the root of Hegel's fatalism. In his philosophy of religion, Hegel uses the dialectic to show that Christianity is the highest form of religion. In the *Philosophy of Right*, it is used to show that constitutional monarchy is the highest form of state. In his system generally, Hegel wishes to use the same mechanism to show that his philosophy is the culmination of the entire western philosophical enterprise. All this is possible because the idealism of Hegel's system determines that the negation of the negation leaves its middle term, social reality, reconciled in its final term, which is a form of thought.[174]

Marx and Engels start out from real social contradictions which give rise to change and so the negation of the negation leaves them with new social conditions that open up the possibility of further change. Thus a real social process, which finds within itself a force opposed to it, is an entirely different situation than is Hegel's dialectic. For Marx and Engels,

> *History* does *nothing*, it "possesses *no* immense wealth", it "wages *no* battles". It is *man*, real, living man who does all that, who possesses and fights; "history" is not, as it were, a person apart, using man as a means to achieve *its own* aims; history is *nothing but* the activity of man pursuing his aims.[175]

Real change must result from any contradictory system, although the outcome of the conflict is not predetermined. Nevertheless, the available solutions will be shaped in specific ways by the preceding contradiction and will issue forth in new pattern of social change. This new pattern will itself depend on how and by whom the preceeding contradiction was resolved.

Notes

1. That Marx and Engels were in broad agreement on the fundamentals of their philosophical approach is not an uncontested assertion. It is not one that I intend to defend directly in this book. I have, however, done so elsewhere. See J Rees, "Engels' Marxism," in J. Rees, ed., *The Revolutionary Ideas of Frederick Engels* (London, 1995).
2. S. Hook, *From Hegel to Marx, Studies in the Intellectual Development of Karl Marx* (Ann Arbor: University of Michigan Press, 1962), 133.
3. Ibid.
4. See D. McLellan, *The Young Hegelians and Karl Marx* (London: Macmillan, 1969), 27; and Hook, *From Hegel to Marx*, 89.
5. Quoted by Hook, *From Hegel to Marx*, 128. Hook adds: "But the important reservation must be made that the fall from grace was very gradual and gathered momentum only as the *Jahrbucher* turned from playing at re-defining Protestantism to an open advocacy of political insurrection in behalf of a democratic republic."
6. L. Kolakowski, *Main Currents of Marxism*, Vol. 1: *The Founders*, (Oxford: Oxford University Press, 1978), 91 and 95.
7. McLellan, *The Young Hegelians*, 39.
8. Quoted in Marx and Engels, *The Holy Family*, in *Marx Engels Collected Works*, (hereafter, *MECW*), Vol. 4 (London: Progress, 1975), 81.
9. K. Marx, *The Poverty of Philosophy* (Moscow: Progress, 1975), 98–99.
10. Marx and Engels, *MECW*, Vol. 5, 36.
11. Ibid., 36–37.
12. Marx and Engels, *MECW*, Vol. 4, 57–58.

13. Ibid., 58.
14. Ibid.
15. K. Marx, "Economic and Philosophical Manuscripts," in *Early Writings* (London: Penguin, 1975), 384–85.
16. K. Marx, "Critique of Hegel's Doctrine of the State," in *Early Writings*, 98.
17. Ibid., 109.
18. K. Marx, "Economic and Philosophical Manuscripts," in *Early Writings*, 382.
19. Ibid., 393.
20. Ibid., 399.
21. Ibid., 398.
22. K. Marx, "Critique of Hegel's Doctrine of the State," in *Early Writings*, 151.
23. As Henri Lefebvre, quoting Marx, put it: "Consequently 'this ideal transcending leaves the object intact in reality.' Hegel opposes non-philosophical immediacy, then accepts its immediate reality philosophically." H. Lefebvre, *Dialectical Materialism* (London: Jonathan Cape, 1968), 65.
24. Marx, "Critique of Hegel's Doctrine of the State," 155.
25. K. Marx, *Economic and Philosophlcal Manuscripts*, in *Early Writings* (London: Pelican, 1975), 381.
26. K. Marx, *On Proudhon*, in *MECW*, Vol. 20 (Moscow: Progress, 1985), 26. Marx also noted, in a letter to Engels in 1868, that "Feuerbach has much on his conscience" in respect of the fact that the "gentlemen in Germany (with the exception of theological reactionaries) believe Hegel's dialectic to be a 'dead dog.'" See *MECW*, Vol. 42 (Moscow, 1987), 520.
27. P. Murray, *Marx's Theory of Scientific Knowledge* (New Jersey: Humanities Press, 1988), 31.
28. Marx, "Critique of Hegel's Doctrine of the State," in *Early Writings*, 152.
29. Ibid., 158.
30. Ibid., 251.
31. Ibid., 394.
32. Marx and Engels, *German Ideology*, in *MECW*, Vol. 5, 30.
33. K. Marx, "Economic and Philosophical Manuscripts," in *Early Writings*, 365.
34. K. Marx, "Theses on Feuerbach," in *Early Writings*, 423.
35. Marx and Engels, *The German Ideology*, 41–42.
36. Ibid., 42.
37. F. Engels, "The Part Played by Labour in the Transition from Ape to Man," in *MECW*, Vol. 25, 453.
38. Marx and Engels, *German Ideology*, 43–44.
39. K. Marx, *Capital*, Vol. I (London: Penguin, 1976), 283.
40. Ibid., 283–84.
41. Ibid., 284.
42. Ibid.
43. K. Marx, "Eighteenth Brumaire of Louis Bonaparte," in *Surveys from Exile* (London: Penguin, 1973), 146.
44. C. J. Arthur, *Dialectics of Labour, Marx and His relation to Hegel* (Oxford: Blackwell, 1986), 5.
45. Ibid., 5–6.
46. F. Jakubowski, *Ideology and Superstructure in Historical Materialism* (London: Pluto Press, 1990), 60.
47. K. Marx, "Theses on Feuerbach," in *Early Works*, 421–22.
48. Hook, *From Hegel to Marx*, 279.

49. Lefebvre, *Dialectical Materialism*, 107.
50. Engels, *Dialectics of Nature*, in *MECW*, Vol. 25, 493.
51. Ibid., 494–95. Engels's emphasis. Bertell Ollman makes some valuable points in this connection: "Naturally, the particular form taken by a dialectical law will vary considerably, depending on its subject. . . . The . . . movements which lie at the core of contradiction, for example, appear very different when applied to the forces of inanimate nature than they do when applied to specifically capitalist phenomena. Striking differences such as these have led some followers of Marx to restrict the laws of the dialectic to social phenomena and to reject as 'unMarxist' what they label 'Engels' dialectic of nature'. Their error, however, is to confuse a particular statement of these laws, usually one appropriate to levels of generality where human consciousness is present, for all possible statements." Ollman goes on to argue that, because contradiction is such a vital concept in Marx's analysis of capitalism, it receives a great deal of attention from Marx's critics. Yet, because contradiction plays "a relatively minor role . . . in the changes that occur in nature . . . this may also help account for the mistaken belief that dialectical laws are only found in society." See B. Ollman, *Dialectical Investigations* (London: Routledge, 1993), 64–65.
52. See J. Ferraro, *Freedom and Determination in History According to Marx and Engels* (New York: Monthly Review Press, 1992), 159.
53. Engels, *Ludwig Feuerbach and the End of Classical German Philosophy* (Peking, 1976), 40.
54. Ibid., 45–46.
55. S. Sayers, "Engels and Materialism," in C. J. Arthur, ed., *Engels Today* (London: MacMillan, 1996), 161.
56. Ibid., 162.
57. Ibid., 163.
58. R. Levins, and R. Lewontin, *The Dialectical Biologist* (Cambridge, MA: Harvard University Press, 1985), 277.
59. Sayers, "Engels and Materialism," 163.
60. Levins and Lewontin, *Dialectical Biologist*. See also Richard Lewontin's brilliant popular application of this approach to one of the most contentious areas of modern science, the study of DNA, in *The Doctrine of DNA* (London: Penguin, 1991). For a more detailed analysis of the contemporary debates surrounding the dialectic of nature, see R. Levins, "When Science Fails Us," in *International Socialism* 72 (London, 1996). This is the transcript of Richard Levin's speech to the 1996 Edinburgh International Science Festival at which Levins was awarded the 1996 Edinburgh Medal. Also see P. McGarr, "Engels and Natural Science," in J. Rees, ed., *Revolutionary Ideas of Frederick Engels*. Also P. McGarr, "Order Out of Chaos," *International Socialism* 48 (London, 1990); and D. Blackie, "Revolution in Science," *International Socialism* 42 (London, 1989).
61. Only in the first forms of communal existence, that is, the clans characteristic of very early human society, were non-exploitative, non-oppressive relations possible. Here social life and the direct struggle for survival (and, therefore, the labor process) were so immediately related, and the product of such work so immediately related to consumption, that no class differentiation was possible. This "primitive communism" rests on the undeveloped level of the productive technique. Only when production was able to provide a surplus, at least for some members of society, does the division of labor develop to the point where classes are formed and where there is a break between domestic

and other labor, that is, the beginning of the oppression of women. Only when the productive process has advanced to the point where the surplus product is so great as to be able to provide for a communism of abundance, rather than the original communism of scarcity, does the abolition of classes, and of the oppression of women, once again become an historical possibility. This is, in essence, the argument of Engels's *The Origins of Private Property, the Family and the State.* Also see C. Harman, "Engels and the Origin of Human Society," in J. Rees, ed., *Revolutionary Ideas of Frederick Engels.*

62. Marx and Engels, *German Ideology*, 431.
63. Ibid., 54.
64. Ibid., 431–32.
65. K. Marx, Preface to *A Contribution to the Critique of Political Economy* (Moscow: Progress, 1970), 20–21.
66. Ibid., 21.
67. Ibid., 21. For a valuable discussion of the base and superstructure debate, see C. Harman, "Base and Superstructure," in *International Socialism* 32 (London, 1986).
68. Marx and Engels, *Communist Manifesto*, in A. P. Mendel, ed., *Essential Works of Marxism* (New York: Bantam, 1971), 13.
69. F. Engels, *Anti-Duhring*, in *MECW*, Vol. 25 (London, 1987), 153.
70. Marx and Engels, *The Holy Family*, in *MECW*, Vol. 4, 81.
71. Ibid., 82.
72. Marx and Engels, *German Ideology*, 60.
73. Ibid., 61.
74. Ibid.
75. Ibid., 53.
76. Ibid., 53–54.
77. Lefebvre, *Dialectical Materialism*, 39.
78. Marx and Engels, *Communist Manifesto*, in A. P. Mendel, ed., *Essential Works of Marxism*, 23–24.
79. Marx and Engels, *Holy Family*, 35.
80. Ibid.
81. Ibid. In this connection, Karl Korsch rightly identified a problem when he argued that simply talking of reciprocal reactions leaves many "hotly disputed questions in the field of historical materialism . . . just as insoluble and just as meaningless as the well-known scholastic disputes about the priority of the hen or the egg." But he was wrong to blame Engels for introducing this problem into marxism. He was also wrong in thinking that these problems will simply disappear if the relations are described in "a concrete, historical and specific manner." This is for the reason that detailed description will simply reveal that in some areas—say the mutually reinforcing dialectic between abstract idealism and abstract empiricism a reciprocal dialectic is at work whereas in others, typically those involving real material change, the impetus for change is provided more by one side of the dialectical contradictions than by the other (as in the example that follows in the main text). For Karl Korsch's views, see "Why I Am a Marxist," in K. Korsch, *Three Essays in Marxism* (London: Pluto Press, 1971), 64.
82. Ibid., 35–36.
83. Hook, *From Marx to Hegel*, 64–65. Hook also makes the valuable point: "The extent, strength and rate of the interaction between the polar elements within

any situation depend upon the specific factors involved. They cannot be *deduced* from the general formula of dialectical movement."

84. Marx and Engels, *Holy Family*, 36.
85. Ibid., 37.
86. Ibid.
87. Marx and Engels, *German Ideology*, 53.
88. F. Engels, Introduction to K. Marx, *The Class Struggles in France*, in *MECW*, Vol. 27 (London, 1990), 520.
89. Marx and Engels, *German Ideology*, 59.
90. Marx, "Economic and Philosophical Manuscripts", in *Early Writings*, 325.
91. Ibid., 326.
92. Ibid., 325–26.
93. Ibid., 327.
94. Ibid.
95. Ibid., 329.
96. This did not commit Marx and Engels to the common view of human nature in which its characteristics remain fixed throughout history. Indeed, it committed them to the view that it was in the nature of humans to change themselves and their circumstances and, therefore, the characterisitics that are commonly described as "human nature" throughout history. See N. Geras, *Marx and Human Nature, the Refutation of a Myth* (London: Verso, 1983) for a useful discussion of these and other issues, albeit one marred by its tortuous presentation.
97. Marx, *Economic and Philosophical Manuscripts*, 330–31.
98. Ibid., 349.
99. Ibid., 359.
100. Ibid., 377.
101. Ibid., 377–79.
102. Marx, *Grundrisse* (London: Penguin, 1973), 832.
103. Marx, *Capital*, Vol. I, 170.
104. Ibid., 171–72.
105. Ibid., 165.
106. Ibid.
107. Ibid., 167–68.
108. Marx, *Grundrisse*, 196–97.
109. Marx, "Economic and Philosophical Manuscripts", in *Early Writings*, 335.
110. Marx, *Grundrisse*, 251.
111. Ibid., 247.
112. Ibid., 245.
113. F. Engels in Marx and Engels, *Selected Correspondence* (Moscow: Progress, 1975), 399.
114. Ibid., 398–99.
115. Ibid.
116. Ibid., 399.
117. Ibid., 400.
118. Ibid.
119. Ibid., 399.
120. K. Marx, *Capital*, Vol. III (London: Lawrence and Wishart, 1959), 817.
121. For a valuable critique of Althusser, see P. Gamble, and A. Walton, *From Alienation to Surplus Value* (London: Sheed and Ward, 1972), chapters 1, 2, and 5.
122. K. Marx, Letter to Joseph Dietzgen, 9 May 1868, in *MECW*, Vol. 43 (Moscow: Progress, 1988), 31.

123. Marx, *Capital*, Vol. I, 744, n. 29.
124. Ibid., 102–3.
125. Ibid., 103.
126. Ibid.
127. Ibid., 93.
128. Ibid., 617.
129. Ibid., 618–619.
130. Ibid.
131. Ibid., 619.
132. Ibid., 928.
133. Ibid., 929.
134. Ibid.
135. Engels, *Anti-Duhring*, 124.
136. Lefebvre, *Dialectical Materialism*, 112–13. Also see Alex Callinicos's useful discussion of "The Dialectics of Progress," in Marx's writings on India: A Callinicos. *Theories and Narratives, Reflections on the Philosophy of History* (Cambridge: Polity Press, 1995), 151–65.
137. Marx, *Grundrisse*, 99.
138. Ibid. Emphasis in the original.
139. Ibid., 99–100. Emphasis in the original.
140. Marx, *Capital*, Vol. III, 244.
141. Ibid.
142. Ibid.
143. Ibid, 245.
144. K. Marx, *Theories of Surplus Value*, Part II (Moscow: Progress, 1968), 504–5.
145. Ibid., 500.
146. K. Marx, *Theories of Surplus Value*, Part III (Moscow: Progress, 1971), 87.
147. Ibid., 88.
148. B. Parekh, *Marx and the Hegelian Dialectic*, in V. K. Roy, and R. C. Sarikwal, eds., *Marxian Sociology*, Vol. I (Delhi, 1979), 83.
149. See R. Dunayevskaya, *Marxism and Freedom from 1776 until Today* (London: Pluto Press, 1975); and *Philosophy and Revolution, from Hegel to Sartre, and from Marx to Mao* (New York, 1973). For C. L. R. James, see *Notes of Dialectics, Hegel, Marx, Lenin* (London: Allison and Busby, 1980).
150. See T. Smith, *The Logic of Marx's Capital, Replies to Hegelian Criticisms* (State University of New York, 1990); and T. Smith, *Dialectical Social Theory and Its Critics, from Hegel to Analytical Marxism to Postmodernism* (State University of New York, 1993), which contains an extremely useful attack on postmodernism and analytical marxism.
151. Smith, *Logic of Marx's Capital*, 96.
152. Ibid.
153. Smith, *Dialectical Social Theory and Its Critics*, 44.
154. See, for instance, ibid., 22 and 96.
155. K. Marx, letter to Kugelmann, 27 June 1870, in *MECW*, Vol. 43 (Moscow: Progress, 1988), 528.
156. Engels to Conrad Schmidt in Marx Engels, *Selected Correspondence*, 457.
157. F. Engels, *Karl Marx, A Contribution to the Critique of Political Economy*, in K. Marx, *Preface and Introduction to A Contribution to the Critique of Political Economy* (Peking, 1976), 55.
158. Ibid., 56.

159. Ibid., emphasis added.
160. Ibid., 58.
161. Ibid., 56–57.
162. Chris Arthur, usually one of the most reliable commentators on the marxist method, is mistakenly skeptical of this approach. See C. J. Arthur, "Engels as an Interpreter of Marx's Economics," in C. J. Arthur, ed., *Engels Today*, 173–209. Arthur's main point is that Engels was wrong to insist on the dialectical development of the capitalist mode of production from simple commodity production, a term that he argues is not present in Marx. Engels was misled by basing himself on Hegel's philosophy of history. Had he based himself instead on Hegel's dialectic of concepts, primarily found in the *Science of Logic*, he would have better understood that the dialectic of capital applies to the finished totality of the capitalist system but not to its emergence from its precapitalist past. This argument, which has some similarities with Tony Smith's approach, has a number of weaknesses. First, it makes more of the separation between logic and history than is in fact the case in Hegel, for whom the two processes were closely linked. Second, it leaves us stranded in the present with no mechanism for understanding how we got here. Third, it assumes that we can understand the present dialectical structure of capitalism without understanding the dialectic of its origin—or at least that such a dialectic is unconnected with the question of simple commodity production. Finally, it underestimates the degree to which Engels (and Marx) understood that a dialectic of the origin of the system and a dialectic of the mature system were different, but related in ways that only the standpoint of the mature system was capable of revealing.
163. Lenin, *Collected Works*, Vol. 38 (Moscow: Progress, 1972), 360–61.
164. Ibid., 320; emphasis in the original. Moreover, it is far from being simply the case that the development of the commodity from cell to system reveals the nature of capitalism. Rather it is the nature of a *specific* commodity, labor-power, that gives us an understanding of capitalism—and even then a whole series of other concepts (accumulation, reproduction, rate of profit, organic composition of capital, and so on) before we have even a general theory of crises.
165. R. Rosdolsky, *The Making of Marx's Capital* (London: Pluto Press, 1977), 114–15. In this connection, Paul Mattick Jr. makes a valuable point: "It is because as conceptions abstractions are not aspects of reality but aspects of the conceptual appropriation of reality that concepts cannot, according to Marx, be said to have a life of their own, to be exhibited at work either in the process of history or in the arrangement of categories in historical construction. The presentation of categories cannot, that is, be said to follow an immanent logic, but must be understood as governed by the effort to account for the fundamental features of the social system under investigation." P Mattick Jr., "Marx's Dialectic," in F. Moseley, ed., *Marx's Method in Capital* (New Jersey: Humanities Press, 1993), 121. Marx's system was both a critique of capitalist society and a critique of the bourgeois science of political economy. But only a reductionist would assume either that a critique of economic reality *is* a critique of its scientific and ideological representation or that a critique of catagories *is*, automatically, a critique of society. In fact, both are necessary.
166. Marx, *Grundrisse*, 460–61.
167. Marx, *Grundrisse*, 101–2.
168. Ibid., 54–55.

169. Ibid., 52.
170. Parekh, *Marx and the Hegelian Dialectic*, 89.
171. Ollman, *Diatectical Investigations*, 17.
172. I have left this formal discussion of the the "three laws" of the dialectic until the conclusion of this chapter, because I believe that, although they are an essential condensation of the dialectic, they cannot be properly understood without the wider context established by the notions of totality, contradiction, and mediation. Nor can they be properly understood without being presented as part of the historical and social analyses in which we find them in the work of Marx and Engels. It was necessary, therefore, that these two approaches should precede, and to some extent replace, the more formal, commonplace innumeration of "dialectical laws." This approach also has the advantage of allowing the reader to approach the issues involved without immediately having to overcome the distortion of the dialectic common in, for instance, the Stalinist tradition which made such ill-use of the "three laws" that an unprejudiced approach to them is still difficult to cultivate.
173. Engels, *Anti-Duhring*, 119.
174. See Parekh, *Marx and the Hegelian Dialectic*, 92.
175. Engels, *Holy Family*, 93.

3

The First Crisis
of Marxism

In the last twenty-five years of the nineteenth century, capitalism developed many of the features that define its modern form. Imperial rivalry became more intense and, in many countries, so did protectionism at home. Monopolies grew in power. "Until the 1870s free competition went almost uncontested; by the end of the century, cartels had already become one of the bases of economic life."[1] Hand in hand with the growth of monopoly went the expansion of the economic, social, and political functions of the state—not least in the creation of professional armies.[2] As a result, the nationalism of the ruling classes increasingly lost any democratic and progressive aspect that it had inherited from the era of bourgeois revolutions and became a retrograde ideology, the hallmark of conservatism and militarism in all the industrialized countries. The roots of mass production, including the mass production of consumer goods, sank deeper into society. Universal suffrage, or at least an extension of the suffrage, became a fact in many, though not all, European countries. Modern, mass political parties, whether conservative or progressive, inevitably followed. In the working class, stable trade unionism advanced, among the unskilled as well as the skilled. As it did so, it lost its local character and increasingly became a nationally organized phenomena. In both the socialist parties and the trade unions, a full-time bureaucracy mushroomed.

At the same time, socialist and marxist ideas gained a mass following in a number of European countries—among them Germany, France, Hungary, Belgium, Italy, Spain, and Russia. This support was, for the first time, organized into national political parties, the most powerful of which was the German Social Democratic Party (SPD). These parties were, after 1889, drawn together in the Second International.[3] Some twenty-five years later, after an era of passing motions condemning war, militarism, and nationalism, the International collapsed as the parties of which it was composed each supported their own ruling class in the mutual slaughter of working people known as the First World War.

126

The rise and fall of the Second International is the indispensable context necessary to understand the debates about the marxist method which take place in this period. And the debates themselves are crucial to understanding the nature of the dialectic because they mark the first attempt to substitute reformism in practice and economic determinism in theory for the genuine marxist tradition. In the hands of Eduard Bernstein (1850–1932) and Karl Kautsky (1854–1938), two of the leading figures of the German SPD, the revolutionary nature of marxism was increasingly turned in a reformist direction, and the philosophical underpinnings of the theory was either abandoned or distorted out of all recognition. And even the most determined defenders of the dialectic, the Russian marxist Georgi Plekhanov (1856–1918) and the Polish revolutionary Rosa Luxemburg (1871–1919), were forced by changed circumstances to develop the marxist method in quite new ways.

There is one crucial area in which the larger social changes (growth of trade unionism, political parties, enlarged suffrage) and the theoretical debates that raged in this period become fused. This is the issue of socialist organization. In the Second International we see the debates over the marxist method and debates over the nature, aims, strategy, and tactics of revolutionary organization more closely connected than ever before. The changes in society and the growth of socialist organization made it inevitable that theoretical debates began to have much more immediate political and organizational ramifications. Equally, arguments over the nature of the changes in society often had a strong philosophical dimension.

The most important crucible for this debate was the German SPD. The forerunner of the SPD, the Social Democratic and Labour Party was led by Marx's disciples Wilhelm Liebknecht and August Bebel. Bismarck's anti-socialist laws were enacted in 1878, ten years after the party was formed at the Gotha congress by the merger of Marx's followers with the reformist tendency led by Lassalle. The anti-socialist laws drove the party into illegality until 1890, although SPD members could still stand in elections as individuals. The existence of the laws obliged the party to adopt a more oppositional pose. Repression forced it, for the first time, to take marxist ideas seriously and to repudiate, at least verbally, its former illusions in parliamentary means of struggle. It nevertheless emerged from the period of the anti-socialist laws with a much enlarged electoral base: in 1881, it had won 311,961 votes, rising to 1,427,298 votes in 1890. In 1891, the party adopted a marxist program, *The Erfurt Programme*. It was the biggest and seemingly most successful of the parties in the International. Bernstein and Kautsky had known Marx and Engels personally and were generally considered their intellectual and political inheritors.

In fact, the SPD was a long way from being a genuinely marxist organization. *The Erfurt Programme* itself was divided into two parts. One, written by Kautsky and based on the *Communist Manifesto*, contained a lengthy analysis of capitalism and a broad demand for its transformation into a socialist society. The second section written by Bernstein, however, contained demands for a number of immediate reforms—universal suffrage, direct taxation, the eight-hour day, and so on. The program was clearly designed for a non-revolutionary period, but its structure allowed it to be understood very differently by the competing currents that still ran side by side in the SPD. As the classic history of the SPD explains:

> To the revolutionaries, the idealists, it said in effect, "Patience! The time is not yet. Remember history is on your side." To the reformists . . . it said, "Reforms are the first task. Pursue them. But remember, you must fight for them. And the faith in the bright new society is a weapon in your struggle. Do not ignore it."[4]

Such ambiguity would have been less damaging if, in the years that followed, the pattern of class struggle had polarized debate on terms favorable to the left wing of the SPD, as it had done in the years of the anti-socialist laws. But events tended to reinforce the right-wing interpretation of the Erfurt synthesis. German capitalism enjoyed a period of expansion until after the turn of the century, and real wages rose from the low levels of the 1860s and 1870s. The working day was shortened in some industries after 1900. The German state was able to grant some reforms. In the whole of the 1890s, a mere 500,000 workers took strike action.[5]

Yet the SPD was not part of the established order. Electoral laws discriminated in favor of the middle and upper classes, systematically under-representing the SPD in local and national parliaments. Censorship of the party press was still enforced. A policeman sat on the platform of every SPD meeting to ensure that restrictions on freedom of speech were not broken. Between 1890 and 1912, SPD members were sentenced to a total of 1,244 years in prison, including 164 years of hard labor.[6] So although conditions were obviously not revolutionary, neither were they such that workers saw no need for socialist organization. Indeed, throughout this period, they flooded into and voted for the SPD in ever-increasing numbers: the SPD received 10.1 percent of the vote in the Reichstag elections of 1887, 19.7 percent in 1890, 23.3 percent in 1893, 27.7 percent in 1898, and 31.7 percent in 1903.[7]

And the SPD was much more than a vote-gathering machine. Excluded from German society, workers looked on the SPD as their own "state within a state." The SPD "developed vigorous women's and youth groups and a wide selection of newspapers and periodicals, ranging from high theoretical reviews to children's magazines."[8] Trade unions and consumer cooperatives were linked to the party, and so were "the 200,000 members of the German

Federation of Worker Choirs in 1914 and the 130,000 members of the Workers' Cycling Club 'Solidarity' (1910)," not to mention the members of the Worker Stamp Collectors and the Worker Rabbit Breeders. Parties like the SPD "might include virtually every association in which workers participated, from cradle to grave."[9]

Clearly the practice of slow, patient reformist work was established long before Eduard Bernstein gave it a finished formulation in a series of articles, beginning in 1897, and culminating in his book *The Preconditions of Socialism*, published in 1899.[10]

BERNSTEIN, REFORMISM, AND THE ABANDONMENT OF THE DIALECTIC

Eduard Bernstein had impeccable radical credentials. He fled Germany for Switzerland just before the anti-socialist laws were passed. He first travelled to London to meet Engels in 1880. He did so again in 1887, this time to live, after the German government brought pressure to bear on their Swiss counterpart. He edited *Der Sozialdemokrat* in London's Kentish Town from where it was smuggled into Germany, as all SPD publications had to be. Until Engels's death in 1895, Bernstein was a loyal collaborator, defending Engels's strategic vision for the SPD—legal tactics as part of a revolutionary policy:

> Engels was thinking in terms of strictly legal and parliamentary activity within the framework of a revolutionary strategy; and he was clear that the strategy had to be a revolutionary one because, for him, it was axiomatic that the bourgeoisie would not sit back and allow the proletariat to legislate capitalism out of existence.[11]

But within a year of Engels's death, and despite being named his literary executor, Bernstein was advancing an entirely different reformist strategy. "While such things are impossible to prove it appears likely that Berstein's close friendship with the older man postponed his lapse into the Revisionist heresy."[12] Bernstein's new strategy had more in common with the Fabianism with which he had come into contact in Britain, much to Engels's dismay, than it did with any variant of revolutionary socialism. By the time *The Preconditions of Socialism* was published, Bernstein had developed an analysis that constituted "a full scale attack on Marx's system."[13]

Bernstein argued, in words repeated by today's reformists, that capitalism was becoming less prone to economic crises because cartels and monopolies, the increased speed of communication, and the growth of the credit system all weakened the anarchic tendencies of the market. He thought that the economy (through the spread of share ownership and consumer cooperatives) and the state (through the widening of the suffrage) were more open to democratic control. He thought that Marx's theory of value was a fiction that could be replaced by mainstream, market-derived economic concepts. And he concluded that the SPD should amend its theory so that it aligned with its practice and could declare itself a democratic party of social reform.

The materialist conception of history was abandoned because, Bernstein argued, it was a rigid determinism in which "matter moves of necessity in accordance with certain laws . . . and . . . since the movement of matter determines the formation of ideas and the directions of the will, these too are necessitated, as are all human events." For Bernstein, marxism was as strict in its fatalism as Protestant predestinarianism:

> The materialist is thus a Calvinist without God. If he does not believe in predestination ordained by divinity, he does and must believe that . . . the totality of the given material and the power relations of its parts [are] determined beforehand.[14]

Bernstein then goes on, using the letters that Engels wrote late in life to explain the relationship between material and ideological elements in social development, effectively to dissolve the real meaning of Marx's conception of history. Bernstein portrayed any notion of material determination as *determinism*. Consequently, he misrepresented Engels's attack on the later as an argument for abandoning the former. To have understood the relationship between the subjective and objective strands of the historical process that Engels was trying to illuminate would have required some inkling of the dialectical method. But it was precisely this aspect of marxism that Bernstein argued had to be removed root and branch.

In most of the areas where Bernstein wanted to revise marxism, he could use partial quotations or citations from the writings of Marx and Engels, torn from their historical and theoretical context, to bolster his case. But in his rejection of the dialectic, Bernstein's revisionism took the form of an absolute and unqualified rejection of Marx and Engels. As Bernstein himself admitted, "My way of thinking would make me a member of the school of positivist philosophy and sociology."[15]

Bernstein's rejection of the dialectic was based on the fact that it offended his understanding of the scientific method drawn from what he imagined to be the procedures of the natural sciences:

> . . . as soon as we leave the solid ground of empirically verifiable facts and think beyond them, we enter the world of derived concepts, and if we then follow the laws of the dialectic, as laid down by Hegel, we will, before we know it, find ourselves once again enmeshed in the "self-development of the concept". Herein lies the great scientific danger of the Hegelian logic of contradiction . . . as soon as developments are deductively anticipated on the basis of these principles, the danger of arbitrary construction begins.[16]

The weakness of Bernstein's theoretical grasp is evident here. He does not seem to realize that *all* science generalizes and abstracts from "empirically verifiable facts." Indeed, the very concept of "fact" is itself an abstraction, because no one has ever eaten, tasted, smelt, seen, or heard a "fact," which is a mental generalization that distinguishes actually existing phenomena from imaginary conceptions. Similarly, *all* science "deductively anticipates" developments—what else is an hypothesis tested by experimentation? The dialectic is, among other things, a way of investigating and understanding the relationship between abstractions and reality. And the "danger of arbitrary construction" is far greater using an empirical method which thinks that it is dealing with facts when it is actually dealing with abstractions than it is with a method that properly distinguishes between the two and then seeks to explain the relationship between them.

These questions of theory, however, were not Bernstein's main concern. Although he argued that the "Hegelian dialectic . . . is the treacherous element in Marxist doctrine, the pitfall that lies in the way of any logical consideration of things," he was not primarily opposed to the dialectic on philosophical grounds.[17] Bernstein's main objection to the dialectic was that it provided support for Marx's theory of revolution.

Marx and Engels's stress on the leap in historical continuity represented by social revolution, their insistence on the explosive, contradictory nature of capitalist society, their determination to combine the subjective and the objective elements of historical change in a conscious revolutionary strategy was, for Bernstein, the strand of putschism in their thought. It led them to overestimate revolutionary possibilities and, when these did not materialize, to sanction a notion of revolution carried out by a minority substituting itself for the activity of the mass of the working class. This strategy Bernstein derided as Blanquism, named after the inveterate organizer of conspiratorial secret societies, and Babouvist, after Babeuf, who is popularly believed to have organized a similar conspiracy during the Great French Revolution.[18]

So it was that Bernstein rejected Marx's notion of permanent revolution, developed as part of his analysis of the revolutions of 1848, as "historical self-deception" on a scale that "a run-of-the-mill political visionary could hardly . . . better." Such a policy "would have been incomprehensible if it were not seen as resulting from a remnant of Hegelian contradiction dialectics."[19] At a time when few marxists were familiar with Marx's early works, Bernstein singles out Marx's *Contribution to the Critique of Hegel's Philosophy of Law* as leading "directly to Blanquism." He insists that "Marx and Engels, working on the basis of the radical Hegelian dialectic, arrived at a doctrine very similar to Blanquism."[20]

The fact that Marx and Engels time and again reject putsches does not deter Bernstein: "To reject putsches does not therefore amount to liberating oneself from Blanquism." Marx and Engels's writings, from the time of the Communist League, are, "apart from the rejection of putsches . . . permeated throughout with . . . a Blanquist or Babouvist spirit." Furthermore, Bernstein argued,

> In *The Communist Manifesto*, it is significant that of all the socialist literature only the writings of Babeuf escape criticism. . . . The programme of revolutionary action in the *Manifesto* is Blanquist through and through.[21]

In these writings, according to Bernstein, "the requirements of modern economic life were totally disregarded, and the relative strengths of classes and their state of development were completely overlooked." The result was that "proletarian terrorism . . . was extolled as a miraculous force which was to propel the conditions of production to that level of development perceived as the precondition for the socialist transformation of society."[22]

The main point to be made here is not that even a very inattentive reader of the *Communist Manifesto* and the other works that Bernstein criticizes, *The Class Struggles in France* and *The Eighteenth Brumaire*, will find there a very careful analysis of both the economic preconditions for socialism and "the relative strengths of the classes." Nor is it to highlight the many passages that explicitly reject the notion of an "elite" revolution, such as Marx and Engels's famous remark that the proletarian revolution is "the self-conscious movement of the immense majority in the interests of the immense majority." Rather the point that concerns us here is how this rejection of revolution is tied to Bernstein's rejection of the dialectic:

> The great things Marx and Engels achieved were achieved not because of the dialectic but in spite of it. When, on the other hand, they heedlessly passed over the grossest errors of Blanquism, it is primarily the Hegelian element in their own theory which is to blame.[23]

Bernstein saw that Marx's notion of social contradiction was linked to his revolutionary politics. He replaced it with the idea of co-operation in theory and class collaboration in practice: "I am not of the opinion that the struggle of opposites is the basis of all development. The co-operation of related forces is of great significance as well."[24]

In all this, it is not hard to see that what is intended is the complete elimination of revolution as a serious strategy for socialists. Bernstein claims that a workers' revolution was premature given the social conditions of the 1840s and 1850s and could only lead to putschism. Equally, he asserts, social conditions have, by the mid-1890s at the latest, also made revolution unnecessary and reform the only sensible strategy. There seems, on Bernstein's account, only a brief historical moment, perhaps somewhere in the 1860s, when revolutions were possible.

The form of this argument, we should note, is as rigidly deterministic as anything in Bernstein's own caricature of marxism. As Bernstein's biographer, Peter Gay, notes, "Bernstein moved the dialectical method from the centre of the Marxist system and substituted evolutionism as the core of Marxism."[25] There obviously is no room for the self-emancipation of the working class in a schema in which economic development excludes revolutionary action as, on the one hand, precipitate, and, on the other, superfluous. But Bernstein's collapse into reformist economic determinism was only one consequence of his rejection of the dialectic. The second consequence was that the subjective factor in history, having been banished from any effective role in the class struggle, returned as a moral imperative.

Bernstein admitted that Rosa Luxemburg was correct in seeing that his theory now inevitably involved a purely ethical aspect:

> ... she objected that on my interpretation socialism would cease to be an objective historical necessity and would be given an idealist basis. Although her line of reasoning ... ends with a completely arbitrary identification of idealism with utopianism, she nevertheless hits the mark. I do not, indeed, make the victory of socialism depend on its "immanent economic necessity". On the contrary, I hold that it is neither possible not necessary to give the victory of socialism a purely materialistic basis.[26]

As a complement to his own undialectical determinism, Bernstein invoked Kant as the bearer of an alternative moral motivation for socialism:

> I cannot subscribe to [Marx's] proposition: "the working class has no ideals to actualise." ... It was with this in mind that I once invoked the spirit of the great Konigsberg philosopher ... against the cant which sought to get a hold on the labour movement and to which the Hegelian dialectic offers a comfortable refuge. ... Social Democracy needs a Kant ... to show where its apparent materialism is the highest and therefore the most easily misleading ideology, and to show that contempt for the ideal and the magnifying of material factors ... is self-deception.[27]

Or, as he put it elsewhere, "Under this banner—Kant, not Hegel—the working class fights for its emancipation today."[28] But how much Bernstein really understood of Kant's philosophy is debatable; he certainly made no great use of it in *The Preconditions of Socialism*. In all likelihood, he took the slogans of the then fashionable neo-Kantian revival, which had been strong in German universities, particularly Marburg, since the 1870s. Neo-Kantianism was in fact a retreat from the views of Kant himself, because its proponents banished any effective notion of the thing in itself and, therefore, held a position closer to the subjective idealism of Berkeley. A number of leading academics with broadly progressive views were at the forefront of this movement. Bernstein was friendly with some of them, and "neo-Kantianism reached its peak in the decade in which Bernstein worked out, published, and defended his views."[29]

Bernstein himself "abandoned dialectical materialism and approached, but did not adopt, neo-Kantianism." In fact, he "stood between the two schools and really belongs to a third: Naturalism," which combined empiricism and "a keen interest in naturalistic ethics."[30] In short, Bernstein found neo-Kantianism a useful rallying cry against the dialectic. But there was, nevertheless, much common ground shared by Bernstein's rejection of "determinism" and neo-Kantian philosophy:

> If socialism demanded conscious struggle for its introduction. . . . Bernstein concluded it was not grounded in causal determinism and could be justified only as an ethical ideal. In this manner, the theorist of empirically minded pragmatic revisionism found common language with the neo-Kantians.[31]

Others were to use neo-Kantianism more intelligently and systematically, but in Bernstein's hands this trend revealed itself in its crudest, most elitist form. For Bernstein, "in legislation, the intellect governs the emotion" whereas "in a revolution, emotion governs the intellect." And because "the working class . . . has not attained a high degree of mental independence through training in self-governing bodies," it followed that "the dictatorship of the proletariat means the dictatorship of club orators and literati." Consequently, the working class is "not yet sufficiently developed to take over political power," and so "we must take the workers as they are."[32]

How, in Bernstein's view, were the workers? They were "not as free from prejudices and weaknesses as their flatterers would have us believe," and they "attach very little value to being liberated from those characteristics which seem petty bourgeois . . . but, on the contrary, are very interested in turning the proletarian into the 'petty bourgeois.'" In fact, Bernstein concluded, in a passage that virtually abolishes any prospect of socialism, whether revolutionary or reformist:

> We cannot demand from a class the great majority of whose members live under crowded conditions, are badly educated, and have an uncertain and insufficient income, the high intellectual and moral standard which the organization and existence of a socialist community presupposes. . . . we must not uncritically ascribe to the masses, to the millions, what holds good for the elite, for, say, hundreds of thousands.[33]

Consequently, Bernstein wrote, "I censure everything which tends to corrupt its moral judgement much more severely than I do similar developments in the upper classes. . . . An up-and-coming class needs a healthy morality and no blase decadence."[34]

The most striking aspect of these arguments, apart from their conservative conclusions and patronising tone, is how cruelly Bernstein's rejection of the dialectic takes revenge on the credibility of his case. Having dismissed the idea that capitalism is a contradictory system and that there is, therefore, a process of struggle in the course of which the current consciousness of the majority of the working class can be transformed, Bernstein is left with two unrelated poles—the everyday consciousness of workers and the abstract picture of socialism. The only bridge from one to the other, from the present to the future, are moral lectures on the need for virtue. This is a dualism of which Kant would have been ashamed. It is certainly a regression in social theory beyond the point that Hegel had reached.

This theoretical regression is hardly surprising, because Bernstein's "philosophic case against marxism was really an afterthought; it was appended to his attempt to refute marxist conclusions on empirical grounds."[35]

Yet most of Bernstein's followers did not share his views because they agreed with his theoretical analysis. Bernstein was useful to the trade union and party functionaries who provided the backbone of his support so long as they still needed to fight for dominance in the SPD. Much of this work was achieved while Berstein was still abroad. After his return to Berlin in 1901, "his prestige was at its peak, yet his doctrine soon lost all distinctness at the hands of his followers and was melted down with anti-revolutionary attitudes of all sorts." This process was "greatly furthered by the ascendancy of the trade unions and the bureaucrats in the Social Democratic Party."[36] These "new men who took over the reformist wing of the party from what might be called the 'real revisionists' were distinguished largely by their mediocrity and paucity of social vision."[37] More importantly, they led the German working class to disaster, first in the revolution of 1918–23 and, second, in the fight against fascism. They were not, however, unopposed.

KAUTSKY, CENTRISM, AND THE FAILURE OF MECHANICAL MATERIALISM

Karl Kautsky's claim to represent the marxist tradition was even stronger than that of Eduard Bernstein. Kautsky knew Marx personally. After Marx's death and until 1888 he worked closely with Engels, despite Marx's prophetic judgement that Kautsky was "a small-minded mediocrity who busies himself with statistics, without deriving anything intelligent out of them."[38] Nevertheless, Engels entrusted Kautsky with the preparation of Marx's *Theories of Surplus Value* for publication. His own correspondence with Kautsky fills some four hundred printed pages. Kautsky founded the journal *Die Neue Zeit* in 1883 and edited it for thirty-five years, making it the international authority of the marxist movement. He was the main popularizer of marxism after Engels' death. His commentary on the *Erfurt Programme*, known as *The Class Struggle* in its English translation, ran to nineteen German editions and sixty-seven either complete or partial editions in other languages. Lenin himself translated the *Erfurt Programme* into Russian, and in 1899, when he and Krupskaya received a copy of Kautsky's critique of Bernstein, they put aside all other work to complete a translation in just two weeks.[39]

Contrary to appearances, however, Kautsky was, in fact, the living embodiment of the contradiction between reform and revolution which lay buried in heart of the SPD's *Erfurt Programme*. As Carl Schorske notes, "The drafting of the new programme was a congenial task for Kautsky, the first of a kind he repeatedly performed as long as it was humanly possible: the reconciliation of antagonistic tendencies in Social Democracy by means of theoretical concepts."[40]

There were three main conditions that initially made this task possible. One was the relatively low level of class struggle in the 1890s and the first years of the new century. The second was that the main threat to marxist principles at this time was from the reformist right, from Bernstein. Against this threat Kautsky sided with the revolutionary left, with Rosa Luxemburg, thus reinforcing his credentials as a defender of marxism. Thirdly, even the revolutionary left continued to view the battle against reformism as a *theoretical* argument *within* the SPD, not as an issue that also involved *organizational* questions, perhaps leading to the need for a separate organization. This meant that Kautsky's orthodoxy was rarely put to any practical test. Worse still, Kautsky could continue to appear to hold to revolutionary purity in theory, although in practice the SPD fell more and more completely into the hands of the revisionists.

This divorce between theory and practice was the hallmark of Kautsky's marxism. Indeed, he raised this division to the point where it became the keystone of his understanding of marxism. He insisted, in the absence of any role for practice in the struggle to transform society, that the automatic workings of the historical process were sufficient to explain social change. This determinism had direct political consequences, as Colletti observes:

> German Social Democracy chose the "parliamentary road" at Erfurt, not because it had abandoned the class conception of the state [that would come later], but because its "fatalistic" and "providential" faith in the automatic progress of *economic evolution* gave it the certainty that its eventual rise to power would come about "in a spontaneous, constant, and irresistable way, quite tranquilly, like a natural process."[41]

Of course, this determinism had its roots in Kautsky's intellectual history as well as in the social and historical situation in which he found himself. Darwin's theory of evolution was the first and most important of these formative influences on Kautsky's thought. He was a Darwinian before he was a marxist:

> I already possessed a conception of history before I became acquainted with that of Marx. . . . The beginnings of my historical thinking were naturally formed only a generation after Marx and Engels had arrived at their conception of history: in the 1870s. Darwinism was at that time the theory that occupied the whole world. . . . They [Marx and Engels] started out from *Hegel*; I started out from *Darwin*. The latter occupied my thoughts earlier than Marx, the development of organisms earlier than that of the economy, the struggle for the existence of species and races earlier than the class struggle.

And, as he admitted, he continued to read Marx with spectacles he borrowed from Darwin:

> To be sure, socialist literature soon made me aware of the importance of the economic factor . . . but my interest in the natural factor in history persisted; and I continued my endeavour to relate historical development to the development of organisms.[42]

Kautsky even went so far as to describe marxism as "the materialist theory of Social Evolution"[43] and to argue that his "theory of history was intended to be nothing other than the application of Darwinism to social development."[44] But Kautsky was imbued not just with a Darwinian view of social development, but with the whole ethos of "value-free" scientific procedure as he thought it operated in the physical sciences. He argued that the "materialist conception of history means nothing but the application of this method to society."[45]

A rigid determinism and a systematic reductionism were the inevitable and predictable outcome of this approach. *The Class Struggle*, for instance, tells us:

> The capitalist social system has run its course; its dissolution is now only a question of time. Irresistible economic forces lead with the certainty of doom to the shipwreck of capitalist production. The substitution of a new social order for the existing one is no longer simply desirable, it has become inevitable.[46]

Even when Kautsky is attempting to escape from the logic of his own system, he immediately confounds himself by confirming the most narrow determinism. In *Ethics and the Materialist Conception of History*, for instance, he argues that socialism is "not necessary in the fatalist sense that a higher power will present" it to us,

> but necessary, unavoidable in the sense, that inventors improve technic [*sic*] and the capitalists in their desire for profit revolutionise the whole economic life, as it is also inevitable that workers aim for shorter hours of labour and

higher wages, and that they organise themselves, that they fight the capitalist class and its state, as it is inevitable that they aim for the conquest of political power and the overthrow of capitalist rule. Socialism is inevitable because the class struggle and the victory of the proletariat is inevitable.[47]

The only sense in which this is not "fatalism" is that it does not require the existence of a supernatural being. If it had been merely this caricature of marxism, rather than Marx's own theory, which Bernstein had in mind when he described materialism as "Calvinism without God," no one could deny that he had hit his mark. Kautsky's own approach, at the philosophical level at any rate, left him defenseless in the face of revisionist attacks.[48]

In particular, Kautsky seemed to have little notion of how he might turn aside Bernstein's attack on the dialectic. Kautsky's attitude to the dialectic was of a piece with his whole attitude to marxism—a combination of formal adherence to its phraseology and a systematic attempt to remove its revolutionary content. Specifically, Kautsky wanted to rid the dialectic of any notion of internal contradiction, of leaps and revolutions in social development, and leave behind only a flat, featureless process of peaceful evolution. Gone, too, is any process of mediation between distinct but connected parts of the totality, this being an affront to reductionism.

Quite how fundamentally Kautsky revised Marx and Engels can be seen in his account of the relationship of human beings to the natural world:

> The mind encounters two factors: on the one hand, the body of the organism, which produces the mental functions, a body with certain innate needs and capacities. Let us call it the "ego." On the other hand, there is the environment.... It is this environment that poses the problems the mind has to solve.[49]

Here, Kautsky reduces human beings to their mental functions, the ego, and then sets them in an environment that externally imposes itself on the mind. Marx's conception was very different. First, human beings were part of nature. Second, their consciousness arose from interaction with their own physical needs and the rest of nature. Third, even when consciousness has evolved, it remains fused with human physicality. Practice, the unity of subject and object, is the characteristic expression of this fact. By imposing an undialectical separation on these aspects of human development, Kautsky sets up a vicious circle where "mind" and "environment" chase each other like a dog chasing its tail:

> The resolution of the antagonism between ego and environment consists in adaptation.... Either the ego adapts itself to the environment through certain changes or actions or it is able to shape certain parts of the environment in such a manner that they are adapted to its own purposes or, finally, some mutual adaptation takes place.[50]

The fact that nothing but external causal relations are involved in this example does not stop Kautsky from claiming that this is a dialectical analysis:

> The starting point of each process is an organism, the ego, the affirmation, the "thesis." It is opposed by its environment, the "nonego," the negation of the organism, the "antithesis." The final result is the overcoming of the opposition, the negation of the negation, the renewed affirmation of the organism by adaptation, the "synthesis."[51]

This is a highly formalistic account that has less in common with Marx's notion of negative dialectic, where change and instability are the result of contradiction, than it does with Hegel's dialectic where change is only apparent because the final term of the dialectic simply returns to its beginning. Indeed, Kautsky concludes his analysis with the observation that "thereby the process returns to its starting point, the individual maintains itself." His only qualification is to add that this happens "in such a way that the starting point is raised to a higher level."[52] But that, too, was Hegel's view.

Even this account would not be so misleading if Kautsky were arguing that the individual and the environment are two interpenetrating forces that are part of a wider totality, rather than seeing them as independent physical entities. But Kautsky goes on to argue explicitly that the dialectic should *only* be understood as the reciprocal relationship between two independent factors and not as a dialectic where development is driven by internal contradiction. Kautsky poses the question of whether "movement and development in the world really *always* assume the form of the Hegelian dialectic." His answer retains the term but effectively abandons the real meaning of the dialectic altogether, not just its Hegelian form:

> I consider this assumption to be correct for the organic world, but not at all in the way Engels illustrates it here. He regards movement and development not as the reciprocal effect of two factors, the individual and the environment, on one another but merely as the self-initiated movement of one factor, the individual, and he seeks the antithesis as well as the thesis in the same individual. Evidently, this is still the strong after effect of the Hegelian model.[53]

The immediate result of abandoning the notion of an internally contradictory totality and replacing it with "mutually influencing factor's" approach is that the dualism that characterized philosophy before Marx and Engels is reintroduced to social theory.

The second casualty of this approach, as the quotation above hints, is that the dialectic is said to apply to human beings and to the animal world, but elsewhere the positivist methods of natural science are to hold sway. In Marx's analysis, human beings and nature were a unity of opposites; humans arose from and were part of the natural world but were made distinct from it by their ability to labor consciously. And this conscious labor unites subject and object, human consciousness and the physical world. It followed that the study of nature and the study of human history (including the dialectic) shared certain fundamental characteristics, although the subject matter and, therefore, the form of the method appropriate to it would be different in nature than it was in society. That is, Marx and Engels understood the dialectic dialectically, as a unity of opposites.

Once this notion, the unity of subject and object, has vanished in one sphere, it cannot be restored in others. Most importantly, the working class is no longer seen as the identical subject-object of history. That is, it is no longer seen as a class whose struggle transforms it from being an exploited class lacking in socialist consciousness and unable to control the society that it produces into a class capable of consciously fighting to banish exploitation and able to run society according to its own needs. And without this understanding, Kautsky had no way in which he could link the objective process of historical development with the subjective ability of workers to transform it. In effect, the first part of Marx's famous couplet, "Men make their own history, but not in conditions that they themselves have chosen," was rendered a dead letter. In Kautsky's view, human beings did *not* make their own history, they were merely the pawns of larger historical forces.

Nothing illustrates this more clearly than Kautsky's discussion of freedom and necessity. Kautsky begins by asserting that social development faces humanity with real choices: "Action implies continual choice between various possibilities . . . it means accepting or rejecting, it means defending and opposing."[54] He goes on to distinguish between "the world of the past" where "the sequence of cause and effect (causality) rules" and the world of the future where "the thought of aim (teleology)" is the rule. But this turns out to be a sham distinction, merely "the feeling of freedom" that may be "an indispensable psychological necessity" but that, in reality, "springs from ignorance of the future."

The truth, according to Kautsky, is that "the setting up of aims is not, however, anything which exists outside the sphere of necessity, of cause and effect."[55] Kautsky himself drew the inevitable conclusion: "Even though I set up aims . . . in the sphere of apparent freedom, yet the act of setting up aims itself, from the very moment when I set up the aim, belongs to the past, and can thus in its necessity be recognized as the result of distinct causes."[56] And so, "the world of conscious aims is thus not the world of freedom in opposition to necessity."[57] From this, Kautsky concluded, "What today is felt to be free action will be recognised tomorrow as necessary action."[58] And, finally, "I recognise, despite all apparent freedom, that in the face of nature my action is necessarily conditioned."[59]

Once again, Kautsky, so skeptical of all Hegel's virtues, repeats the elder

Hegel's worst vice: the argument that freedom *is only* the recognition of necessity. Freedom is reduced to the choice between either working with the inevitable force of necessity, or of hurling oneself uselessly against it: "Even if I can only recognise the world on the assumption of necessity . . . whether I shall yield to it, or not, there remains to me as last resort the possibility of withdrawing myself by a voluntary death."[60] Even the passivity and conservatism of Hegel's later system, "what is real is rational," are reproduced in Kautsky's theory.

This approach was, of course, no effective reply to Bernstein. Indeed, neither Kautsky nor his opponents understood Marx's attempt to overcome the false polarity between necessity and freedom by finding how the "ought" emerges from the "is." Neither side appreciated Marx's great discovery of the working class as the subject-object of history, the class that is both a necessary product of historical development and, at the same time, its determining force.[61]

Kautsky could no more see the working class dialectically than he could any other aspect of society. He never saw working class struggle as *self*-emancipation or that the transformation of the consciousness of the working class *is* an essential part of the transformation of society. Kautsky saw workers' consciousness as "a reservoir of knowledge, first acquired and then put into practical use" and not as the point where "the historical process coincides with the awareness of that process." Finally, therefore, he could not see that "the necessity of socialism realises itself as the free, conscious activity of the working class."[62]

Kautsky's all-embracing determinism could not, of course, be entirely consistent in theory or in practice. Sometimes Kautsky is obliged to write things and to behave in ways that suggest room for conscious human activity. His uncritical positivism sometimes results in uncritical idealism. But the main feature of Kautsky's work is its *systematic* nature. It rarely deviates from its rigid central principle. Certainly neither historical events nor various theoretical asides ever result in Kautsky re-evaluating his main approach. Had he been less of a systematizer, the contradictions in his thought might have made Kautsky a more interesting figure. But he remained a prisoner of the "Darwinian" worldview he had first embraced in his youth. And it was this that informed his approach to the questions of strategy and tactics in the SPD.

The facade of Kautsky's marxism began to crack whenever practical issues necessitating a definite course of action were involved, or when a rise in the struggle challenged his passive evolutionist notions, figures to his left provided a more coherent defense against the right wing. Starting in 1905, all these conditions began to come together.

By the middle of the first decade of the century, the reformist's grip on the SPD was tightening. Organizational changes were in train and decisions could not be settled simply by "theoretical debate." Simultaneously, imperialism became an ever-present feature of politics, the tool with which the ruling class wished both to extend its power abroad and, via the promotion of nationalism, divide the working class at home. But also in 1905, as if to prove that a one-dimensional approach to social contradictions would be inadequate, Russia exploded in revolution, and in Germany strike figures for the year exceeded those for the whole of the 1890s. Finally, Rosa Luxemburg emerged as the most articulate figure on the increasingly restive revolutionary left of the SPD.

Kautsky's view of organization was a direct extension of his broader determinism. "Social democracy," he wrote, "is a revolutionary party, but it is not a party that makes revolutions." This is for the simple reason that "we know that it is just as little in our power to make this revolution as it is in the power of our opponents to prevent it."[63] What was necessary was that a unified party organize wider and wider layers of the working class and bring to them the necessary socialist consciousness. This "socialist consciousness is . . . an element imported into the class struggle from outside and is not something that takes shape spontaneously." And so, "without the collaboration of 'intellectuals' this class struggle cannot become a Social Democratic movement."[64]

For Kautsky, the unity of the party was identical with the unity of the class. It was, therefore, illegitimate, under any circumstances, to break this unity. He wrote, "One can be a good comrade without believing in the materialist conception of history, but one is in no sense a good comrade if one does not submit to the congresses of the party."[65] Theoretical differences could only be solved by discussion and debate inside the party but, no matter how serious the division over principles and politics became, never by building a separate party. He thus found it impossible to understand the divisions among Russian marxists over just these issues. As the Russian movement separated into revolutionary Bolsheviks and reformist Mensheviks, Kautsky repeatedly counseled against a split, his only reservation being that "I don't feel very competent on this matter. What concerns us here is an organisational question and I have never been a practical organiser."[66]

This myopia also made it difficult for Kautsky to see the rapid advance of the full-time bureaucracy in the SPD and the increasing power of the trade union leadership within the party in the first ten years of the twentieth century. He seemed to believe that so long as Bernstein and his supporters were beaten in the votes at SPD congresses, as they were at first, and so long as the party remained united, right-wing reformism would be held at bay:

Completely underestimating the real weight of the leaders of the trade union bureaucracy, not only in the unions but potentially in the party, he claimed that in the final analysis . . . "revisionism is a general staff without an army."[67]

The irony was that, as the bureaucrats' control over the organization spread, it was Kautsky who became a general without an army. Worse still, as the level of the struggle and the vociferousness of the left wing grew in the years before the First World War, Kautsky increasingly identified the revolutionaries as the main threat to the unity of the SPD. Over time he became the bulwark between the right-wing leadership and their radical critics.

By 1910, Kautsky was a declared enemy of Luxemburg and the left. Under the pressure of events, his analyses became more dogmatic and right wing. Where once the abstract possibility of armed revolution had been allowed, Kautsky now argued almost undiluted parliamentarianism. Where once he had granted the militaristic nature of capitalism, he now saw the possibility of "ultra-imperialism," in which the cartels and monopolies had so much to lose by war that they would regulate it out of existence. In fact, everywhere that Rosa Luxemburg saw contradictions and called for action, Kautsky saw beneficent evolution and argued passivity.

Kautsky pressed on with this perspective in spite of all contrary evidence. When war broke out, he wanted SPD deputies to vote against war credits, but he went along with the majority when they refused. When the Second International collapsed, he claimed that it was "an instrument of peace, not of war" and that it would be rebuilt once the bloodletting stopped. When the October revolution broke in Russia, he disowned it. When the German revolution split the SPD, he would not stay with the right, nor would he join the Communist Party that Rosa Luxemburg built. Instead, like Bernstein, he stayed with the short-lived centrist Independent Social Democrats (USPD), always with the intention of leading as many as possible back to the SPD. In the mid-1920s, he was writing that,

> The excitement caused by the World War is beginning to subside. The economic abnormalities . . . are beginning to give way once more to normal economic conditions in which the force of economic laws is again manifesting itself . . . the strength of the Social Democratic movement is beginning to grow again, and is resuming its temporarily interrupted victorious advance.[68]

Neither world war nor revolution, nor the collapse of the Wiemar Republic and the rise of the Nazis could alter this mechanical materialism. Yet it had failed as a guide to action more completely than any other theory bearing the name of marxism, with the exception of Stalinism, which inherited many of its theoretical positions.

PLEKHANOV: THE TRAGEDY OF A PIONEER

Georgi Plekhanov and Karl Kautsky are often talked about in the same breath as representatives of the mechanical materialism of Second International. This is unjust. Plekhanov shared some of Kautsky's determinism, but he also possessed a number of strengths that Kautsky did not. He made a real contribution to the development of marxism in his analysis of Russian social development. He understood the need for, and built the first, revolutionary marxist organization in Russia. Unlike Kautsky, he developed a real, if flawed, understanding of philosophical questions. And, of all the figures who emerged in the period between the death of Engels and Lenin's study of Hegel during the First World War, he undoubtedly possessed the best understanding of Hegel.[69]

It is possible, with greater ease than in the case of either Bernstein or Kautsky, to see Plekhanov's strengths and weaknesses as a product of his circumstances. The Russia in which Plekhanov became politically active in the 1870s was one in which semi-feudal rural relations still held the vast majority of society in their grip. Capitalist industry was growing, but the small working class was only just beginning to demonstrate the turbulent revolutionary potential that marked its later development. The tsarist autocracy ruled with a brutality far exceeding that of Bismarck and the kaiser.

Plekhanov first became active in the Narodnik (meaning Friends of the People) movement which, though composed mainly of educated, Westernized intellectuals, looked to the peasant village commune as the basis on which Russia might move directly to the construction of socialism, bypassing the need for a period of capitalist development. Plekhanov's agitational work brought him into contact with workers, although the Narodniks regarded them only as a particularly oppressed section of the peasantry. Indeed, it was at the first political demonstration organized by Russian workers, in front of Kazan Cathedral in December 1876, that Plekhanov made his maiden speech beneath a banner reading "Land and Freedom." He continued to be involved in agitation around strikes as well as in a Narodnik campaign among the Don Cossacks. By 1879, "Plekhanov still believed that the revolution would be brought about by the peasants, but thought that the workers would help them by initiating revolts in the towns." Consequently, "he was now just a step from recognising the decisive role that the working class would inevitably play in the revolution."[70]

Constantly moving house and sleeping with a revolver beneath his pillow, Plekhanov was arrested twice. He escaped on both occasions and fled abroad. His second exile, beginning in 1880, lasted thirty-seven years. It is a decisive element in the tragedy of Plekhanov's development that he became a marxist in isolation from the struggle in Russia. Once in Western Europe, Plekhanov studied geology, anthropology, zoology, organic chemistry—and the works of Marx and Engels. He wrote that reading the *Communist Manifesto* marked "an epoch in my life," and in 1882, he translated it into Russian. In 1883, Plekhanov and other Russian exiles in Geneva founded the first Russian marxist organization, the Emancipation of Labour Group. In the same year, Plekhanov wrote *Socialism and the Political Struggle*, a last attempt to win Narodniks to marxism. This pamphlet, Lenin was later to say, bore comparison with the *Communist Manifesto* in terms of its effect on the Russian working-class movement.

Russia's social development in general, and the level of development of the working-class movement in particular, were both factors that shaped Plekhanov's philosophical work. In Germany, Hegel was treated as a "dead dog" after the 1840s. But in Russia, where social conditions still resembled those which existed in Germany during Hegel's youth, Hegel's reputation remained intact among the intelligentsia. Hegel's philosophy arose from the clash between the weakness of German capitalism and the impact of the Enlightenment and the French Revolution. Its continued appeal for some Russian intellectuals stemmed from a similar pattern of combined and uneven social development:

> The [Russian] intelligensia was the product of cultural contact between two unlike civilizations . . . Russia's tradition-oriented and rigidly stratified society was exposed to the secular, dynamic ideologies that successively arose in the West. Advanced political ideas won a few followers in the eighteenth century and a larger number, including such brilliant figures as Alexander Herzen and Vissarion Belinsky, in the nineteenth. From the standpoint of Western values, the intelligensia found Russian life barbaric. The fulfillment of their aspirations demanded a radical revision of its foundations.[71]

Herzen (1812–70) and Belinsky (1811–48) were, as Plekhanov realized, significant intellectual forerunners of his own approach. Neither were followers of Marx, but both were aware of Marx's writings as early as the 1840s. It was Herzen who first described Hegel's philosophy as "the algebra of revolution." And it was Belinsky who, towards the end of the 1830s, abandoned "moralism," "subjectivism," and "abstract heroicism" and embraced Hegel's notion that there was an objective course in human affairs to which the individual must submit. Plekhanov, who was related to Belinsky, clearly understood this as a parallel with his own rejection of Narodnik politics and his embrace of marxism:

> The Marxism adopted by Plekhanov and his comrades could also be called a variant of reconciliation with reality (the reality of Russian capitalism) in the name of historical necessity. . . . It is interesting to note that in his unfinished *History of Russian Social Thought* Plekhanov had intended

to draw this parallel between Belinsky's reconciliation with reality and Russian Marxism.[72]

But for an initial period, this aspect of Plekhanov's thought was more of a strength than a weakness. Against the Narodniks, who emphasized isolated individual acts of terrorism combined with pedagogical work among the masses, Plekhanov's insistence on analyzing the objective course of historical development was a huge advance. And when, later, Plekhanov entered the lists against Bernstein and his Russian imitators, the Economists, his grasp of marxism allowed him to reply to them more effectively than Kautsky. He was clear, for instance, that "even orthodox Marxists" are often satisfied with "extremely vague conceptions of dialectics." And he went on,

> It must be admitted that in the polemics aroused by the "critical" efforts of Mr. Bernstein and Co., the majority of orthodox Marxists proved to be weakest precisely in defence of *dialectics*. This weakness must be eliminated; we are duty bound to repulse decisively all the attacks of our enemies on our logical stronghold.[73]

Plekhanov's clarity was, in part at least, a result of the fact that his marxism emerged from a Hegelian tradition suited to the task of analyzing the highly contradictory reality of Russian society. Thus, Plekhanov developed certain strands of thought that ran contrary to the dominant determinism of Second International marxism.

Here there is only space to examine some of the issues on which Plekhanov says a great deal that is still of interest. Plekhanov, unlike Kautsky, had a keen critical appreciation of Hegel's legacy. He could see, for instance, that Hegel's philosophy would never again receive the acclaim it had from mainstream academics in the aftermath of the French revolution:

> ... we can foretell that although there will be a revival of interest in Hegel among educated classes, they will never adopt towards him the attitude of profound sympathy that he was the object of 60 years ago in the countries of German culture. On the contrary, bourgeois scientists will undertake a feverish "critical revision" of Hegel's philosophy and many doctors' diplomas will be obtained fighting the late professors "extremes" and "arbitrary logic."[74]

And Plekhanov was one of the first marxists to pour scorn on the idea that the dialectic in Hegel can be simplistically reduced to the thesis-antithesis-synthesis triad:

> Your pardon, reader, we do not mention the triad for the simple reason that it does not at all play in Hegel's work the part which is attributed to it by people who have not the least idea of the philosophy of that thinker. . . . Filled with sacred simplicity, these light-hearted people are convinced that

the whole argumentation of the German idealists was reduced to references to the triad; that whatever theoretical difficulties the old man came
up against, he ... with a tranquil smile, immediately built up a syllogism ... This is simply lunatic nonsense.[75]

Plekhanov went on to note, as few enough even among modern scholars
have, that "the 'triad' only *follows* from one of Hegel's principles: it does not
in the least serve him as the main principle itself."[76] And Plekhanov was also
one of the first to note that Hegelian contradictions by no means progress in
a rigidly tripartite manner. There are often two or four elements involved in
the process.[77]

Until Plekhanov made the point that reciprocal action is only a subsidiary
part of the dialectic, marxists had to rely on scattered passages in the work
of Marx and Engels to appreciate this important point. Kautsky, and many
others since, treated reciprocity and dialectical interaction as if they were
synonymous. Plekhanov, drawing on those passages in Hegel examined in
chapter 1, provides what remains the clearest refutation of this position in
the marxist tradition.

The argument from reciprocity simply states that "right [law] influences
religion, religion influences right, and each of them and both together influence philosophy and art, which in turn, affecting each other, also affect
right, religion and so on." Although "doubtless there is a measure of truth
in this," Plekhanov writes, "the trouble is that it explains nothing at all."
Those who talk in this way "completely forget that there must be one common source out of which all these aspects ... that are interrelated arise."
Without some notion of what underlies the totality of interactions, "this
system proves to be deprived of all foundation, to be hanging in the air"
and, consequently, "fails to explain anything."[78]

To see the importance of this point, one only has to recall the Althusserian
attempt to construct a non-reductionist marxism by means of this kind of
"interaction." Similarly, many of the New Left reacted against the reductionist
analyses associated with Stalinism by adopting a similar approach. Plekhanov's
critique is a useful reminder that the "reciprocal interaction" approach can
only ever be a partial antidote to reductionism. Final explanations that avoid
reductionism must always be sought in the material contradictions which
structure the relations between the different aspects of the social totality.[79]

Plekhanov was also careful, despite the overall deterministic cast of his
thought, to avoid the vulgarized Darwinism that characterized Kautsky's thought.
Plekhanov warned that simply transferring evolutionary patterns to social
history risked losing sight of the sudden convulsions and leaps in the historical process that were an integral part of any dialectical approach.[80] He criticized those who argue,

...that neither in nature nor history are there any leaps. When they speak of the *origin* of some phenomena or social institution, they represent matters as though this phenomena or institution were once upon a time very tiny, quite unnoticeable, and then gradually grew up. When it is a question of *destroying* this or that phenomena and institution, they presuppose, on the contrary, its gradual diminution, continuing up to the point where the phenomena becomes quite unnoticeable on account of its microscopic dimensions.

As Plekhanov notes, "evolution conceived in this way explains absolutely nothing," because "it presupposes what it has to explain."[81] Furthermore, "German idealist philosophy decisively revolted against such a misshapen conception of evolution. Hegel bitingly ridiculed it, and demonstrated irrefutably that both in nature and in society *leaps* constituted just as essential a stage of evolution as gradual quantative changes."[82]

There are also some important passages in Plekhanov's writings that recall the philosophical underpinning which Marx gave to his notion of working-class self-emancipation. Here, for instance, Plekhanov distinguishes the dialectic of nature from that in society by developing an understanding of the role played by human subjectivity:

> ...man becomes a *"subject"* only in history, because only in the latter is his *self-consciousness* developed. To confine oneself to examining man as a member of the animal kingdom means to confine oneself to examining him as an *"object"*, to leave out of account his historical development, his social "practice", concrete human activity. But to leave all this out of account means to make materialism *"dry, gloomy, melancholy"* (Goethe). More than that, it means making materialism . . . *fatalistic*, condemning man to complete subordination to blind matter.[83]

Plekhanov goes on to substantiate this point, making use of Marx's early writings in a way in which few other marxists of this period were able to do:

> Marx noticed this failing of French materialism, and even of Feuerbach's, and set himself the task of correcting it. His "economic" materialism is the reply to the question of how the "sensuous activity" of man develops his *self-consciousness*, how the *subjective side of history* comes about. When this question is answered even in part, materialism . . . will free itself from its characteristic fatalism.[84]

In other passages, Plekhanov seems to advance tentatively, on the basis of this understanding, a conception of society as a contradictory totality which gives rise to alternative courses of action between which it is necessary for human beings to choose—and that in making such choices questions of organization, politics, and theory can be decisive. For instance, although

Plekhanov argues that every class "adapts its 'ideals' to its economic needs," he goes on to say:

> But this adaptation can take place in various ways, and why it takes place in this way, not in that, is explained not by the situation of the given class taken in isolation, but by all the particular features of the relations between this class and its antagonist (or antagonists). With the appearance of classes, *contradiction becomes not only a motive force, but also a formative principle.*[85]

This is a conclusion of the first importance, and it foreshadows Luxemburg and Lenin's approach to the question of the dialectic. But, unfortunately, such passages do not set the dominant tone of Plekhanov's approach. Much more numerous are the passages that treat the dialectic as a process of linear development. Plekhanov describes the process of change from one mode of production to the next, but only rarely touches on the internal contradictions that drive this process forward. Plekhanov's account of the dialectic stresses the aspects of constant change and totality but substitutes a linear notion of material determination where an approach that stresses contradiction is most needed.

Above all, Plekhanov does not seem consistently to hold onto the relationship between, on the one hand, the process by which objective historical development raises the possibility of a new mode of production replacing the old and, on the other, the subjective element inherent in the battle between the classes of the old society. He does not seem to understand that where the birth of the new society depends on the outcome of the battle between the classes, there must always exist the possibility that progress will be frustrated. Rather he chooses to stress that the contradiction between the new social forces and the old world will inevitably be resolved in favor of the former:

> Some members of society defend the old order: these are the people of stagnation. Others—to whom the old order is not advantageous—stand for progress; their psychology changes in the direction of those relations of production which in time will replace the old economic relations, now growing out of date.[86]

This is a doubly determinist formulation. First, it assumes an identity of economic interest and consciousness, whereas both historical experience and Marx's theory of alienation give good grounds for thinking that many people whose economic interests do not lie with the existence of the current system are not necessarily fully or automatically conscious of this fact. Second, it seems to suggest that the old economic relations will naturally disappear with the passage of time. Indeed, Plekhanov substantiates this second claim with a passage that might have been taken directly from Hegel's *Philosophy of History*:

... on the basis of the new economy there takes place the flowering of the new psychology. For a certain time this harmony remains unbroken, and even becomes stronger and stronger. But little by little the first shoots of a new discord make their appearance; the psychology of the foremost class ... again outlines old methods of production: without for a moment ceasing to adapt itself to economy, it again adapts itself to the *new* relations of production, constituting the germ of the future economy.[87]

In a linear notion of development the element of contradiction on which most stress rests is that between what is past and what is future and not, as in some of the first passages quoted above, on the contradictory elements coexisting in the present which will determine whether contemporary society will be superceded by progress or reaction. This essentially conservative notion—change as unilinear sequence—recurs time and again in Plekhanov's work. He writes, for instance,

The psychology of society is always expedient in relation to its economy, always corresponds to it, is always determined by it. ... Economy itself is something derivative, just like psychology. And that is the very reason why the economy of every progressing society *changes*: the new state of productive forces brings with it new economic structure just as it does a new psychology, a new "spirit of the age."

Plekhanov goes on to say that "only in popular speech could one talk about the economy as the *prime cause*," because, in fact, "it is itself a consequence, a 'function' of the productive forces."[88] This approach provided an important underpinning for Plekhanov's stages theory of Russian social development, and this, in turn, predisposed him to reject the possibility of a workers' revolution in Russia.

There is, of course, a relationship between the development of the productive forces and the totality of social development, but it can only be grasped dialectically—and this is what Plekhanov fails to do, in spite of his knowledge of Hegel. In fact, it is precisely at this point that Plekhanov's knowledge of Hegel becomes more of a hindrance than a help.

Plekhanov knew Hegel and was a skilled interpreter of his thought. But what he did not fully understand was *Marx's critique of Hegel*. This he took, despite occasional flashes of insight, to be mainly an assertion of materialism much in the spirit of Feuerbach. He did not understand Marx's double critique, a critique of uncritical positivism as well as of uncritical idealism. Plekhanov therefore tended, first, to allow two strands of thought to remain unreconciled within his system, and, second, when forced to provide a final explanation of social change, he relapsed into deterministic formulations. When he did this, he adapted the most fatalistic of Hegel's formulations to describe his own reductionism, thus giving the semblance of a dialectical approach while in fact rejecting its most essential features.

The point at which this weakness in Plekhanov's method is most easily seen is in his discussion of freedom and necessity. Plekhanov, like Kautsky, simply borrows Hegel's position that freedom *is* necessity—although Plekhanov, unlike Kautsky, is conscious of the debt:

> Hegel finally solved the antinomy between freedom and necessity. He proved that we are free only insofar as we know the laws of nature and socio-historical development and insofar as *we, submitting to them,* rely upon them.[89]

Plekhanov does not deny, any more than did Hegel, that "men consciously follow their private personal ends." But "out of the sum total of their individual actions there arise certain social results which perhaps they did not at all desire, and certainly did not foresee." Thus, generally, there is not freedom but necessity—Hegel's "ruse of reason" operating through the particular aims of individual human beings but beyond their collective comprehension. Freedom must, therefore, be redefined so that it equals knowledge of "the direction of the forces of society." Such knowledge must be the privilege of an elite, because it is unavailable to any class collectively. For Plekhanov, being one of those who enjoyed such knowledge of the forces that drive society, "it will only remain for me to rely on their resultant to achieve my ends."[90]

In failing to appreciate completely the force of Marx and Engels's critique of Hegel, Plekhanov also abandoned their notion of the workers' collective ability to change the course of history. In reproducing the dominant themes of Hegel's determinism in materialist form, he also reproduced Hegel's fatalistic conservatism. These ramifications became all the more obvious as the struggle in Russia posed new problems of revolutionary strategy and tactics. As Plekhanov's biographer has noted,

> Taking his Marxian writings as a whole, one sees that Plekhanov's account of the movement to socialism unmistakably depended upon a "natural" evolutionary process, in conformity with law. . . . he did not quite manage to bring voluntarism into a perfect balance with determinism—even at the level of logical argument. How much more likely it was that imbalances might arise at the level of practice.[91]

The strengths of Plekhanov's marxism were the vitality that it took from struggle in Russia and the influence of Hegel in his understanding of general marxist principles. But the longer his exile lasted, the less nourishment Plekhanov drew directly from the struggle. Plekhanov was not, like Lenin during his exile, connected by a thousand strands to the labor movement in Russia. Moreover, the whole nature of the problems faced by the Russian labor movement changed dramatically during this same period. The general question of the development of capitalism in Russia, whose understanding Plekhanov had pioneered, mostly required the application of very general marxist principles.

But the precise nature, the exact class relations and the precise forms of organization necessary to relate to the increasing combativity of the labor movement now required a further step forward in theory and in practice. This could not be taken simply on the basis of those same general principles.

Other Russian marxists met these challenges by developing more concrete dialectical analyses. Trotsky pioneered the theory of combined and uneven development; Lenin refashioned the theory of the party, although even he was not to see its general significance until years later. But Plekhanov, having done so much to achieve the initial stage of development, remained stranded in the past. And the more he reiterated old generalities in changed circumstances the further he departed from revolutionary marxism: first parting company with Lenin's activist notion of the party, then with the notion that a workers' revolution was possible, then with the internationalist position on the First World War and, ultimately, with the October revolution itself.[92] Ironically, Plekhanov provided his own epitaph: "It was Hegel who said that any philosophy may be reduced to *empty formalism*, if one confines oneself to the simple repetition of its fundamental principles."[93]

ROSA LUXEMBURG: THE DIALECTIC IN ACTION

It was Rosa Luxemburg's great good fortune to be an outsider. Born in Poland, she joined a revolutionary organization at the age of sixteen. Hunted by the police, she fled Poland in 1889, moving first to Zurich to attend university. Within a couple of years, she had become the leading theoretician of the Social Democratic Party of Poland and Lithuania, a position that she retained until her murder by the army during the German revolution. She was a leading participant in the Second International from the moment she first attended a congress in 1893.[94]

In 1898, she moved to Germany and became a frequent contributor to Kautsky's *Neue Zeit*. But although she was part of the Second International, she was, like Lenin, not shaped by it in the same way as were Bernstein, Kautsky, and, even, Plekhanov. Her links with the more volatile political developments in Poland and Russia must have helped shape her commitment to revolutionary activity. Time after time Luxemburg is found in the thick the struggle and, consequently, also in prison. When she looked at events in Germany, she judged them with the yardstick taken from the struggle further east. In a dialectical reversal foreign to the leaders of the Second International, she saw that the struggle in the less developed countries showed the more developed countries their future.

Luxemburg never wrote her "Logic," a treatise specifically on the marxist method, but it would be wrong to conclude from this that it was not an absolutely central concern for her. In nearly everything she wrote, she specifically refers to the dialectical method and to the ways in which her opponents' lack of it produces errors in theory and in practice. As Lelio Basso makes clear: "It is useless to search in her writings for long discussions on historical materialism, on the pre-eminence of the economic 'factor' over the political 'factor', or on other similar themes so largely debated by adversaries and advocates of Marxism alike." This is because "Luxemburg . . . almost never stopped to review and repeat the principles of Marxism, but rather attempted to show them in action in the course of her analyses of contemporary phenomena and in the practical indications that she drew from these analyses."[95]

Nothing could make this point as clearly as Luxemburg's intervention in the debate with Bernstein. Her approach showed her grasp of the marxist method to be qualitatively superior to that of Kautsky or Plekhanov.

Bernstein's attack on the dialectic had been an important part of his justification for abandoning a revolutionary perspective, but it was not his main or strongest point. Neither was it the issue around which most debate took place, in part because Kautsky and others did not, as Plekhanov noted, understand its full significance. But, however that may be, Bernstein's central charge was that both the political and economic institutions of capitalist society were evolving toward socialism. Consequently, all that the SPD need do is to keep up the pressure for reform, knowing that they were swimming with the tide of social progress.

Kautsky tried to counter this argument by busying himself with mostly empirical arguments that refuted this or that justification or conclusion of Bernstein's case. However valuable this might be, it could not, on its own, do much damage to Bernstein's approach as long as it was contained by Kautsky's own evolutionary framework. If Bernstein, in effect, was arguing that social progress was already upon us, Kautsky was merely arguing that social progress would *soon* be on us—and that it would occur without us having to do very much about it. In both cases, the practical conclusions were similar: avoid "revolution-mongering" (as Bernstein called it), strengthen the trade union struggle, and campaign for an SPD government.

The coincidence of Bernstein's and Kautsky's positions is nowhere more clearly expressed than in their attitude to the revolution itself. Bernstein, we know, wanted to embrace reformism and jettison any talk of revolution. Kautsky's attitude was, characteristically, ambivalent. Kautsky took refuge in general statements that could not on their own offer a guide to action. He insisted that revolutionaries could not enact a revolution by decree and that, although reforms were not a substitute for social transformation, they were a vital part of the preparatory struggle. In any case, he argued, taking political power would not bring about socialism unless capitalism had already developed to the point where it would provide the productive capacity necessary.

But Kautsky's temporizing was beside the point. What was required to refute Bernstein was not a blueprint or a timetable for insurrection, nor did it
require a rejection of the involvement of revolutionaries in the battle for
partial economic or political gains. What was required was definite answer
to the following questions: Has capitalist society overcome its inherent contradictions? Is socialism to be achieved by gradual reform, or is the system
still prone to crises in which a working class revolution is necessary to avoid
social retrogression? Kautsky's inability to answer this question inevitably
drew him to the reformist camp:

> Kautsky's refusal to prejudge the character and duration of the revolution
> was quite reasonable on the premiss that the proletariat must wait for the
> ripening of conditions under capitalism. But a party which calls itself revo-
> lutionary cannot act rationally if, on whatever grounds, it refuses to pre-
> judge the meaning of the term "revolution."[96]

The fault lay in Kautsky's deterministic approach, because objective conditions are only one part of the necessary preconditions of revolution:

> For this reason Kautsky's centrist position, based on his scientific attitude
> and reluctance to take decisions without rational foundation, amounted in
> practice to acceptance of the reformist standpoint. The theory of a revo-
> lution prepared by capitalism itself and not by the proletariat was a reflec-
> tion, in Kautsky's doctrine, of the practical situation of the party, which
> adhered to revolutionary phraseology in its programme but took no ac-
> tion suggesting that it meant what it said.[97]

It shows the great power of Luxemburg's understanding of the marxist
method that from the outset she refused to accept the terms of debate agreed
to by Bernstein and Kautsky, even though she and Kautsky were both opposed to Bernstein at this time.

Luxemburg rejected Bernstein's contention that capitalism was becoming
increasingly crisis free and democratic, but the *way* in which she did so was
entirely different to Kautsky's method. She rejected the simplistic evolutionary approach common to both Bernstein and Kautsky. When Bernstein was
confronted with contradictory social trends—the spread of universal suffrage
and imperialism, the alternation of periods of expansion and crises—he simply chose to take the progressive aspects as reality and dismiss the regressive
elements as accidental blemishes, argued Luxemburg. In short, he failed to
grasp the contradictory nature of society. Luxemberg's treatment of Bernstein's
"mechanical view" of crises makes the point:

> For him crises are simply derangements of the economic mechanism. With
> their cessation, he thinks, the mechanism could function well. But the
> fact is that crises are not "derangements" in the usual sense of the word.

They are "derangements" of the economic mechanism without which capitalist economy could not develop at all. For if crises constitute the only method possible in capitalism—and therefore the normal method—of solving the conflict existing between the unlimited extension of production and the narrow limit of the world market, then crises are an organic manifestation inseparable from capitalist economy.[98]

Luxemburg's defense of the marxist theory of the state also depended on her ability to see how two contradictory social trends were united in one institution. She starts by arguing that the further capitalist economic development advances the more the state loses its character as a representative of the whole society. It is transformed into a pure ruling class institution. Luxemburg then goes on, developing the analysis beyond the point then common among marxists, to show how the "democratizing" of the state and its class character were combined. This was obviously a crucial question given the changes in the state institutions then taking place in the advanced capitalist countries—and the polemical use to which these facts were being put by the revisionists. Luxemburg's argument is that the state is now penetrating more deeply into the body of society than ever before and, at the same time, quite contrary to the appearance created by the widening of the suffrage, reserving more and more of its powers to those state institutions beyond the reach of the legislature (for instance: the civil service, the military, the executive):

> These two qualities [the representative and the class character] distinguish themselves more from each other and find themselves in a contradictory relation in the very nature of the state. This contradiction becomes progressively sharper. For, on the one hand, we have a growth in the functions of a general interest on the part of the state, its intervention in social life, its "control" over society. But, on the other hand, its class character obliges that state to move the pivot of its activity and its means of coercion more and more into domains which are useful only to the class character of the bourgeoisie . . . as is the case of militarism and tariff and colonial policies.[99]

Luxemburg goes on, in a point crucial to understanding the development of the state in the twentieth century, to say that the elements of "social control" are inevitably and increasingly dominated by those aspects of a wholly class character. This brings her to a damning rebuttal of Bernstein: "The extension of democracy, which Bernstein sees as a means of realising socialism by degrees, does not contradict but, on the contrary, corresponds perfectly to the transformation realised in the nature of the state."[100] Her summary runs right to the heart of the reformist case as it was then put by Bernstein, later by Kautsky, and afterward by reformists of every stripe:

In this society, the representative institutions, democratic in form, are in content the instruments of the ruling class . . . as soon as democracy shows the tendency to negate its class character and become transformed into an instrument of the real interests of the populations, the democratic forms are sacrificed by the bourgeoisie and its state representatives.

The conclusion that socialists should draw were equally clear:

That is why the conquest of a parliamentary reformist majority is a calculation which, entirely in the spirit of bourgeois liberalism, preoccupies itself with one side—the formal side—of democracy, but does not take into account the other side, its real content. All in all, parliamentarianism is not a directly socialist element impregnating gradually the whole capitalist society. It is, on the contrary, a specific form of the bourgeois class state, helping to ripen and develop the existing class antagonisms of capitalism.[101]

What Luxemburg objected to in Bernstein's method was that:

Bernstein's theory does not seize these manifestations of contemporary economic life as they appear in their organic relationship with the whole of capitalist development, with the complete economic mechanism of capitalism. His theory pulls these details out of their living economic context. It treats them as the *disjecta membra* (separate parts) of a lifeless machine.[102]

Thus, in two beautifully concrete analyses, Luxemburg highlighted how Bernstein separated contradictory elements that belonged together to present an harmonious picture of capitalist development. Luxemburg's analysis restates the contradiction, thereby establishing a structure with greater explanatory power and, simultaneously, reintegrates this analysis with a revolutionary strategy. On her own account, it was just as important to focus on the *contradictory* nature of capitalism as it was to stress that capitalist relations formed an *interconnected whole*:

If we ignore the irreconcilable contradictions and concentrate our attention only on the fact that the proletariat and bourgeoisie live on the same soil, it is not hard to accept the idea of the so-called national interests for the defence of national industry . . . and "a reasonable" colonial policy (Bernstein . . .) .

The result of ignoring contradictions in this way would be:

Everything [in the party] is turned upside down: its programme, its tactic, its attitude toward the state, toward the bourgeoisie, toward foreign policy, toward militarism. From a revolutionary and internationalist party, the social democrats are transformed into a national, small bourgeois, social-reformistic party.[103]

Written in 1899, this proved a prophetic forecast of the SPD's development over the next fifteen years. At every juncture in this period, Luxemburg proved the superiority of her method over that of her fellow leaders in the SPD. The Russian revolution of 1905 influenced Kautsky as well as Luxemburg, temporarily inclining him to the left. But Kautsky simply did not possess an approach that would really enable him to integrate the experience of 1905 into a wider theory of revolution. Luxemburg did. Her masterly description of the relationship between economic and political strikes demonstrates how completely Luxemburg rejected this "repulsive web around my brain," as she called Kautsky's fatalistic marxism.[104] She first spells out how the economic struggle passes over into a political struggle:

> The earlier mass and general strikes had originated from individual coalescing wage struggles which, in the general temper of the revolutionary situation and under the influence of the social democratic agitation, rapidly became political demonstrations; the economic factor and the scattered condition of trade unionism were the starting point; all-embracing class action and political direction the result.[105]

Luxemburg then goes on to show how "the movement was now reversed" and "action soon fell into an unending series of local, partial economic strikes in separate districts." But rather than see this merely as a retreat, Luxemburg shows how this phase of economic struggle prepared the way for a second and even more powerful general movement, because it involved ever deeper layers of the working class in action:

> ... the whole long scale runs from the regular trade union struggle of a picked and tested troop of the proletariat drawn from large-scale industry, to the formless protest of a handful of rural proletarians, and to the first slight stirrings of an agitated military garrison, from the well-educated and elegant revolt in cuffs and white collars in the counting house of a bank to the shy-bold murmurings of a clumsy meeting of dissatisfied policemen in a smoke-grimed dark and dirty guardroom.[106]

In this great act of dialectical imagination, Luxemburg paused to lambast "the theory of the lovers of 'orderly and well-disciplined' struggles, according to plan and to scheme, according to those especially who always know better from afar 'how it should have been done.'" The leaders of the SPD were her intended target, those who perpetually put off any talk of mass strikes because "the funds and the organisation of the unions were not yet ready."

When Luxemburg made her general case against reformism, she demonstrated the same refusal to separate contradictory elements. She famously rejected Bernstein's argument that "the final goal is nothing, the movement everything," by showing how the movement and its goal could not be torn apart. She chose to define the relationship between means and ends precisely and, on that basis, to arrive at a course of action designed to resolve the contradiction on terms favorable to the working class:

... people who pronounce themselves in favour of the method of legis-
lative reform *in place of and in contradistinction to* the conquest of political
power and social revolution, do not really choose a more tranquil, calmer
and slower road to the *same* goal, but a *different* goal. ... If we follow the
political conceptions of revisionism ... our programme becomes not the
realization of *socialism* but the reform of *capitalism*: not the suppression of
the system of wage labour, but the diminution of exploitation, that is, the
suppression of the abuses of capitalism instead of the suppression of
capitalism itself.[107]

Luxemburg developed her argument by showing that Bernstein had arrived at his conclusions by mistaking the subjective and objective significance of the day-to-day battles in which revolutionaries must necessarily
involve themselves. Bernstein imagined that such partial battles for reform
could work an *objective* change in the nature of the system, whereas Luxemburg
believed that they could not. For her, the importance of battles for reform
was that they worked a change on the *subjective* precondition for socialism—
the class consciousness of workers. In the battle for partial advances, workers
would learn that their own strength lay in collective organization and struggle. Consequently, they would learn the nature of the system, including its
ultimately irreformable nature. From success in small battles, workers would
become conscious of the subjective ability to wage, and the objective necessity of, the fight for a revolutionary transformation of the system. Luxemburg's
own summary of this point has never been bettered:

> It is not true that socialism will arise automatically from the daily struggle of the
> working class. Socialism will be a consequence of (1) the growing contradictions of
> the capitalist economy and (2) the comprehension by the working class of the
> unavoidability of the suppression of these contradictions through a social transfor-
> mation. When, in the manner of revisionism, the first condition is denied
> and the second rejected, the labour movement finds itself reduced to a
> simple co-operative and reformist movement. We move here in a straight
> line toward the total abandonment of the class viewpoint.[108]

Luxemburg's whole refutation of Bernstein depended on showing how an
undialectical analysis leads to mistakes in theory and practice so it is not
surprising that she deliberately and explicitly attacks his abandonment of the
marxist method:

> When he directs his keenest arrows against our dialectic system, he is
> really attacking the specific mode of thought employed by the conscious
> proletariat in its struggle for liberation. It is an attempt to break the sword
> that has helped the proletariat to pierce the darkness of its future. It is an
> attempt to shatter the intellectual arm with the aid of which the prole-
> tariat, though materially under the yoke of the bourgeoisie, is yet enabled
> to triumph over the bourgeoisie.[109]

Luxemburg did much more than reassert a general commitment to the dialectic, much more even than develop a number of concrete analyses that refuted revisionism and restated the revolutionary position in contemporary terms. She also provided an effective answer to the determinism that beset every other leading figure in the Second International, except Lenin. In reply to the belief in the inevitability of historical progress shared by Bernstein, Kautsky, and Plekhanov, Luxemburg deliberately recalled Marx's famous phrase in *The Eighteenth Brumaire of Louis Bonaparte*. She wrote:

> Man does not make history of his own volition, but he makes history nevertheless. The proletariat is dependent in its actions upon the degree of maturity to which social evolution has advanced. But again, social evolution is not a thing apart from the proletariat; it is in the same measure its driving force and its cause as well as its product and its effect. And though we can no more skip a period in our historical development than a man can jump over his own shadow, it lies within our power to accelerate or to retard it.[110]

Basso, quoting Luxemburg, expounds the meaning of her analysis:

> ... nothing is inevitable, and nothing is arbitrary. Nothing is inevitable because there are no mechanical laws, but only tendencies that can be thwarted, and because, in the last analysis history is made by the conscious will of men that creates the economic conditions which shape the objective tendencies. Nothing is arbitrary, because the conscious will of man is itself formed in the midst of the historical process. It is conditioned by the objective circumstances in which it moves and cannot separate itself from the tendencies of development, from the "logic of the objective historical process" that "precedes the logic of its protagonists."[111]

This is a very different notion of historical necessity to that which dominated the Second International. It does not abandon the notion of objective limits on the possibilities of human action, but neither does it obliterate the essential element of conscious action by the working class in the achievement of socialism. It thereby reinstates the notion of working-class self-emancipation at the core of revolutionary socialism.

In fact, Luxemburg believed that there was rather more at stake than, as the quotation above has it, the "power to accelerate or to retard" social development: rather, she believed that the whole future course of humanity was caught in a contradiction from which it could only be extricated if the conscious activity of the working class exploited that power which historical development had given it.

> Historic development moves in contradictions, and for every necessity puts its opposite into the world as well. The capitalist state of society is doubtless a historic necessity, but so also is the revolt of the working class

against it. Capital is a historic necessity, but in the same measure is its gravedigger, the socialist proletariat. The world rule of imperialism is a historic necessity, but likewise is its overthrow by the proletarian international. Side by side two historic necessities exist in constant conflict with each other.[112]

Indeed, we might reformulate Luxemburg's point as follows: the conscious activity of workers is unavoidable *because* historical development presents us with junctures at which the objective conditions can develop in only one of two basic directions. At such turning points, the difference between the classes is *not* that one has "history on its side," at least not in the sense that objective developments will only admit one course of action. Both classes have the power to determine events. The alternative will be decided by that class which is best able to organize itself and can most clearly formulate its aims in such a way that it can lead the whole society in one direction rather than another. In the maelstrom of the First World War, Luxemburg saw one such moment of choice in the following terms:

Frederick Engels once said: "Capitalist society faces a dilemma, either an advance to socialism or a revision to barbarism." . . . Thus we stand today, as Frederick Engels prophesied more than a generation ago, before the awful proposition: either the triumph of imperialism and the destruction of all culture, and, as in ancient Rome, depopulation, desolation, degeneration, a vast cemetery; or the victory of socialism, that is, the conscious struggle of the international proletariat against imperialism, against its methods, against war. This is the struggle of world history, its inevitable choice, whose scales are trembling in the balance awaiting the decision of the proletariat. Upon it depends the future of culture and humanity.[113]

When Luxemburg wrote these lines, the names of the Somme, Auschwitz, the Gulag, and Hiroshima were not yet capable of summoning in popular consciousness the precise definition of barbarism that they provide today. Neither could Luxemburg count dates, nor name the places—Germany 1918–23, Hungary 1919, China 1927, Spain 1936, Hungary again in 1956, France in 1968—where the alternative to such horror again hung in the balance. She did, nevertheless, provide the unique service of reformulating the marxist dialectic in such terms that future generations might recognize such crossroads when they appear again.

It is all the more tragic, therefore, that her achievement has been belittled by commentators, mostly Stalinist in origin, who have argued that Luxemburg was a "spontaneist" who believed that the laws of history would automatically produce revolts among the working class. The accusation is, therefore, that Luxemburg was as determinist as those she fought against in the Second International and that this led her to underestimate the need for socialist organization. "Zinoviev was the first to make this claim"[114] as head of the Communist International; by 1925, Ruth Fischer's campaign to "Bolshevise" (that is, to bring under Stalinist control) the German Communist Party was being fought under the banner of combating Rosa Luxemburg as "the fount of all errors, all theories of spontaneity, all erroneous conceptions of organisational problems."[115] This campaign lacked all credibility where Luxemburg's political work was concerned and so attention was focussed on her economic theory as the supposed site of her determinism.

The Accumulation of Capital, Luxemburg's great contribution to economic theory, had argued that capitalism could only continue to exist so long as it was able to expand into the non-capitalist hinterland. Marx, Luxemburg argued, had failed to see that when, as a result of the development of imperialism, the capitalist system was the *only*, rather than simply the *predominant*, economic reality, it would collapse under the weight of its own contradictions. Luxemburg's critics took this position to be a variant of the determinism common in the Second International. They assumed that she meant, as Kautsky had, that the collapse of capitalism was automatically the same as its replacement by socialism. Thus, they connected this economic analysis with Luxemburg's praise for workers' capacity to learn in struggle and her supposed disregard for organizational issues.

Luxemburg's economic analysis had the great virtue of drawing attention to the vital inter-relationship between the drive for imperialist expansion and the general health of the system, especially in its heartlands. In doing so, she emphasized precisely what Bernstein and Kautsky wanted to deny—that imperialism was both integral to the system and a factor that would increasingly destabilize capitalism. In this she was right. But in *predicating* the stability of the system on its relations with the non-capitalist world she was wrong, because there are internal mechanisms that also result in capitalist crises. The economic argument against Luxemburg is not of central concern here.[116] The key question in this context is whether Luxemburg's argument did actually have the deterministic aspect that its critics allege.

The crucial point here is that Luxemburg did not at all understand the notion of "capitalist collapse" in the manner of Kautsky. First, although she thought that the longer the system existed the more crisis ridden and destructive it would become, she only understood its "collapse" as an extreme possibility. In *The Accumulation of Capital* she wrote:

> Here, as everywhere in history, theory renders its greatest service only if it shows us the *tendency* of development, the final logical point towards which this development objectively proceeds. This point can only be reached to the degree that the preceding periods of historical evolution have been carried to their extreme consequences. It becomes even less *necessary* that this point be reached, the more actively the proletariat, which at present

embodies the social consciousness, intervenes in the blind interaction of forces. Under this aspect as well, the proper interpretation of Marxist theory offers the proletariat the most fruitful orientations and the most powerful stimulus.[117]

Second, and most importantly of all, Luxemburg did not think that the collapse of capitalism would automatically or inevitably usher in the socialist era. For her the question of collapse was another way of posing the question "socialism or barbarism"? It was a way of dramatizing the social regression that would begin to overtake society unless workers took power and reconstituted society on a different basis. In this, she posed the question in the same way that Marx and Engels had done when they wrote in the *Communist Manifesto* that a social crisis can either be resolved by "a social revolution or the common ruin of the contending classes." As one commentator notes:

> For Luxemburg, therefore, what the inevitability of capitalist collapse proves is not the redundancy, but the urgent indispensability, of conscious revolutionary struggle on the part of the working class. It is because of that inevitability, and not despite it, that such a struggle is required. It is also because of that inevitability that Luxemburg can meaningfully speak of there being an alternative to socialism. For what else, other than catastrophe, could that alternative be?[118]

We need only add some thoughts on what such a "catastrophe" or "collapse" might look like. For us, though not for Luxemburg, it might be imagined as one final cataclysm in which society is thrown back into a new dark age—that is the special nightmare of the generations that have lived in the shadow of nuclear war. More recently, the prospect has opened before us of a similar point being reached as a result of the environmental damage done by capitalist development.

But for Luxemburg, to whom these horrors were unknown, collapse signified a longer process of social decay—of wars, bloody national and ethnic conflicts, mass unemployment, the retrogression of welfare provision, and the decline of science and culture. In Luxemburg's words, "a string of political and social disasters and convulsions . . . punctuated by periodical economic catastrophes or crises." It is unnecessary to conceive such regression in absolute terms—that running water will become a thing of the past in advanced capitalist countries, or that cars and trains will be replaced by horses. To establish that society is regressing, it is enough to point out that technical "progress" turned the rack and the whip of the Spanish Inquisition into the gas chambers of the Nazis, supplied by I. G. Farben, and that the starvation of the middle ages was the result of the weakness of the productive forces, not the result of a system that is "technically" capable of preventing it but does not do so because it will not turn a profit for those who run it.

Regression is a situation in which society turns the means of progress into methods of destruction. Barbarism can be the product of progress, not just some primitive state to which we may revert if we do not halt the process before it reaches its limit.

Given this understanding, it is hardly likely that Luxemburg could conclude that questions of organization were of little importance, and indeed she did not. Her whole effort was geared to convincing an organization, the SPD, to adopt a revolutionary perspective. The same prospect that appears to society as two roads of social development appears to the organizations of the working class as a choice of strategy. To refuse the revolutionary strategy is, inevitably, to be driven to defend some variant of its opposite. As Luxemburg wrote during the First World War, "Faced with the alternative: for or against the war, the social democrats were forced by the iron logic of history to throw all their weight into the balance of war from the moment when they abandoned their position against the war."[119] This could hardly be written by someone who underestimated the importance of revolutionary organization.

Luxemburg did make a crucial error about revolutionary organization. But it did not stem from her method—she was neither a spontaneist nor a determinist. Neither is it correct to see her mistakes on the question of the party as rooted in her analysis of capitalism—this *heightened* the importance she attached to conscious, organized intervention in historical development. To look in either of these two areas is to look at the wrong level of generality. Luxemburg understood the need for a party. What she misunderstood was *the type of party* that it was necessary to build before the revolutionary crisis itself developed. Her model was the SPD. Her mistake was to believe that it could be won to revolutionary socialism and not to see that it would have to be replaced by an independent organization not dependent on the bureaucracy of the trade unions.

In making this mistake, Luxemburg was in good company. Every other marxist of her generation made the same mistake. Even Lenin did not understand that the SPD and the Second International were bankrupt until 1914, and this was despite the fact that he had, in the practice of the Bolshevik party, developed an alternative vision of revolutionary organization. Lenin never recommended that the revolutionary wing of the SPD split away to form a separate organization, as he had split with the Mensheviks. The reason for Luxemburg and Lenin's position is not hard to see—the SPD appeared practically coextensive with the working class. To split from it was not the same as the split between the Bolsheviks and the Mensheviks where the rival organizations were of comparable size. No one could claim that the Bolsheviks were "outside the movement" in the same way that such a claim might have been made against people who left the SPD.

Nevertheless, for all the mitigating circumstances, the objective possibility existed after 1904 for an independent revolutionary organization to be built. The level of struggle rose, the crisis of society deepened, imperialism threatened war, and the pace of the SPD's march to the right quickened. And Luxemburg had one great advantage over Lenin, as he himself later admitted. She realized how hopelessly compromised with reformism was the so-called "marxist centre" led by Kautsky. That is, the irreformability of the SPD was clearer to Luxemburg earlier than it was to Lenin. The need for an alternative revolutionary organization was "in the air." On this vital question, Luxemburg's sense of dialectical development deserted her. She did not see how today's revolutionary minority could become the mass revolutionary party of tomorrow by developing in partial separation from the consciousness of the majority of the working class. Nor did she see that centralism and spontaneity are not necessarily inversely related. Marked by the bureaucratic centralism of the SPD, she did not see, even after she split from the SPD, that in Lenin's party centralism was a method of spreading and generalizing the spontaneous revolts of the class beyond the point in time and place where they first originate. As such, it is a lever to achieve the self-emancipation of the class, not a substitute for self-emancipation.

CONCLUSION

The enormous changes that overtook capitalist society in the thirty years before the First World War marked the opening of a new era. Imperialism, mass suffrage and the growth of reformism faced marxists with questions that assumed a quite different form from that in which they had confronted Marx and Engels. But among all these issues, the organizational question was the key to the development of marxism in the period of the Second International. Reform or revolution, imperialism and internationalism—these were questions that now arose directly as questions of strategy and tactics. Division over such issues always ran back to the question of what sort of organization the various combatants thought they were trying to build. But although these were the most important determinants of the positions taken by Bernstein, Kautsky, Plekhanov, and Luxemburg, they were not the only ones.

Bernstein, Kautsky, Plekhanov, and Luxemburg all confronted these new problems with theoretical conceptions they had inherited from the past. These, too, played a crucial role in their ability to analyze changed circumstances. Where this inheritance was weakest, with Bernstein, capitulation to some attenuated version of the dominant ideology was swift. In Kautsky and Plekhanov the root was deeper, but ultimately insufficiently strong to adapt itself to the needs of the day. In Luxemburg, the marxist method was most powerful of all; it was the most capable of meeting new challenges, because it was the most capable of conducting new analyses and of distinguishing the fundamental from the merely phenomenal. She, least of all, was prey to the twin temptations of either casting aside the cornerstones of marxism simply because capitalism had changed its form, or of repeating old formulas that no longer provided a concrete analysis of the concrete situation. This last skill was her decisive advantage over Plekhanov.

But it was Lenin who combined Luxemburg's strengths with one other vital factor: persistent, unrelenting, close personal involvement with the task of building a genuinely revolutionary organization. This strength proved to be decisive. Others could claim to outshine Lenin in this or that respect— Plekhanov in his understanding of Hegel before 1914, Luxemburg in her grasp of the nature of reformism in the West, Trotsky on the nature of the Russian revolution, for instance. But Lenin's grasp of the fundamentals of marxism was sufficiently strong, and his grasp of the dialectic of party and class so superior, that he was able to overcome his weaknesses as he developed in the struggle. But without Lenin's conception of the party, Luxemburg and Trotsky's strengths could not be effectively brought to bear on the course of the class struggle. With his conception of the party, Lenin could learn from Luxemburg and Trotksy and make what he had learned effective in the struggle. This is where Lenin's decisive intellectual and practical advantage lies. Lenin's conception of the party is the crucible in which the objective and subjective strands of the historical process are formed into a conscious strategy for revolution, the last missing link in Luxemburg's dialectic.

Notes

1. L. Colletti, "Bernstein and the Marxism of the Second International," in *From Rousseau to Lenin* (London: New Left Books, 1972), 58.
2. And, at the beginning of the twentieth century, that holy of holies for the capitalist state, the secret service.
3. The First International, organized by Marx and Engels, was founded in 1864. It declined after the defeat of the Paris Commune in 1871 and was formally abandoned in 1876.
4. C. E. Schorske, *German Social Democracy, 1905–1917, the Development of the Great Schism* (Cambridge, MA: Harvard University Press, 1955), 6.
5. C. Harman, *The Lost Revolution, Germany 1918–1923* (London: Bookmarks, 1982), 15–17.
6. Ibid., 14.
7. Schorske, *German Social Democracy*, 7.
8. J. Joll, *Europe since 1870* (London: Pelican, 1976), 60.
9. E. Hobsbawm, *The Age of Empire, 1875–1914* (London: Weidenfeld and Nicolson, 1987), 131.
10. This book is also known by the title *Evolutionary Socialism*.
11. H. Tudor, Introduction to E. Bernstein, *The Preconditions of Socialism* (Cambridge: Cambridge University Press, 1993), xxii.

12. P. Gay, *The Dilemma of Democratic Socialism, Eduard Bernstein's Challenge to Marx* (New York: Columbia University Press, 1952), 55.

13. Ibid., 131.

14. Bernstein, *Preconditions of Socialism*, 13.

15. Quoted in Gay, *Dilemma of Democratic Socialism*, 153, fn71. Gay disagrees with Bernstein's own assessment on the grounds that Bernstein's interest in ethics is at odds with positivism, although he is willing to say that Bernstein's unilinear view of progress was "closely akin to the view of the 19th century positivists" (136). It is the argument of this account that Bernstein's positivism gave rise to the ethical element in his thought. The unacknowledged contradiction between the two elements of his thought were the inevitable consequence of abandoning a dialectical notion of subject and object.

16. Bernstein, *Preconditions of Socialism*, 30–31.

17. Ibid., 36.

18. It is not even obviously the case that this popular attitude to Babeuf is correct. See I. Birchall, "The Babeuf Bicentenary—Conspiracy or Revolutionary Party," *International Socialism* 72 (London, 1996).

19. Bernstein, *Preconditions of Socialism*, 32.

20. Ibid., 37–38.

21. Ibid., 38–39.

22. Ibid., 40.

23. Ibid., 46.

24. Quoted in Gay, *Dilemma of Democratic Socialism*, 137.

25. Ibid., 133.

26. Bernstein, *Preconditions of Socialism*, 200.

27. Ibid., 209.

28. Quoted in Gay, *Dilemma of Democratic Socialism*, 151.

29. Ibid., 143.

30. Ibid., 152.

31. A. Walicki, *Marxism and the Leap to the Kingdom of Freedom* (California: Stanford University Press, 1995), 212.

32. Bernstein, *Preconditions of Socialism*, 205–6.

33. Ibid., 208.

34. Ibid., 209.

35. Gay, *Dilemma of Democratic Socialism*, 152.

36. Ibid., 251.

37. Ibid., 256.

38. Marx to J. Longuet, 11 April 1881, cited in H. Sheehan, *Marxism and the Philosophy of Science* (New Jersey: Humanities Press, 1985), 67.

39. M. Donald, *Marxism and Revolution, Karl Kautsky and the Russian Marxists* (New Haven, CT: Yale University Press, 1993), 6.

40. Schorske, *German Social Democracy*, 5.

41. Colletti, "Bernstein and the Marxism of the Second International," 105.

42. K. Kautsky, *The Materialist Conception of History* (New Haven, CT: Yale University Press, 1988), 6.

43. K. Kautsky, *Ethics and the Materialist Conception of History* (Chicago: CH Kerr, 1906), 117.

44. K. Kautsky, quoted in M. Salvadori, *Karl Kautsky and the Socialist Revolution 1880–1938* (London: Verso, 1990), 23.

45. Kautsky, *The Materialist Conception on History*, 19.

46. K. Kautsky, *The Class Struggle* (Chicago: CH Kerr, 1910), 117.
47. K. Kautsky, *Ethics and the Materialist Conception of History*, 206.
48. L. Kolakowski, a bitter opponent of marxism, nevertheless finds that "a striking feature of Kautsky's work is the complete lack of understanding of philosophical problems." See *The Main Current of Marxism*, Vol. II: *The Golden Age* (Oxford: Oxford University Press, 1978), 35.
49. Kautsky, *Materialist Conception of History*, 34.
50. Ibid..
51. Ibid., 34–35.
52. Ibid., 35.
53. Ibid., 36.
54. Kautsky, *Ethics and the Materialist Conception of History*, 60.
55. Ibid., 61.
56. Ibid., 61–62.
57. Ibid., 62.
58. Ibid., 64.
59. Ibid., 63.
60. Ibid., 60.
61. See in this connection Kolakowski, *Main Current of Marxism*, 41. Kolakowski may not agree with Marx on this point, but at least he understands the point Marx was making.
62. Ibid.
63. Kautsky, quoted in Salvadori, *Karl Kautsky*, 40.
64. Ibid., 76–77.
65. Ibid., 127.
66. Kautsky, quoted in Donald, *Marxism and Revolution*, 47.
67. Salvadori, *Karl Kautsky*, 100.
68. Kautsky, *The Materialist Conception of History*, lxix–lxx.
69. Leszek Kolakowski's claim that Plekhanov's "picture of Hegel is mainly taken from Engels" and is "much over-simplified and seems to be based on fragmentary and cursory reading" is completely inaccurate as even a passing familiarity with Plekhanov's work demonstrates. Even the brief account of some of the major themes in Plekhanov's writings given in this chapter should also be enough to dispel this illusion. A more serious point, made by Lenin not Kolakowski, is that Plekhanov knew Hegel more from his political philosophy and his philosophy of history than from the *Science of Logic*.
70. T. Cliff, "Plekhanov: Father of Russian Marxism," in *A Socialist Review* (London, 1965), 297.
71. S. H. Baron, *Plekhanov, the Father of Russian Marxism* (California: Stanford University Press, 1963), 3.
72. Walicki, *Marxism and the Leap*, 237.
73. G. Plekhanov, *Selected Philosophical Works*, Vol. III (Moscow: Progress, 1976), 55.
74. G. Plekhanov, *Selected Philosophical Works*, Vol. 1 (London, 1961), 456.
75. G. Plekhanov, *In Defence of Materialism* (London: Lawrence and Wishart, 1947), 99. This title is in fact Plekhanov's original. *The Development of the Monist View of History*, the title by which this text is usually known, was only adopted to escape the attentions of the censor. For the same reason, Plekhanov took the pseudonym N. Beltov for this publication.
76. Ibid., 100.
77. Ibid., 114.

78. G. Plekhanov, *Selected Philosophical Works*, Vol. 1 (London, 1961), 458–61.
79. This was not, however, Plekhanov's solution to the problem. Instead, he tended to eliminate the contradictory nature of the material base and, therefore, to reduce the various interactions to the base in a deterministic manner. Nevertheless, he correctly identified the limits of the "interactive relations" approach where many at the time (and since) have seen no problem.
80. Plekhanov, *Selected Philosophical Works*, Vol. I, 480.
81. Plekhanov, *In Defence of Materialism*, 96.
82. Ibid., 97. All of which means that it is an exaggeration to say, as Kevin Anderson does, that Plekhanov conducts "a rather tepid and qualified critique of evolutionism." Plekhanov may have, inconsistently, held a social evolutionist view, but he did not reduce this to natural evolution. Neither is it true that "the concept of contradiction" is "completely missing." The point is, as I argue below, that Plekhanov's dialectic is rather too Hegelian and, at the same time, too deterministic. These two elements remained unreconciled in Plekhanov's work, making it more contradictory and more interesting than Anderson allows. His point that "Plekhanov's concept of 'leaps' is barren of any notion of a human subject" is more to the point. See K. Anderson, *Lenin, Hegel and Western Marxism* (Chicago: University of Illinois Press, 1995), 17. On this point, see Walicki, *Marxism and the Leap*, 240: "All these ideas derived from Engels, not from Kautsky . . . [and] enabled Plekhanov to draw directly on from Hegel and to develop his concept of necessity as dialectical, teleological, and rational, that is, in conscious opposition to the mechanistic determinism of the natural sciences."
83. Ibid., 222–23. Plekhanov's "philosophy of history retained some semblance of the Marxian scheme of self-enriching alienation." Walicki, *Marxism and the Leap*, 240.
84. Ibid., 223.
85. Ibid., 215.
86. Ibid., 192.
87. Ibid., 193.
88. Ibid., 189. Other similar formulations are to be found, for example, in Plekhanov's discussion of Ricardo and Bastiat (194), of Brunetiere (208 and 213), of the French utopians (209), and of the English Revolution and the Enlightenment (211).
89. Plekhanov, *Selected Philosophical Works*, Vol. I, 476–77. See also the commentary on Plekhanov's notion of freedom and necessity in Colletti, "Bernstein and the Marxism of the Second International," 68–72.
90. Plekhanov, *In Defence of Materialism*, 128–30.
91. Baron, *Plekhanov, the Father of Russian Marxism*, 116.
92. The only exception, the partial alliance between Plekhanov and Lenin after the 1905 revolution, proves the point. As the revolutionary wave subsided into a period of reaction and as the influence of neo-Kantian ideas grew in the Russian Social Democratic and Labor Party (see chap. 4), Lenin and Plekhanov found common cause in defending general marxist principles against the new idealism.
93. Ibid., 224.
94. See T. Cliff, *Rosa Luxemburg* (1959; Bookmarks edition, London, 1983), 19–24. Also see P. Frolich, *Rosa Luxemburg* (London: Pluto Press, 1972); and P. Nettl, *Rosa Luxemburg* (Oxford, 1969).
95. L. Basso, "Rosa Luxemburg: The Dialectical Method," *International Socialist Journal* (November 1966), 520. I largely follow the argument of Basso's study in this discussion of Luxemburg, although Basso's own politics were closer to

those of the "Marxist centre" against whom Luxemburg fought than they were
to those of the classical marxist tradition.

96. Kolakowski, *Main Current's of Marxism*, 46.
97. Ibid., 46–47.
98. R. Luxemburg, *Social Reform or Revolution*, in M. A. Waters, *Rosa Luxemburg Speaks* (New York: Pathfinder, 1970), 61–62.
99. Ibid., 55–56.
100. Ibid., 56.
101. Ibid.
102. Ibid., 61.
103. R. Luxemburg, quoted in L. Basso, "Rosa Luxemburg," 517.
104. See R. Abraham, *Rosa Luxemburg* (Oxford: Berg Publishers, 1989), 90.
105. R. Luxemburg, *The Mass Strike, the Political Party and the Trade Unions*, in M. A. Waters, *Rosa Luxemburg Speaks*, 170.
106. Ibid., 171.
107. Luxemburg, *Social Reform of Revolution*, 79.
108. Ibid., 59.
109. Ibid., 86.
110. R. Luxemburg, *The Crisis in Social Democracy*, in *Rosa Luxemburg Speaks*, 269. This translation uses the word "righteousness" where I, following Basso's usage in "Rosa Luxemburg" cited above, and for the sake of clarity, have substituted the word "maturity."
111. Basso, "Rosa Luxemburg," 523.
112. Luxemburg, *The Crisis of Social Democracy*, 324–25.
113. Ibid., 269.
114. Frolich, *Rosa Luxemburg*, 140.
115. Quoted in N. Geras, *The Legacy of Rosa Luxemburg* (London: Verso, 1976), 16–17.
116. For a full explanation of Luxemburg's position and an account of its strengths and weaknesses, see Cliff, *Rosa Luxemburg*, 70–86. However, it is worth noting the oddity that so dialectical a thinker should locate the key fault line in the system as running between the system and its periphery rather than within the system itself.
117. Luxemburg, quoted in L. Basso, "Rosa Luxemburg," 522.
118. Geras, *Legacy of Rosa Luxemburg*, 31. Geras provides a valuable account of the relationship between Luxemburg's theory of accumulation and her notion that the development of capitalism poses a choice of socialism or barbarism. It is marred only by his apparent belief that he is the first to do so whereas the connection is made explicitly by Basso, "Rosa Luxemburg," and forms the backdrop for Cliff's defense of Luxemburg. And Geras, like Basso, failed to match his subject's ability to unite theory and practice—he came to back Western imperialism in the 1991 Gulf war, for instance.
119. Luxemburg, quoted in L Basso, "Rosa Luxemburg," 525.

4

Lenin and Philosophy

One of the most powerful and enduring images of Lenin portrays him as a cunning, practical organizer with little interest in political theory other than as a justification for whatever action he found expedient at the given moment.[1] Yet this account is difficult to reconcile with the facts. It was, after all, Lenin who made one of the most detailed assessments of the prospects for Russian capitalism, *The Development of Capitalism in Russia*, at the very beginning of his political career. And it was the same Lenin who, faced with an unprecedented world war, made notes running over some eight hundred printed pages before finishing his own study of imperialism. Similar research accompanied his path-breaking analysis of the marxist theory of the state in *State and Revolution*.

The same enormous intellectual effort went into Lenin's philosophical studies, although Lenin himself was modest about his abilities as a philosopher. But he had, though many commentaries still overlook the fact, read Kant, Hegel, Fichte, and the Hegelian marxist Antonio Labriola by the time of his Siberian exile in the 1890s.[2] He was in fact deeply committed to the idea that political practice must be rooted in close study of social, economic, and philosophical facts and theories. As he famously put it, "Without revolutionary theory there can be no revolutionary practice."

Lenin made two major philosophical statements. *Materialism and Empiriocriticism* was written in 1908 as part of a factional struggle in the Bolshevik party while the *Philosophical Notebooks*, written in 1914 but unpublished while Lenin was alive, mark his reaction to the outbreak of the First World War and the collapse of the Second International. *Materialism and Empiriocriticism* was an important defense of marxism in the face of an obscure idealist retreat connected, both philosophically and politically, to the impasse that tsarist society had reached and to the defeat of the 1905 revolution.

But *Materialism and Empirio-criticism* is a flawed work, as Lenin implicitly recognizes in his *Philosophical Notebooks*. In 1908, the broader philosophical tradition from within which Lenin wrote was still that of the Second International. By 1914 the International had collapsed in the face of prowar national chauvinism. Lenin embarked on a root-and-branch criticism of Second International marxism, including its philosophical framework. The frag-

170

mentary record of this massive reappraisal is preserved in the *Philosophical Notebooks*, which provide a far more effective account of the dialectic than that found in *Materialism and Empirio-criticism*.

It would, however, be a mistake simply to leave the issue with this stark opposition between the Lenin of 1914 and the Lenin of the earlier period. There was a real break in Lenin's understanding of the marxist method in 1914, which is examined below, but his new approach was not as complete a departure from the past as some writers have assumed. As Paul Le Blanc notes, "Some have seen almost an 'epistemological break' in 1914 that divides Lenin's thought more fundamentally than he himself would have accepted."[3]

The truth is more complex. Lenin's philosophical formation did not begin with *Materialism and Empirio-criticism*. Indeed, the concentration on his highly polemical formulations in this work obscures the elements of continuity between Lenin's earlier comments on the dialectic and the ideas that he developed in 1914.

EARLY FORMULATIONS

If we are to be accurate about Lenin's philosophical ideas before 1914 we have to understand that they were formed much more by Plekhanov than by Kautsky, by the best method that Second International marxism had to offer, not the worst. Thus, Lenin never shared the crude Darwinian distortion of the dialectic developed by Kautsky, nor did he have a dismissive or shallow attitude toward Hegel.

As early as 1894, in his *What the "Friends of the People" Are and How They Fight the Social Democrats*, Lenin spent considerable time arguing against the Narodniks precisely on the question of the dialectic. In answer to the Narodnik writer Mikhailovsky, Lenin argues that marxism is "based, firstly, on the materialist conception of history, and, secondly, on the dialectical method." Mikhailovsky had revived Duhring's criticism of Marx: that Marx relied on Hegelian triads as an abstract framework into which he forced the real pattern of historical development. Lenin replied using arguments drawn from Marx's *Capital*, Engels's *Anti-Duhring*, and Plekhanov.

Lenin concluded that Mikhailovsky "ascribed to Marx the incredible absurdity of having tried to prove the necessity of the doom of capitalism by means of triads." He had ignored "the fact that the dialectical method does not consist in triads at all, but that it consists precisely in the rejection of the methods of idealism and subjectivism in sociology."[4] Even when defending marxism against the charge of Hegelianism, Lenin was careful to make a study of Marx and Engels's position on the dialectic, even if, in this work, he did little to develop it.

Even where Lenin formally repeats the same mistaken arguments that we find in Plekhanov, he sometimes amends them in significant ways. In *The*

Economic Content of Narodism (1895), for instance, Lenin repeats the view that "Freedom is the appreciation of necessity," but he quickly adds, following Engels rather than Plekhanov, "far from assuming fatalism, determinism in fact provides a basis for reasonable action." Lenin argues that marxism's critics "could not understand even such an elementary question as freedom of will," because they "confused determinism with fatalism."[5]

This activist note is the key element that distinguishes Lenin's formulations from those of Plekhanov. Even in passages where Lenin is most closely following the formulations common in Plekhanov, the line of argument will suddenly shift to introduce a quite distinctive element. The following point, for instance, contains a brilliant summary of the dialectic which is utterly at odds with the determinism of the Second International:

> The objectivist speaks of the necessity of a given historical process; the materialist gives an exact picture of the given socio-economic formation and the antagonistic relations to which it gives rise. When demonstrating the necessity for a given series of facts, the objectivist always runs the risk of becoming an apologist for these facts: the materialist discloses the class contradictions and in so doing defines his standpoint. The objectivist speaks of "insurmountable historical tendencies"; the materialist speaks of the class which "directs" the given economic system, giving rise to such and such forms of counteraction by other classes. . . . He does not limit himself to speaking of the necessity of a process, but ascertains *exactly what class* determines that necessity.

Lenin's insistence on saying concretely what class agency is at the heart of any social development necessarily leads to abandoning fatalism in favour of a commitment to action:

> . . . the materialist would not content himself with stating the "insurmountable historical tendencies", but would point to the existence of certain classes which determine the content of the given system and preclude the possibility of any solution except by the action of the producers themselves . . . materialism includes partisanship, so to speak, and enjoins the direct and open adoption of the standpoint of a definite social group in any assessment of events.[6]

This approach speaks volumes for how much Lenin gained theoretically from the practical struggle to build an activist revolutionary party. The concrete and pressing necessity to develop a clear assessment of objective conditions to shape a revolutionary strategy gave Lenin's thought a practical, anti-determinist element from the beginning. It is true this approach was not always consistent at the level of philosophical method until 1914, as it is also true that, for specific reasons, it was still less in evidence in *Materialism and Empirio-criticism*. But this should not blind us to the fact that it was a vital element in Lenin's thought, and decisive for his practice, before 1914. It is also the key to understanding that Lenin was not starting from the beginning when he reread Hegel in 1914.[7]

THE FIGHT FOR MATERIALISM

Lenin was reluctant to make philosophical issues a matter of debate inside the Bolshevik party. As early as 1904, one of Lenin's co-workers in the leadership of the Bolsheviks, A. A. Bogdanov, had published philosophical views with which Lenin disagreed. But Lenin made no public response, although in 1906, when Bogdanov sent him the last of his three volumes on *Empiriomonism*, Lenin did reply with a private letter—"a declaration of love, a little letter on philosophy which took up three notebooks." As late as 1908, Lenin was still insistent that "this philosophical controversy is not a factional one and . . . should not be so." He explained: "In the summer and autumn of 1904, Bogdanov and I reached a complete agreement, as *Bolsheviks*, and formed a tacit bloc, which tacitly ruled out philosophy as a neutral field, that existed all through the revolution and enabled us in that revolution to carry out together the tactics of revolutionary Social Democracy."[8]

Two things changed Lenin's mind. Both of them were connected to the defeat of the 1905 revolution in Russia. First, the defeat of the 1905 revolution, like all such defeats, carried confusion and demoralization into the ranks of the revolutionaries. This resulted in divisions among the Bolsheviks, divisions that grew wider the longer the period of reaction lasted. In the first instance, these were over tactical issues. Bogdanov and his co-thinkers, among them the future Commissar for Education Lunarcharsky and the writer Maxim Gorky, wanted either to boycott the Duma, the tsar's restricted franchise parliament, or to maintain such tight control over the Bolshevik deputies as to amount to the same thing.

Lenin himself had been in favor of boycotting the Duma in 1905 when, at the height of the revolution, the workers' councils had been challenging for power. Now, with the workers' councils crushed, Lenin found his own words quoted against him by Bogdanov. In addition, the boycottists wanted nothing to do with the legal unions which were obliged to register with the police, whereas Lenin urged the Bolsheviks to use every forum, no matter how restricted, to make contact with workers.

Second, it quickly became clear that the split between Lenin and Bogdanov involved much more than tactical issues, however important those issues might be. The dispute also involved key questions about the marxist method. Bogdanov and his adherents were part of a bright young intellectual coterie drawn to Lenin by his audacity in the revolutionary period. They felt Russia's backwardness, both economic and intellectual, very keenly. They followed every new development in Western science and art and were enthusiastic about incorporating these new insights into marxism. The forward rush of the revolution had helped unite the leadership of the Bolsheviks on strategic questions and so such intellectual differences could be left to private disagreement. But when defeat magnified every tactical disagreement, forcing revolutionaries to derive fresh strategies from a re-examination of the fundamentals of marxism, theoretical differences were bound to become more important. As Tony Cliff explains:

> With politics apparently failing to overcome the horrors of the Tsarist regime, escape into the realm of philosophical speculation became the fashion. And in the absence of any contact with a real mass movement, everything had to be proved from scratch—nothing in the traditions of the movement, none of its fundamentals, was immune from constant questioning.[9]

The beginning of this intellectual trend can be traced back to the publication of the influential essay collection *Problems of Idealism* in 1903. But the immediate trigger for open debate was the publication, in 1908, of *Studies in Marxist Philosophy*, a collection of articles by Bogdanov, Lunarcharsky, and their co-thinkers. Lenin's decision to tackle Bogdanov on both the tactical and the philosophical fronts was a surprise even to his own supporters:

> When Ilyich began to quarrel with Bogdanov on the issue of *empiriomonism*, we threw up our hands and decided Lenin had gone slightly out of his mind. The moment was critical. The revolution was subsiding. We were confronted by the need for a radical change in our tactics; yet at that time Ilyich immersed himself in the Bibliotheque Nationale [in Paris], sitting there for whole days, and wrote a philosophical book as a result. The scoffing was endless.[10]

Lenin must have been further alarmed at Bogdanov's plan to hold a school to train Bolshevik cadre at Gorky's home on Capri. "The philosophical orientation of Bogdanov . . . had a profound appeal for the newly radicalised young workers with an intellectual bent and was in harmony with the psychology of a number of militant Bolshevik committeemen"—including Joseph Stalin who, in 1908, praised Bogdanov for indicating "individual blunders of Ilyich" and for being an impressive alternative to "the other part ('orthodox') of our faction, headed by Ilyich."[11]

Lenin replied with *Materialism and Empirio-criticism* and his own school held outside Paris. Bogdanov was eventually expelled from the Bolsheviks in 1909, shortly after the publication of *Materialism and Empirio-criticism*.

These events within the Bolshevik party took place against a much wider canvas. In the early years of the century the Russian intelligensia, in common with many of their class across Europe, "showed a marked tendency to abandon positivism, scientism and materialism, which had for so long been the dominant modes of thought."[12] Philosophical fashion took a subjectivist, personal, and sometimes religious turn. Among the Western philosophers appearing in Russian translation were Windelband, Nietzsche, Bergson, Husserl, and Max Stirner, "the prophet of egocentric anarchism." The mood spread well beyond the confines of those interested in philosophy:

> In poetry symbolism and "decadence" flourished. . . . Interest in religion, mysticism, oriental cults, and occultism was almost universal. . . . Pessimism, Satanism, apocalyptic prophecies, the search for mystic and metaphysical depths, love of the fantastic, eroticism, psychology and self-analysis—all these merged into a single modernistic culture.[13]

This air of intellectual crisis was, in Europe, ultimately a product of the atmosphere of impending doom that attended the years before the First World War. In Russia, the crisis was all the greater because of the impasse that tsarism had reached. It was heightened by the defeat of the 1905 revolution: "The disillusionment following the defeat of the 1905 revolution did much to strengthen this mood and bring it to bear in sectors that had heretofore not felt the force of it."[14]

So the ideas with which Bogdanov was trying to marry marxism had been circulating in the intellectual chaos that had engulfed the European radical intelligentsia since at least the turn of the century, although they probably reached their peak with the publication of the *Landmarks* collection of articles in 1909. These essays denounced the militant materialism of Plekhanov and his intellectual forerunners. Populists and marxists, it was said, ignored spiritual and ethical issues. The Russian intelligensia should abandon its "irreverent, anti-governmental" attitudes and its repudiation of "the idea of individual responsibility," argued Peter Struve, the man who, a mere eleven years earlier, had composed the manifesto of the first congress of the Russian Social Democratic and Labour Party.[15]

One corner of this intellectual panorama was occupied by a rebirth of interest in the views of Immanuel Kant, following the centenary of his death in 1904. The neo-Kantian movement was the philosophical background to the debate between Lenin and Bogdanov. But the factor that gave neo-Kantian ideas particular force was the way in which they interacted with the revolution that was taking place in the physical sciences.

This revolution also reached its peak in 1905 when Einstein presented three papers to the *Annals of Physics*. One described the particle theory of light, laying the basis for quantum theory. The other two papers were on relativity. Einstein's discoveries destroyed the conventional wisdom, based on Newton's laws of physics, that nature was composed of discrete stable pieces of matter. Now the world proved to be made up of infinitesimally small, sub-atomic particles. Time and space were proved to be relative, not absolute, concepts.

Looking back, it is easier for us than it was for contemporaries to see that this was a revolution in how we understand physical reality, not a theory that contended that physical reality no longer existed. But some physicists at the time, including some of those most closely associated with the new discoveries, did not make this distinction very clearly. Shocked that Einstein had *reinterpreted* the world in a radically new way, they drew the conclusion that *all* we know about the world is our sensations and conceptions. And this is the point where the revolution in science seemed to give powerful evidence in favor of a neo-Kantian epistemology with its emphasis on the unbridgeable gap between our sense perceptions and the real world.

In both physics and philosophy, it seemed that proof of the objective existence of the world was missing—the only knowable reality was our mental concepts about the world. Correspondence between thought and reality was no longer necessarily possible, let alone guaranteed. And so a scientific advance, which should have helped to undercut the growing mood of irrationalism among sections of the Russian intelligentsia, was dragooned into bolstering idealism.

Bogdanov drew inspiration from the theories of physicist Ernst Mach and philosopher Richard Avenarius. Mach, to whom Einstein had acknowledged his debt, had been a participant in the debates that dramatically reshaped physics in the first decade of the century. Initially influenced by Kant, he went on to contend that any idea of a "thing-in-itself" was "superfluous," thus retreating from Kant's ambiguous idealism to the pure idealism of Berkeley and Hume whom he thought "far more consistent thinkers than Kant."[16] Mach thought that,

> Science was an attempt to organise sensations in the most concise possible way . . . not to discover the truth about the world. . . .
> Mach's unifying concept was experience rather than matter. Experience in and through sensations was the only meaningful epistemological category, excluding any notion of source, cause or reference. Physical objects were only relatively constant groupings of sensations.[17]

Mach tried to avoid the charge of idealism by insisting that he was not treating material objects as if they were mental states, merely declaring questions of the relationship between mind and matter as irrelevant, because we cannot distinguish one sort of sensation, those induced in us by so-called matter, from those induced in us by the processes of thought:

> Thus I see no antithesis of the physical and the psychical, but I see a simple identity relative to these elements. In the sensual realm of my consciousness every object is both physical and psychical at the same time.[18]

The Zurich philosopher Richard Avenarius was engaged in a similar quest to overcome the contradictions of Kant's dichotomy between the world of thought and the material world, the thing-in-itself:

Above all he sought to refute the . . . distinction between "mental impressions" and inaccessible "things in themselves." . . . Once we shake off the illusion that we have an "inner consciousness" in which "external objects" are mysteriously present—objects which exist independently of the fact that they are "given", but which we cannot know in any other way— we are freed from all the traditional questions and categories of philosophy, the disputes between realism and spiritualism, and the insoluble problems inherent in the notions of substance, force and causality.[19]

Or, as Lenin put it, "Averarius . . . falls back on the time-worn argument of subjective idealism, that thought and reality are inseparable, because reality can only be conceived in thought."[20]

The act of understanding, in this schema, becomes simply a biological reflex. Advances in thought are simply more efficient methods by which the brain orders the stream of impulses that it receives from the senses. The aim of thought is not to know the truth about the world, but to economize on the effort needed to process the information received by the senses—"the whole purpose of scientific knowledge is reduced to biological utility."[21] Avenarius, like Mach, wanted to avoid charges of idealism by simply ruling them inadmissable to his conceptual framework, but "although it was Avenarius's object to free philosophy from the dualism of 'mind' and 'matter' by reducing all Being to experience in which the self and the object are present on equal terms, he was unable to avoid drawing conclusions that brought him under suspicion of "subjectivism" or inconsistency."[22]

The most striking thing about Mach and Avenarius's thought is precisely this idealism. By abolishing the "thing-in-itself" in the name of undifferentiated experience, they had cut the tethers that held Kant's philosophy to a relationship with the real world.

But any philosophy that does not properly account for the relationship between the material world and the process of thought ends up reproducing the problems of idealism and vulgar materialism in an unacknowledged, unintegrated, and contradictory manner. Avenarius and Mach, for instance, produced a theory whose dominant motif was a thoroughgoing idealism but that also contained vulgar materialism, such as the reduction of the act of cognition to a biological reflex.

Bogdanov's philosophy was almost entirely derivative of Mach and Avenarius's ideas. Like them, he believed nature is not an independently existing reality but merely a "collectively organised experience."[23] For Bogdanov, "the question of the conformity of experience to anything outside itself was meaningless, as experience encompassed all there was, there being nothing outside it."[24] He could, therefore, rewrite Marx's famous dictum so that it read: "*social being and social consciousness are, in the exact meaning of these terms, identical.*"[25]

The difference between subjectivity and objectivity, in Bogdanov's view, was that the former is the perception held by an individual whereas the latter is a perception held in common by a whole society. A pseudo-marxist twist was given to this theory by claiming that any contradictions in society's understanding of the world were a result of class divisions and that these would disappear under socialism. Bogdanov also concurred with Mach and Avenarius's biological reductionism—knowledge became simply an instrument whose purpose was to assist technical progress in the most efficient manner, a kind of "Taylorism of the mind" that left no room for any conception of truth which was based on the conformity of our judgments with an independent reality.

Bogdanov seems to have thought that this cocktail of ideas was the epitome of marxism because it stressed that the labor saving drive for "efficient" concepts was the motor of progress and that human creativity is the crucial element in organizing our experience to make the most efficient use of the data supplied by our senses. This last point connected Bogdanov's philosophical views with his attitude toward building the Bolshevik party:

> Bogdanov . . . and the other Russian empiriocritics believed their "activist" epistemology was well attuned to the spirit of Bolshevism and to its general idea that the revolution would not break out of itself when economic conditions were ripe, but that it depended on the will-power of a group of organisers. Bogdanov, to whom "organisation" was an obsession, used the term with equal freedom in regard to party matters and principles of epistemology.[26]

This combination of idealism, crude materialism, and abstract ultra-leftism stayed with Bogdanov all his life—after the October revolution, he became an advocate of both Proletkult and "proletarian science."

In *Materialism and Empirio-criticism*, Lenin exposes the mistaken philosophical conclusions that Mach, Avenarius, and Bogdanov drew from the revolution in science. It is the great strength of *Materialism and Empirio-criticism* that it was clearly able to disentangle the new physics from the philosophical misuse to which it was being put, even by some of the scientists most closely associated with it. In his discussion of the "Recent Revolution in Natural Science," Lenin insists that the new science has "served the philosophers as an excuse to desert materialism for idealism." In an atmosphere of rapidly changing conceptions of the world, where "one hypothesis yields place to another,"

> Nothing whatever is known of the positive electron; only three months ago (June 22, 1908) Jean Becquerel reported to the French Academy of Science that he had succeeded in discovering this "new component part of matter." How could idealist philosophy refrain from taking advantage of such an opportunity, when "matter" was still being "sought" by the human mind and was therefore no more than a "symbol," etc.[27]

The new science, Lenin argues, is "proclaimed a collaborator of idealism," because it has:

> Destroyed the old theory of the structure of matter, shattered the atom and discovered new forms of material motion, so unlike the old, so totally uninvestigated and unstudied, so unusual and "miraculous," that it permits nature to be presented as *non-material* (spiritual, mental, psychical) motion. Yesterday's limit to our knowledge of the infinitesimal particles of matter has disappeared, hence—concludes the idealist philosopher—matter has disappeared (but thought remains).[28]

Again, we can see how the revolution in science could feed the idealist revival in philosophy—even the president of the British Association was complaining, "the question at issue is whether the hypotheses which are at the base of the scientific theories now most generally accepted, are to be regarded as accurate descriptions of the constitution of the universe around us, or merely convenient fictions."[29] And French physicist Louis Houllevique declared, "The atom dematerialises, matter disappears."[30]

Lenin insisted on distinguishing the philosophical *category* of matter from particular *theories* about the structure of matter. *Materialism and Empirio-criticism* simultaneously welcomes the revolution in science while rejecting the idealist theory of knowledge, the epistemology, being built on these foundations:

> *Not a single one* of these professors, who are capable of making very valuable contributions in the special fields of chemistry, history, or physics, *can be trusted one iota* when it comes to philosophy. Why? For the same reason that *not a single* professor of political economy, who may be capable of very valuable contributions in the field of factual and specialised investigations, can be trusted *one iota* when it comes to the general theory of political economy. For in modern society the latter is as much a *partisan* science as is *epistemology*.[31]

Against Mach and Bogdanov and in his evaluation of the revolution in physics, Lenin was right. It was indeed Mach and Bogdanov's "ignorance of dialectics" that allowed them to "slip into idealism." Lenin was right to highlight the link between Bogdanov's adoption of idealism and his failure to react correctly to the downturn in the level of the struggle in Russia. And it has certainly proved to be the case that "the physical idealism" in vogue when Lenin wrote was, as he argued, a "transitory infatuation," adhered to by only "a minority of the new physicists . . . influenced by the breakdown of old theories . . . [and] the crisis in the new physics."[32]

Lenin's achievement was to call a halt to the idealist trend that Bogdanov represented by simply insisting time and again:

> The existence of matter does not depend on sensation. Matter is primary. Sensation, thought, consciousness are the supreme product of matter organised

in a particular way. Such are the views of materialism in general, and of Marx and Engels in particular.[33]

And Lenin was not slow to exploit the contradiction between Bogdanov's idealist framework and the undigested materialism that he attempted to introduce into it:

Since you base yourself *only* on sensations you do not correct the "one-sidedness" of your idealism by the term "element," but only confuse the issue and cravenly hide from your own theory.... For, if elements are sensations, you have no right even for a moment to accept the existence of "elements" *independently* of my nerves and my mind. But if you do admit physical objects that are independent of my nerves and my sensations and that cause sensations only by acting upon my retina—you are disgracefully abandoning your "one-sided" idealism and adopting the standpoint of "one-sided" materialism![34]

When Lenin moved beyond this defense of materialism to give a positive account of marxist philosophy, his theory became much less dialectical than his treatment of the relationship between the new physics and the philosophical ideas of his opponents. One root of this weakness was that Lenin, too, suffered from the defeat of the revolutionary wave and the decline in the level of class struggle. As Tony Cliff notes,

Lenin's own work, *Materialism and Empirio-criticism,* however, also suffered from the lack of real contact with a live movement. (One need only compare it with the magnificent, dialectically terse, and lively *Philosophical Notebooks,* Vol. 38 of Lenin's *Collected Works.*) It is significant that he never repeated its arguments in later pamphlets and articles, as he always did with other his writings. No special articles in the press elaborated the theses of this book. Nor is it referred to in any of Lenin's writings, including his vast correspondence, after 1909.[35]

This circumstantial source of weakness combined with another factor: the impact of the intellectual tradition in which Lenin worked. This was the world of Second International marxism. Lenin was still half a dozen years away from his final break from the Second International in 1914, and although, in practice, the Bolshevik party was being forged on a revolutionary basis quite different to the reformism of the Second International as a whole it was by no means clear that this would eventually lead to a complete re-evaluation of the traditions of the International in every aspect—from tactics to philosophy. It was still quite possible to place oneself on the far left of the International on questions of tactics, organization, and political theory without necessarily rejecting the overall account of the marxist method given by Second International theorists such as Kautsky and Plekhanov.

Such ambiguity marked the thought of all the great marxists of the period.

Rosa Luxemburg fought the leaders of the International over the issues of reform or revolution and the mass strike, but she never re-examined the question of the revolutionary party. Trotsky's theory of permanent revolution was a decisive break with the mechanistic stages theory of the Second International, yet he remained a member of the International and continued to share its vision of party organization. The peculiarities of Russian society helped Lenin to come to the conclusion that a vanguard party was necessary, but he did not generalize the Bolshevik experience until after the outbreak of the First World War.

In none of these cases was the break with the Second International total, either practically or theoretically, and so it is not surprising that the most abstract levels of marxism, questions of the marxist method, remained substantially untouched by these upheavals. Indeed, it was only after 1914, when the full extent of the degeneration in the International was completely exposed, that root and branch criticism became unavoidable.

Thus Lenin's account of marxism in *Materialism and Empirio-criticism*, although often more subtle and flexible than those of Kautsky, nevertheless still bore the mark of Second International marxism. Indeed, Plekhanov was Lenin's ally in the debate with the Machists. The point at which this weakness manifested itself most strongly is in the 'copy theory of knowledge' which Lenin defends in *Materialism and Empirio-criticism*. Lenin insists that the theoretical vision in our heads is a simple copy of the real world. For instance, he explains the difference between Newtonian mechanics and the new physics in these terms:

> ... it is ... beyond question that mechanics was a copy of real motions of moderate velocity, while the new physics is a copy of real motions of enormous velocity. The recognition of theory as a copy, as an approximate copy of objective reality, is materialism.[36]

Time after time Lenin repeats that knowledge is a simple reflection of material reality:

> Our sensation, our consciousness is only *an image* of the external world, and it is obvious that an image cannot exist independently of that which images it. Materialism *deliberately* makes the "naive" belief of mankind the foundation of its theory of knowledge.[37]

Our thoughts are, Lenin bluntly insists, "copies, photographs, images, mirror-reflections of things."[38] It is this identification of marxism with a crude materialist theory of cognition that allows Lenin to rely, albeit for polemical purposes, on the bourgeois materialists of the eighteenth century for authority in his battle with the Machists. But, revolutionary as the eighteenth-century materialists might have been in their day, it should be clear that after Hegel, let alone Marx, their conception of materialism was one-sided.

Lenin's reliance on the methodological framework current in the Second International prevents him from making this point. Consequently, Lenin's formulations border on the belief that knowledge of the world is achieved simply by the metal reproduction of its immediate appearance.

This was not Marx's view. Indeed, he asserted that it was "the philistine's and vulgar economist's *way of looking at things*" that "stems from, namely, from the fact that it is only the direct *form of manifestation* of relations that is reflected in their brains and not their *inner connection*."[39]

When Marx argues that science is necessary because the appearance of society is different to its underlying structure, he is pointing to the fact that a conceptual effort is necessary to uncover the real causes of change that lie beneath the surface. In the introduction to the *Grundrisse*, Marx explains some of what this method involves:

> When we consider a given country politico-economically . . . it seems correct to begin with the real and the concrete, with the real precondition, thus to begin, in economics, with e.g. the population, which is the foundation and the subject of the entire social act of production. However, on closer examination this proves false. The population is an abstraction if I leave out, for example, the classes of which it is composed. These classes in turn are an empty phrase if I am not familiar with the elements on which they rest. e.g. wage labour, capital etc. These latter in turn presuppose exchange, division of labour, prices, etc. For example, capital is nothing without wage labour, without value, money, price etc. Thus, if I were to begin with the population, this would be a chaotic conception of the whole, and I would then, by means of further determination, move analytically towards ever simpler concepts, from the imagined concrete towards ever thinner abstractions until I had arrived at the simplest determinations. From there the journey would have to be retraced until I had finally arrived at the population again, but this time not as the chaotic conception of the whole, but as a rich totality of many determinations and relations.[40]

This process is doubly necessary under capitalism, both in scientific thought and the struggle for political consciousness, because the workings of the market tend to disguise the real nature of the class relations that lie at its heart. It is, therefore, inconceivable that Marx could have endorsed a crude copy theory of knowledge. Such a theory would simply reproduce the surface appearance of society—a chaotic conception of the whole—and would therefore fail to reveal the underlying structure. This underlying structure is not to be counterposed to the surface appearance: uncovering the real structure of society reveals why society appears to us as it does; it explains why appearance and essence are necessarily different but at the same time why the later gives rise to the former.

Yet Lenin's copy theory of knowledge has its defenders. David Hillel

Ruben's *Marxism and Materialism* is one of the few works to mount a defense of *Materialism and Empirio-criticism* on this issue.[41] But the manner in which Ruben conducts his defense turns out to concede all the criticisms commonly leveled at this theory.

Ruben's account turns on distinguishing between a *correspondence theory of knowledge* and a *reflection theory of perception*. The first is simply the broad assertion that our ideas are capable of reproducing in thought the real structure of the world. But the second argues that this process is a more or less direct product of sense perception:

> To say that a theory reflects or portrays real structures is to make a claim about reflective beliefs or concepts. It is to make a claim about the correspondence between theories, beliefs, statements, on the one hand, and reality on the other. It is to imply nothing whatever about perceptual correspondence. Indeed, in so far as the theoretical entities referred to by such beliefs or statements are unobservable, there are no corresponding perceptions or sensations for them. Theories about subatomic particles, force fields, abstract labour, or social relations of production, are true when what they say is so . . . [but] there are no . . . direct sensations, images, or impressions of these things at all.[42]

In a correspondence theory of knowledge, some version of which is essential to any materialism, there is room for a specific interpretive effort, a theoretical element, to intervene between perception and consciousness. In a reflection theory, however, consciousness is reduced to perception.

Ruben admits that a reflection theory is inadequate. But he also admits that *Materialism and Empirio-criticism* elides the two theories. Indeed, Ruben argues that the "main weakness" of the book is "the conflation by Lenin of a correspondence theory of *knowledge* and correspondence theory of *perception*"[43] and that "there is no doubt that Lenin does hold a reflection theory of perception."[44] This then is a defense that admits the main charge. And because a dialectical approach handles the relationship between theory and reality in a manner which neither requires that we abandon the correspondence of the two, nor reduces the former to the latter, it has an inherent claim to superiority over more mechanical approaches. Lenin himself realized the inadequacy of his approach and made a return to Marx's method on this issue in 1914.

To rediscover this method, Lenin would have to retrace Marx's critique of Hegel. The outbreak of the First World War and the collapse of the Second International were the occasion for Lenin's fundamental re-examination of the origins of marxism.

THE FIGHT FOR A DIALECTICAL METHOD

The outbreak of the First World War did not surprise Lenin, but the collapse of the Second International came as a complete shock. So much so that Lenin thought the copy of *Vorwarts*, the German Social Democratic Party's paper, which announced that SPD parliamentary deputies had voted for the kaiser's war credits, must be a forgery. The shock discovery that the International was rotten to its core required not just the development of a consistent, internationalist anti-war policy, not just the proclamation of the need for a new International, but also a review of the fundamental tenets of the marxism on which the Second International had supposedly been based.

Nadezhda Krupskaya, Lenin's wife and lifelong political collaborator, recalled Lenin's response to this crisis:

> While developing a passionate struggle against the betrayal of the cause by the Second International, Ilyich at the same time began, immediately upon his arrival in Berne, preparing an essay on "Karl Marx" for *Granat's Encyclopedic Dictionary*. In this essay he begins by explaining his exposition of the teachings of Marx with an explanation of his philosophy, dividing it into two parts: "Philosophic Materialism" and "Dialectics."

This was, as Krupskaya notes, a sharp departure from the normal approach:

> This was not the usual way of presenting Marx's teachings. Before writing the chapters on philosophic materialism and dialectics Ilyich again diligently reread Hegel and other philosophers and continued these studies even after he had finished the essay. The aim of his work in the realm of philosophy was to master the method of transforming philosophy into a concrete guide to action.[45]

Lenin's essay on Marx was written between July and November 1914. But, as Krupskaya tells, his study of Hegel continued after the draft was sent to the *Granat's Encyclopedia*. Lenin's thoughts on the dialectic were clearly still developing. He read the sections of Hegel's *Logic* that deal with "Subjectivity" and the "Doctrine of the Notion" in the first half of December 1914. On 4 January 1915, he wrote to the *Encyclopedia's* publishers:

> By the way, will there not still be time for certain corrections in the section of dialectics. . . . I have been studying this question of dialectics for the last month and a half and I think I could add something to it if there were time.[46]

So what had Lenin discovered in his rereading of Hegel that forced him to recast his understanding of the dialectic? First, he found a philosophy very different and very much more important than the mechanical materialism of the Second International had led him to believe. In his notes on the very sections of the *Logic* which he had been reading just before he wrote to the publishers of the *Encyclopedia*, Lenin offers "two aphorisms concerning the question of the criticism of modern Kantianism, Machism, etc." These are:

1. Plekhanov criticises Kantianism (and agnosticism in general) more from a vulgar-materialist standpoint than from a dialectical-materialist standpoint, *insofar as* he merely *rejects* their views *a limine* [from the threshold], but does not *correct* them (as Hegel corrects Kant), deepening, generalising and extending them, showing the *connection* and *transitions* of each and every concept.

2. Marxists criticised (at the beginning of the 20th century) the Kantians and Humists more in the manner of Feuerbach (and Buchner) than of Hegel.[47]

This was more than criticism of Second International marxism, it was self-criticism. Lenin had been closely allied with Plekhanov in the battle against "Machism and modern Kantianism" and he, like Plekhanov, had advocated a marxist epistemology which had more in common with Feuerbach's materialism than Hegel's dialectics. A third aphorism pushes the point home:

It is impossible completely to understand Marx's *Capital*, and especially its first chapter, without having thoroughly studied and understood the *whole* of Hegel's *Logic*. Consequently, half a century later none of the Marxists understood Marx!![48]

Lenin continually returns to the fact that Plekhanov ignored Hegel's most important writings, especially in relation to his theory of knowledge:

Dialectics *is* the theory of knowledge of (Hegel and) Marxism. This is the "aspect" of the matter (it is not "an aspect" but the *essence* of the matter) to which Plekhanov, not to speak of other Marxists, paid no attention.[49]

And again, next to the instruction "to be elaborated," Lenin wrote:

Plekhanov wrote on philosophy (dialectics) probably about 1,000 pages (Beltov + against Bogdanov + against Kantianism + fundamental questions, etc., etc.). Among them, *about* the large *Logic, in connection with* it, *its* thought (i.e., dialectics *proper*, as a philosophical science) nil!![50]

In fact, Lenin was so struck by the force of Hegel's system that he concluded, "intelligent idealism is closer to intelligent materialism than stupid materialism," adding, to make the point clearer, "dialectical materialism instead of intelligent; metaphysical, undeveloped, dead, crude, rigid instead of stupid."[51] But there is much more in Lenin's reconsideration of Hegel than a break with his past. In these fragmentary notes, Lenin formulates some of the most precise definitions of key concepts in marxist philosophy available anywhere. The dialectic itself, for instance, has never been better explained:

The splitting of a single whole and the cognition of its contradictory parts . . . is the *essence* (one of the "essentials," one of the principal, if not the principal, characteristics or features) of dialectics. That is precisely how Hegel, too, puts the matter.[52]

Lenin notes that "this aspect of dialectics (e.g., Plekhanov) usually receives inadequate attention: the identity of opposites is taken as the sum-total of *examples*." Lenin's worry is that previous explanations of dialectics have simply shown that reality forms a totality and that things which are assumed to be opposites are in reality connected with one another. But they have not stressed that reality is a *contradictory totality* or that it is the mutually antagonistic relationship between the parts of the totality which are the motor force of its change and development. When Lenin defined his view of the dialectic in three points, he emphasized, besides totality and the unity of analysis and synthesis, "the contradictory nature of the thing itself (the other of itself), the contradictory forces and tendencies in each phenomena."[53]

A contemporary example of an *un*contradictory totality might be the view of the world held by some ecologists who stress the interconnectedness of human beings and nature, science and reality, etc., but have no notion of *contradiction* and therefore no notion of internally developed change. The desire for change is, therefore, merely a pious wish or a moral command introduced from the outside but having no organic connection with the totality of relationships previously described. The totality, therefore, remains a dead totality. Lenin clearly saw that Second International marxism had developed a similarly false conception of the totality that eradicated the concept of internal contradiction. For Lenin the key was,

> the recognition (discovery) of the contradictory, *mutually exclusive*, opposite tendencies in *all* phenomena and processes of nature (*including* mind and society). . . . Development is the "struggle" of opposites.[54]

Indeed, when Lenin asked himself, "What distinguished the dialectical transition from the undialectical transition?" he answered, "The leap. The contradiction. The interruption of gradualness."[55] On this basis, Lenin argues that "the two basic conceptions of development" are 1) change as gradual increase or decrease, or repetition or, 2) change as the result of struggle between opposites. The first leaves the ultimate cause of change hidden or else attributes it to something external to the system, like God. The second, dialectical solution to the problem of change points to internal contradiction and, therefore, to "self-movement":

> The first conception is lifeless, pale and dry. The second is living. The second *alone* furnishes the key to the "self-movement" of everything existing; it alone furnishes the key to the "leaps," to the "break in continuity," to the "transformation into the opposite," to the destruction of the old and the emergence of the new.[56]

Here perhaps we can catch a glimmer of the political concerns that motivated Lenin's reworking of his marxist method; here he had found a method
that could cope with the sudden transformation of the Second International
into its opposite, the unexpected "leap" in the course of historical development and the "destruction of the old and the emergence of the new."

Having rediscovered the essence of dialectics, Lenin went on to refurbish
some of the key terms of the marxist method. The distinction between the
day-to-day appearance of reality and its underlying structure, between appearance and essence, now took on a new importance for Lenin. In *Materialism and Empirio-criticism* Lenin's copy theory of consciousness had militated
against any great stress on this issue because, if consciousness is simply the
mirror-image of reality, reality must be assumed to be easily and immediately accessible in its surface appearance. Marx, as we have seen, gave this
issue more prominence. Lenin now followed suit.

The important thing about a marxist understanding of the distinction between the appearance of things and their essence is twofold: 1) by delving
beneath the mass of surface phenomena, it is possible to see the essential
relations governing historical change—thus beneath the appearance of a free
and fair market transaction it is possible to see the exploitative relations of
class society, but, 2) this does not mean that surface appearances can simply
be dismissed as ephemeral events of no consequence. In revealing the essential relations in society, it is also possible to explain more fully than before
why they appear in a form different to their real nature. To explain, for
instance, why it is that the exploitative class relations at the point of production appear as the exchange of "a fair day's work for a fair day's pay" in
the polished surface of the labor market.

In making the distinction between appearance and essence but at the same
time insisting on their connection, by insisting on the importance of finding
the underlying structure of events but at the same time not pretending that
their day-to-day appearance is somehow unreal or irrelevant, Lenin was
rediscovering an essential part both of Marx's method and of his description
of capitalist society. Lenin summarizes the situation with a characteristically
apt metaphor:

> the unessential, seeming, superficial, vanishes more often, does not hold so
> "tightly," does not "sit so firmly" as "Essence." [Approximately:] the move-
> ment of a river—the foam above and the deep currents below. *But even the
> foam is an expression of essence.*[57]

On the basis of this understanding Lenin taxes his old enemies, the Machists
among others, with a new criticism which found no place in *Materialism and
Empirio-criticism*:

The more petty philosophers dispute whether essence *or* that which is immediately given should be taken as basis (Kant, Hume, all the Machists). Instead of *or*, Hegel puts *and*, explaining the concrete content of this "and."[58]

Lenin argues that Hegel does not see the appearance or semblance of things as mere mist to be blown away by understanding the "true" reality. There is a deeper reality, but it must be able to account for the contradiction between it and the way it appears: "Hegel is for the 'objective validity' . . . of Semblance, 'of that which is immediately given.'"[59] This approach to the question of essence and appearance becomes central to Lenin's new conception of the relationship between thought and reality. Whereas *Materialism and Empirio-criticism* held them in rigid opposition, the one the mirror of the other, the notebooks on Hegel develop a more sophisticated understanding. Lenin's first breakthrough is to apply his understanding of the reality of appearance to the question of consciousness. Commenting on a passage of Hegel's, Lenin writes:

Is not the thought here that semblance is also objective, for it contains *one of the aspects* of the *objective* world? Not only *Wesen* [essence], but *Schein* [appearance], too, is objective. There is a difference between the subjective and objective, BUT IT, TOO, HAS ITS LIMITS.[60]

The idea that consciousness and reality were not the simple polarities described in *Materialism and Empiro-criticism*, that there was objective unity as well as difference here, was obviously a blinding discovery for Lenin, as his bold-type capital letters testify. Later Lenin spells out his new understanding:

Logical concepts are subjective so long as they remain "abstract," in their abstract form, but at the same time they express the things-in-themselves. Nature is *both* concrete *and* abstract, *both* phenomena *and* essence, *both* moment *and* relation. Human concepts are subjective in their abstractness, separateness, but objective as a whole, in the process, in the sum-total, in the tendency in the source.[61]

What Lenin is driving at is a point similar to that made by Marx when he argued that ideas become a material force when they seize the masses. Indeed, Lenin himself later wrote, "Ideas become a power when they grip the people," as he observed the process at work in 1917.[62] That is, there comes a point where consciousness ceases to be merely a subjective opinion about the world but enters, through collective practice, into the objective constitution of the world. When he caught the glimmer of a similar idea in Hegel, Lenin remarked:

The thought of the ideal passing into the real is *profound*: very important for history. But also in the personal life of a man it is clear that this contains much truth. Against vulgar materialism. NB. The difference of the ideal from the material is also not unconditional, not *uberschwenglich* [inordinate].[63]

What does this conception of consciousness mean for Lenin's theory of knowledge? It required that Lenin make a considerable, though not complete, break with the ideas contained in *Materialism and Empirio-criticism*. First, let's look at what *did not* change. Lenin, of course, remained a materialist. He continued to insist that material reality existed independently of human thought and, indeed, that the very ability to think was a product of natural development: "Concepts, and the art of operating with concepts are not inborn, but is the result of 2,000 years of the development of natural science and philosophy."[64] Thus, "men's ends are engendered by the objective world and presuppose it,—they find it as something given, present,"[65] consequently, "the dialectic of *things* produces the dialectics of *ideas*, and not vice versa."[66]

It is important not to lose sight of the fact that Lenin never abandoned this commitment to materialism. This is especially the case, because some otherwise valuable analyses of Lenin's *Philosophical Notebooks*, most recently Kevin Anderson's *Lenin, Hegel and Western Marxism*, tend to underestimate this element of continuity in Lenin's thought.[67]

Yet these broad statements of materialism were only the beginning of the problem, not its solution. They could not, for instance, furnish an account of the relationship between the dialectic of ideas and the dialectic of reality, which Lenin obviously no longer conceived in the linear and one-dimensional pattern outlined in *Materialism and Empirio-criticism*. The language of "copies" and "photographs" is entirely absent from the *Philosophical Notebooks*. Lenin still sometimes talks of consciousness reflecting reality in a general sense, but the term is rarely used without substantial qualification:

> The *reflection* of nature in man's thought must be understood not "lifelessly," not "abstractly," *not devoid of movement, **not without contradictions***, but in the eternal *process* of movement, the arising of contradictions and their solution.[68]

Indeed, Lenin insists that, "Man cannot comprehend = reflect = mirror nature *as a whole*, in its completeness, its "immediate totality," he can only *eternally* come closer to this creating abstractions, concepts, laws, a scientific picture of the world, etc., etc." This is impossible partly because gaining knowledge is a infinite process, as Lenin had already noted in *Materialism and Empirio-criticism*.[69] But now Lenin adds that it is also impossible because knowledge requires an active process of abstraction capable of discriminating between essence and appearance. This process is simply not possible using a crude copy theory of consciousness. Lenin himself makes the point:

> Logic is the science of cognition. It is the theory of knowledge. Knowledge is the reflection of nature by man. But this is not a simple, not an immediate, not a complete reflection, but the process of a series of abstractions, the

formation and development of concepts, laws, etc., and these concepts, laws, etc., . . . *embrace* conditionally, approximately, the universal, law governed character of eternally moving and developing nature.[70]

Thus, Lenin develops a more active and independent role for consciousness than the framework of *Materialism and Empirio-criticism* could allow. He even went so far as to exclaim, "Man's consciousness not only reflects the world, but creates it."[71] That sentiment could never have found its way into *Materialism and Empirio-criticism*, if only because Bogdanov would have seized on it as contradicting Lenin's whole line of argument. Such ideas required a dialectical theory of cognition to root them in a marxist framework, and this was precisely what *Materialism and Empirio-criticism* lacked.

But wasn't Lenin purchasing this more independent role for consciousness at the expense of scientific precision? How can we know that our consciousness really corresponds to the world if it is only an "approximate," "conditional," and abstract representation of reality? Lenin's answer has two aspects. First, abstraction can be a method of seeing reality more clearly, as we saw in relation to the question of essence and appearance, and, second, consciousness must issue in practical activity, which will furnish the proof of whether or not our conceptions of the world are accurate.

> Thought proceeding from the concrete to the abstract . . . does not get away from the truth but comes closer to it. The abstraction of *matter*, of a *law* of nature, the abstraction of *value*, etc., in short *all* scientific abstractions reflect nature more deeply, truly and *completely*. From living perception to abstract thought, *and from this to practice*,—such is the dialectical path of the cognition of *truth*, of the cognition of objective reality.[72]

The second leg of this process, the movement to practice, is crucial because what is involved is a fusion of intellectual understanding and objective existence. Human action, in the sense that Marx understood the question in his analysis of human labor, is not simply an extension of thought nor merely an objective occurrence in the external world, like the wind blowing the branch of a tree. It is a *conscious act*. In conscious activity, human beings overcome the abstractness of thought by integrating it with concrete, immediate reality in all its complexity—this is the moment when we see whether thought really does assume an objective form, whether it really can create the world, or whether it has mistaken the nature of reality and therefore is unable to enter the historical chain as an objective force which, in the case of the class struggle, seizes the masses. This is Lenin's meaning when he writes *"practice is higher than (theoretical) knowledge,* for it has not only the dignity of universality, but also of immediate actuality."[73] Or, in a slightly elaborated version of the same point:

The activity of man, who has made an objective picture of the world for himself, **changes** external actuality, abolishes its determinedness (= alters some sides or other, qualities, of it), thus removes from it the features of Semblance, externality and nullity, and makes it as being in and for itself (= objectively true).[74]

We can see here how for Lenin practice overcomes the distinction between subjective and objective and the gap between essence and appearance. The ground for this theoretical discovery had been laid by Lenin's theory of the party, always the most dialectical and the most important element in his marxism. The whole conception of a party that is part of, but for long periods separated from, the majority of the working class demands a dialectic that understands the unity of opposites, the essential nature of practice, and the concrete historical nature of development.[75]

Lenin's remarkable rediscovery of "Hegelian" Marxism gave him the tools with which to reconstruct his method in the light of this party building experience. And it did so at just the point where the failure of the Second International tradition onto which it had previously been grafted had become blindingly obvious. In fact, Lenin's attack on Kautsky's pro-imperialism specifically points to his failure to understand the dialectic:

Kautsky is exploiting the *hope* for a *new* peaceful era of capitalism to justify the adhesion of the opportunists and the official Social Democratic parties to the bourgeoisie, and their rejection of the revolutionary, i.e., proletarian tactics in the *present stormy era*. . . . Marxist dialectics, as the last word in the scientific evolutionary method, excludes any isolated examination of an object.[76]

And of Plekhanov's support for the war, Lenin wrote:

Plekhanov has set a new record in the noble sport of substituting sophistry for dialectics. The sophist grabs at one of many "arguments"; it was Hegel who long ago very properly observed that "arguments" can be found to prove anything in the world. Dialectics calls for the many-sided investigation into a given social phenomena in its development, and for the external and apparent to be reduced to the fundamental motive forces, to the development of the productive forces and the class struggle. . . . With reference to wars the main thesis of dialectics, which has been so shamelessly distorted by Plekhanov to please the bourgeoisie, is that *"war is simply the continuation of politics by other* (i.e., violent) *means."* Such is the formula of Clausewitz, one of the greatest writers on the history of war, whose thinking was stimulated by Hegel.[77]

It was much more than the application of dialectics to the study of war that Lenin took from his reading of Hegel. It infused the whole of his thought and remained with him for the rest of his life. As Michael Lowy argues:

It is not difficult to find the red thread leading from the category of sum total to the theory of the weakest link in the imperialist chain; from the interpenetration of opposites to the transformation of the democratic revolution into the socialist revolution; from the dialectical conception of causality to the refusal to define the character of the Russian Revolution solely by Russia's "economically backward base"; from the critique of vulgar evolutionism to the "break in continuity" in 1917.[78]

Of course, Lenin did not predict or deduce the Russian revolution as a result of his study of Hegel. But his relearning of the dialectic did make him more alive to the possibilities, more capable of discovering, concretely and empirically, the forms of action that could overcome the contradictions with which he was faced. His attitude to the workers' state is a case in point: In *Two Tactics of the Social Democracy in the Democratic Revolution* (1905), Lenin had criticized the Paris Commune for being unable to "distinguish between the elements of a democratic revolution and a socialist revolution," because "it confused the tasks of fighting for republic with those of fighting for socialism." But by 1917, Lenin had done away with this approach. The Commune became, in *State and Revolution*, the model for carrying through, simultaneously, a democratic and a socialist revolution.[79]

This new approach was to serve Lenin once again, as Krupskaya noted, in "his brief remarks about the dialectical approach to all phenomena, made in 1921 in the course of the controversies with Trotsky and Bukharin concerning the trade unions." They were "the best evidence of how much Ilyich had gained in this respect from his studies in philosophy."[80] Indeed, two sections of Lenin's *Once Again on the Trade Unions*, some seventeen pages, are devoted to the dialectic.[81]

The 1921 debate concerned the degree to which the trade unions should be integrated with the state. Lenin believed that even in a workers' state, especially one that was, as he put it, a worker's and a peasant's state with bureaucratic distortions, workers still needed unions that had enough autonomy to defend themselves from their own state. Trotsky, although he had originally proposed a position close to the one that Lenin now argued, came to defend the idea that the unions should be more closely tied to the state machine in order to overcome the devastation caused by the civil war. Bukharin occupied a "buffer" position between Lenin and Trotsky.

Lenin's criticism of Trotsky was that he had forgotten that "politics must take precedence over economics," because "without a correct political approach to the matter the given class will be unable to stay on top, *and, consequently*, will be incapable of solving *its production problem* either."[82]

Lenin's attitude to Bukharin is more interesting from a methodological point of view. Lenin charges Bukharin with eclecticism:

The gist of his theoretical mistake is the substitution of eclecticism for the dialectical interplay of politics and economics (which we find in Marxism). His theoretical attitude is: "on the one hand, and on the other," "the one and the other." That is eclecticism. Dialectics requires an all-round consideration of relationships in their concrete development but not a patchwork of bits and pieces.[83]

Bukharin had tried to dismiss the differences between Lenin and Trotsky by insisting that their positions were not contradictory. Bukharin said:

Comrades, many of you may find that the current controversy suggests something like this: two men come in and invite each other to define the tumbler on the lectern. One says: "it is a glass cylinder, and a curse on anyone who says different." The other says: "A tumbler is a drinking vessel, and a curse on anyone who says different."[84]

For Lenin this represented "the standpoint of formal or scholastic logic, not of dialectical or Marxist logic." His reply to Bukharin shows not just the mastery of the dialectic which he had acquired in his study of Hegel, but the profound materialist understanding with which he transformed Hegel's categories, making them concrete and precise:

A tumbler is assuredly both a glass cylinder and a drinking vessel. But there are more than these facets to it; there are an infinite number of them, an infinite number of "medacies" and inter-relationships with the rest of the world. A tumbler is a heavy object which can be used as a missile, a receptacle for a captured butterfly, or a valuable object with an artistic engraving or design, and this has nothing at all to do with whether or not it can be used for drinking, is made of glass, is cylindrical or not quite, and so on and so forth.[85]

Lenin complains that Bukharin has simply taken the definitions supplied by formal logic and combined them at random, just as in the trade union debate he randomly combined elements of Lenin's position with elements of Trotsky's. Lenin argues that dialectical logic demands that we should go further:

Firstly, if we are to have true knowledge of an object we must look at and examine all its facets, its connections and its "medacies." That is something we cannot ever hope to achieve completely, but the rule of comprehensiveness is a safeguard against mistakes and rigidity.

Thus, Lenin makes polemical use of Hegel's notions of totality and mediation. He goes on:

Secondly, dialectical logic requires that an object should be taken in development, in change, in "self-movement" (as Hegel sometimes puts it). This is not immediately obvious in respect of such an object as a tumbler, but it, too, is in flux, and this holds especially true for its purpose, use and *connection* with the surrounding world.

Lenin argued, thirdly, that only such a notion could act as "a criterion of truth and a practical indicator of its connection with human wants." He concludes, "fourthly, dialectical logic holds that 'truth is always concrete, never abstract,' as the late Plekhanov liked to say after Hegel."[86] This last point is decisive in a materialist dialectic, and Lenin is at pains to hammer the point home with a political example:

> I know next to nothing about the insurgents and revolutionaries of South China. . . . Since there are these uprisings, it is not too far-fetched to assume a controversy going on between Chinese No. 1, who says that insurrection is a product of a most acute nation-wide class struggle, and Chinese No. 2, who says that insurrection is an art. That is all I need to know in order to write a theses *a la* Bukharin: "On the one hand, . . . on the other hand." The one has failed to reckon with the art "factor," and the other, with the "acuteness factor," etc. Because no *concrete* study has been made of *this particular* controversy, question, approach, etc., the result is a dead and empty eclecticism.[87]

In place of this approach, Lenin insists that there must be "a correct solution of the political question of the 'trends within the trade union movement,' the relationship between classes, between politics and economics, the specific role of the state, the Party, the trade unions . . . etc."[88] This is the only way of avoiding both Bukharin's eclecticism and Trotsky's "one-track thinking." It was, no doubt, partly this debate that Lenin had in mind when he wrote in his testament that Bukharin's "theoretical views can only with the greatest doubt be regarded as fully Marxian, for there is something scholastic about him. (He has never learned, and I think never fully understood the dialectic)."[89]

Lenin's commitment to the dialectic remained with him in his last article on philosophy, written in 1922 for the journal *Pod Znamenem Marksizma* (*Under the Banner of Marxism*). Lenin urged that,

> . . . the contributors to *Pod Znamenem Marksizma* must arrange for the systematic study of Hegelian dialectics from a materialist standpoint. . . .
> Taking as our basis Marx's method of applying materialistically conceived Hegelian dialectics, we can and should elaborate this dialectics from all aspects, print in the journal excerpts from Hegel's principal works, interpret them materialistically and comment on them with the help of examples of the way Marx applied dialectics in the sphere of economic and political relations, which recent history, especially modern imperialist war and revolution, provides in unusual abundance. In my opinion the editors and contributors of *Pod Znamenem Marksizma* should be a kind of "Society of Materialist Friends of Hegelian Dialectics."[90]

AFTER LENIN

The full extent of Lenin's renewal of the marxist method was not known during the Russian revolution and still less survived his death in 1924. Philosophical debate, however, flourished in the aftermath of the October revolution. Machism underwent something of a revival, and those who had been prominent opponents of Lenin found themselves in leading positions in the Soviet state. Lunarcharsky became, as we have noted, commissar for education. Bogdanov became a prominent member of the Communist Academy, and Pokrovsky was the first director of the Institute of Red Professors. But the two main schools of thought were the Mechanists and the group associated with Abram Deborin.

Mechanism was an extreme form of positivism—an "extremely empiricist, anti-theoretical temper of thought, a tendency to stand on the 'bare facts' and to believe that they needed no further elaboration."[91] Its advocates were convinced that

> the exploratory resources of science are able to provide a complete account of objective reality. They held that science employs reductive procedures able, in principle, to reveal exhaustively the nature not only of physical objects, but also of living organisms and psychological phenomena.[92]

This approach had an affinity with the positivist strand of Bogdanov's thought. Indeed, Bogdanov associated himself with the Mechanists. The Mechanists, however, were less keen to associate themselves with Bogdanov, partly because they genuinely had little sympathy with his idealist theory of knowledge and partly because his having been the target of Lenin's earlier polemic put him beyond the pale in the increasingly factional disputes of the mid-1920s. Bukharin was also a supporter of the Mechanist trend, a position that drew a rebuke from Lenin, contained in the will that Stalin suppressed after his death, that Bukharin had "never really understood the dialectic."

The young philosophers who gathered around A. M. Deborin at the Institute of Red Professors claimed to be the very antithesis of the Mechanists. They were absolutely opposed to down-playing the role of philosophy and were committed, following Lenin's advice, to the rehabilitation of Hegel and to the materialist understanding of the dialectic. Indeed, compared with the crude scientism of the Mechanists, the Deborin group were the height of philosophical sophistication. But, ultimately, for all their trumpeting of Hegel and the dialectic, they were formalists. Their understanding of the dialectic was composed of a fixed litany of formulations drained of content and unamenable to challenge by mere facts. The Deborinite understanding of the dialectic exhibited the same sclerosis that overtook Plekhanov and the theorists of the Second International who, while formally adhering to the dialectic, in fact drained it of any real content and divorced it from the living contradictions of the world around them. Unsurprisingly, Deborin had been one of those who joined the attack against George Lukacs and Karl Korsch in the early 1920s. In the Deborinites' hands, the dialectic became a ready-made formula to be applied to any problem, not a living method that could only be verified by constantly examining and re-examining the real development of society and nature.

What in fact was happening to Soviet philosophy was that, as the real basis of a dialectical unity, the revolution itself, degenerated, two one-sided camps emerged—the crude empiricists opposed by the abstract Hegelians. The two camps were not equally worthless in philosophical terms—the Deborinites were wrong in a more sophisticated way than the Mechanists—but both were ultimately incapable of maintaining the dialectical tradition that Lenin had rediscovered. Any last possibility of holding on to that insight was lost in the intrigues of the late 1920s and the early 1930s as Stalin consolidated his power.

In 1929, the Deborinites used their positions of power inside the state apparatus to defeat their opponents. The stick used to beat the Mechanists was hardly philosophical. As Stalin abandoned the New Economic Policy and embarked on forced collectivization of peasant farms, Bukharin, who supported a policy of even greater concessions to the peasantry, became the main enemy. Bukharin was an ally of the Mechanists. Consequently, the Mechanists were branded as gradualists and determinists. Bukharin was a "right deviationist" and a Mechanist. Crushing one meant crushing both.

Those who rose by manipulative means also fell from power by the same means. Within a year, some of Deborin's erstwhile allies, Mitin and Yudin, were using the same methods of abuse and slander against him. The Deborinites were accused of having fought the "right-deviation" but neglected the party's other enemy, Trotsky's "left-deviation." In 1930, Stalin himself dubbed the Deborinites "Menshevising Idealists," and they would later be described as "Trotskyite agents on the philosophical front."[93] There was no more truth in this than there was in the claim that every Mechanist must be a follower of Bukharin's economic policy. But by this stage what passed for theory had ceased to have any connection with political practice, other than as a weapon in the hands of the powerful. In January 1931, the Deborinite review, *Under the Banner of Marxism*, was condemned by resolution of the Central Committee. In philosophy, as in all other areas of social and intellectual life, the rise of Stalinism strangled a vital, vibrant revolutionary culture reducing it to the cynical, self-serving creed of a new and brutal ruling class.

With Lenin's death, the defeat of the left opposition, and Lukacs's accommodation to Stalinism, the genuine study of the marxist dialectic was driven underground until Trotsky returned to the question in the 1930s.

Notes

1. This was the view of the right-wing historians of the Russian revolution, such as Leonard Shapiro, during the Cold War. But it is still very much alive today. See, for instance, O. Figes, *The People's Tragedy* (London: Jonathan Cape, 1996). The contrary view is best put in T. Cliff, *Lenin* 3 vols. (London: Bookmarks, 1985–87). See also M. Liebman, *Leninism under Lenin* (London: Merlin, 1975); N. Harding, *Lenin's Political Thought, Theory and Practice in the Democratic and Socialist Revolutions* (London: Macmillan 1983); and Paul Le Blanc, *Lenin and the Revolutionary Party* (New Jersey: Humanities Press, 1993).

2. Lenin found Labriola's *Essays on the Materialistic Conception of History* to be "a very sensible and interesting book." See G. Weber, and H. Weber, *Lenin, Life and Works* (London: Macmillan 1980).

3. P. Le Blanc, *Lenin and the Revolutionary Party*, 209. Kevin Anderson's *Lenin, Hegel and Western Marxism, a Critical Study* (Chicago: University of Illinois Press, 1995) is the most recent example of the approach to which Le Blanc refers. Anderson is following a tradition originated by Raya Dunayevskaya and her followers. More extreme formulations are to be found in N. Valentinov, *Encounters with Lenin*, quoted in D. H. Ruben, *Marxism and Materialism, a Study in Marxist Theory of Knowledge* (Sussex and New Jersey: Harvester and Humanities Press 1977), 166. But even in very valuable works such as Michael Lowy's "From the 'Logic' of Hegel to the Finland Station In Petrograd" in his *On Changing the World* (New Jersey: Humanities Press 1993), there can sometimes be elements of this argument, see especially 79–81.

4. V. I. Lenin, *Collected Works*, Vol. I (Moscow: Progress, 1960), 182–83.

5. Ibid., 420.

6. Ibid., 400–401.

7. This element in Lenin's thought also refutes the line of argument advanced in 1938 by Anton Pannekoek's *Lenin as Philosopher* (London: Merlin, 1975). Pannekoek rightly points to the faults in some of the mechanical materialist arguments that Lenin deploys against Bogdanov. Nevertheless, Pannekoek's book has many more weaknesses than virtues. First, he explains the weaknesses in Lenin's approach as a result of "middle class materialism," which still has an appeal in backward Russia, where it is rehabilitated as marxism long after it has fulfilled its role as the ideology of the revolutionary bourgeoisie in Western Europe. This, however, is an even more crude reductionism than that with which Pannekoek taxes Lenin. There were, after all, plenty of mechanical materialists in the Second International in Western Europe, and Lenin was still a Russian when he refurbished the dialectic in 1914. The real roots of Lenin's approach in 1914 are not only the general material circumstances but *the way in which these were mediated by the Marxism of the Second International, the aftermath of the 1905 revolution and the precise situation in the Bolshevik Party.* Pannekoek is equally wrong in assuming that Lenin did not locate philosophical problems within the class contradictions of society, as even the brief examination in the main text of his arguments against the Narodniks makes clear. Finally, Pannekoek had no better positive account of the dialectic with which to replace Lenin's approach—and this in 1938, after Lukacs, after Korsch, after Gramsci!

8. See T. Cliff, *Lenin*, Vol. I, *Building the Party* (London: Pluto Press, 1975), 288.

9. Ibid., 290.

10. M. N. Pokrovsky, the Bolshevik historian then allied with Bogdanov, reporting on the reaction among Bolsheviks, quoted in Le Blanc, *Lenin and the Revolutionary Party*, 160.
11. See Le Blanc, *Lenin and the Revolutionary Party*, 163.
12. L. Kolakowski, *Main Currents in Marxism 2. The Golden Age* (Oxford: Oxford University Press, 1978), 419.
13. Ibid., 420.
14. H. Sheehan, *Marxism and the Philosophy of Science, a Critical History* (New Jersey: Humanities Press, 1985), 120.
15. See N. Harding, *Leninism* (London: Macmillan, 1996), 219–20.
16. Quoted in Sheehan, *Marxism and the Philosophy of Science*, 122.
17. Ibid., 123.
18. E. Mach, *Analyse der Empfindungen*, quoted in A. Pannekoek, *Lenin as Philosopher* (London: Merlin, 1975), 52.
19. Kolakowski, *Main Currents in Marxism 2*, 424–25.
20. Lenin, *Materialism and Empirio-criticism* (Peking, 1972), 72.
21. Kolakowski, *Main Currents in Marxism 2*, 429.
22. Ibid., 427.
23. See ibid., 435.
24. Sheehan, *Marxism and the Philosophy of Science*, 125.
25. Bogdanov, quoted in Lenin, *Materialism and Empirio-criticism* 390. The italics are Bogdanov's.
26. Kolakowski, *Main Currents in Marxism 2*, 441.
27. Lenin, *Materialism and Empirio-criticism*, 342.
28. Ibid., 340.
29. Quoted in ibid., 329.
30. Quoted in Sheehan, *Marxism and the Philosophy of Science*, 120.
31. Lenin, *Materialism and Empirio-criticism*, 415.
32. Ibid., 434.
33. Ibid., 51.
34. Ibid., 50.
35. Cliff, *Lenin*, 291. See also Anderson, *Lenin, Hegel and Western Marxism*, 19: "When he allowed the book to be republished in 1920, Lenin did write that its subject was 'the philosophy of Marxism, dialectical materialism.' However, he makes it clear that this was not so much 'in general' or for the world marxist movement but rather mainly in reference to a critique of his old opponent Bogdanov's concept of 'proletarian culture,' which was gaining a following among Soviet youth and intellectuals in the early 1920s."
36. Lenin, *Materialism and Empirio-criticism*, 317.
37. Ibid., 69.
38. Ibid., 276.
39. Marx and Engels, *Selected Correspondence* (Moscow: Progress, 1965), 191. (Letter from Marx to Engels, 27 June 1867.)
40. Marx, *Grundrisse* (London: Penguin, 1973), 100.
41. A defense of *Materialism and Empirio-criticism* is also to be found in chap. 5 of Sebastiano Timpanaro's *On Materialism* (London: Verso 1975). Timpanaro does not conduct his defense of Lenin directly, but by attacking Karl Korsch's views on Lenin. This is easy meat, because Korsch became an anti-Leninist in the late 1920s. Even before this, and although his earlier writings contain much that is interesting, he was a much weaker theoretician than Lukacs with whom he was

identified. Timpanaro's other evasive strategy is to claim that the specific conditions of idealist renaissance that Lenin set his face against at the time of *Materialism and Empirio-criticism* are a permanent feature of twentieth-century thought, thus justifying the extension of Lenin's approach: "The 'historical period' which justifies Lenin's work is, therefore, a *long historical period* already encompassing almost half the twentieth century and with no sign that it is drawing to a close" (230). This is, to say the least, a one-sided approach, because the hallmark of Second International marxism and Stalinism is not idealism but crude materialism, which is why the latter was able to misuse Lenin's book as its primer for so long.

42. Ruben, *Marxism and Materialism*, 177.
43. Ibid., 176.
44. Ibid., 177.
45. N. Krupskaya, *Memories of Lenin* (London: Lawrence and Wishart, 1970), 255.
46. Lenin quoted in R. Dunayevskaya, *Marxism and Freedom* (London: Pluto Press 1971), 169.
47. Lenin, *Collected Works*, Vol. 38 (Moscow: Progress, 1972), 179.
48. Ibid., 180.
49. Ibid., 362.
50. Ibid., 277.
51. Ibid., 276.
52. Ibid., 359.
53. Ibid., 221.
54. Ibid., 360.
55. Ibid., 284.
56. Ibid., 360.
57. Ibid., 130.
58. Ibid., 134.
59. Ibid.
60. Ibid., 98.
61. Ibid., 208.
62. Lenin, *Collected Works*, Vol. 26 (Moscow: Progress, 1964), 163.
63. Lenin, *Collected Works*, Vol. 38, 114.
64. Ibid., 264.
65. Ibid., 189.
66. Ibid., 196.
67. Anderson, *Lenin, Hegel and Western Marxism*. In the first half of his book Anderson provides a careful and long overdue comparison between Lenin's notes and the original works of Hegel on which the notes are based. But Anderson is mistaken in following Raya Dunayevskaya's tendency to dismiss Plekhanov as a typical representative of Second International marxism, which, as I have shown in chapter 3, he was not. This makes it impossible for Anderson to explain why Lenin continued to find some aspects of Plekhanov's work valuable while still being critical of his understanding of the dialectic. The result is that he again follows the later Dunayevskaya in accusing Lenin of bad faith in not more publicly breaking with Plekhanov's views and announcing his own philosophical conversion.

Anderson is even further from the mark when he projects the failures of Second International determinism back onto Frederick Engels (see, for instance, 39, 46, 59, 95, 102). In the fancifully titled section "'On the Question of Dialectics': Lenin Critiques Engels," Anderson accuses Engels of drawing "too close an affinity between the movement of inanimate matter and the self-development of human consciousness and activity" (106). Yet the only point that Lenin makes is that Engels has made an understandable simplification "in the interests of popularisation." Furthermore, as I show in chapter 2 and elsewhere (see J. Rees, "Engels' Marxism," in J. Rees, ed., *The Revolutionary Ideas of Frederick Engels, International Socialism* 65 [London, 1995]), Engels was in fact the person who distinguished clearly between the nature of the dialectic in inanimate nature and in society.

68. Lenin, *Collected Works*, Vol. 38, 195. Also "in human concepts nature is reflected *in a distinctive way* (this NB: in a *distinctive* and *dialectical* way!!)," 285.

69. In *Materialism and Empirio-criticism*, Lenin wrote: "In the theory of knowledge, as in every other sphere we must think dialectically, that is, we must not regard our knowledge as ready-made and unalterable, but must determine how *knowledge* emerges from *ignorance*, how incomplete, inexact knowledge becomes more complete and more exact." For a discussion of this point, see N. Harding, *Leninism*, 224.

70. Lenin, *Collected Works*, Vol. 38, 182.

71. Ibid., 212.

72. Ibid., 171.

73. Ibid., 213.

74. Ibid., 218.

75. The root of an important part of Lenin's appreciation of the dialectic is therefore to be found in his theory of the party, quite contrary to the views of Kevin Anderson for whom "Lenin's conception of the state and revolution remains a somewhat contradictory and ambivalent one because of his failure to work out a dialectical critique of his earlier concept of the party to lead. The latter, which remained part of Bolshevism even in 1917 ... led back toward centralization, bureaucracy and the indefinite perpetuation of the single-party state." Anderson, *Lenin, Hegel and Western Marxism*, 169 (also see 23, 147, 165–68, 245). This analysis is doubly wrong. First, it ignores the significant changes in Lenin's theory of the party during the 1905 revolution. Second, in a characteristic reduction common among the "super-Hegelians" of the Dunayevskaya school, it deduces real events from concepts—in this case the rise of Stalinism from Lenin's concept of the party—rather than examining the real dialectic of social forces which led to the *destruction* of Lenin's party in the late 1920s. On this, see Cliff, *Lenin*; Liebman, *Leninism under Lenin* and Le Blanc, *Lenin and the Revolutionary Party*.

76. Quoted in Anderson, *Lenin, Hegel and Western Marxism*, 110.

77. Quoted in ibid.

78. Lowy, *On Changing the World*, 84.

79. See ibid., 81 and 84–87.

80. Krupskaya, *Memories of Lenin*, 255.

81. Lenin, *Collected Works*, Vol. 32 (Moscow: Progress, 1965), 83–100.

82. Ibid., 83–84.

83. Ibid., 91.

84. Quoted in ibid., 93.

85. Ibid.

86. Ibid., 94.

87. Ibid., 95.

88. Ibid., 99.

89. Lenin, *Collected Works*, Vol. 36, (Moscow: Progress, 1965) 595. Lenin may also have been thinking of Bukharin's attitude to the national question and to the

imperialist state. In both cases, Bukharin tended to see undifferentiated totalities and linear tendencies of development where Lenin saw contradictory developments, as Anderson, *Lenin, Hegel and Western Marxism*, (159) rightly notes.

90. Lenin, *On the Significance of Militant Materialism*, in *Selected Works* (Moscow: Progress, 1968), 658.
91. Sheehan, *Marxism and the Philosophy of Science*, 167.
92. D. Bakhurst, *Consciousness and Revolution in Soviet Philosophy from the Bolsheviks to Evald Ilyenkov* (Cambridge: Cambridge University Press, 1991), 31–32.
93. Ibid., 48–49.

5

The Legacy of Lukacs

George Lukacs was a revolutionary socialist for, at most, a decade. He became a marxist through his experience of the First World War and the revolutions that followed it. This was a time when Bolshevik theory and practice were little known and even less understood outside Russia. The almost universally accepted form of marxism was that of the Second International. Lukacs's reading of, at first, Hegel, Marx, and Luxemburg, and, later, of Lenin, allowed him to reconstruct a version of marxism remarkably close to that of its founders. And he tailored that interpretation so that it met the needs of an era of imperialist war, monopoly capitalism, mass reformism, revolution, and counterrevolution. His *History and Class Consciousness* and *Lenin* remain remarkable achievements. But in two respects, they also carry the mark of their conditions of birth.

First, they were born in the greatest period of revolutionary advance the world has ever seen. They assume extreme forms of crisis and class struggle. This, like many of the classic writings of the revolutionary tradition, is their strength. It also means that they require an effort of reinterpretation if they are to be made to speak to generations who have seen more struggles, but not lived through any more victories, than the generation of 1917.

Second, *History and Class Consciousness* and *Lenin* were written by a man who did not know the Marx and Engels or the Lenin and Trotsky that we know. Marx's *1844 Manuscripts* and *Grundrisse*, both crucial to any clear understanding of alienation, were not available until 1930 and 1939, respectively. Lenin's *Philosophical Notebooks* were not printed until 1929. Even *Materialism and Empirio-criticism* did not appear between its original publication in 1909 and the early 1920s, and Lukacs did not read it until its translation into German in 1927. Theoretically, Lukacs was working with sources much less extensive than later generations.

These two conditions impose certain obligations on any new account of Lukacs's work. Any exposition is inevitably also an interpretation. And the interpretation of Lukacs presented here has deliberately been refracted through the experience of the classical marxist tradition. Consequently, it gives more emphasis to some aspects of Lukacs's work than to others, highlights parts of his work that only became controversial long after they were first published, and seeks to support the weaknesses in Lukacs's views with complimentary arguments drawn from other sources. I have tried to indicate where this has been the case and where I have differed from other interpretations. Although I have not violated the integrity of what Lukacs's actually wrote, some may object to this method of interpretation. But this is, ultimately, an antiquarian's argument. The real question is, Does *this interpretation* of Lukacs provide the best available account of class consciousness, the possibilities for socialist revolution, and of the marxist dialectic?

Whatever the answer to this question may be, it is at least certain that Lukacs's two books, *History and Class Consciousness*, published in 1923, and *Lenin*, written in 1924, provided a startling restatement of the marxist method at a time when it had suffered grievous damage at the hands of the theoreticians of the Second International.

Lukacs generalized and developed his analysis on the basis established by Marx and Engels. Lukacs's ability to do this rested, more than is often acknowledged, on his experience of the First World War, the collapse of the Second International, and the Russian revolution and revolutions and counterrevolutions in Germany and in his native Hungary. These posed questions about the crisis of capitalism, the rapid, mass transformation of workers' consciousness, the creation and destruction of revolutions and revolutionary organizations on a scale that Marx and Engels could only imagine.

THE HUNGARIAN REVOLUTION AND THE FORMATION OF LUKACS'S THOUGHT

George Lukacs became a marxist under the impact of the First World War and the Russian revolution. He joined the newly formed Hungarian Communist Party in December 1918. He was thirty-three years old and already the author of two books of literary criticism, *The Soul and the Forms* (1911) and *The Theory of the Novel* (1916). Until Lukacs became a marxist, his attitude toward bourgeois society was one of ethical rejection and intellectual disdain. Today, a whole academic industry devotes itself to trying to trace the connections between the pre-marxist literary theorist and the man who wrote *History and Class Consciousness* and *Lenin*.[1] Consequently, the events that form Lukacs's personal and intellectual biography have been examined in minute detail.

The result is that the decisive experience of Lukacs's life—participation in the Hungarian revolution and, through the Third International, the international revolutionary movement, which swept Europe after the First World War—is systematically downplayed in most accounts of his life. This, in turn, leads writers either to minimize the significance of *History and Class Consciousness* or to misunderstand its meaning, which can only be clearly seen against the background of the Hungarian, the German, and the Russian revolutions.[2] Intellectual influences play their part, of course. But the new use to which a writer puts them can only be understood against the history of his times and the new problems with which he is faced. Istvan Meszaros, Lukacs's friend and pupil, expresses the point well:

> Whatever the limits of adaptability of the individual philosopher might be, the point is that he does not learn from books the important issues of his time, but lives them. . . . it would be foolish to deny that the assimilated influences are *influences*. . . . nevertheless in this relationship the historical situation itself has primacy over intellectual influences. What separates the important philosopher from the clever eclectic is the historical irrelevance of the latter's merely academic synthesis as compared to the ultimate practical significance of the first.[3]

And so it is vital to turn to Hungarian society as it hurtled toward war and revolution in the first decades of the century. Hungarian capitalism was late developing, but, by the turn of the century, the bourgeoisie were rapidly gaining in strength against the old feudal and bureaucratic layers of the ruling class. It was also asserting its independence from its imperial partner, the Austrian ruling class. But, as the bourgeoisie grew in strength, so did the working class: "The strikes of 1907 and 1912 were serious enough to terrify the bourgeoisie."[4] At the same time, the peasants and agricultural laborers demanded land reform. There were widespread harvester strikes between 1894–1904, followed by bloody reprisals and trials.[5] In addition, there was increasing resistance to Hungarian domination of national minorities.

Most "educated opinion" wanted to see Hungary modernized by copying the advanced parliamentary democracies. The titles of the two leading periodicals, *The West* and *Twentieth Century*, tell their own story. Initially, this trend looked favorably on the socialist movement. This is less surprising than it might seem. The Hungarian Social Democratic Party (SDP) was a deeply conservative organization, its leaders as desirous of aping the German SPD as the bourgeoisie was of aping their Western counterparts.

The SDP leaders had little interest in ideology or political theory—"positivism was the establishment creed and Social Democratic bible."[6] Verbally the SDP leaders were marxists, but in practice their economic demands never rose above immediate trade union issues, partly because membership of a trade union automatically meant membership of the party. Politically the party aimed at no more than achieving universal suffrage. "Whatever radicalism there was in the working classes . . . was in spite of and not because of the socialist leadership."[7] This was a conservative party even by the standards of the Second International. A delegate to the International's 1907 Stuttgart Congress reported: "At the annual elections of [SDP] national officers . . .

personal popularity, qualities of 'sober deliberation,' and an intellectual mediocrity were at a premium in the eyes of union delegates."[8] The SDP's leaders "had become accustomed over the years to defeat and dared not rally organised workers for fear that the government, under the guise of martial law, would destroy the party's organisations."[9]

These circumstances are important to recall when confronting the argument that, during frequent periods of study in Berlin and Heidelberg between 1909 and the end of the First World War, Lukacs simply absorbed the influences of those by whom he was taught and with whom he worked, for example, sociologist Max Weber, neo-Kantian philosophers Windelband and Rickert, among others. Lukacs's attitude to German culture appears much more complex when Hungarian conditions are kept in mind—and worth investigating, because it shows him to be critical of both positivist and romantic thought even though he had not yet found an alternative synthesis. As one commentator notes, "Lukacs had originally arrived on the scene at a time when it was very generally held that the only choice open to one who could accept neither traditional metaphysics nor religious faith lay between the positivism of empirical science and the vitalism . . . of irrationalists such as Nietzsche or Bergson."[10]

Lukacs's whole experience of, and previous reaction to, the impasse of Hungarian society inoculated him against easy acceptance of either of these two currents. He had already brushed with the authorities when they closed the Thalia Theatre Company with which he was involved. He had also supported what was progressive in *Twentieth Century* and *The West* and shown some interest in socialist ideas and organization, so he was unlikely to fall for the irrationalist creed. He was an equally stern critic of the positivism of the "enlightened bourgeoisie" and, therefore, was also unlikely to be an uncritical pupil of, for instance, Max Weber. Therefore, Lukacs confronted German culture with the paradoxes of Hungarian social development in the forefront of his mind.[11]

As yet, Lukacs only knew what he was against, not what could replace it. His intellectual impasse reflected the social impasse of Hungarian society—an old imperial bureaucracy, a conservative bourgeoisie, and a compliant and sclerotic SDP opposed only by poorly organized groups of revolutionaries without systematic contact with the working class. The stalemate in political life was the root of Lukacs's "romantic anti-capitalism"—the phrase he used to describe his position at this time.

The outbreak of the First World War only deepened the social and intellectual crisis, at least at first. In Hungary, there was "unprecedented squalor and splendor side-by-side in wartime Budapest."[12] The SDP, like their German model, enthusiastically supported the imperial war effort. The left socialists worked underground producing anti-war and pacifist propaganda, but it was not until November 1917 that the Hungarian Socialist Group emerged to produce "the first truly revolutionary document that appeared in Hungary during the war," a leaflet that contained the politics of the Zimmerwald left with whom Lenin, critically, aligned himself. The paralysis that Lukacs had felt before the war now turned to despair:

> When the War started, I said Germany and Austro-Hungary will probably defeat Russia and destroy Tsarism: that is good. France and England will probably defeat Germany and Austro-Hungary and destroy the Hohenzollerns and the Habsburgs: that is good. But who will save us from English and French culture? My despair at this question found no answer.[13]

The despair of which Lukacs speaks was not totally immobilizing.[14] It was during the war that Lukacs first read Rosa Luxemburg and works of marxist economics, but the decisive turning point came with the news of the Russian revolution:

> Only the Russian revolution really opened the window to the future; the fall of Tsarism brought a glimpse of it, and with the collapse of capitalism it appeared in full view. At that time our knowledge of the facts and the principles underlying them was of the slightest and very unreliable. Despite this we saw—at last! at last!—a way for mankind to escape from war and capitalism.[15]

This dramatic change of direction was only carried out in the most general terms. It was accompanied by many ghosts from Lukacs's intellectual past. His own recollections of this period have the ring of truth:

> I think that it would be departing from the truth if I were to attempt to iron out the glaring contradictions of this period by artificially constructing an organic development and fitting it into the correct pigeon-hole in the "history of ideas." If Faust could have two souls within his breast, why should not a normal person unite conflicting intellectual trends within himself when he finds himself changing from one class to another in the middle of a world crisis? . . . my ideas hovered between the acquisition of Marxism and political activism on the one hand, and the constant intensification of my purely idealistic ethical preoccupations on the other.[16]

Lukacs made rapid intellectual progress between 1917 and joining the Hungarian Communist Party twelve days after it was formed in December of the following year. However, the Hungarian revolution and the consciousness of the Hungarian working class made even faster progress.

Despite the SDP's decision to support a wartime coaltion government, the mood hardened inside the working class and, in January 1918, a general strike led by railworkers began. Some 150,000 demonstrated in Budapest, shouting "Long Live the Workers' Councils!" and "Greetings to Soviet Russia!"

The SDP tried to call the strike off, but the metal workers' unions, the rail unions, and the defense plants held out. Only the resignation of the SDP executive got them back to work. The rail workshops were soon on strike again. The army intervened and shot three strikers dead. A new general strike was called, although not before the leaders of the left were arrested. The general strike lasted from 22 June to 27 June before the SDP again called it off in return for minor economic concessions.

The intensification of the class struggle was too much for the government and, in October 1918, the war cabinet fell. In what became known as the Autumn Rose Revolution, on 1 November, Count Karolyi formed a government that included SDP ministers. The Karolyi government was inherently unstable. On the one side, the victors of the First World War obliged Karolyi to cede half of Hungarian territory, precipitating shortages of grain, textiles, and shoes. On the other side, peasant uprisings broke out, and, in the towns, especially in Budapest, there were riots. Real power lay not with Karolyi but with the Workers' and Soldiers' Councils.

The old state bureaucracy and officer corps remained intact, but as historian R. L. Tokes writes, "The dual power situation that emerged in the wake of the October revolution in Hungary was similar in many respects to the one following the February revolution in Russia."[17] Nevertheless, there were also vitally important differences with the Russian revolution. The Hungarian SDP dominated the Workers' Councils just as their Menshevik counterparts had at first in Russia, but, if anything, the Hungarians were even more conservative. The SDP "was not prepared to strike out on its own, but had chosen to remain an inferior partner in the new governmental structure." Kunfi, an SDP cabinet member, called for a "six week suspension of class struggle."[18]

The second, vital difference between the two revolutions was that the revolutionary left was incomparably weaker in Hungary than the Bolsheviks had been in Russia. The Workers' Council was dominated by 239 SDP trade union delegates out of a total of 365 delegates. The SDP initially barred the revolutionary socialists, the left-wing engineers, and the syndicalists from the council, leaving the left with a foothold only in the Soldiers' Council. As late as 17 November, a majority of a meeting of fifty representatives from revolutionary organizations refused to set up an independent organization, settling instead for a political club inside the SDP. It was only later in the same month that the Hungarian Communist Party (CP) was founded by Bela Kun.[19] Lukacs joined the CP almost immediately when it was still well short of one hundred members.

In the revolutionary atmosphere of early 1919, the CP grew rapidly, winning over revolutionary syndicalists, engineer socialists, and key sections of the manual working class. But it was still not able to challenge effectively the hegemony of the SDP. The CP certainly did not have a majority in the Workers' Councils when, less than three months after its formation, it called for an insurrection in early February 1919. In response, the SDP threatened to purge the unions of "communist splitters." The CP tried to retreat, but, on 20 February, four policemen were killed in a demonstration. The SDP took the opportunity to crack down, closing the CP headquarters, seizing its printing press, and arresting its leaders.[20]

The CP had blundered badly, but the situation was not irretrievable. The SDP made the mistake of allowing the police to beat Bela Kun unconscious in front of a newspaper journalist. Within six hours the tabloid *Evening* spread the news in impressive detail.[21]

On 18 March, several thousand steel workers voted to fight for the release of the communists, with arms if necessary. The printers' union voted for a two-day strike, the first directed not at the employers but at the "socialist" government. The Soldiers' Council and the Budapest militia fell under CP control.[22]

The final blow to the government came from the Entente. Colonel Vyx, the Entente representative in Budapest, visited Karolyi on 19 March and handed him a note virtually demanding that the whole country, except for a twenty-mile area around the capital, be put under Entente occupation. The government crumbled.[23]

The bourgeoisie now played their last card—handing power to a SDP government. But the SDP could only be effective if they could control the CP.[24] On 21 March, Kun's socialist jailers visited him and he agreed to *merge* the CP and the SDP and form a "revolutionary" government. There was opposition to the merger in the CP, but Kun talked them down in a series of face-to-face confrontations. It was a decision that doomed the Hungarian Republic from birth. The CP were given just one out of the twelve commissars in the new government, and only seven out of twenty-one deputy commissars. "It took the Hungarian SDP just seven days to fully absorb the CP's secretariat, agitprop apparatus and network of clandestine factory cells."[25]

It was against precisely this danger that Lenin had warned.[26] But Kun reassured Lenin, and Lenin accepted his assurances, at least for the time being.[27] Kun was not alone in believing that he had taken the right road.[28] Practically the entire CP leadership, including Lukacs who had edited the party paper while Kun was in prison and was deputy commissar for education in the new government, agreed. Indeed, Lukacs wrote a "Luxemburgist" article, titled "Party and Class," lauding the merger of the SDP and the CP as the spontaneous restoration of proletarian unity.[29]

The merger was, of course, a disaster for the revolution and for the CP, although the new government did succeed, at least temporarily, in defeating an Entente invasion.[30] This success only undermined the socialists' tolerance for the CP, who failed to strengthen their own base because their hands were tied by the merger of the two parties.[31]

At the party congress that opened on 12 June, the CP had between 60 and 90 of the 221 delegates. The delegates voted to give the trade union stewards' conference a veto over the actions of the party.[32] The congress was hostile both to peasant demands for land and to the demands of national minorities. Neither was this just the work of the SDP majority; the CP believed that Lenin's policy of giving land to the peasants was an unnecessary concession that the Hungarian Soviet Republic should avoid. Equally Kun believed that the cautious policy toward nationalization adopted by the Bolsheviks should be replaced by wholesale nationalization.

The results of such policies were all too predictable: the working class remained under reformist leadership, but with a communist gloss; the peasants and the nationalities were driven into the camp of counterrevolution by the government's attitude. The Entente threatened again.[33] The right-wing socialists deserted the government and, after setbacks at the front, the remains of the government also resigned and handed power to an Entente-backed government. Admiral Horthy's white terror followed rapidly, executing 5,000 and jailing 75,000, while another 100,000 fled the country. Lukacs stayed behind for two months to organize the CP underground before fleeing to Vienna.[34]

LUKACS AND THE LESSONS OF THE HUNGARIAN SOVIET REPUBLIC

It is common to describe Lukacs as an ultra-left in this period, but actually his politics were an amalgam of right- and left-wing misunderstandings of the relationship between the revolutionary party and the working class. His "Luxemburgist" conception of the party was, if anything, a right-wing interpretation,.because it deprecated independent organization. This was justified by the "left-wing" assumption that the raw experience of the class struggle would automatically combine with those who merely intellectually opposed the old reformist leadership, enabling the party to be organically reformed from within.[35] This was what Lukacs believed had happened when the CP and the SDP merged. This conception of the party was joined to an ultra-left attitude to a number of strategic questions: land reform, parliamentarianism, nationalization, and so on.

It was not until Lukacs's exile in Vienna that he began to systematically rework his understanding of marxism. The leadership of the Hungarian CP were Leninists in name only—they knew virtually nothing of Lenin's work. Only a few of Lenin's pamphlets were available, and even those were poor translations. Lukacs himself recalls, "it was not until my emigration to Vienna that I was able to make a thorough study of Lenin's theory." By the time Lenin criticised Lukacs's ultra-left article titled "On the Question of Parliamentarianism" as "very poor," Lukacs had read *"Left Wing" Communism* and "had already been wholly convinced by his arguments on the question of parliamentary participation there: so his criticism of my article did not change anything very much for me. I already knew it was wrong."[36] Lukacs's views about Hungarian politics changed first. It took longer for him to generalize to the international situation and abandon ultra-left tactics altogether. The last vestiges of ultra-leftism were eradicated from his thought during the debate in the Third International that followed the 1921 March Action in Germany, of which Lukacs had been a critical supporter.

History and Class Consciousness, written in late 1922, was a reflection on three revolutions—the Hungarian, the Russian, and the German—shot through with a new understanding of marxism based on Lukacs's studies in exile. Some of the essays in *History and Class Consciousness* had been published in earlier drafts during the final part of Lukacs's ultra-left phase, although the two most important studies, "Reification and the Consciousness of the Proletariat" and "Towards a Methodology of the Problem of Organisation," were written later, in 1922. Even the earlier essays were substantially reworked for inclusion in *History and Class Consciousness* in ways that distanced them from Lukacs's first formulations.[37] In its final form, and taken together with Lukacs's *Lenin*, it is one of the unsurpassed philosophical generalizations of the experience of the most revolutionary era in the history of the international working class.

LUKACS ON ALIENATION AND THE DIVISION OF LABOR

One central concern of both *History and Class Consciousness* and *Lenin* is to restate and generalize Marx and Engels's insights into the formation of class consciousness. Lukacs gives a clear indication that he has grasped Marx's distinction, discussed in chapter 2, between commodity fetishism and alienation:

> There is both an objective and a subjective side to this phenomena. *Objectively* a world of objects and relations between things springs into being (the world of commodities and their movements on the market). The laws governing these objects are indeed gradually discovered by man, but even so they confront him as invisible forces that generate their own power. . . . *Subjectively* . . . a man's activity becomes estranged from himself, it turns into a commodity which, subject to the non-human objectivity of the natural laws of society, must go its own way independently of man just like any consumer article.[38]

In a society of generalized commodity exchange, as Marx's labor theory of value makes clear, the value of the commodities exchanged must be capable of reduction to a common element: the amount of labor time crystallized in their production. Thus, labor under capitalism has itself become measurable, comparable, abstract, and exchangeable—therefore, so many hours of labor embodied in this car are exchanged for so many hours of labor embodied in those sacks of grain. But with this development, notes Lukacs, comes the division of labor, not just in the immediate process of production but in every aspect of society:

> ... the capitalist division of labour existing both as the presupposition and the product of capitalist production, is born only in the course of the development of the capitalist system. Only then does it become a category of society influencing decisively the objective form of things and people in the society thus emerging, their relation to nature and the possible relations of men to each other.[39]

This process is most clearly observable at the point of production where "the process of labour is progressively broken down into abstract, rational, specialised operations so that the worker loses contact with the finished product and his work is reduced to the mechanical repetition of a specialised set of actions" and so "an objectively calculable work-stint . . . confronts the worker as a fixed and established reality."[40] Consequently, "the human qualities and idiosyncracies of the worker appear increasingly as *mere sources of error* when contrasted with these abstract special laws functioning according to rational predictions."[41]

This process reaches far beyond its point of origin, the workplace, and penetrates every part of society. And the older the system becomes, the more the market seeks to meet every human need via the mechanism of commodity exchange. Lukacs quotes sociologist Max Weber's description of capitalist society:

> The relative independence of the artisan (or cottage craftsman), of the landowning peasant, the owner of a benefice, the knight and vassal was based on the fact that he himself owned the tools, supplies, financial resources or weapons with the aid of which he fulfilled his economic, political or military function and from which he lived while his duty was being discharged. Similarly, the hierarchic dependence of the worker, the clerk, the technical assistant, the assistant in an academic institute *and* the civil servant and soldier has a comparable basis: namely that the tools, supplies and financial resources essential both for the business-concern and for economic survival are in the hands . . . of the entrepreneur and . . . the political master.[42]

The same process of specialization and division of labor that marks capitalism at the point of production also separates politics from economics and different aspects of the political process from each other. This helps the bourgeoisie impose a reified, petrified order on the unruly class relations of their society by means of Ford-like production line techniques that stress the inevitability of the whole process. Lukacs again quotes Max Weber to make his point: Capitalism "requires for its survival a system of justice and an administration whose workings can be *rationally calculated*, at least in principle, just as the probable performance of a *machine* can be calculated." For this reason, it is unable "to tolerate the dispensing of justice according to the judge's sense of fair play *in individual cases* or any other irrational means or principles of administering the law." Weber argues that "modern businesses with their fixed capital and their exact calculations are much too sensitive to legal and administrative irrationalities" to accept anything less than a "bureaucratic state with its rational laws where . . . the judge is more or less an automatic statute dispensing machine in which you insert the files together with the necessary costs and dues at the top, whereupon he will eject the judgement together with more or less cogent reasons for it at the bottom."[43] Bureaucracy is necessarily the hallmark of the capitalist system:

> Bureaucracy implies the adjustment of one's way of life, mode of work and hence of consciousness, to the general socio-economic premises of the capitalist economy, similar to that which we have observed in the case of the worker in particular business concerns. The formal standardisation of justice, the state, the civil service etc., signifies objectively and factually a comparable reduction of all social functions to their elements. . . . this results in an inhuman, standardised division of labour analogous to that which we have found in industry.[44]

Bureaucracy is marked not only by the sterility, uniformity, and repetitiveness of its workings, but also by its remoteness and indifference to the real nature of the issues with which it is supposed to be dealing. Every problem that bureaucracy touches, irrespective of the real human relations involved, is evacuated of all its individual characteristics and reduced to its formal properties, so that it can be processed by the bureaucratic machine.

> This phenomena can be seen at its most grotesque in journalism. Here it is precisely subjectivity itself, knowledge, temperament and powers of expression that are reduced to an abstract mechanism functioning autonomously and divorced both from the personality of their "owner" and from the material and concrete nature of the subject matter in hand. The journalist's "lack of convictions", the prostitution of his experiences and beliefs is comprehensible only as the apogee of capitalist reification.[45]

Marriage, too, is an institution which buries individuality under formal, regulated, reified structures—hence its legal and contractual nature. Kant described the situation "with the naively cynical frankness peculiar to great thinkers," says Lukacs. "Sexual community is the use made by one person of the sexual organs and faculties of another . . . marriage . . . is the union of two people with a view to the mutual possession of each other's sexual attributes for the duration of their lives."[46] Hence bourgeois morality and the legal system treat transgression of the marriage contract as they treat transgression of any property law. For example, adultery is fraud, the fraudulent acquisition of sex; rape is theft, the stealing of sex. Any wider social or historical causes or consequences are eliminated as even the most personal of relationships are reduced to their formal, legal—and, consequently, bureaucratically amenable—side.

Thus alienation and commodity fetishism "stamps its imprint upon the whole consciousness of man; his qualities and abilities are no longer an organic part of his personality, they are things which he can 'own' or 'dispose of' like the various objects of the external world."[47] One only has to think of the way in which the lives and personalities of film, music, and sports stars are turned into commodities to see this process at one extreme. To see what this means at the other extreme it is only necessary to recall the way in which the fashion industry and the media transform this commodification of "stars" into a general alienation effecting even the poorest, whose lives are supposed to be enhanced by the vicarious pleasure of adopting the cheap replicas of the clothes, makeup, and lifestyles of the rich and famous.

In such a system, individuality and freedom are reduced to "playing the system," that is, the manipulation of the rules to your own best advantage. This is necessarily the sham freedom experienced by the roulette player—he or she knows the rules of the game and will, therefore, have an advantage over someone who knows them less well, but the whole process is not under the conscious control of anyone. Consequently, no real freedom, no real control over destiny, is possible, because no single capitalist or group of capitalists, let alone workers, can control the system as a whole. Thus, rigid bureaucracy and division of labor rule the parts of the system, but chaos rules the system as a whole: "the capitalist process of rationalisation based on private economic calculation requires that every manifestation of life shall exhibit this very interaction between details which are subject to laws and a totality ruled by chance."[48]

This is why each new area created by the division of labor, although it has its roots in the economic structure of capitalism, also develops its own special principles of organization:

> It has already been pointed out that the division of labour disrupts every organically unified process of work and life and breaks it down into its components. This enables the artificially isolated partial functions to be performed in the most rational manner by "specialists" who are specially adapted mentally and physically for the purpose. This has the effect of making these partial functions autonomous and so they tend to develop

through their own momentum and in accordance with their own special laws independently of the other partial functions of society (or of that part of society to which they belong).[49]

This is an insight of great significance. It furnishes us with an account of the basis on which so many key divisions in bourgeois society arise— between politics and economics, law and government, executive and administration, mental and manual labour, art and science, and the military and civil institutions of state. It does so in a way that allows us to see clearly their roots in the economic structure of society while at the same time showing why this very same economic structure tends to give rise to other spheres that cannot crudely and immediately be reduced to their economic origins, which develop, so to speak, a life of their own.

Lukacs has some interesting things to say about the way parliamentary democracies embody the kind of attitudes to which commodity fetishism gives rise. Lukacs points out that if we accept the surface appearance of formal, bourgeois democracy, it can seem to justify a reformist political strategy:

> From this standpoint the most developed bourgeois form of rule—democracy—appears . . . to be the embodiment of this democracy itself in which it need only be ensured that the majority of the population is won to the "ideals" of social democracy through peaceful agitation. From this it would follow that the transition from bourgeois to proletarian democracy is not necessarily revolutionary.[50]

But this approach "conceals the class character" of bourgeois democracy, and it does so in the same way that the seemingly equal and fair exchanges of the marketplace disguise the underlying reality of exploitation. In this case, the separation of politics and economics, written into the structure of capitalism, makes the parliamentary democratic fraud possible:

> The moment of deception lies in *the undialectical concept of "the majority."* Because the representation of the interests of the overwhelming majority of the population is the essence of working class rule, many workers suffer from the illusion that a purely formal democracy, in which every citizen is equally valid, is the most suitable instrument. . . . But this fails to take into account the simple—simple!—detail that men are not just citizens or isolated atoms within the totality of the state, but are always concrete human beings who occupy specific positions within social production.[51]

The effect of ignoring the social and economic dimension of workers' existence is to allow the formal equality of bourgeois democracy to "*pulverise bourgeois society politically*—which is not merely an advantage to the bourgeoisie but precisely the decisive condition of its class rule."[52] Lukacs is well aware that bourgeois rule "rests in the last instance on force," but for a society to experience even limited stability the willing consent of at least a large minority of the population is vital. Bourgeois democracy alone would be "by no means enough to achieve this." But bourgeois democracy does not stand alone:

> It is ... only the political culmination of a social system whose other elements include the ideological separation of economics and politics, the creation of a bureaucratic state apparatus which gives large sections of the petty bourgeoisie a material and moral interest in the stability of the state, a bourgeois party system, press, schools system, religion, etc. With a more or less conscious division of labour, all these further the aim of preventing the formation of an independent ideology among the oppressed classes of the population which would correspond to their own class interests; of binding the individual members of these classes to the system as single individuals, as mere "citizens," to an abstract state reigning over and above all classes; *of disorganising these classes as classes* and pulverising them into atoms easily manipulated by the bourgeoisie.[53]

The aim of any genuine working-class organization, including revolutionary parties and trade unions, should be to help workers in their struggle to overcome this fragmentation and to see the connections between different aspects of society. But it is the workers' council that can fulfill this task most completely because it is the organized form of workers' power, a worker's state as a weapon against the bourgeois state. The first task of a workers state is, of course, a practical one. "The crushing of the bourgeoisie, the smashing of its state apparatus, the destruction of its press, etc., is a vital necessity for the proletarian revolution because the bourgeoisie by no means renounces it efforts to re-establish its economic and political dominance after its initial defeats."[54] The experience of the Hungarian revolution had shown that any "concessions which in this case were without exception also concessions to the Social Democrats, served only to strengthen the power consciousness of the former ruling classes and to postpone and even put an end to their inner willingness to accept the rule of the proletariat."[55] It is only by showing such determination that the working class can make its allies from other classes, and its own more hesitant members, believe that it really can take power. In Hungary,

> ... [the] retreat of the soviets before the bourgeoisie had even more disastrous implications for the ideology of the broad masses of the petty bourgeoisie. It is characteristic of them that they regard the state as something general and universal, as an absolutely supreme institution. Apart from adroit economic policy which is often enough to neutralise the individual groups of the petty bourgeoisie it is evident, then, that much depends on the proletariat itself. Will it succeed in giving its state such authority to meet half-way the faith in authority of such strata of the population. . . . If the proletariat hesitates, if it lacks a sustaining faith in

its own mission to rule, it can drive these groups back into the arms of the bourgeoisie and even to open counter-revolution.[56]

The workers' council is an organization designed to maximize the unity and striking power of the working class because:

> the Soviet system . . . bind[s] together those moments of social life which capitalism fragments. . . . The Soviet system, for example, always establishes the indivisible unity of economics and politics by relating the concrete existence of men—their immediate daily interests, etc.—to the essential questions of society as a whole. It also establishes unity in objective reality where bourgeois class interests created the "division of labour"; above all, the unity of the power "apparatus" (army, police, government, the law, etc.) and "the people."[57]

It was in this context that Lukacs wrote, "The workers' council spells the political and economic defeat of reification."[58]

Lukacs's work gives us a more systematic and concrete account of the institutional forms of class consciousness. But he is also concerned to show how these structures shape the consciousness of the bourgeoisie and the working class in different ways, giving rise to profoundly different attitudes to the experience of alienation and commodity fetishism.

THE IDEOLOGY OF THE BOURGEOISIE

The class position of the bourgeoisie circumscribes its ability to understand the society of which it is a part. The bourgeoisie oppresses and exploits other classes, but it does not control society. The rules of market competition benefit the bourgeoisie, but the bourgeoisie do not consciously make the rules. The bourgeoisie can no more prevent periodic economic crises than can the working class; it, too, is subject to an alien force it cannot control. The bourgeoisie is alienated, but, as Marx argued, they are happy in their alienation, because it confirms their own social power. For the bourgeoisie to address the fundamental contradiction that produces alienation would be to declare its own dissolution as a class:

> . . . the bourgeoisie was quite unable to perfect . . . its own science of classes: the reef on which it foundered was its failure to discover even a theoretical solution to the problem of crises. The fact that a scientifically acceptable solution does exist is of no avail. For to accept that solution, even in theory, would be tantamount to observing society *from a standpoint other than that of the bourgeoisie*. And no class can do that—unless it is willing to abdicate its power freely. Thus the barrier which converts the class consciousness of the bourgeoisie into "false" consciousness is objective; it is the class situation itself. It is the objective result of the economic set-up, and is neither arbitrary, subjective nor psychological.[59]

A true understanding of society stands in opposition to class interest of the bourgeoisie. One immediate effect is to divorce the bourgeoisie's theory from its social practice:

> It is true that the bourgeoisie acts as a class in the objective evolution of society. But it understands the process (which it is itself instigating) as something external which is subject to objective laws which it can only experience passively.[60]

This is not to say, obviously, that the bourgeoisie does not break strikes, fight wars, and so on. But it does so in the more or less sincere belief that it is merely carrying out the dictates of a system over which it has no control—an argument that contains an important element of truth. This fatalism reflects the social position of the bourgeoisie which is a class united only in opposition to the working class but divided against itself by the competition and by the division of labor that its own system produces. Thus, bourgeois ideology, unable to comprehend the true totality of social relations without announcing its own dissolution, characteristically reacts in two ways: It either tries to give an account of the social totality in idealist, frequently mystical, terms, or it retreats into specialized study of those partial aspects of the system over which some regulation is possible, without ever trying to give an explanation of their relationship to each other or to the social whole. Often both elements are incoherently combined in the work of a single theorist or school.

Lukacs explores this false but unavoidable polarity in bourgeois ideology by examining the history of western philosophy. Lukacs has a particular vision of what lies at the core of this tradition. From "Descartes, to Hobbes, Spinoza, Leibniz there is a . . . central strand, rich in variations . . . that the object of cognition can be known by us for the reason that, and to the degree in which, it has been created by ourselves."[61] But how can a philosophical tradition which asserts that, if we are to understand the world at all, we need to grasp the process by which we make the world, flourish in a society where this very process is systematically hidden by the mechanisms of alienation and commodity fetishism? In asking this question, the western philosophical tradition merely reproduces the problem of alienation at a more rarified level. As a result of not being able to answer the question adequately, of not being able to see society as a historically created, contradictory totality, philosophy is constantly pushed back into reflecting the reified surface appearance of society. Consequently, it is tossed between two poles—matter and mind, necessity and freedom, materialism ·and idealism, objectivity and subjectivity, fatalism and voluntarism.

One aspect of the empiricist approach is to focus on the specific laws governing parts of the system without ever being able to develop these to the point where a general account of society is possible. This leads to "positing as the aim of philosophy the understanding of the phenomena of isolated, highly specialised areas by means of abstract rational systems, perfectly adapted to them and without making the attempt to achieve a unified mastery of the whole realm of the knowable."[62] Since, contrary to its reified appearance, society is a whole and not simply a collection of discrete parts, a crisis inevitably afflicts bourgeois science when it tries to reach beyond its own self-imposed compartmentalism. Such a crisis in the empirical approach to the world often issues in its opposite—an attempt to re-create the lost totality of the real world in the realm of thought. As Lukacs says of Kant's philosophy, "If it was not to renounce its understanding of the whole it had to take the road that leads inwards."[63] Thus, the pole of empiricism transforms itself into its opposite, the pole of idealism—the belief that the totality of society only exists in thought, in other words, a secular faith that asserts that human beings can create the world but has no rational explanation of how this can actually be done.

Kant's philosophy ran aground on this contradiction, asserting that all we could know of the world was the world as it appeared in our thoughts and that there were strict limits to the correspondence between the world as seen in thought and the "thing in itself" or the world as it really existed. Hegel labored mightily to overcome this contradiction. Indeed, he discovered where such a unity could be found: "Classical philosophy did indeed advance to the point . . . in which philosophically the underlying order and connections between things were to be found, namely history."[64] The historical process is the site where mind and matter and objectivity and subjectivity are united, because "historical evolution annuls the autonomy of individual factors," and "by compelling the knowledge which ostensibly does these factors justice to construct its conceptual system upon what is qualitatively unique and new in phenomena, it forces it at the same time to refuse to allow any of these elements to remain at the level of mere concrete uniqueness." Instead, "the concrete and total historical process is the only point of view from which understanding becomes possible."[65]

There is more than one way of seeing this unity and, in particular, more than one candidate for the historical agency through which such a unity could be achieved. It was Hegel's greatest achievement to pose the correct question, but it was his inevitable weakness (given the era, the class position, and the philosophical tradition within which he worked) that he chose to see "the spirit of the nation" (that is, nationalism and nationhood) as the only real embodiment of the World Spirit, as the agency of historical change. Hegel's great discovery was that history is source and solution of philosophical problems. It "signals a change in the relation between theory and practice and between freedom and necessity" because "the idea that we have made reality loses its more or less fictitious character: we have . . . made our own history and if we are able to regard the whole of reality as history (i.e. as *our* history, for there is no other), we shall have raised ourselves in fact to the position from which reality can be understood as our 'action.'" But it is still necessary "to discover the site from which to resolve all these problems and also to exhibit *concretely* the 'we' which is the subject of history, that 'we' whose action is in fact history."[66]

It was Marx's great discovery to see that history was driven forward, not by the spirit of great nations, but by class struggle. With the development of capitalism, a class had been created through whose struggle the course of history could become comprehensible.

THE CONSCIOUSNESS OF THE WORKING CLASS

The insuperable barrier into which every attempt to understand society from the point of view of the bourgeoisie runs is the class interests of the bourgeoisie. If the bourgeoisie were to break through the reified appearance of capitalist society, it would have ripped the mask from its own crisis-ridden system and so be forced to admit that its fundamental faults can only be remedied by ending the rule of the bourgeoisie. The bourgeoisie would have to announce its own dissolution. There is no such barrier between the class interests of the working class and a clear, scientific understanding of society. When the working class breaks through the same reified appearance, it sees its own labor as the basis on which society rests. Its liberation is seen to be the liberation of humanity from a chronically, necessarily crisis-racked world.

> This image of a frozen reality that nevertheless is caught up in an unremitting, ghostly movement at once becomes meaningful when this reality is dissolved into the process of which man is the driving force. This can be seen only from the standpoint of the proletariat because the meaning of these tendencies is the abolition of capitalism and so for the bourgeoisie to become conscious of them would be tantamount to suicide.[67]

The unique position of the working class is a result of the fact that labor power is the commodity on whose sale the whole system rests. Workers are a "living commodity" and therefore have the ability to become conscious of the real nature of a world based on the sale of commodities. Workers experience, as no other class does, the reality of exploitation, the real human relation that stands behind the seemingly natural and inevitable workings of the market. They alone stand at the vantage point from which it is possible to see that history can be made and need not be passively experienced as if we were all merely cogs in some great machine. And because the working class stands at "the Archimedean point from which the whole of reality can be overthrown," it has the possibility of seeing the connections between theory and practice, politics and economics, the parts and the whole in a way that is not possible for any other class. Lukacs summarized this position by saying that the working class is both the subject and object of history, both the creation and the creator of the historical process.

But there is all the difference in the world between workers being in position from which it is *possible* to gain this consciousness of society and workers *actually developing* such consciousness. "What change has been brought about . . . by the possibility of taking up a point of view at all towards society," asks Lukacs. His reply: "'In the first instance' nothing at all. For the proletariat makes its appearance as the product of the capitalist order." Consequently, "the forms in which it exists are . . . the repositories of reification in its acutest and direst form and they issue in the most extreme dehumanisation."[68] So the key question is: How do workers move from the everyday consciousness, which is dominated by commodity fetishism, to the consciousness that is possible, given the workers' class position and the class interests that flow from that position?

It is often asserted that it is at this point that Lukacs's whole account of class consciousness fails. Gareth Stedman Jones, for instance, argues that Lukacs's theory either leaves the consciousness of the working class imprisoned within the iron cage of commodity fetishism, or it must assert that workers have a perpetually revolutionary consciousness. There is nothing to show "what determines the proletariat's swing from one to the other of these two all-or-nothing poles."[69] Consequently, Lukacs must either put his faith in "the final cataclysmic economic collapse of capitalism that will usher in the socialist revolution," or he must rely on the revolutionary party "to be magically proof against this ideological crisis . . . endowed with the power to recall the class to its true historical vocation." Thus, Lukacs is accused of "economist spontaneism" or "organisational voluntarism."[70] In fact, neither of these charges can withstand the contact with what Lukacs actually wrote in *History and Class Consciousness*. Lukacs does give an important role to both economic crises and the revolutionary party, but they are not introduced externally, like some good fairy whose wand merely has to touch the brow of the alienated worker to transform him into a marxist revolutionary.

Part of Lukacs's answer is to repeat the point that Marx made in the *Communist Manifesto* when he described how the workings of capitalism create its own gravedigger by "concentrating masses of workers in large factories, of mechanising and standardising the processes of work and levelling down the standard of living." These are the *indispensable precondition* without which "the proletariat would never have become a class and if they had not been continually intensified—by the natural workings of capitalism—it would never have developed into the decisive factor in human history."[71] Nevertheless, this only explains the sociological formation of the working class, not the process by which it becomes conscious. To use Marx's terms, it shows how it becomes "a class in itself" but not how it becomes "a class for itself." To understand this, the crux of the whole problem, we have to look again at the workers' experience of exploitation at the point of production.

A central contradiction of capitalism is, as we have seen, that the system treats the workers' labor power as if it were just another commodity to be used for as long, and at whatever intensity, the purchaser, the capitalist, desires. From the point of view of the market, which is also the point of view of the workers so long they accept the laws of the market as eternal and unavoidable, the capitalist is within his rights.

But the law of the market blesses the seller as well as the purchaser, sanctifies the sellers' right to demand whatever price he likes for his product, and to sell only so much as he chooses to sell. Moreover, the product that the worker sells, labor power, is a very peculiar product. When the capitalist buys a tin of beans, the seller does not accompany him to his kitchen and continue to haggle over the price he should pay for the beans or the quantity of beans that he should consume. But, much as the capitalist might wish to, he cannot separate the owner of labor power from labor power itself. This fact inconvenienced Henry Ford so much that he asked, "How come every time I want a pair of hands I get a human being?" The worker brazenly accompanies his labor power right into the workplace and stands protectively by it, continuing to argue with the capitalist day-in, day-out about the terms of its sale. Unsurprisingly, worker and capitalist do not see this process from the same viewpoint. Lukacs quotes Marx to reinforce his argument:

> We see then, that, apart from extremely elastic bounds, the nature of the exchange of commodities itself imposes no limit to the working day, no limit to surplus-labour. The capitalist maintains his right as a purchaser when he tries to make the working day as long as possible, and to make, whenever possible, two working days out of one. On the other hand, the peculiar nature of the commodity sold implies a limit to its consumption by the purchaser, and the laborer maintains his right as a seller when he wishes to reduce the working day to one of normal duration. There is here, therefore, an antimony, right against right, both equally bearing the seal of the law of exchanges. Between equal rights force decides. Hence it is that in the history of capitalist production, the determination of the working day, presents itself as a result of a struggle, a struggle between collective capital, i.e. the class of capitalists, and collective labor, i.e. the working class.[72]

This is, therefore, the point where the grip of commodity fetishism is prised open: The "laws of the market" cannot resolve the contradiction that is thrown up in every workplace on every working day, "for this is the point where the 'eternal laws' of capitalist economics fail and become dialectical and are thus compelled to yield up the decisions regarding the fate of history to the conscious actions of men." Consequently, it is here that "we find in concentrated form the basic issue of the class struggle: the problem of *force*."[73] It is from this first awakening that working-class consciousness develops:

> ... the special objective character of labour as a commodity, its "use-value" (i.e. its ability to yield surplus produce) which like every use-value is submerged without trace in the quantative exchange categories of capitalism, now awakens and becomes a *social reality*. . . . Now that this core is revealed it becomes possible to recognise the fetish character *of every commodity* based on the commodity character of labour power: in every case we find its core, the relation between men, entering into the evolution of society.[74]

This "antithesis with all its implications is only the *beginning* of the complex process of mediation whose goal is the knowledge of society as a historical totality."[75] It is a long ascent from the fundamental contradiction of capitalist society to revolutionary consciousness. Nevertheless, having seen the reality of commodity exchange with regard to themselves, workers can use this insight to unravel all the other mystifications of human relations that have taken on the appearance of relations between things—from the state and the bureaucracy to marriage and sexuality.

Before moving on, it is worthwhile pausing to examine a somewhat obscure and controversial formulation in which Lukacs expresses his conception of consciousness:

> ... as the mere contradiction is raised to a consciously dialectical contradiction, as the act of becoming conscious turns into *point of transition to practice*, we see once more in greater concreteness the character of proletarian dialectics as we have often described it: namely, since consciousness here is not the knowledge of an opposed object but is the self-consciousness of the object *the act of consciousness overthrows the objective form of its object*.[76]

The final phrase of this quotation, "the act of consciousness overthrows the objective form of its object," has sometimes been taken to mean that Lukacs thought that, for instance, realizing that the state is a product of alienation is the same as actually getting rid of the state. Of course, Lukacs meant no such thing. He realized, with Marx, that "to supercede private property as it actually exists, *real* communist activity is necessary."[77] Indeed, *History and Class Consciousness* makes an identical point, even though Lukacs had not read Marx's formulation:

> It is evident that however clearly we may have grasped the fact that society consists of processes, however thoroughly we may have unmasked the fiction of its rigid reification, this does not mean that we are able to

annul the "reality" of this fiction in capitalist society *in practice*. The moments in which this insight *can* really be converted into practice are determined by the developments of society. Thus proletarian thought is in the first place a *theory of praxis* which only gradually (and indeed often spasmodically) transforms itself into a *practical theory* that overturns the real world. The individual stages of this process . . . alone would be able to show . . . the intimate dialectical process of interaction between sociohistorical situation and the class consciousness of the proletariat.[78]

What Lukacs really meant by "consciousness overthrowing the objective form" was that the habit of treating class relations as inevitable givens (objective) had been replaced by a consciousness that sees them as historical, and therefore alterable, creations. Such a change in worker's perceptions is a step away from reified thought and a step toward revolutionary consciousness. Such a step can be the result of action, but it is also the precondition of further *class-conscious* action. Or as Lukacs puts it:

> . . . class consciousness must develop a dialectical contradiction between its immediate interests and its long-term objectives, and between discrete factors and the whole. For the discrete factor, the concrete situation with its concrete demands is by its very nature an integral part of the existing capitalist society; it is governed by the laws of that society and is subject to its economic structure. Only when the immediate interests are integrated into a total view and related to the final goal of the process do they become revolutionary, pointing concretely and consciously beyond the confines of capitalist society.[79]

The speed with which the connections between partial struggles and partial gains in class consciousness can generalize into a more complete revolutionary consciousness depends, not exclusively but nevertheless to an important degree, on the depth of the economic crisis. The more ruthlessly the capitalist class is obliged to attack the wages and conditions of the working class, the more likely it is that the contradiction at the heart of the productive process will reveal the true nature of capitalist society to those who have to sell their labor-power. An economic crisis suddenly reminds all the haughtily independent fiefdoms of capitalist society, with their own private modes of thought and action, of their crude blood relation with the monarchical power of the economy that sustains them. The economic crisis does not abolish the separate spheres of government and arts, legal and social life, and so on, but it makes their interrelations easier for workers to see and harder for the bourgeoisie to disguise. Nevertheless, the whole point of Lukacs's book was to demonstrate that even the deepest economic crises do not *automatically* produce the consciousness and organization necessary for workers to take power. In passages that echo with phrases from Marx and Luxemburg, Lukacs wrote:

For socialism would never happen "by itself", and as the result of an inevitable natural economic development. The natural laws of capitalism do indeed lead inevitably to its ultimate crisis but at the end of *its* road would be the destruction of all civilisation and a new barbarism.[80]

... the "natural laws" governing the economic process ... only determine the crisis itself, giving it dimensions which frustrate the "peaceful" advance of capitalism. However, if left to develop (along capitalist lines) they would not lead to the simple downfall of capitalism or to the smooth transition to socialism. They would lead over a long period of crises, civil wars and imperialist world wars on an ever-increasing scale to "the mutual destruction of the opposing classes" and to a new barbarism.[81]

Without the intervention of the working class, the capitalist class is "in a position to break the deadlock and to start the machine going again." And "the measures taken by the bourgeoisie to break the deadlock of the crisis and which in the abstract (i.e. but for the intervention of the proletariat) are as available to it as in former crises, now become the arena where class warfare is openly waged."[82] Hence the action of the working class "blocks capitalism's way out of the crisis," giving rise to a revolutionary opportunity. Even so, it still remains true that "in this situation the fate of the proletariat, and hence the whole future of humanity, hangs on whether or not it will take *the step that has now become objectively possible*."[83] Lukacs's point is sometimes treated, even in marxist circles, as if it were heretical. In fact, Lenin made a very similar, if more concrete, observation:

... revolutionaries sometimes try to prove that the crisis is absolutely insoluble.

This is a mistake. The bourgeoisie ... are committing folly after folly, thus aggravating the situation.... But nobody can "prove" that it is absolutely impossible for them to pacify a minority of the exploited with some petty concessions and suppress some movement or uprising of some section of the oppressed and exploited. To try to "prove" in advance that there is "absolutely" no way out of the situation would be sheer pedantry or playing with concepts and catchwords. Practice alone can serve as real "proof" in this and similar questions. All over the world the bourgeois system is experiencing a tremendous revolutionary crisis. The revolutionary parties must now "prove" in practice that they have sufficient understanding and organisation, contact with the exploited masses, and determination and skill to utilise the crisis for a successful, a victorious, revolution.[84]

Lukacs was well aware from his own experience that changes in class consciousness were always uneven: workers in different countries, industries, unions, and workplaces went into battles of different intensity at different times and emerged with different degrees of class consciousness. The emergence of a clear class consciousness does not happen "at a single stroke and in a coherent manner. For there are not merely national and 'social' stages involved but there are also gradations within the class consciousness of workers in the same strata."[85] It was the task of revolutionary organization to try and overcome this unevenness:

> The more or less chaotic ups and downs in the evolution of consciousness, the alternation of outbreaks which reveal a maturity of class consciousness far superior to anything foreseen by theory with half-lethargic conditions of stasis, of passivity, of merely subterranean progress finds itself opposed by a conscious effort to relate the "final goal" to the immediate exigencies of the moment. Thus in the theory of the party the process, the dialectic of class consciousness becomes a dialectic that is consciously deployed.[86]

But different types of political organization can retard as well as advance this process. Consequently, the question of political organization was a central concern for Lukacs as he applied his theory to concrete questions of class struggle.

REFORMIST ORGANIZATION AND REVOLUTIONARY ORGANIZATION

The explanation of class consciousness in the work of Marx, Engels, and Lukacs does not suffer the same one-sidedness as those which rely exclusively on pointing to ruling class control of the ideological levers in society—the so-called "dominant ideology thesis." This is because it starts from the real class experience of life under capitalism and shows both how this predisposes workers to accept the system, how key institutional and ideological divisions in society reflect its economic structure, and also how this pattern is disrupted by the inescapable contradiction at the heart of capitalism. In the wake of his experience in the Hungarian revolution and his assimilation of the lessons of the Russian revolution, Lukacs was insistent that any such general analysis must come to organizational conclusions. Indeed, he was insistent that the analysis itself was radically incomplete without an understanding of how the general formation of class consciousness was mediated by political organization:

> Organisation is the form of mediation between theory and practice. And, as in every dialectical relationship, the terms of the relation only acquire concreteness and reality in and by virtue of this mediation.[87]

So, to provide a more concrete picture of class consciousness, it is now necessary to show how the economic, political, and ideological struggle gives rise to and is shaped by political organization.

From the general analysis outlined above, it is not difficult to see the effect that reformist politics and organization have on working-class consciousness. It is precisely because the economic and social preconditions for revolution are often realized before workers are conscious of the revolutionary opportunity before them that the struggle against reformist political currents, which inhibit the development of such a consciousness, is so important:

> . . . the Menshevik [i.e. reformist] worker's parties and the unions they control . . . now consciously labour to ensure that the merely spontaneous movements of the proletariat (with their dependence on an immediate provocation, their fragmentation along professional and local lines etc.) should remain on the level of pure spontaneity. They strive to prevent them from turning their attention to the totality, whether this be territorial, professional etc., or whether it involves synthesising the economic movement with the political one.[88]

In this process Lukacs saw a division of labor between trade unions and reformist parties: "the unions tend to take on the task of atomising and de-politicising the movement and concealing its relation to the totality," whereas the reformist parties "perform the task of establishing the reification in the consciousness of the proletariat both ideologically and on the level of organisation."[89] In fact, the very separation between the economic struggle and the political struggle, embodied in the division between the unions and the reformist parties, "precludes any really effective action encompassing society in its totality, for this itself is based on the mutual interaction of both these factors."[90]

There is always a danger that the advances in consciousness that the working class gains through struggle will relapse into an understanding of society based on discrete spheres of life. "With the growth of social democracy," argues Lukacs, "this threat has acquired a real political organisation which artificially cancels out the mediations so laboriously won and forces the proletariat back into its immediate existence where it is merely a component of capitalist society and not *at the same time* the motor that drives it to its doom and destruction."[91] And because social democracy lives within the fragmented world presented by the day-to-day appearance of capitalism, it is unable to see the connection between the immediate struggle and the total struggle to change society. It, therefore, "must concede defeat on every particular issue also," because it has renounced the only standpoint that could enable it to combat the "overwhelming resources of knowledge, culture and routine which the bourgeoisie undoubtedly possesses and will continue to possess as long as it remains the ruling class."[92]

Lukacs's overall point is that the politics and structures of reformist organization tends to reinforce the reified picture of the world engendered by the process of capitalist production and exchange. This is even true during those periods of political and economic crisis when the working class is beginning to break from the old ideas. If such transformations in workers' consciousness are to fulfill their potential, it is essential that they are reflected in attempts to build an organization. Indeed, it is vital "that part of the proletariat that spontaneously rebels against its leaders' behaviour . . . and longs for revolutionary leadership *must assemble in an organisation.* The genuine revolutionary parties and groups which thus arise must contrive to win the confidence of the great masses and remove them from the power of the opportunists by their *actions* (and furthermore it is absolutely essential that they acquire their *own revolutionary party organisations*)."[93]

It was the contrast between the experience of Rosa Luxemburg and her supporters and that of Lenin and the Bolsheviks that made Lukacs so insistent on this issue. Luxemburg had fought a political and theoretical battle against right-wing revisionism *inside* the German reformist party, the SPD, but it was not until the revolution was actually underway that she formed an independent organization. The result was that, unlike Lenin and the Bolsheviks, Rosa Luxemburg's party was too small and too inexperienced to effect the outcome of the revolution decisively. As Lukacs notes,

> Lenin and Rosa Luxemburg were agreed *politically* and *theoretically* about the need to combat opportunism. The conflict between them lay in their answers to the question whether or not the campaign against opportunism should be conducted as an *intellectual* struggle *within* the revolutionary party of the proletariat or whether it was to be resolved on the level of organisation.[94]

The consequence of following Rosa Luxemburg's approach was that it "put the whole emphasis on convincing the supporters of opportunism and on achieving a majority *within* the party." The result is that "a war against *opportunism as a tendency* cannot crystallize out: the terrain of the 'intellectual conflicts' changes from one issue to the next and with it changes the composition of rival groups."[95] And so "it follows that the struggle against opportunism will disintegrate *into a series of individual skirmishes* in which the ally of yesterday can become the opponent of today and vice versa." Without a politically unified organization, it is impossible to judge whether the theory of the organization is correct and whether its strategy and tactics are effective:

> Only an analysis oriented towards organisation can make possible a genuine criticism of theory from the point of view of practice. If theory is directly juxtaposed to an organised action without its being made clear how it is supposed to affect it, i.e. without clearly expressing their connectedness in terms of organisation, then theory can only be criticised with regard to its own internal contradictions. This aspect of the problem

of organisation enables us to understand why opportunism has always shown
the very greatest reluctance to deduce organisational consequences from
theoretical disagreements.[96]

Of course, Lukacs's insistence on the independence of the revolutionary
party did not mean that the party should not relate to non-party workers,
attempt to lead them, and increase their political confidence and combativity.
Indeed, it was precisely because the reformist organization blunted the politics of the revolutionaries, forcing them into internal party struggles with
the right wing, that Lukacs saw reformism as incapable of relating to the
struggles of workers. And Lukacs was clear that the party's relationship with
the class was a two-way affair: the party had to learn from, as well as lead,
the class. But unless the spontaneously arising lessons of the class struggle
were embodied in organization, they could never be made permanent:

> A communist organisation . . . can only be created through struggle, it
> can only be realised if the justice and the necessity of this form of unity
> are accepted by every member as a result of his own experience.
> What is essential, therefore, is the interaction of spontaneity and con-
> scious control. . . . Thus, Engels describes how certain forms of military
> action originated spontaneously in the instincts of the soldiers as a reac-
> tion to the exigencies of the situation. This happened without any theo-
> retical preparation, and indeed often conflicted with the prevalent theories
> and hence existing military organisations. Despite this they prevailed and
> only afterwards were incorporated into the organisations concerned.[97]

In his *Lenin*, Lukacs makes a similar point: "In no sense is it the party's role
to impose any kind of abstract, cleverly devised tactics upon the masses. On
the contrary, it must continuously *learn* from their struggle and their conduct of it." The revolutionary party "must unite the spontaneous discoveries
of the masses, which originate in their correct class instincts, with the totality of the revolutionary struggle, and bring them to consciousness."[98] Lukacs
argued that changes in the level of struggle would have a profound effect
not just on the strategy and tactics of a revolutionary party but also on
every aspect of its organization:

> If the revolution leaves a particular phase behind, it would not be possible
> to adapt oneself to the exigencies of the new situation merely by chang-
> ing one's tactics, or even by changing the form of the organisation (e.g.
> exchanging illegal methods for legal ones). What is needed in addition is
> a reshuffle in the party hierarchy: the selection of personnel must be ex-
> actly suited to the new phase of struggle. Of course, this cannot be put
> into practice without "errors" or crises. The Communist Party would be
> a fantastical utopian island of the blessed reposing in the ocean of capital-
> ism if its progress were not constantly attended by such dangers.[99]

So far Lukacs's conception of the role of the party has been explained in terms of its difference from reformist organization, its importance in overcoming the unevenness in working-class consciousness, and in terms of the relationship between spontaneity and organization. But Lukacs's conception of the revolutionary process was more detailed than this, encompassing accounts of the role of the petty bourgeoisie, oppressed nationalities, parliamentary institutions and the state.

THE PROCESS OF REVOLUTION

At the heart of Lukacs's conception of revolution was the idea that, although only a strategy based on the power of the working class could ensure success, any such strategy must take account of the fact that the revolution would mobilize masses of the petty bourgeoisie and the oppressed nationalities against the old order. The way in which these other classes and nationalities were brought into alliance with the revolution was a life or death question, as Lukacs knew from his own experience. In the Russian revolution, the Bolshevik party had fiercely defended its own independence and that of the working class, but it had also developed a strategy of giving land to the peasants and independence to the oppressed nationalities and so ensured their loyalty to the revolution. In contrast, the Hungarian Communist Party and the reformist party had merged, thus compromising the political independence of the working class and never adequately resolving the question of dual power, and, at the same time, it had refused to grant land to the peasantry. The result was catastrophic for the revolution.

Lukacs begins his analysis of the petty bourgeoisie by describing the furthest limits of their class consciousness according to their position in the process of production, just as he had derived the contradictions of bourgeois thought and the potentialities of working-class consciousness according to their relationship to the economic structure of society. And, as with the two main classes, Lukacs is not, in the first instance, concerned with the immediate, actually existing consciousness of the petty bourgeoisie but with the objective limits of their consciousness as determined by their class position.

The petty bourgeoisie, unlike the bourgeoisie, are not a ruling class. They do not experience the system as *their* system. But, unlike the working class, there is nothing in their experience that, in itself, can drive them to break with the system, either in theory or in practice. Left to their own devices, they cannot develop a consciousness that graduates beyond the most immediate attempts to gratify their own egoistic interests: "These intermediate strata . . . are themselves—socially—blind . . . as a result of this they always represent particular class interests which do not even pretend to be the objective interests of the whole of society."[100] They are incapable of generating a consciousness that connects their own interests with the wider needs of society. This is why, to this day and despite their numerical decline, the mentality of the small shopkeeper is still the original model for the consciousness of this whole class.

In reality, however, the consciousness of the petty bourgeoisie is never left to its own devices. It is always buffeted and shaped by the changes in the fortunes and consciousness of the two major classes. The consciousness of the middle classes cannot, therefore, be reduced to a single position, or even to a single set of contradictions, emanating directly from their own place in the productive process:

> ... their actions are determined by factors external to themselves ... nothing that they do is implicit in their inner nature. Instead everything hinges on the behaviour of the classes capable of consciousness: the bourgeoisie, and the proletariat.[101]

Under "normal" circumstances, the petty bourgeoisie will gravitate toward the ruling class—sometimes outbidding its master in right-wing rhetoric, sometimes gently chastising the bourgeoisie for its harsh treatment of "the little man" or its lack of concern for "the social fabric"—but remaining basically loyal to the system. The bourgeoisie and its state, being a tiny minority of society, necessarily placates and seduces such intermediate layers and classes to facilitate its rule:

> The exercise of power by a minority can only perpetuate itself if it can contrive to carry the classes not directly and immediately affected by the revolution along with it ideologically. It must attempt to gain their support or at least their neutrality.[102]

This is especially true of the capitalist class which, unlike the aristocracy of feudal times, is in the first instance an economic class whose conditions of existence do not automatically confer political power as well. Capitalism separates politics and economics, for the ruling class as well as the working class (though not to the same degree), in a way that many precapitalist societies did not. Consequently, the bourgeoisie, even in the making of the classical bourgeois revolutions, often "delegates" its political functions, including the staffing of the state machine, to the petty bourgeoisie:

> The bourgeoisie had far less of an *immediate* control of the actual springs of power than had ruling classes in the past. ... On the one hand, the bourgeoisie had to rely much more strongly on its ability to make peace or achieve a compromise with the opposing classes that held power before it so as to use the power-apparatus they controlled for its own ends. On the other hand, it found itself compelled to place the actual exercise of force (the army, petty bureaucracy, etc.) in the hands of petty bourgeois, peasants, the members of subject nations, etc.[103]

Under conditions of economic expansion and political quietude, the bourgeoisie finds it relatively easy to gather around it this protective skirt of intermediate classes. And, of course, this process cannot but have an effect on the class consciousness of the working class, or at least those layers of it which are in greatest contact with the petty bourgeoisie, particularly the leaders, functionaries, and those most influenced by trade union and reformist party bureaucracies. But in conditions of economic and political crisis, the petty bourgeoisie's loyalty to the system comes under strain. Their "naive, unthought-out loyalty to the social system led by the bourgeoisie" is shaken. "Broader and broader strata separate out from the—seemingly—solid edifice of bourgeois society; they bring confusion into the ranks of the bourgeoisie, they unleash movements which do not themselves proceed in the direction of socialism but which through the violence of the impact they make do hasten the realisation of the preconditions of socialism: namely, the collapse of the bourgeoisie." This is a "situation which causes ever wider rifts in bourgeois society and which drives the proletariat on to revolution whether it would or not."[104]

Lukacs's attitude to the role of oppressed nationalities in the revolution follows a broadly similar pattern. First of all, he notes that there is nothing *inherent* in the position of an oppressed nationality which predisposes it to look favorably on a socialist revolution:

> If . . . other strata of the population become involved in the revolution they may advance it under certain circumstances. But it is just as easy for them to deflect it in a counter-revolutionary direction. For in the class situation of these strata (petty bourgeoisie, peasants, oppressed nationalities, etc.) there is nothing nor can there be anything to make their actions lead inevitably towards the proletarian revolution.[105]

In the case of oppressed nations, this is increasingly the case as the capitalist system ages. As capitalism struggled to emerge in opposition to the old feudal order, most of the struggles for national liberation had an implicitly progressive character. But "the movements for the unity of Germany and Italy were the last of these objectively revolutionary struggles."[106] Simply because this process has turned these countries into imperialist powers, this "does not mean that its significance as a nation-building factor ceased for the whole of the rest of the world." Indeed, the problem of the role of the oppressed nations in the socialist revolution has not disappeared; "on the contrary, *continuing capitalist development created national movements among all the hitherto 'unhistoric' nations of Europe.*" This means that socialists have to look at the problem in a new light:

> The difference is that their "struggles for national liberation" are now no longer merely struggles against their own feudalism and feudal absolutism—

that is to say only implicitly progressive—for *they are forced into the context of imperialist rivalry between the world powers.* Their historical significance, their evaluation, therefore depends on what concrete part they play in this concrete whole.[107]

Or, as *History and Class Consciousness* expresses the same thought:

> Forces that work towards revolution today may very well operate in the reverse direction tomorrow. And it is vital to note that these changes of direction do not simply follow mechanically from the class situation or even from the ideology of the stratum concerned. They are determined decisively by the constantly changing relations of the totality of the historical situation and the social forces at work. So that it is no very great paradox to assert that, for instance, Kemal Pasha may represent a revolutionary constellation of forces in certain circumstances whilst a great "workers' party" may be counter-revolutionary.[108]

Of course, Lukacs understood that ensuring that the petty bourgeoisie, the peasantry, and the oppressed nationalities fought on the side of the working class and not against it was of the very greatest importance:

> For, as the proletariat can liberate itself only by destroying class society, it is *forced* to conduct its war of liberation *on behalf* of every suppressed and exploited sector of the population. But whether the *latter* find themselves fighting on the side of the proletariat or in the camp of its opponents . . . depends . . . very much upon whether the revolutionary party of the proletariat has chosen the correct tactics.[109]

In his short book on Lenin, Lukacs outlines the difference that this choice of tactics can make:

> The approach of a revolutionary period is . . . heralded by all the dissatisfied elements of the old society seeking to join, or at least to make contact with, the proletariat. But precisely this can bring with it hidden dangers. If the proletarian party is not organised so that the correct and appropriate class policy is assured, these allies—who always multiply in a revolutionary situation—can bring confusion rather than support. For the other oppressed sections of society (peasants, petty bourgeoisie, and intellectuals) naturally do not strive for the same ends as the proletariat. The working class, provided it knows what it wants and what its class interest dictate, can free both itself and these other groups from social bondage. But if the party . . . is uncertain of the direction the class should take . . . then these other groups will deflect it from its path. Their alliance, which would have benefited the revolution if the proletarian party had been sure of its class organization, can then instead be of the greatest danger to it.[110]

To avert this last danger, Lenin's conception of the party contains two fixed poles: "the strictest selection of party members on the basis of their proletarian class consciousness, and total solidarity with and support for all the oppressed and exploited within capitalist society." As a consequence of this, Lenin "dialectically united exclusive singleness of purpose, and universality—the leadership of the revolution in strictly proletarian terms and its general national (and international) character." By contrast, the reformist conception of the party weakened "both these poles, confused them, reduced them to compromises, and united them *within the party itself.*"[111]

These general propositions had, naturally, to be expressed in specific tactical proposals. Lukacs showed in his discussion of Rosa Luxemburg's attitude to the national question that he had absorbed this lesson of the Russian revolution. He insisted that the internationalist instincts of the oppressed nationalities "cannot be aroused by intellectual utopians who behave as if the socialist world to come had already arrived and the nationality problem no longer existed."[112] Instead, Lukacs followed Lenin in insisting:

> It can be aroused only by the *practical proof that the victorious proletariat of an oppressor nation has broken with the oppressive tendencies of imperialism with all its consequences to the point where it accepts the right of self-determination "including national independence."*[113]

The ultimate test of a revolutionary party was whether it could bind the working class and its allies together to smash the bourgeois state.

Thus Lukacs's theory of class consciousness, although never reaching the level of concreteness to be found in Lenin, Luxemburg, Gramsci, and Trotsky, has provided a powerful general picture of what it is that makes workers liable to accept bourgeois ideology. It, therefore, provides a framework within which more partial explanations can be situated. And it has derived from that general picture some important observations about the institutions and characteristic forms taken by the ideology of the bourgeoisie and the class consciousness of the working class. Nor has it stopped at extending this analysis to other classes in capitalist society. It has also made working-class organization a decisive factor in the struggle for socialism. But for all its achievements, Lukacs's theory has been subject to ferocious criticism.

THE CRITICS OF LUKACS

Criticism of *History and Class Consciousness* has been heavy and sustained ever since the book was first published, becoming particularly intense after the first English translation appeared in 1971. In the mid-1920s, the book unsuccessfully swam against the rising tide of the Stalinist bureaucracy and the rapidly atrophying philosophical culture to which it gave rise. *History and Class Consciousness* was widely denounced within a Third International falling under Stalin's influence. Lukacs soon made his peace with Stalinism.

His passage to Stalinism inevitably required him to repudiate his own masterwork because *History and Class Consciousness* itself was imbued with the politics of the revolutionary era. Nevertheless not everything was lost, despite Lukacs's frequent bouts of Stalinist "self-criticism." Indeed, after he read Marx's *Economic and Philosophical Manuscripts* for the first time in Moscow in the late 1920s, Lukacs was able to make labor much more central to his philosophy than he had done in the early 1920s. This new perspective gives a powerful new dimension to his *The Young Hegel*, and it is a useful lens through which the modern reader can study *History and Class Consciousness*.[114]

Despite this, after the mid-1920s, the great systematic interpretation of marxism embodied in *History and Class Consciousness* and *Lenin* was a broken mirror—reflections of the old majesty could sometimes be glimpsed in the shards of Lukacs's later writings, but Lukacs himself could never recompose the totality of the system. That task could only be performed by spirits still in touch with a genuine revolutionary movement.[115]

The English translation was launched amid much interest in "Western Marxism," of which Lukacs was assumed to be a founder. This interest was fueled by the events of 1956—Lukacs identified with the Hungarian revolution and took a post in the Nagy government before it was crushed by Russian tanks. Interest continued to build throughout the wave of struggle which began in the 1960s and lasted into the mid-1970s.[116] In the left-wing theoretical discussions of the 1970s two broad camps could be distinguished. One represented the forces of the New Left, among whom were many orthodox Trotskyists. Here there was a stress, not all of it positive, on the "young Marx," on a humanist, activist marxism. It distinguished itself from an older, corrupted Stalinism.

In these discussions, there have been two types of criticism leveled at Lukacs. One concerns Lukacs's view of the marxist method; the second concerns Lukacs's substantive account of how class consciousness is formed. The remainder of this section deals with the critics of Lukacs's conception of class consciousness, the next section looks at the complimentary work of Antonio Gramsci, and the final section examines weaknesses in Lukacs's understanding of the marxist method.

One of the most frequent objections to Lukacs's notion of class consciousness is that it makes the ability to see the truth about society depend on class position. Gareth Stedman Jones insists that for Lukacs "all truth is relative to the standpoint of individual classes,"[117] and Kolakowski argues that "it is not clear how we can avoid the conclusion that in his view not only is truth revealed solely from a particular class angle, but that nothing is true at all except in the class consciousness that is identical with the practical revolutionary movement—in other words, participation in the movement equals possession of the truth."[118] For Terry Eagleton, there is "a logical problem" with Lukacs's idea that the working class can discern the truth about society: "For if the working class is the potential bearer of such consciousness, from what point is *this* judgement made?" Following Bhikhu Parekh, Eagleton argues that

> to claim that only the proletarian perspective allows one to grasp the truth of society as a whole already assumes that one knows what it is. It would seem that truth is either wholly internal to the consciousness of working class, in which case it cannot be assessed *as* truth and the claim simply becomes dogmatic; or one is caught in the impossible paradox of judging the truth from outside the truth itself, in which case the claim that this form of consciousness is true simply undercuts itself.[119]

In a certain sense, of course, all truth *is* relative—it is just that some theories do not acknowledge this elementary fact. There is no final, faultless, criterion for truth which hovers, like god, outside the historical process. Neither is there any privileged scientific method which is not shaped by the contours of the society of which it is a part. All that exists are some theories which are less internally contradictory and have greater explanatory power than others. The real question is from which vantage point, using what methods and tested by which criteria, are we likely to see more of the truth about our history?

On this understanding, the charge of relativism against Lukacs would hold only if: 1) his picture were one in which the ideology of a particular class was both homogenous and automatically reducible to its class position, 2) there was no disjunction, either analytically or historically, between the emergence of marxism as a body of theory and, even, the revolutionary consciousness of the working class and, 3) if there were no conception of practice as the test of theory.

In fact, it would be impossible for Lukacs's theory, properly understood, simply to reduce the truth to the consciousness of the working class. First, there is the obvious point that the actually existing consciousness of the working class is partially trapped within the structures of commodity fetishism and, therefore, by definition, unable to comprehend the truth about society. Second, as we have seen, when workers do begin to break from contradictory pro-capitalist consciousness they do so unevenly, and so the potential to see the truth always emerges among some workers who then find themselves in a contradictory relationship with other members of their own class. There can be no question, therefore, of simply equating the truth with the consciousness of the working class.

Even if we imagine a homogeneous, revolutionary working class, it would still need to generalize beyond its immediate experience to gain a truthful, scientific insight into the nature of society. If the truth is the totality, then it is the totality of working-class experience, internationally and historically, which gives access to the truth. No single experience of struggle alone, no matter how intense, can reveal this. The struggle can open up a path to the truth, but only an act of theoretical generalization, which builds on this basis, can form an adequate theory. Thus, theory develops its own particular concepts—the dialectic, surplus value, oppression, and so on—which condense and interpret real experience.

The fact that a body of theory can be seen as a summation of the historical experience of the working class does not alter the fact that this experience can only be available as theory and never as an immediate experience. In short, no one can be simultaneously present in, say, the Paris Commune, the 1905 Russian revolution, and Paris in 1968. But they will more readily comprehend the meaning of these events, and therefore of their society as a whole, from the class position of the proletariat than from that of the bourgeoisie. And when we move beyond the question of individual cognition to the issue of the consciousness of whole classes, then we can see that it is impossible for a ruling class *as a whole* to vacate its position in society and see the world from the point of view of another class.

If, then, the immediate struggle is always mediated by the cumulative experience of past struggle and its codification in theory, there can be no question of reducing consciousness to immediate class position or of reducing theory to immediate consciousness, even in a revolutionary situation. If theory is not "automatically" true by virtue of the class position of those who hold it, how are we to be sure that our theory is correct? The answer is that there is a point where the theory and the consciousness of the working class meet—in practice. Conscious human labor, in this case the theoretically informed struggle of the working class against the capitalist system, is the ultimate proving ground. History, the place where human beings create their own world, the point where subjective and objective meet, is the final arbiter. The Spanish Inquisition may still have its advocates, but their case has been dismissed with the only kind of finality that humanity can offer: the ideas that they represented are historical relics powerless to affect the world.

Thus, although it is true to say that only the working class, as a class, has the potential to see the truth about society, it is not true that this potential can simply be reduced to the immediate consciousness of the working class, let alone that "participation in the movement equals possession of the truth" as Kolakowski asserts. The class position of the proletariat, in particular the peaks in the history of working-class struggle, are a vantage point from which the working class can *generalize* to an understanding of society, to a theory of society.

Therefore, it is not that the validity of marxism *only* flows from the immediate practice of the working class. It is a theoretical generalization based on the historical experience of the working class, and therefore a theory of society as a whole rather than merely the history of the oppressed. Consequently, its validity must be proven by its superior explanatory power—more internally coherent, more widely applicable, capable of greater empirical verification—in comparison with its competitors. Indeed, this is a condition of it entering the chain of historical forces as an effective power. It is a condition of it being "proved in practice." If it is not superior to other theories in this sense, it will not "seize the masses," will not become a material force, will not be realized in practice.

The answer to Terry Eagleton's conundrum is that because marxism is the *theoretical summation* of working-class experience historically and internationally, it does provide a vantage point from which the truth of class consciousness can be judged. It is, therefore, possible to "judge the truth from outside the truth" without abandoning the point of view of the working class. Neither does this mean adopting the dogmatic attitude that "already assumes that one knows what the truth is," because the truth of the judgment about class consciousness can only finally be attested by the results of the struggle—only when theory "has become part of the consciousness of the proletariat and has been made practical by it," as Lukacs puts it. Theory and practice are independent moments, and so one can be the judge of the other, but ultimately they are parts of a single whole, moments of a single process called history.[120]

A second objection often raised against Lukacs is that his theory does not allow for the way in which the contending classes influence each other. The working class has one pure consciousness, shaped by its relationship to the means of production; and the ruling class has an opposed, pure consciousness, based on its relationship to the means of production, and, so the argument runs, there is no interaction between the two. So Stedman Jones objects that "there has never existed the type of *pristine* ideological sway which he [Lukacs] proposes." He goes on to quote Althusserian Nicos Poulantzas: "The dominant ideology does not simply reflect the life conditions of the dominant class subject 'pure and simple', but the political relationship in a social formation between the dominant and the dominated classes".[121] Terry Eagleton makes a similar point when he objects that "class is not just some kind of collectivised individual equipped with all sorts of attributes ascribed by humanist thought to the individual person: consciousness, unity, autonomy, self-determination and so on." Instead, Eagleton argues, classes are "complex, internally conflictive 'blocs,' rather than homogenous bodies," which display "unevenness and contradictoriness."[122] Even Colin Sparks, in a generally more favorable treatment of Lukacs, agrees on this point: "If the conception of history admits, in theory, only two possible world-visions ... then the study of differing intellectual currents within a class becomes of secondary importance."[123]

Yet these criticisms, insofar as they are directed at Lukacs's conception of working-class consciousness, are so wide of the target as to be positively perverse. A number of writers have testified to Lukacs's central concern with the uneven nature of working-class consciousness, the whole point of which was to demonstrate that workers' consciousness needed to overcome the impact of ruling ideas upon it and to break with the organized forms in which such ideas were embodied, such as reformist parties.

As Jorge Larrain states:

> ... it is simply a mistake to believe that for Lukacs ideologies are seen as "number plates carried on the backs of class subjects"—as Poulantzas puts it—if this characterisation implies any genetic relationship between the class and its ideology.... In fact, for Lukacs the class psychological consciousness, spontaneously developed by the class, does not constitute its real ideology and can be entirely at variance with it.[124]

Although Lukacs tended to see shifts in workers' consciousness in overly dramatic terms, he did also acknowledge that consciousness is necessarily uneven. He understood that it was divided between revolutionary and reformist consciousness, influenced by petty bourgeois currents and buffeted by spontaneous attempts to overcome trade union sectionalism. All this, as we have seen, is specifically analyzed in *History and Class Consciousness* and *Lenin*.

Bourgeois ideology is also, though for different reasons, driven by contradiction, only able to form a partial picture of how society works. This is necessarily the case for a class divided against itself by competition and unable to control fully the system over which it presides. Lukacs notes that the division of labor which arises on this basis gives different aspects of society, for instance, the legal system, their own mode of operation which is not immediately reducible to what happens in the other parts of the system. Naturally, the ideology of such a class can be forced to make concessions to pressure from below, especially in those periods of crisis when the natural ideological allies of the bourgeoisie, the petty bourgeoisie, are pulled toward the working class in the way described by Lukacs.

The grain of truth in Poulantzas's argument is that Lukacs saw the ideology of the ruling class as more homogenous and less liable to influence by other class forces than the ideology of the working class and that there were narrow limits beyond which bourgeois ideology could not be bent. But in arguing against Lukacs on this point, his critics are being too clever for their own good. Lukacs's conception of class consciousness combines a clear sense of the limits within which consciousness can change with an equally clearly articulated conception of the possibilities for conflict and contradiction within the ideology of a particular class. The difficulty with the position outlined by Lukacs's critics is that it provides the latter only at the cost of abandoning the former. In short, they dissolve the objective limits of class consciousness into a permanent flux of intersecting ideological currents, making secondary conflicts within the consciousness of particular class the hinge on which analysis turns.

The political ramifications of this approach are obvious. Poulantzas's wish to assert the permeability of ruling-class consciousness was, for instance, connected with his later support for the Eurocommunist strategy of reforming capitalism from within—"the long march through the institutions" of the bourgeois society. Poulantzas's critique of Lukacs is simultaneously a critique of classical marxist theory, an attempt to abandon *State and Revolution* by criticizing *History and Class Consciousness*.

A third criticism of Lukacs is that "his reasoning . . . is conducted on a level of rarefied abstraction that rarely makes contact with the relevant facts of historical actuality"[125] and that he "pays scant attention to the material institutions through which ideologies are produced and disseminated."[126] Stedman Jones, as usual, puts the case at its most extreme: *History and Class Consciousness* has "very little reference to, or awareness of the real history of either the capitalist mode of production or working class struggle";[127] it provides for no role for class formations that have survived from earlier modes of production;[128] contains "very little . . . on the bourgeois state";[129] and "never provides a concrete analysis of a concrete situation."[130]

The majority of these criticisms are untenable. Lukacs's whole analysis is predicated on the historical specificity of capitalism compared with other modes of production. Long passages of the book are devoted to demonstrating how capitalism emerged from feudalism. Even the most rarified passages of *History and Class Consciousness*, the central section of the essay "Reification and the Consciousness of the Proletariat," deals with the development of bourgeois philosophy *in the context of the bourgeoisie's transition from a revolutionary class to a stable ruling class.* Likewise, Lukacs's lengthy analysis of the role played by revolutionary parties, workers' councils, reformist parties, and trade unions—surely some of the most important "institutions through which ideologies are produced"—can only be ignored by treating the final three essays in *History and Class Consciousness* and *Lenin* as if they had nothing to do with the central essay on reification when, on the contrary, they are obviously intended to concretize the analysis.[131]

But whether or not Lukacs himself was always as concrete as he might have been, it can be shown that Lukacs's system is *inherently* historical in its approach. Lukacs realized, as did Marx, that capitalism formed a *system* in which discoverable laws governed the relationships between the different parts of the system. But, of course, these laws were the product of an historical process and are changed by the further development of this process. The knack lies in analyzing the interaction between system and process.[132] The result is that any understanding of society must be based on a dialectical interaction between the structural facets of the system and the myriad of events that form the stream of the historical process: "Thus the succession and internal order of the categories constitute neither a purely logical sequence, nor are they organised merely in accordance with the facts of history."[133]

Consequently, even though *History and Class Consciousness* was primarily concerned to outline "the structural components of the present," it was necessarily and simultaneously also an historical account of the formation of the system. The irony is that Althusserian structuralism, on which most of Lukacs's critics depend, never even approached this level of analysis, retreating into a sterile world of pure structures in which the real historical process was as welcome as a leper at the lord mayor's banquet.[134]

Lukacs's weakness was that he did not extend his general framework into a sufficiently concrete account of the historically developed forms of contradictory consciousness. Bourgeois ideology varies significantly according to historical circumstance—fascism and reformism, for instance, are obviously not twins despite both being forms of bourgeois ideology. And not all forms of bourgeois ideology grip the working class equally. Such grip as bourgeois ideology does command is certainly not static, unchanging, or unalterable. To account for these important variations in consciousness is an important challenge for any marxist. The general approach that Lukacs provided is indispensable for meeting this challenge. But it needs to be supplemented with insights which, for example, are to be found in the work of Antonio Gramsci.

GRAMSCI'S CONCEPT OF CONTRADICTORY CONSCIOUSNESS

George Lukacs and Antonio Gramsci (1891–1937) could not have come from more different backgrounds. Gramsci came from poor provincial origins in Sardinia; his education was difficult and often interrupted by poverty and illness. His revolutionary activity began earlier than Lukacs, giving him the decisive advantage of real immersion in a mass workers' movement.

But Lukacs and Gramsci also have some close similarities. Gramsci's intense hostility to the reformism of the Second International at first led him to adopt "spontaneist" political positions. Even when he rethought these attitudes, he retained a deep aversion to reformism, but then coupled it with an abiding commitment to building a revolutionary workers' party—although much modern commentary seeks to diminish the fact.[135] Philosophically, he was indebted to the Hegelian tradition. He was influenced by the idealist philosopher Benedetto Croce's reading of Hegel. Antonio Labriola's Hegelian marxism became a recurring point of reference in Gramsci's writing. Gramsci attended the philosophy classes of Professor Annibale Pastore in Turin, who recorded that his own conception of the Hegelian dialectic went beyond the idea that it was "fixed in an eternal trichotomy of thesis, antithesis and synthesis". His "original discovery" was that "the incubation of material conditions in the womb of existing society [is] the point of disruption between thesis and antithesis." Pastore remembers that,

> Gramsci grasped the originality of the notion at once, and saw it as a new and critical insight into the meaning of crisis and revolution. He had been a Crocean originally, but now was very restless. . . . He wanted to understand how culture developed, for revolutionary reasons: the ultimately practical significance of theoretical life. He wanted to find out how thinking can lead to actions (the technique of propaganda), how thought can make people's hands move, and how and in what sense ideas themselves may be actions.[136]

It is this "practical" aspect that is Gramsci's decisive advantage over Lukacs. In many purely "philosophical" respects—his understanding of Hegel, the precision with which he used the dialectic, his clarity about the overall limits of class consciousness, his understanding of commodity fetishism—he was inferior to Lukacs.[137] But he did have a much greater feel for the concrete ways in which philosophical ideas interact with both the social circumstances and the existing ideologies of the various classes in capitalist society.

In particular, Gramsci understood contradictory consciousness as something *within* classes, sections of classes, and, even, single individuals. Lukacs, by contrast, tended to express the same idea much more abstractly, merely as *uneven* consciousness between discrete layers of the class. Even though Lukacs's broader theory was quite capable of generating a more complex picture, it was in fact Gramsci who did so, despite a weaker general theory.

Although couched in language obscure enough not to alert the censor, Gramsci's writings during his decade in Mussolini's jails captured the lessons he learned during the revolutionary years after the First World War. In the following passage, he describes the struggle for political consciousness that takes place in every worker's mind, especially during periods of heightened class conflict:

> The active man-in-the-mass has a practical activity, but has no clear theoretical consciousness of his practical activity, which nonetheless still involves understanding the world in so far as he transforms it. His theoretical consciousness can indeed be historically in opposition to his activity. One might almost say that he has two theoretical consciousnesses (or one contradictory consciousness): one which is implicit in his activity and which really unites him with his fellow-workers in the practical transformation of the real world; and one, superficially explicit or verbal, which he has inherited from the past and uncritically absorbed.[138]

It is not difficult to see how this notion of "superficial verbal" consciousness marries up with Lukacs's idea of false consciousness derived from the experience of commodity fetishism, nor to see in Gramsci's "practical consciousness" the idea of a non-alienated consciousness emerging in the process of struggle against the power of capital described by Lukacs. But Gramsci's analysis turns away from these more abstract discussions of the determinants of class consciousness in favor of the institutions and ideologies that do battle for the worker's allegiance:

> ... this verbal conception ... holds together a specific social group, it influences moral conduct and the direction of the will, with varying efficacity but often powerfully enough to produce a situation in which the contradictory consciousness does not permit of any action, any decision or any choice, and produces a position of moral and political passivity. Critical understanding of self takes place therefore through struggle of political "hegemonies" and of opposing directions, first in the ethical field and then in that of politics proper, in order to arrive at the working out at a higher level of one's own conception of reality.[139]

Gramsci, therefore, concludes that "political consciousness ... is the first stage towards the further progressive self-consciousness in which theory and practice will finally be one."

This general framework led Gramsci to a lifelong study of various ideologies: Catholicism, folklore, cultural theories, the limits of trade union and reformist consciousness, the popular appeal of fascism, and so on. Gramsci was concerned to direct attention to the various forms of "primitive" revolt among the exploited and oppressed—populism, social banditry, expressions of millenarianism and mysticism in the countryside, urban insurrectionism, utopian socialism, and cultural revolt in the cities.[140]

These spontaneous and impure forms of consciousness mixed together "common sense"—"the day-to-day ideology of the bourgeoisie", with "good sense"—the elements of progressive consciousness won from the everyday experience of the oppressed. It was the task of marxists to intervene in the class struggle, both practically and ideologically, and to help in the formulation of a more coherent class consciousness.

Such work could only be successful if the working class and its party were capable of creating "organic intellectuals," rooted in the life of the masses, speaking their language, and able to use every turn of events to raise their consciousness. The creation of such a cadre was often a painstaking, long term job: "Creating a group of independent intellectuals is not an easy thing; it requires a long process, with actions and reactions, coming together and drifting apart and the growth of very numerous and complex new formations."[141]

Nevertheless, the task was necessary because an economic crisis, even a revolutionary situation, would not in itself be enough to create the consciousness capable of leading to an overthrow of the system: "It may be ruled out that immediate economic crises of themselves produce fundamental historical events; they can simply create a terrain more favourable to the dissemination of certain modes of thought, and certain ways of posing and resolving questions involving the entire subsequent development of national life."[142]

From Gramsci's idea of contradictory consciousness, from his study of its various concrete forms, from his outline of ways in which marxists can intervene to make it more coherent, and from many other insights not discussed here, the classical marxist tradition has gained a great deal.

But even in the area of his greatest strength Gramsci's theory has an important shortcoming. Gramsci never made any consistent study of the economic roots of class consciousness. He, therefore, elaborated no notion either of alienation or commodity fetishism. Thus, for all the subtlety of his concrete description, he provided no overall explanation for where the conservative or the progressive sides of contradictory consciousness originated. Indeed, he tended to assume that force of ruling-class ideas among the working class was simply the result of the ruling classes' control of the press, the education system, and so on.

> So long as there exists a bourgeois regime, with a monopoly of the press in the hands of capitalism and thus the possibility of the government and the political parties to impose political issues according to their interests, presented as the general interest ... so long as the most impudent lies against communism are diffused at will, it is inevitable that the working class will remain fragmented.[143]

This kind of approach, as we saw in chapter 2, was only half of Marx's explanation, because it could only account for why the ruling class had the power to disseminate its ideas, but not fully account for why workers' accept them. And, by extension, Gramsci's notion of what force is capable of resisting bourgeois ideology, for all his attempts to base it on the elements of "good sense" among the masses ultimately relied on an external impulse from the party and the "organic intellectuals" it managed to create: Boggs notes the "increasing preoccupation with this 'external element' (the role of the intellectuals, the function of the party) that informs Gramsci's writings in the *Prison Notebooks*."[144] These formulations are strangely reminiscent of those developed, but later significantly modified as being too one-sided, by Lenin in *What Is to Be Done?*

To provide a fully convincing explanation of contradictory consciousness, a theory of alienation and commodity fetishism is necessary. Such a theory explains the elements of both bourgeois and working-class consciousness which *pre-exist* in the objective economic and social conditions of the working class. It is to these that both the bourgeoisie and the socialists can appeal in their attempts to influence working-class consciousness. Moreover, it draws attention to the inherent conflicts at the heart of this mechanism which allow elements of resistance, both practical and ideological, constantly to re-emerge. It, therefore, provides the secure economic and social foundation for Gramsci's observations about ideology which his own account failed to provide. This is why, although Gramsci's insights can help concretize Lukacs's theory, they depend on Lukacs's work for their ultimate ground.

LUKACS AND THE MARXIST METHOD

The marxist method has, in Lukacs's account, three key terms: immediacy, totality, and mediation. Immediacy is the condition in which we confront the world in our day-to-day lives. It is the raw experience of daily life, or what empiricists call reality. But, as we have seen, the immediate, reified appearance of capitalist society is very different to its underlying structure. The immediate reality of capitalist society—the "facts" to which empiricists appeal—can seem to endorse the inevitability of the market and all the other forms of commodity fetishism that Marx and Lukacs describe. The true reality, or "essence" to use Hegel's terminology, is very different—a world of exploitation and class struggle. Understanding this division, says Lukacs, is the beginning of wisdom:

> If the facts are to be understood, this distinction between their real existence and their inner core must be grasped clearly and precisely. This distinction is the first premise of a truly scientific study which in Marx's words, "would be superfluous if the outward appearance of things coincided with their essence." Thus we must detach the phenomena from the form in which they are immediately given and discover the intervening links which connect them to their core, their essence.[145]

This approach does not mean that Lukacs has a contemptuous attitude toward the facts, simply ignoring what is inconvenient in the name of some mystical insight into a deeper reality. His point is that isolated, discrete facts, or even partial theories, can only be fully understood in the context of the whole. Only by grasping the totality, the second key concept in Lukacs's account of the marxist method, will we be able to *explain* why the appearance of society and its inner workings are so different. Indeed, given the workings of commodity fetishism, the appearance of society is *necessarily* different from its true reality. So, for Lukacs, the marxist method must explain "the facts" in terms of the deeper reality, not simply ignore them.

What is required to overcome immediacy? "To leave empirical reality behind," argues Lukacs, "can only mean that the objects of the empirical world are to be understood as aspects of a totality, i.e. as the aspects of a total social situation caught up in a process of historical change." Lukacs, like Marx, followed Hegel's maxim that "the truth is the whole." And, because this totality is the historical process, it is important not to see "the facts" as static segments that must be related to an equally unchanging whole, but to see "facts" as dynamic processes related to a constantly changing totality. Or, as Lukacs expresses it, "the *developing tendencies of history constitute a higher reality than the empirical facts.*"[146]

Nevertheless, it is not possible simply to pick out a particular social process, say, the breakdown of Prince Charles's marriage, and relate it *directly* to the historical evolution of capitalism in its entirety. The relationship between every partial process or isolated fact and the totality is always a *mediated* relationship. Mediation, the third term in Lukacs's dialectic, involves looking at the various subordinate totalities into which the individual processes must be integrated before they can be absorbed into the global process of historical change.

In the case of the breakdown of the Prince of Wales's marriage, we would have to look at the particular evolution of the monarchy under the specific conditions of British capitalism in the late twentieth century, at the impact that changing sexual mores and attitudes toward women have had on the monarchy, at the part played by the onset of the recession of the late 1980s and early 1990s and its impact on class consciousness, on the role of the press, and so on (conversely, the history of British capitalism could be told through the particular history of the British monarchy, because every part of the totality reflects, at a particular angle, the total process of which it is a part). Thus, mediation is not just an intellectual tool but also a real historical process. Indeed, it is only the fact that mediation exists as a social reality that allows its intellectual counterpart to exist:

> Thus the category of mediation is a lever with which to overcome the mere immediacy of the empirical world and as such is not something (subjective) foisted on to the objects from outside, it is no value judgement or "ought" opposed to their "is" *It is rather the manifestation of their objective structure.* . . . Mediation would not be possible were if it not for the fact that the empirical existence of objects is itself mediated and only appears to be unmediated in so far as the awareness of mediation is lacking so that the objects are torn from the complex of their true determinants and placed in artificial isolation.[147]

Mediation also has another very important role to play in the unfolding of the historical process. Lukacs sees the present as the mediating moment between the past and the future, "the mediation between the concrete, i.e. historical past, and the equally concrete, i.e. historical future." The present is where the dialectically understood past can be transformed in accordance with a theory that has grasped the "developing tendencies of history." We must stop seeing society as in a static state of "being," to use Hegel's term, and see it as in a process of change, of "becoming." To see the present in this way is to stop it dissolving into "a continuous, intangible moment, immediacy slipping away" and to seize it as "the focus of decision and of the birth of the new":

> As long as man concentrates his interest contemplatively upon the past *or* the future, both ossify into an alien existence. And between the subject and the object lies the unbridgeable "pernicious chasm" of the present. Man must be able to comprehend the present as a becoming. He can do this by seeing in it the tendencies out of whose dialectical opposition he can *make* the future.[148]

Thus, Lukacs is not content with a method that leaves its user in a passive, contemplative attitude toward the fate of society. To adopt the marxist method implies political activity. Indeed, it can only be fully comprehended in the course of such activity. It is easy to see why, from this point of view, Lukacs is unhappy with traditional "reflection" theories of consciousness which assume that our ideas simply mirror reality in the way that a photograph reproduces its object. In the first place, because appearance and reality are opposed, a reflection theory of consciousness is likely simply to reproduce the reified surface of society, not its inner structure. Second, a reflection theory tends to assume simplistically that the patterns of intellectual development mirror those in reality. But for Lukacs, although thought and reality are part of the same process, they also develop their own specific features, just as the world of art moves according to its own laws as well as being subject to those which govern the economic structure. To reduce one to the other is a classic example of an *unmediated* relationship:

> ... thought and existence are not identical in the sense that they "correspond" to each other, or "reflect" each other, that they "run parallel" to each other or "coincide" with each other (all expressions that conceal a rigid duality). Their identity is that they are aspects of one and the same real historical and dialectical process. What is "reflected" in the consciousness of the proletariat is the new positive reality arising out of the dialectical contradictions of capitalism.[149]

Finally, the result of reducing thought to existence is that it runs the risk of turning into fatalism. If thought simply reflects reality, what role can consciousness have in changing that reality? Lukacs argues:

> ... when the truth of becoming is the future that is to be created but has not been born, when it is the new that resides in the tendencies that (with our conscious aid) will be realised, then the question of whether thought is a reflection appears quite senseless. It is true that reality is the criterion for the correctness of thought. But reality is not, it becomes—and to become the participation of thought is needed.[150]

Lukacs is not objecting to a theory that demands that our ideas correspond to reality; he is merely arguing that a reflection theory is too simplistic to account for a situation in which appearance and reality diverge and where consciousness itself is an active part of reality. By ignoring these complexities, reflection theories produce all the old dualism characteristic of bourgeois ideology, complete with either the contemplative or the voluntarist attitude toward reality that it entails.

But although Lukacs's interpretation of the marxist method was superior to its best known alternative, it still suffered from a number of shortcomings. The first of these concerns Lukacs's description of marxist orthodoxy as referring "exclusively to *method*." Lukacs formulates this point in an extreme form on the very first page of *History and Class Consciousness*. He argues that even if "recent research had disproved once and for all every one of Marx's individual theses," no marxist should worry, because marxism is "not the 'belief' in this or that thesis, not the exegesis of a 'sacred' book," but only a question of the dialectical method.

This view may have something to recommend it as a polemical response to the positivism rampant in the Second International, but it creates as many problems as it solves. There is, for instance, an objection on which common sense and dialectics agree: What is the use of a pristine method that continually delivers predictions which are proved false? And proved false, presumably, by bad old empirical methods at that. Or, put dialectically, method and result must bear the same structure and cannot, therefore, be separated in the manner Lukacs proposes. Neither is there, on Lukacs's definition, any necessary or continuing connection between marxism and the struggle of the working class. Indeed, such an approach risks resurrecting the old division between thought and reality for which Lukacs criticizes reflection theory.

In fact, method and theory can only find their ultimate verification in the struggle of the working class, as *History and Class Consciousness* goes on to demonstrate in some detail. A more satisfactory summary of the real definition contained in the substantive analysis of *History and Class Consciousness* would be Engels's view that marxism "is the theory of the conditions of the liberation of the proletariat." Indeed, the very first sentence of Lukacs's *Lenin* paraphrases Engels: "Historical materialism is the theory of proletarian revolution." The fact that Lukacs could correct his definition of marxism, bringing it into alignment with the content of his theory, demonstrates that here we are dealing with an important but secondary question which does not effect the essentials of what Lukacs has to say. This is not the case with the next issue raised by Lukacs's description of the marxist method.

One surprising aspect of Lukacs's views about the key elements of the marxist method—immediacy, mediation, and totality—is that he makes no mention of contradiction, a concept usually assumed to be at the heart of

Marx's view of the dialectic. Indeed, Lukacs has a tendency, again more marked in the earlier rather than the later essays of *History and Class Consciousness*, to make totality alone the decisive characteristic of the marxist method: "*The primacy of the category of totality is the bearer of the principle of revolution is science.*"[151] It is not hard to see why Lukacs adopts this definition, distinguishing marxism from the fragmented and partial nature of bourgeois ideology and from the economic reductionism current in the Second International. But totality alone is not the defining characteristic of the marxist method.

Many other social theories also involve seeing the world as a totality. Religions of various kinds often insist on seeing the world as expressions of a single, albeit mystical, essence. A variety of ecological and green theorists argue that all natural and human life are part of an interconnected ecosystem. Functionalist sociological theorists see society as an interrelated system. Even conservative ideologies have their own conception of totality linked to ideas of blood, family, and nationhood.

It could be argued in defense of Lukacs's use of totality that all these are examples of *unmediated* totalities in which the facts of everyday life are simply held against the backcloth of some grand theory without ever demonstrating the real connections between the two. They are, therefore, not totalities in the real sense—because every real totality is a mediated totality—but mystical and irrational attempts to counterfeit a genuine account of how society develops. This point is perfectly valid, but it ignores another equally important point. All these false totalities are *static*. None can explain why the totality changes and develops over time. They simply produce the same features generation after generation or, at best, assume a cyclical development, that is, a situation in which there is change but no progress, only repetition.

For a totality to be capable of generating change independently, it must be internally contradictory. Contradiction is the motor of progress—in marxism such contradictions are class contradictions. Similarly, for there to be changes in the consciousness of the working class, it, too, must embody a contradiction. We have seen from Lukacs's account of how working-class consciousness changes, of the effect of the battle over the length of the working day and so on, that he clearly identified such a contradiction at this level of analysis. For instance, on the very page where he describes the battle over the working day as the hinge on which class consciousness turns, as the point where the reified relations of the market give way to the force of the class struggle, Lukacs says that such a movement "must direct itself to the qualitatively new factors arising from the dialectical contradictions: it must be a movement of mediations advancing from the present to the future."[152] And there are many other instances in the description of the class struggle contained in *History and Class Consciousness* where particular contradictions are given a key role.[153] But Lukacs did not raise this insight to the point where he made it the defining characteristic of the marxist method. In this respect, Lenin's definition in the *Philosophical Notebooks*, previously cited, is superior: "The splitting of a single whole and the cognition of its contradictory parts . . . is the *essence* . . . of dialectics."[154]

This definition has the virtue of focusing attention on contradiction and conflict, the dynamic at the heart of the totality, encouraging attempts to find the key link in the whole chain—the possessor of which can move the chain in its entirety. Lukacs's weakness in respect of this methodological question has its counterpart in a weakness in his view of alienation.

For Marx and Engels, the ability to create objects through labor—be they physical objects such as a table, or institutions like a workers' council, or intellectual systems like marxism—was fundamental to their definition of what it meant to be a human being. To "objectify" oneself by the creation and alteration of the natural and social world was what distinguished humans from animals. It was only under certain specific historical conditions that this natural characteristic of humanity could be experienced as alienation. Those conditions, as we have seen, are at their most extreme in capitalist society where the products of human labor—including its social, political, and intellectual aspects—confront us as alien objects, not as confirmation of our nature but as distortions of our nature.

The distinction between objectification and alienation was one of the crucial advances that Marx made over Hegel. It was Hegel's belief that it was changes in consciousness that were ultimately the motor force of history which led him to the view that any attempt to give physical shape to thought, to embody thought in the structures and institutions of the real world, was a form of alienation. Objectification and alienation were, therefore, identical. In this context, alienation became a universal condition of human existence, not the condition imposed on humanity by a particular mode of production.[155] In Hegel, alienation was absolute and unchangeable; in Marx, it was historical and transitory. But Marx's crucial distinction between alienation and objectification appeared in his *1844 Manuscripts*, which were unknown and unpublished when Lukacs wrote *History and Class Consciousness*. Lukacs's sources were his wartime reading of Hegel and the account of commodity fetishism contained in *Capital* and *A Contribution to a Critique of Political Economy*. Consequently, Lukacs tends to use objectification and alienation as interchangeable terms. On this issue, Lukacs is his own fiercest critic, as a glance at the relevant section of his 1967 preface to *History and Class Consciousness* confirms.[156]

In fact, Lukacs admits more weaknesses than the text of *History and Class Consciousness* actually contains. Although Lukacs makes no methodological distinction between alienation and objectification, he does use the term objectification in both a positive and a negative sense. Frequently, objectification is used as a synonym for alienation, as when Lukacs describes the objectification of workers' labor power as "something opposed to their total personality," so that "the personality can do no more than look on helplessly while its own existence is reduced to an isolated particle and fed into an alien system."[157] But equally there are a number of passages where Lukacs sees objectification in the same positive light that Marx recognized. For instance, "the trust that the spontaneously revolutionary masses" feel for the revolutionary party "is nourished by the feeling that the party is the objectification of their own will . . . the visible incarnation of their class consciousness."[158] And, in an important passage, Lukacs makes it clear that he understands that objectivity is historically variable:

> . . . to eliminate the objectivity attributed both to social institutions inimical to man and to their historical evolution means the restoration of this objectivity to their underlying basis, to relations between men; it does not involve the elimination of the laws of objectivity independent of the will of men and in particular of the wills and thoughts of individual men. It simply means that this objectivity is the self-objectification of human society at a particular stage of its development; its laws hold good only within the historical context which produced them and which is in turn determined by them.[159]

This is clearly a very different conception than that which seeks to banish objectivity once and for all as inevitably stained with the mark of alienation. Here the thought is that objectification, which takes place on its natural basis, as conscious product of unalienated relations between men, is quite different from relations that are dominated by institutions which function according to the unconscious and uncontrolled laws. Thus Lukacs's confusion on this point, though dangerous, is more terminological than substantive. It does, however, point to a more serious weakness in Lukacs's attitude to human labor and, therefore, to the dialectic of nature.

Marx and Engels had seen human labor as a natural facility, originating in nature, developing historically to the point where it can transform nature, consequently also developing its own specific characteristics but yet still part of nature. Marx and Engels's attitude is well summarized by Franz Jakubowski:

> Nature and man form a unity. Just as man is a product of nature (as well as the product of human labour), so too the nature which surrounds him is produced, in its present form, by human society. Once man is considered a social being, nature too is recognised as human and social. Nature is the basis for his presence in the world, the link with other men, an aspect of his social existence: "Society is the consummated oneness in substance of man and nature . . . the naturalism of man and the humanism of nature both brought to fulfillment."[160]

At first sight, it seems as if Lukacs has completely departed from this conception, insisting on a radical separation of the social and natural worlds. In a notorious passage in *History and Class Consciousness*, Lukacs criticizes Engels for arguing that experimentation in the natural sciences is the same as practice in the social world. Lukacs argues that political practice, the struggle of the working class, involves the object of society coming to consciousness, transforming the social structure from within. It is the very opposite of the passive contemplation of the workings of natural laws or, even, the external manipulation of material by experimentation. It was this vision of science, projected onto society, which had been at the root of the deterministic marxism of the Second International.[161]

From this argument, it is often assumed that Lukacs rejects any conception of a dialectic in nature, although he pays little specific attention to this broader issue as opposed to the narrower question of the experimental method in his critique of Engels. Yet there are other passages in *History and Class Consciousness* where Lukacs gives a very different impression. In his discussion of Hegel, for instance, Lukacs points out that Hegel was wrong simply to try and project his dialectic of consciousness onto the natural world. But even Hegel, Lukacs then goes on to note, did "perceive clearly at times that the dialectics of nature can never become anything more exalted than a dialectics of movement witnessed by the detached observer." This comment opens the possibility of interpreting Lukacs's attitude to Engels in a rather different light. It was not so much that Lukacs objected to the idea of a dialectics of nature, more that he objected to the idea that such a dialectic would have the same structure as that which operated in the social sphere— in particular, he objected to the idea that laboratory experimentation and social practice were identical. Lukacs's conclusion is decisive in revealing his meaning:

> From this we deduce the necessity of separating the merely objective dialectics of nature from those of society. For in the dialectics of society the subject is included in the reciprocal relationship in which theory and practice become dialectical with reference to one another. (It goes without saying that the growth of *knowledge* about nature is a social phenomena and therefore to be included in the second dialectical type.) Moreover, if the dialectical method is to be consolidated concretely it is essential that the different types of dialectics should be set out in concrete fashion. . . . However, even to outline a typology of these dialectical forms would be well beyond the scope of this study.[162]

So Lukacs's argument is not against a dialectic of nature. In fact, a moment's thought about the structure of Lukacs's theory of consciousness should be enough to reveal that it would have been impossible for him to have made the presence of consciousness the factor that divided dialectical from non-dialectical systems. For long periods, the capitalist economy works in a way that is beyond the consciousness of its participants, yet Lukacs is in no doubt that capitalism has a dialectical structure. In this instance, there is a similarity between the dialectic in society and that in nature:

> ... classical economics with its system of laws is closer to the natural sciences than to any other. The economic system whose essence and laws it investigates does in fact show marked similarities with the objective structure of that Nature which is the object of study of physics and the other natural sciences.[163]

But Lukacs *was* arguing against seeing the two forms of the dialectic as identical. He rightly saw that the presence of consciousness, or the possibility of consciousness, marks a qualitative difference between the dialectic in society and that in nature.

The main problem with Lukacs's view of nature is not that he saw it as undialectical. Rather, it is that he was not clear about the connection between the dialectic of nature and that in society. Both were dialectical, but in sufficiently different ways, Lukacs seems to have thought, for him not to have to look closely at how the one impinged on the other. Indeed, Lukacs's almost exclusive concern with the dialectic in society led him to concentrate on how changes in society influenced nature, but not on how changes in nature influenced society. "Nature," Lukacs insisted, "is a social category," because "natural relations are socially conditioned ... they change when society changes," even if over a much longer time scale, which, therefore, gives the impression that natural laws are "eternal."[164] This attitude was reinforced by the correct appreciation that the more capitalism developed the more natural limits receded, tending to reducing everything to a social level.[165]

Yet none of this abolishes the problem that the natural realm is a persistent element in human history, that human beings will remain partly subject to its laws, and that it is, therefore, inadmissable to compartmentalize the dialectic in the way that, by a sin of omission, Lukacs did. Had Lukacs clearly understood human labor as the original form of conscious, unalienated practice—and its ultimate origins in a natural world that preceded consciousness—he would have been able to avoid the ambiguity involved in his attitude to objectification and to strengthen his conception of the dialectic by putting the question of contradiction and its resolution in practice more explicitly at its core. And he would also have been able to avoid the mistake that he made in his attitude toward the dialectic of nature.

Notes

1. G. Lukacs, *History and Class Consciousness* (London: Merlin, 1974); and *Lenin, a Study in the Unity of His Thought* (London: New Left Books, 1977).
2. For example, G. Lichtheim, *Lukacs* (London: Fontana, 1970). M. Gluck, *Georg Lukacs and His Generation 1900–1918* (Cambridge, MA: Harvard, 1991) concentrates solely on the period before the Soviet Republic. G. H. R. Parkinson's *Georg Lukacs* (London: Routledge and Kegan Paul 1977) deals with the Hungarian revolution in three pages and *History and Class Consciousness* in a single chapter. A. Kadarkay's *Georg Lukacs, Life, Thought and Politics* (Oxford: Blackwell, 1991) has been widely praised but, leaving aside the author's Cold War politics and self-important prose style, the book devotes only twenty-eight of its 538 pages to *History and Class Consciousness* and only a minority of these discuss the content of the book. Even M. Lowy's otherwise very valuable *Georg Lukacs— From Romanticism to Bolshevism* (London: New Left Books, 1979) is flawed by its concentration on Lukacs's pre-marxist intellectual circle and by the author's admission that "it is not possible to study *History and Class Consciousness* systematically given the limitations of space." A. Arato and P. Breines's *The Young Lukacs* (London: Pluto Press, 1979) does have a serious analysis of *History and Class Consciousness* and the debate that it sparked in the Comintern, but again devotes too much space to Lukacs's intellectual family tree and too little to the reality of the Hungarian and Russian Revolutions. This is one area, at least, where Lukacs is not his own worst critic, because he always insisted on the centrality of the revolutionary years. See, for instance, the 1967 Preface to *History and Class Consciousness*. An important discussion of Lukacs's legacy is to be found in the debate that took place between Peter Binns, Alex Callinicos, and Chris Harman in *International Socialism*. See P. Binns, "What Are the Tasks of Marxism in Philosophy?" *International Socialism* 17 (London, 1982); A. Callinicos, "Marxism and Philosophy: A Reply", *International Socialism* 19 (London, 1983) and C. Harman, "Philosophy and Revolution," *International Socialism* 21 (London, 1983).
3. I. Meszaros, *Lukacs Concept of the Dialectic* (London: Merlin, 1972), 20–21.
4. P. Kenez, "Coalition Politics in the Hungarian Soviet Republic," in A. C. Janos, and W. B. Slottman, eds., *Revolution in Perspective—Essays on the Hungarian Soviet Republic of 1919* (California: University of California Press, 1971), 65.
5. See R. L. Tokes, *Bela Kun and the Hungarian Soviet Republic* (London: Pall Mall, 1967), 5.
6. Lichtheim, *Lukacs*, 25.
7. Kenez, 'Coalition Politics . . .', 65
8. Quoted in Tokes, *Bela Kun*, 7.
9. Ibid., 30.
10. Lichtheim, *Lukacs*, 26.
11. As Meszaros argues: "It cannot be stressed enough: we are not concerned with the influences of neo-Kantianism, etc. The young Lukacs reached out for them in the spirit of his own situation and assimilated them in his own way, in a comprehensive synthesis not in the least recognisable in the work of any one of his friends and teachers. Max Weber, to name but the most significant of them, was well aware of the originality of the young Hungarian philosopher, and regarded him more as an intellectual equal than a pupil." Meszaros, *Lukacs'*, 30.
12. Tokes, *Bela Kun*, 26–27.

13. G. Lukacs, in I. Eorsi, ed., *Georg Lukacs, Record of a Life* (London: Verso, 1983), 175.
14. Although *The Theory of the Novel* was a product of this desperate mood, "it did call for the overthrow of the world that produced the culture it analysed" (ibid.). Lukacs was still preoccupied with ethics, but "my ethics tended in the direction of praxis, action, and hence towards politics"—an orientation encouraged by his socialist mentor, Szabo.
15. Preface to *History and Class Consciousness*, xi.
16. Ibid., x.
17. Tokes, *Bela Kun*, 89.
18. Ibid., 87 and 89. Kunfi's call came despite intensifying class struggle—in early 1919 there were factory and land seizures and daily street demonstrations in Budapest. The SDP called just two demonstrations during the four and a half months that the Karolyi government lasted.
19. Bela Kun was a Hungarian prisoner of war in Russia who had become a Bolshevik and organized a Hungarian "party" among other prisoners.
20. The Communist Party (CP) leaders knew of their impending arrest, but, unlike the Bolshevik leaders during the July days, they refused to go into hiding, because they were too fearful of their reputations and insufficiently sure of working-class support for their party.
21. Lajos Kassak, a contemporary diarist, recorded: "If the officials thought they could suppress the movement by arresting the communist leaders, they were fatally mistaken. The movement was not strong enough to assume power . . . but the arrest and beating of its leaders was as if fuel were poured on slowly burning embers." Quoted in Tokes, *Bela Kun*, 125. The SDP then proceeded to add insult to injury by holding a memorial rally for the policemen killed on the 20 February demonstration. It mobilized 250,000—but the anti-government reaction was stronger.
22. Meanwhile, *every day* four hundred people visited Bela Kun—no wonder his jailers heard him singing the *Internationale* in his cell.
23. Karolyi told his Council of Ministers: "None but a purely Social Democratic government can maintain order. . . . The actual power has, indeed, for months been exclusively in the hands of the organised workers . . . only a purely socialist government can stand against the more and more ruthless attacks of the Communists." Quoted in O. Jaszi, *Revolution and Counter-Revolution in Hungary* (London: P. S. King, 1924), 94.
24. Ibid. "In Karolyi's view the new Social Democratic government should now come to an agreement with the Communists to ensure that there should be no disorders in the country so long as it was conducting this struggle against the imperialist invaders." This calculation involved more than the domestic challenge posed by the CP, although that was still growing—on one contemporary estimate the Vyx note had caused 30,000 iron workers to join the CP. There was also an international dimension to the bourgeoisie's and the SDP's desire to co-opt the CP. The government's military experts thought that it was only a matter of weeks before the Russian Red Army would break through Romanian lines and reach Hungary's eastern borders. One SDP leader, Garbai, hurried to the Budapest Workers' Council to explain the SDP's cynical "left" turn: "We must take . . . from the East what has been denied to us by the West. . . . The army of the Russian proletariat is approaching rapidly. A bourgeois government . . . will not be able to cope with these new developments . . .

the Communist comrades immediately must be released from prison and tomorrow . . . we shall announce to the entire world that the proletariat of this
country has taken the guidance of Hungary and at the same time offered its
fraternal alliance to the Soviet Russian government." Quoted in Tokes, *Bela
Kun*, 133–34. It was a last act of desperation, and it depended on the stupidity,
inexperience, and gullibility of the CP leadership if it was to work. Unfortunately, these were qualities that Bela Kun and his compatriots possessed in
abundance.

25. Tokes, *Bela Kun*, 146.

26. In a radio message to Bela Kun on 23 March, Lenin demanded: "Please inform
us what real guarantees you have that the new Hungarian government will
actually be a communist, and not simply a socialist government, i.e., one of
traitor-socialists.

    Have the Communists a majority in the government? When will the Con-
gress of Soviets take place? What does the socialists recognition of the dictatorship of the proletariat really amount to?" V. I. Lenin, *Collected Works*, Vol.
29, (Moscow: Progress, 1965) 227.

27. Ibid., 243, 269–71. Lenin seems to have believed that the unique international
situation had enabled the Hungarian working class to seize power without a
decisive settling of accounts with the SPD.

28. "The ease with which they sacrificed their organisation followed from the
Hungarian Communists' conception of the party, which was more Luxemburgist
than Leninist . . . it would be anachronistic to think of the Hungarian party at
that time as a Bolshevist organisation." Kenez, 'Coalition Politics' . . ., 70.

29. "Party and Class" is reproduced in G. Lukacs, *Tactics and Ethics, Political Writings
1919–1929* (London: New Left Books, 1972), 28–36.

30. Although in mid-April the Hungarian Red Army collapsed and the Romanians
looked as if they might take Budapest, the Budapest Workers' Council raised
50,000 volunteers and pushed back the Romanians. In the fighting, in which
Lukacs was a political commissar at the front, the Hungarian forces recaptured
every city on the Hungarian plain by June 1919.

31. The CP held just 2 of the 7 secretariats in the merged party. Just as in the old
SDP, trade unionists were automatically members of the party. In the local
soviet elections of 7 April 1919, CP candidates were in a minority of 5 to 1.
Budapest elected 46 SDP candidates and 18 CP candidates. Had the CP still
been in opposition, this would have been a good base from which to keep the
pressure on the reformists. But the future of the CP was now irrevocably
linked to the fate of the government—and the government was run on SDP
terms.

32. The SDP delegates were vicious in the debates with the minority of CP members. One typical contribution argued: "You can say many things about the
old Hungarian Social Democratic Party, but not that it allowed a herd of
parvenus to infest its leadership. . . . Just as we have never permitted young
punks to dictate party policies to us, we shall not allow a gang of young,
decadent, psychologically disturbed degenerates to write our party literature or
carry out party agitation." See, Tokes, *Bela Kun*, 183.

33. This time the situation of the Russian Red Army worked against the CP. By
mid-May, the rising of Grigoriev's Cossacks and a new White offensive by
Denikin had dashed hopes of a thrust toward Hungary.

34. The Third International identified four key failures of the Hungarian Soviet

Republic: 1) the decision to merge the SDP and the CP, 2) the agrarian policy, 3) failure to win the middle classes on the tactical question of "no annexations," 4) the policy of immediate and widespread nationalization. Lukacs absorbed these lessons, but not all at the same speed.

35. Lukacs himself puts this down to the fact that "vestiges of Ervin Szabo's syndicalism lived on in me." See *Georg Lukacs, Record of a Life*, 59.
36. Ibid., 177.
37. For a carefully argued and fully documented account of the "radical alteration" and "virtual rewriting" of these essays, see Lowy, *Georg Lukacs—from Romanticism to Bolshevism*, chap. 4, esp. 173–76. Lowy is generally good on the shifts in Lukacs's political positions, but his book is flawed in other ways. See note 2 above and my review of Lowy in *Socialist Review* (London) no. 89 (July/August 1986), 33–34.
38. Lukacs, *History and Class Consciousness*, 87.
39. Ibid., 87–88.
40. Ibid., 88.
41. Ibid., 89.
42. Ibid., 95.
43. Ibid., 96.
44. Ibid., 98.
45. Ibid., 100.
46. Ibid., 100.
47. Ibid.
48. Ibid., 102.
49. Ibid., 103.
50. Lukacs, *Lenin*, 64.
51. Ibid., 65.
52. Ibid.
53. Ibid., 66.
54. Ibid., 67.
55. Lukacs, *History and Class Consciousness*, 266.
56. Ibid., 266–67.
57. Lukacs, *Lenin*, 67.
58. Lukacs, *History and Class Consciousness*, 80.
59. Ibid., 54.
60. Ibid., 63.
61. Ibid., 112.
62. Ibid., 120.
63. Ibid., 122.
64. Ibid., 143.
65. Ibid., 144–45.
66. Ibid., 145.
67. Ibid., 181.
68. Ibid., 149.
69. G. Stedman Jones, "The Marxism of the Early Lukacs," in *Western Marxism, A Critical Reader* (London: New Left Books, 1977), 42.
70. Ibid., 42–43.
71. Lukacs, *History and Class Consciousness*, 173.
72. Ibid., 178–79. The quotation is from *Capital*, Vol. I.
73. Ibid., 178.

74. Ibid., 169.
75. Ibid.
76. Ibid.
77. Marx, *Economic and Philosophical Manuscripts in Early Writings*, (London: Penguin, 1975), 365.
78. Lukacs, *History and Class Consciousness*, 205–206.
79. Ibid., 71.
80. Ibid., 282. See also the whole essay "Critical Observations on Rosa Luxemburg's 'Critique of the Russian Revolution,'" still one of the best defenses of the Russian revolution, and many other passages are devoted to this issue.
81. Ibid., 306.
82. Ibid., 224–45.
83. Ibid., 75.
84. V. I. Lenin, "Report on the World Political Situation and the Basic Tasks of the Communist International," in *The Communist International in Lenin's Time, Proceedings and Documents of the Second Congress*, Vol. I (New York: Pathfinder, 1991), 118–19.
85. Lukacs, *History and Class Consciousness*, 78.
86. Ibid., 328.
87. Ibid., 299.
88. Ibid., 310.
89. Ibid.
90. Ibid., 195.
91. Ibid., 196.
92. Ibid., 197.
93. Ibid., 289.
94. Ibid., 284.
95. Ibid., 286.
96. Ibid., 300–301.
97. Ibid., 317.
98. Lukacs, *Lenin*, 36.
99. Lukacs, *History and Class Consciousness*, 336.
100. Ibid., 308.
101. Ibid.
102. Ibid., 307.
103. Ibid.
104. Ibid., 289–90.
105. Ibid., 304.
106. Lukacs, *Lenin*, 45.
107. Ibid., 46.
108. Lukacs, *History and Class Consciousness*, 311.
109. Ibid., 324–25.
110. Lukacs, *Lenin*, 30.
111. Ibid.
112. Lukacs, *History and Class Consciousness*, 276.
113. Ibid. Lukacs also understood, again following Lenin, that "this slogan must be counterbalanced by the slogan of 'belonging together', of federation." However, even a victorious revolution "does not free the proletariat from contamination by capitalist and nationalist ideologies, and if it is to pass through the transitional ideological phase, then it will need both slogans *together*."

114. Had Lukacs emphasized this aspect earlier (which is present in *History and Class Consciousness*, but not as its central organizing principle), he might well have been able to avoid the ambiguity on the issues of the dialectic of nature and on the distinction between alienation and objectification which is analyzed in the last section of this chapter. The key, of course, is that labor provides both the distinction from, and the continuity between, humans and the rest of nature.

115. One of the best representatives of which is *Ideology and Superstructure in Historical Materialism* (London: Pluto Press, 1990) by Trotskyist Franz Jakubowski.

116. English language interest in Lukacs was promoted by the first translation of an extract of *History and Class Consciousness* in 1957 by the American International Socialist League, run by former Trotskyists, Hal Draper among them. Soon after the first French translation appeared and circulated among the left in Britain. Also influential was *The Hidden God* written by Lukacs-inspired theorist Lucian Goldman. In the spring and summer issues of *International Socialism* (nos. 24 and 25 of the first series) for 1966, a translation by Mary Phillips of the first chapter of *History and Class Consciousness*, "What Is Orthodox Marxism?" appeared. The editor's introduction described the book as deserving to be "one of the most famous marxist classics of this century," and, while noting Lukacs's adherence to Stalinism, argued that the book was "in essence a central critique of the ideology and philosophy that dominates East and West alike, and a reaffirmation of the supreme synthesis, dialectical materialism." Goldman's essay, "Is There a Marxist Sociology," appeared in *International Socialism* 34 (first series), and Ian Birchall's "Lukacs as a Literary Critic" appeared in *International Socialism* 36 (old series). My thanks to Chris Harman for the information contained in this note.

117. Stedman Jones in *Western Marxism*, 37.

118. L. Kolakowski, *Main Current of Marxism*, Vol. 3 (Oxford: Oxford University Press 1978), 277.

119. T. Eagleton, *Ideology* (London: Verso, 1991), 97.

120. In an important passage in the *Prison Notebooks*, Gramsci seems to be suggesting a similar line of argument: "It might seem that there can exist an extra-historical and extra-human objectivity. But who is to be the judge of such objectivity? Who is able to put himself in this kind of 'standpoint of the cosmos in itself' and what could such a standpoint mean? It can indeed be maintained that here we are dealing with a hangover of the concept of God."

Gramsci then goes on to cite the following formulation of Engels's *Anti-Duhring* as containing "the correct conception in that it has recourse to history and to man in order to demonstrate objective reality: 'The real unity of the world consists in its materiality, and this is proved not by a few juggling phrases but by a long and tedious development of philosophy and natural science.'"

Gramsci then continues: "Objective always means 'humanly objective' which can be held to correspond exactly to 'historically subjective': in other words, objective would mean 'universal subjective.' Man knows objectively in so far as knowledge is real for the whole human race *historically* unified in a single unitary cultural system. But this process of historical unification takes place through the disappearance of the internal contradictions which tear apart human society, while these contradictions themselves are the condition of the formation of groups and for the birth of ideologies which are not concretely universal but are immediately rendered transient by the practical origin of its substance. There exists therefore a struggle for objectivity (to free oneself from partial and fallacious ideologies) and this struggle is the same as the struggle for the cultural unification of the human race." See *Selections from the Prison Notebooks* (London: Lawrence and Wishart, 1971) 445.

The struggle to which Gramsci refers is, of course, the struggle of the working class, the "universal class" to use Marx's phrase. There is a "struggle for objectivity" precisely because the immediate consciousness of the class has to rise to the level of universality implicit in its objective class position. And this struggle can only be successful if the historical and international experience of the class—and the total view of society constructed on this basis (marxism)—is brought into a dialectical relationship with the day-to-day struggle of the class.

121. Stedman Jones, *Western Marxism*, 40–41.
122. Eagleton, *Ideology*, 102.
123. C. Sparks, "Georg Lukacs," in *Working Papers in Cultural Studies*, no. 4 (Birmingham University, 1973), 83. For a similar criticism, see G. Novack, *Polemics in Marxist Philosophy* (New York: Monad, 1978), 125.
124. J. Larrain, *Marxism and Ideology* (New Jersey: Humanities Press, 1983), 75. Also see A. Arato, and P. Breines, *The Young Lukacs and the Origins of Western Marxism* (London: Pluto Press, 1979); and J. McCarney, *The Real World of Ideology* (New Jersey and Sussex: Humanities Press and Harvester, 1980).
125. Novack, *Polemics Marxism and Ideology*, 124.
126. Larrain, 85.
127. Stedman Jones, *Western Marxism*, 38.
128. Ibid., 39.
129. Ibid., 44.
130. Ibid., 43.
131. In this context, it is interesting to note that Eric Hobsbawm's essay "Notes on Class Consciousness," inspired by the English edition of *History and Class Consciousness*, while eschewing any philosophical issues, manages to reconstruct a thoroughly empirical and historical picture of class consciousness that closely corresponds to that given by Lukacs. The essay is reprinted in E. Hobsbawm, *Worlds of Labour* (London: Weidenfeld, 1984).
132. As Lukacs puts it: "On the one hand, all the categories in which human existence is constructed must appear as the determinants of that existence itself (and not merely of the description of that existence)." In other words, a simple aggregate of historical facts or narrative of events will not do. We have to distill from the infinity of historical events those elements which are essential, not merely idiosyncracies or irrelevancies but "the determinants of existence," that is, a system or structure. But this system cannot simply be an abstract conception that forces its attentions on a reluctant historical reality. "On the other hand," Lukacs says, the concepts of such a system, "their succession, their coherence and their connections must appear as aspects of the historical process itself, as structural components of the present." *History and Class Consciousness*, 159.
133. Lukacs, *History and Class Consciousness*, 159.
134. There is a theory of class consciousness which simply attempts to dismiss altogether the problem with which Lukacs was grappling. It asserts that workers do not actually share ruling class values and that there is no real contradiction between working-class interests and working-class consciousness. Sociologist Michael Mann has argued that studies of working-class consciousness show little fundamental agreement with the establishment ideology: "Value consensus does not exist to any significant extent." Workers may be resigned to their fate, argues a study of ChemCo workers, but they "do not affirm *or* deny" the

values of "capitalist hegemony." Sociologists Abercrombie, Hill, and Turner argue that "the penetration of ideology into the subordinate classes has generally been slight . . . the main role of the dominant ideology has been to secure the cohesion and reproduction of the *ruling* class, not to integrate the masses within the existing social order." For a sympathetic account of Mann and Abercrombie, Hill and Turner, see A. Callinicos, *Making History* (Cambridge: Polity Press, 1987), 140–47.

This view has some important virtues. It draws attention to the fact that the hold of ruling-class ideology on the working class is always partial and tenuous. And it highlights the countercurrents of resistance to bourgeois ideas that, even in the worst times, command the support of a minority of workers. For socialists, it is certainly attractive to think that workers do not positively believe bourgeois ideology but merely go along with it for want of an alternative. Unfortunately, there are two major objections to this view: 1) it is only partly·true, and 2) to the extent that it is true, it only *describes* the state of workers' consciousness but does not *explain* where such contradictions originate.

In fact, there are often large sections of the working class—Tory voters, strike breakers, racists, volunteers for the First World War—whose actions cannot be explained simply by claiming that they are begrudgingly going along with ruling-class ideology. To support the party that openly champions the ruling class, to scab on a strike, to shoot or physically attack fellow workers requires more than a passive feeling that "nothing can be changed." It may be that these are all examples that are only true of a minority of the working class. But other ideas, say sexist or nationalistic ideas or positive support for reformism, itself a form of bourgeois ideology, are a feature of most workers' intellectual vocabulary. They cannot simply be wished away. Certainly alienation plays its part, but the result of alienation is not merely surly submission. It often takes the form of workers trying to overcome their exclusion from official society by conforming all the more completely, in action as well as in thought, to its values.

135. See C. Harman, *Gramsci versus Reformism* (London: Bookmarks, 1983).

136. Quoted in G. Fiori, *Antonio Gramsci, Life of a Revolutionary* (London: Verso, 1990), 92–93.

137. See M. A. Finocchario, *Gramsci and the History of Dialectical Thought* (Cambridge: Cambridge University Press, 1988). For example, on the relationship between thesis and antithesis, Gramsci wrongly argues against the idea that "in the dialectical process the thesis should be conserved by the antithesis," but that instead "in real history the antithesis tends to destroy the thesis" (170). Also see Gramsci's inability to see how the general notion of combined and uneven economic development must result in a political program of permanent revolution (165). None of this should, however, obscure the fact that there are many other, more numerous, valuable insights into the dialectic in Gramsci's writing.

138. A. Gramsci, *Selections from the Prison Notebooks* (London: Lawrence and Wishart, 1971), 333.

139. Ibid.

140. See C. Boggs, *Gramsci's Marxism* (London: Pluto Press, 1976), 64. Boggs provides a readable introduction to Gramsci's thought, marred by his determination, quite contrary to Gramsci's own political position, to use it as a critique of Leninism.

141. Gramsci, *Selections from Prison Notebooks*, 395–96.
142. Ibid., 184.
143. Gramsci, quoted in Boggs, *Gramsci's Marxism*, 71.
144. C. Boggs, *Gramsci's Marxism*, 69–70.
145. Lukacs, *History and Class Consciousness*, 8.
146. Ibid., 181.
147. Ibid., 162–63.
148. Ibid., 204.
149. Ibid.
150. Ibid.
151. Ibid., 27. Lukacs also asserts "it is not the primacy of economic motives in historical explanation that constitutes the decisive difference between Marxism and bourgeois thought, but the point of view of the totality" (27). Lukacs is right that economic determination is not, on its own, the defining characteristic of Marxism—many crude reductionists of all stripes would happily subscribe to marxism if that were true. But he is wrong in making totality into an equally one-sided criteria. On totality also see 8, 15, 28–29.
152. Ibid., 179.
153. See, for instance, ibid., 62, where Lukacs talks of "the deepest contradictions in capitalism . . . as they appear in the consciousness of the bourgeoisie," or 71 where he describes the "dialectical contradiction between its [the working class] immediate interests and its long-term objectives, and between the discrete factors and the whole."
154. V. I. Lenin, *Collected Works*, Vol. 38 (Moscow: Progress, 1972), 359.
155. Existentialism made the same error, even retreating to a position less contradictory, and therefore less valuable, than Hegel's view.
156. Lukacs, *History and Class Consciousness*, xxii–xxiv.
157. Ibid., 90.
158. Ibid., 42.
159. Ibid., 49. Also see 84 where Lukacs argues that "commodity fetishism is a *specific* problem of our age" and, in the same paragraph, that "the distinction between a society where this [commodity] form is dominant, permeating every expression of life, and a society where it only makes an episodic appearance is essentially one of quality. For depending on which is the case, all subjective and objective phenomena is the societies concerned are objectified in qualitatively different ways."
160. Jakubowski, *Ideology and Superstructure*, 29.
161. Lukacs, *History and Class Consciousness*, 132–33.
162. Ibid., 207.
163. Ibid., 231–32.
164. Ibid., 234–35.
165. See ibid., 237.

6

Trotsky and the Dialectic of History

Even his most determined enemies grant that Leon Trotsky was a great revolutionary, a reputation assured by his leadership of the Workers', Peasants', and Soldiers' Soviet in the Russian revolutions of 1905 and 1917 and of the Red Army in the Russian civil war. But Trotsky's status as a theoretician is less secure, at least among academics. That same strange alliance of conservatives and Stalinist supporters of the former USSR who have failed to eradicate the facts of Trotsky's life have been more successful in denying the intellectual contribution that he made to the marxist tradition.

Trotsky was one of the great original thinkers of the marxist tradition. The theory of permanent revolution predicted the course of the Russian revolution eleven years before it broke out. His analysis of Germany foresaw the dangers of nazism when many, on the left as well as the right, remained blind. His writings on art and literature gained respect from the unlikely figures of F. R. Leavis and T. S. Eliot. Trotsky's monumental *History of the Russian Revolution*, moved even the conservative historian A. L. Rowse to say "his gift is so brilliant and incisive that one is continually reminded of Carlyle."[1]

But even among those who are willing to grant all this, Trotsky has never had much of a reputation as a pioneer of the marxist method. In the postwar period, Marx's philosophy has become an object of almost obsessional study. The philosophy of both Lukacs and Gramsci have produced endless debate. Even Lenin's *Materialism and Empirocriticism* and his *Philosophical Notebooks* have received some attention. But Trotsky, it was assumed, even by some of his admirers, had little to contribute in this field.[2] For Merleau Ponty, "Trotsky was not a philosopher; and when he speaks philosophically it is by taking up again and making his own the most banal naturalism."[3] Kevin Anderson argues that Trotsky adhered to "a crude form of scientific materialism," which shows "either indifference or hostility toward Hegel."[4]

These charges were always unjust. The evidence of Trotsky's fine dialectical method was obvious not just in his explicit statements from the 1920s

262

and late 1930s but also from his theory of permanent revolution and his writings on history and art. In 1986, however, new proof of Trotsky's original contribution to the marxist method emerged when *Trotsky's Notebooks, 1933–35, Writings on Lenin, Dialectics and Evolutionism* were published for the first time. They place Trotsky very firmly in the "Hegelian" marxist tradition.

Trotsky's notebooks on dialectics and his other related writings provide more than a defense of the materialist conception of history. They provide an account of the marxist method that resolutely refuses all crude reductionism and that articulates a dialectical method which is sophisticated enough to give proper weight to all the different political, ideological, and philosophical elements within society without lapsing into idealism. These elements were part of Trotsky's approach from his earliest encounters with marxism, as his own account of his earliest marxist influences demonstrates.

THE INFLUENCE OF ANTONIO LABRIOLA

In his autobiography, *My Life*, Trotsky pays tribute to the influence that the work of Antonio Labriola (1843–1904) had on his development as a marxist. In January 1898, Trotsky was arrested by the tsarist authorities and, while imprisoned, began a study of freemasonry. In his search for an explanation of "this strange movement," Trotsky recalls that he at first "resisted the theory of historical materialism . . . and held to that of the multiplicity of historical factors, which, as we know, even today is the most widely accepted theory in social science."[5]

As this theory is still influential today—its approach not only underlies much sociology but also the Althusserian and "cultural materialist" varieties of marxism developed by Raymond Williams and other New Left theorists. It is worth looking at Trotsky's definition of it. In this method, argues Trotsky,

> People denote as "factors" the various aspects of their social activity, endow this concept with a super-social character, and then superstitiously interpret their own activity as the result of the interaction of these independent forces. Where did the factors come from, that is, under the influence of what conditions did they evolve from primitive human society? With these questions, the official eclectic theory does not concern itself.[6]

The appeal of this approach is that it appears to provide a non-determinist explanation of social change by stressing the ideological factor, the cultural factor, the political factor, and so on, as well as the economic factor. Trotsky's objection is not simply that it dissolves any real explanation of how these factors arose but also that the whole structure of factors then replaces human activity as the motive force of history. Consequently, the theory ends up replacing economic determinism with structural determinism. Labriola's influence was decisive in winning Trotsky from this approach. He recalls,

It was in my cell that I read with delight two well-known essays by an old Italian Hegelian-Marxist, Antonio Labriola, which reached the prison in a French translation. Unlike most Latin writers, Labriola mastered the materialist dialectics, if not in politics—in which he was helpless—at least in the philosophy of history. . . . He made short work, and in marvelous style, of the theory of multiple factors.[7]

Labriola's work stayed with Trotsky all his life—"although thirty years have gone by since I read his essays, the general trend of his argument is still firmly entrenched in my memory." So what was it in Labriola's work that Trotsky found so useful?

In Labriola's *Essays on the Materialistic Conception of History* (1896), Trotsky found a brilliant outline of Marx and Engels's method, practically unique in the Second International of the day for its careful restatement of a dialectical approach to the study of history [8] Labriola was certainly a materialist and his famous aphorism, which Trotsky remembered in *My Life*, "Ideas do not fall from heaven, and nothing comes to us in a dream" encapsulates his commitment to this fundamental aspect of marxism. Labriola was, therefore, absolutely opposed to idealist explanations of social change, but he combined this with a stress on the role of human labor mostly missing from his contemporaries' accounts of marxism:

Man has made his history not by a metaphorical evolution nor with a view of walking on a line of preconceived progress. He has made it by creating his own conditions, that is to say, by creating through his labour an artificial environment, by developing successively his technical aptitudes and by accumulating and transforming the products of his activity and this new environment.[9]

According to Labriola's account, this approach should be called scientific "provided we do not thus confuse ourselves with positivists, sometimes embarrassing guests, who assume to themselves a monopoly of science." Although "our intentions are nothing less than the theoretical expression and practical explanation of the data offered us," marxists, unlike positivists, realize that this explanation is "of the process which is being accomplished among us and about us and which has its whole existence in the objective relations of social life of which we are the subject and the object, the cause and the effect."[10]

Starting from this dialectical perspective, Labriola was as hostile to determinist distortions of marxism as he was to the positivists. He ridiculed the idea that the economic structure is "a simple mechanism whence emerge, as immediate, automatic and mechanical effects, institutions, laws, customs, thoughts, sentiments, ideologies. From this substructure to all the rest, the process of derivation and of mediation is very complicated, often subtle, tortuous and not always legible."[11]

Though the mediations between economic structures and superstructures might be complex, Labriola was unwilling simply to dissolve them into a mass of competing factors. It is this argument, which denies both crude determinism and a rootless conglomeration of sociological categories, that Trotsky remembered so vividly. Labriola, who was himself a considerable Hegel scholar, mounts a critique of the factors theory which recalls Hegel's discussion of shortcomings of the notion of reciprocity.[12] He criticizes those who take "separately and in a distinct fashion on the one side the economic forms and categories, and, on the other, for example, law, legislation, politics, customs," and "proceed to study the reciprocal influences of the different sides of life in an abstract fashion."[13]

Labriola's position is quite different; it is "the organic conception of history." This approach does not separate "the factors of an organism" and so "destroys them in so far as they are elements contributing to the unity of the whole." Instead, it "permits us to understand history, which only distinguishes and separates the elements to find again in them the objective necessity of their co-operation toward the total result."[14] Thus Labriola reinvents the idea of a mediated totality in opposition to an undialectical attempt to dismember the complex relationship between economic context and human consciousness and activity.

It is not that Labriola denies the need to establish distinctions between different spheres of social life: "The complete whole is the stage on which the events unfold, but if the narrative is to have solidity, vividness and perspective there must be points of departure and ways of interpretation."[15] The danger occurs when this process—which is ultimately rooted in the real division of labor in class, particularly capitalist, society—is allowed to ossify into a fixed system of categories. "In this consists the first origin of those abstractions, which little by little take away from the different parts of a given social *complexus* their quality of simple sides or aspects of a whole, and it is their ensuing generalization which little by little leads to the doctrine of factors."

Labriola saw that such frozen images of a fluid reality "arise in the mind as a sequence of the abstraction and generalizations of immediate aspects of apparent movement" and are, therefore, simply "of an equal value with that of all other empirical concepts." They will "persist until they are reduced or eliminated by a new experience, or until they are absorbed by a conception more general, genetic, evolutionary or dialectic."[16]

The experiences and theories that are capable of overcoming this stupefaction of theory emerge from a social totality, which is riven by contradiction and which, therefore, will not eternally conform to the circular, static model described by the factors theory. Labriola's stress on the element of contradiction, rare enough among marxists in the 1890s, is reinforced by his citation of the then almost forgotten maxim of Marx, "It is the antagonisms which are the principal cause of progress."[17]

It was from this narrow channel of continuity with the historical materialism of Marx and Engels that Trotsky drew his early inspiration. He was to make direct use of Labriola's critique of the factors theory in one of his clashes with the Stalinist bureaucracy.

A POLEMIC AGAINST THE STALINIST BUREAUCRACY

Trotsky mostly elaborated and defended his vision of the marxist method against the backdrop of the growth of Stalinism. Stalinism and the marxism of the Second International had much in common. They both elaborated a fatalistic, closed form of the dialectic which justified the status quo. They both needed to iron out the volatility, uniqueness, and unevenness in the world that the dialectic was first developed to explain.

Trotsky's materialist analysis, unlike Hegel's idealism, dealt with real history unfolding in time and space, not just the timeless patterns of consciousness. It, therefore, needed to develop concepts that were either undeveloped or unknown in Hegel. Trotsky's concepts of combined and uneven development, his notion of a "differentiated unity," and his distinction between the form of the dialectic in nature and the dialectic in history are an important contribution to this task. These themes emerge fully in Trotsky's notebooks on dialectics and his other philosophical writings in the 1930s. But the same line of thought, plus a dramatic demonstration of the use to which he put the method he found in Labriola's work, can be found in his "Philosophical Tendencies of Bureaucratism."

This work was written in December 1928 but remained unpublished during Trotsky's lifetime. It was intended to be part of a "historico-polemical work" aimed at Stalin's *Problems of Leninism* and Zinoviev's *Leninism*, works representative of "the official ideology of the era of reaction." Trotsky's analysis of the philosophical position of Stalinism grows directly out Labriola's account of the origins of the multiple factors theory in the division of labor inherent in capitalist society. Where Labriola saw the division of labor, and the separate elements of economic, social, and political life that arose from it, reflected uncritically in the factors theory, Trotsky sees the same process taken to the extreme in the outlook of the bureaucracy:

> The most appropriate system of thought for a bureaucracy is the theory of multiple causality, a multiplicity of "factors." This theory arises on the broadest basis out of the social division of labour itself, in particular out of the separation of mental and manual labour. . . . But the perfected form of the multiple-factor theory, which transforms human society, and in its wake the entire world, into the product of the interplay (or what we might call the interdepartmental relations) of various factors or administrative forces, each of which is assigned its own special province or area of jurisdiction—this kind of system can be elevated to the status of a "pearl

of creation" only if there is present a bureaucratic hierarchy which, with all its ministries and departments, has raised itself over and above society.[18]

The supreme virtue of this approach, as far as the Stalinist bureaucracy was concerned, or indeed for any bureaucratically organized layer in any capitalist state, is that it requires a force that will guide and coordinate the various more or less autonomous factors, just as the bureaucracy itself needs a dictator to oversee its separate departments:

> In essence the multiple-factors theory cannot get along without a deity. It simply dispenses the divine omnipotence among the various lesser rulers with more or less equal powers—economics, politics, law, morality, science, religion, aesthetics, etc.[19]

The factors theory is doubly compromised in Trotsky's view because apparent pluralism always relapses into a hidden reductionism. If we want a method that can both provide a rational account of development without crushing the obvious heterogeneity of the world, we must look elsewhere. Trotsky's own account of social causation begins by acknowledging, as Labriola had done, that we cannot do without differentiation and distinction:

> Materialism does not simply reject factors, just as dialectics does not simply reject logic. Materialism makes use of factors as a system of classification of phenomena which have arisen historically . . . out of the underlying productive forces and relations of society and from the natural, historical, i.e., *material*, foundations of nature.[20]

The knack is not to allow this perfectly necessary procedure to congeal into a "crude fetishization of the distinct, homogeneous factors (economics, politics, law, science, art, religion) which weave the fabric of history through their interaction and combination."[21]

Trotsky then proceeds to give a number of examples of the way in which we can relate one area of reality to others without either abandoning materialism or becoming determinists. Thus natural phenomena and social phenomena are related, but not reducible to one another; historical materialism itself is the "application of materialist dialectics to a distinct, although enormous, part of the universe," yet dialectics is not reducible to historical materialism. These are themes that Trotsky develops more fully in his writings in the 1930s. But in the "Philosophical Tendencies of Bureaucratism," the best example of this notion of "differentiated unity," as he will later call it, is his discussion of the relationship between theory and practice.

Trotsky seizes on Stalin's definition of Leninism as "the primacy of practice before theory." If Stalin's definition is correct, argues Trotsky,

> . . . are the empiricists not right—they who guide themselves by "direct" practice as the highest court of authority? Are they not, then, the most

consistent materialists? No, they represent a caricature of materialism. To be guided by theory is to be guided by generalizations based on preceding practical experience of humanity in order to cope as successfully as possible with one or other practical problem of the present day. Thus, through theory we discover precisely the primacy of practice-as-a-whole over particular aspects of practice.[22]

Stalin was completely unable to grasp this dialectic of the whole and the part, of the theoretical summation of past activity brought to bear as the guide for present activity. Stalin "absolutely fails to understand that theory—genuine theory or theory on a large scale—does not take shape in *direct* connection with the practical tasks of the day." Theory can only be effective if it is both detached from *and* brought into relation with current tasks. Theory is,

> the consolidation and generalization of all human practical activity and experience, embracing different historical periods in their materially determined sequence. It is only because theory is not inseparably linked with the practical tasks contemporary to it, but rises above them, that it has the gift of seeing ahead, that is, is able to prepare to link itself with the future practical activity and to train people who will be equal to future political tasks.[23]

Trotsky thus defended a view of marxism that grounded ideological changes in natural, material, economic, and social development. But it did so in a way that, because such changes always take place "through people, through the agency of human beings," opened up the possibility of conscious intervention in the historical process. This is just the thing that Stalin's "ultrapractical" caricature of Leninism would deny, leaving explanation, always after the fact, to "multiple factors."

THE STRUCTURE OF THE DIALECTIC

The notion that the dialectic adds nothing to marxism is still common enough even among marxists. Trotsky dealt directly with this kind of objection to the dialectic in the course of a debate inside the American Socialist Workers Party in the 1930s.[24] Even Trotsky's closest supporters were surprised by his determination to address this issue.

George Novack remembers traveling by train to Mexico City with Trotsky when he first took asylum there in 1937. The conversation turned to philosophy and to those in the Socialist Workers Party (SWP) who wished to abandon dialectical laws as useless pieces of theoretical baggage that substitute metaphysical obscurities for genuine scientific analysis. Trotsky became "tense and agitated," insisting that the struggle against this "repudiation of dialectical materialism" should be "taken up immediately" and that "nothing is more important than this."

Novack was "somewhat surprised." He had good reason, as he records. Trotsky was the center of attention as the principle defendant in the Moscow show trials and as a result of his dramatic voyage into exile. He was "fighting for his reputation, liberty and life against the powerful government of Stalin." After having been imprisoned in silence for months by the Norwegian authorities, he had just stepped off a tanker in which he had been held, again cut off from the outside world, for weeks. "Yet," says Novack, "on the first day . . . he spent more than an hour explaining how important it was for a Marxist movement to have a correct philosophical method and to defend dialectical materialism."[25]

The substance of the debate inside the American SWP about which Trotsky was so concerned, the class nature of Russia, does not directly concern us here.[26] But the context of the debate is important. Trotsky's central opponent, James Burnham, like many in the SWP at this time, was an intellectual drawn to the American Communist Party in the 1930s. They were horrified by the great slump and the rise of nazism and inspired by the resistance of the Republicans in the Spanish Civil War. A minority of these were also disgusted by the Moscow Trial and puzzled by a Popular Front tactic which meant welcoming Roosevelt's New Deal. Edmund Wilson, Sidney Hook, James T. Farrell, and many others were briefly drawn by "the dramatic pathos of Trotsky's struggle and to his eloquence and literary genius. Trotskyism became something of a vogue."[27]

Trotsky was always wary of this superficial popularity, and, as the Second World War grew nearer, the arguments with his intellectual fellow travellers grew more intense. Isaac Deutscher catches something of the atmosphere:

> Never yet had any cause looked as hopeless as Trotsky's began to look to the professors, authors, and literary critics who were deserting him. They came to feel that by opting for Trotskyism they had needlessly involved themselves in the huge, remote, obscure and dangerous business of the Russian revolution; and that this was bringing them into conflict with the way of life and the climate of ideas which prevailed in their universities, editorial offices, and literary coteries. It was one thing to lend one's name to a Committee for the Defence of Leon Trotsky and to protest at the purges, but quite another to subscribe to the Manifestoes of the Fourth International and to echo Trotsky's call for the conversion of the forthcoming world war into a global civil war.[28]

Under circumstances where a whole layer of intellectuals were breaking with their former attachment to marxism, it is not surprising that the dialectic, the marxist method, should come into question.

In fact, an early episode in this saga had already raised the question of the Hegelian influence in marxism. Some left intellectuals had probed Trotsky about his role in supressing the Kronstadt rising, claiming that it showed the cynical immorality of Bolshevism's doctrine that the end justifies the means. American philosopher John Dewey was one of those who traced this supposed failing to marxism's "Hegelian origins." Trotsky's response, *Their Morals and Ours*, was a masterpiece of polemical writing. It demonstrated with great dialectical verve that only certain means could achieve socialist goals. Lying, deceit, and dishonesty could never "impart solidarity and unity to revolutionary workers," consequently, the Bolsheviks were the "most honest political party in the whole of history."[29]

In the subsequent months, as the debate moved from the historical question of Kronstadt to the then current question of Russia, the issue of the dialectic became more central. Burnham attacked the dialectic again and again, using formulations almost identical to those used to attack it today. He found Engels's writings on the dialectic "confused or outmoded by subsequent scientific investigation." Burnham saw Hegel as "the century dead arch-muddler of human thought" and insisted that:

> Hegelian dialectics has nothing whatever to do with science. *How* the sciences have influenced the forms of thought no one will ever discover by spending even a lifetime on the tortuous syntax of the reactionary absolutist, Hegel.[30]

Burnham favored modern science and empiricism, which "are the monopoly of no man or group or class, but a common human possession."[31] In any case, he argued:

> There is no sense *at all* in which dialectics (even if it were not, as it is, scientifically meaningless) is fundamental in politics, none at all. An opinion on dialectics is no more fundamental for *politics* than an opinion on non-Euclidean geometry or relativity physics.[32]

Therefore, it made no difference if "*every* revolutionist believed in dialectics and *everyone* who was against the revolution disbelieved [because] this fact . . . would not have the slightest relevance to the question of the truth, falsity, or scientific meaninglessness of dialectics."[33]

Trotsky's reply to these arguments contains a convincing explanation of why the dialectic is an essential part of marxism. Trotsky first sketches an account of why

> American "radical" intellectuals accept Marxism without the dialectic (a clock without a spring). . . . The secret is simple. In no other country has there been such a rejection of class struggle as in the land of "unlimited opportunity." The denial of social contradictions as the moving force of development led to the denial of the dialectic as the logic of contradictions in the domain of theoretical thought. Just as in the sphere of politics it was thought possible everybody could be convinced of the correctness of a "just" programme by means of clever syllogisms and society could be

reconstructed through "rational" measures, so in the sphere of theory it was accepted that Aristolian logic, lowered to the level of "common sense," was sufficient for the solving of all problems. Pragmatism, a mixture of rationalism and empiricism, became a national philosophy in the United States.[34]

This historical circumstance was most damaging to the intelligentsia because, argued Trotsky, "the academically trained petty bourgeoisie['s] . . . theoretical prejudices have been given a finished form at the school bench." Academics assume that because they have "succeeded in gaining a great deal of knowledge both useful and useless without the aid of the dialectic they can continue excellently through life without it." But the test of great events always reveals that "in reality they dispense with the dialectic only to the extent that they fail to check, sharpen and theoretically polish their tools of thought."[35]

Trotsky goes on to reply to those who argue that questions of method are not important in reaching correct political conclusions:

What is the meaning of this thoroughly astonishing reasoning? Inasmuch as *some* people through a bad method *sometimes* reach correct conclusions, and inasmuch as some people through a correct method *not infrequently* reach incorrect conclusions, therefore . . . the method is not of great importance. . . . Imagine how a worker would react upon complaining to his foreman that his tools were bad and receiving the reply: With bad tools it is possible to turn out a good job, and with good tools many people only waste material. I am afraid that such a worker, particularly if he is on piece-work, would respond to the foreman with an unacademic phrase.[36]

Trotsky then spells out the essence of the dialectic. He makes some elementary points that bear repetition, because they are still not always understood, even among marxists.

First, Trotsky insists that the dialectic is not an *alternative* to "normal" scientific methods or formal logic. These methods are perfectly valid within certain limits, just as Newtonian physics is perfectly adequate for many purposes. Formal logic, however, like Newtonian physics, has proved inadequate to deal with the "more complicated and drawn out processes." So the dialectic stands in the same relation to formal logic as Newtonian physics stands to relativity theory or, as Trotsky puts it, as "that between higher and lower mathematics."[37]

Second, Trotsky warns against seeing the dialectic as "a magic master key for all questions." The dialectic is not a calculator into which it is possible to punch the problem and allow it to compute the solution. This would be an idealist method. A materialist dialectic must *grow from* a patient, empirical examination of the facts and not be *imposed* on them. Although on occasion Trotsky defined the dialectic as a *method* of analysis, here he is pointing to a deeper truth. A dialectical method is only possible because reality itself is dialectically structured. It is from this material dialectic that the dialectical

method must emerge and against this material dialectic that it must constantly check itself. For Trotsky, the dialectic "does not replace concrete
scientific analysis. But it directs this analysis along the correct road."[38]

Trotsky had already elaborated this point in his 1926 essay, "Culture and
Socialism":

> Dialectics cannot be imposed on the facts; it has to be deduced from
> facts, from their nature and development. Only painstaking work on a
> vast amount of material enabled Marx to advance the dialectical system of
> economics to the conception of value as social labour. Marx's historical
> works were constructed in the same way, and even his newspaper articles
> likewise. Dialectical materialism can be applied to new spheres of knowl-
> edge only by mastering them from within. The purging of bourgeois sci-
> ence presupposes a mastery of bourgeois science. You will get nowhere
> with sweeping criticism or bald commands. Learning and application here
> go hand in hand with critical reworking.[39]

Trotsky saw that it was the inadequacies and contradictions of formal
logic that. drove theorists toward dialectical formulations. Even those who
pride themselves on a "deductive method," which proceeds "through a number
of premises to the necessary conclusion," frequently "break the chain of
syllogisms and, under the influence of purely empirical considerations, arrive
at conclusions which have no connection with the previous logical chain."
Such ad hoc empirical adjustments to the conclusions of formal logic betray
a "primitive form of dialectical thinking." The only way to escape this "primitive" combination of abstract logic and empiricism is to combine these elements "more fully, much better, on a much broader scale, and more
systematically . . .through dialectical thinking."[40]

The reason why formal logic is often forced to abandon its own procedures in the face of the facts is that it attempts to analyze a living, evolving
reality with static concepts. Formally things are defined statically, according
to certain fixed properties—color, weight, size, and so on. This is denoted
by the expression "A is equal to A." Trotsky, following Engels's formulations, gives a "very concise sketch" of the inadequacies of this way of looking at the world:

> In reality "A" is not equal to "A." This is easy to prove if we observe
> these two letters under a lens—they are quite different to each other. But,
> one can object, the question is not the size or the form of the letters,
> since they are only symbols for equal quantities, for instance, a pound of
> sugar. The objection is beside the point; in reality a pound of sugar is
> never equal to a pound of sugar—a more delicate scale always discloses a
> difference. Again one can object: but a pound of sugar is equal to itself.
> Neither is this true—all bodies change uninterruptedly in size, weight,
> colour etc. They are never equal to themselves.[41]

It is not even true, Trotsky continues, that a pound of sugar is equal to itself "at a given moment in time." Even in an infinitesimal moment of time, the pound of sugar is undergoing microscopic changes—"existence itself is an uninterrupted process of transformation." At this point, a word of warning is necessary. A criticism sometimes leveled at this kind of example is that it is trying to *explain* the changes taking place in the pound of sugar. This is obviously not the case. An explanation would have to proceed from the established properties of sugar and the surrounding air, and so on to the laws governing the changes in these properties and their interaction. The example merely shows that, because the sugar is in the process of transformation, no static formal definition will be adequate even to formulate the question, never mind deliver the answer. And because we have to formulate the question dialectically, we are justified in hypothesizing that the answer will be dialectical as well.

The doctrine that "A equals A" is satisfactory only under conditions where the scale of change is not vital to our understanding—as when we buy a pound of sugar. But for more complex tasks in politics, history, and science generally, this will not do. Common sense and formal logic are agreed on static definitions of, for instance, "capitalism," "freedom," or "the state." Much of modern social science is obsessed precisely with this kind of classification and definition, the "motionless imprints of a reality that consists of eternal motion." But "dialectical thinking analyses all phenomena in their continuous change, while determining in the material conditions of those changes that critical limit beyond which 'A ceases to be A.'" This method gives theory a "succulence" that "brings it closer to the living phenomena. Not capitalism in general, but a given capitalism at a given stage of development."[42] Although he recognized that Hegel's dialectic was only an "anticipation" of scientific thought, Trotsky concludes this passage by saying:

> Hegel in his *Logic* established a series of laws: change of quantity into quality, development through contradictions, conflict of content and form, interuption of continuity, change of possibility into inevitability, etc., which are just as important for theoretical thought as the simple syllogism for more elementary tasks.[43]

This brief outline of the dialectic, like Engels's own account, has met with sustained criticism. It is said to be an all-embracing determinism, predicting the inevitable unfolding of history according to spurious dialectical laws. The idea that the dialectic applies to the natural world as well as the social world, which Trotsky clearly believes, has been cited as evidence for this determinism. Nature develops blindly and unconsciously, it is argued, and so any dialectic that applies both to the natural world and the social world must end in denying conscious human agency any role in social change. In the last thirty years, such accusations have been the common coin of idealists and empiricists alike, of structuralists, Althusserians, postmodernists, and analytical marxists.

Trotsky did not meet such criticisms at the time of the debate in the American SWP. He was mostly concerned with the substantive issue of the class nature of Russia and touched on dialectics only in outline. But some years earlier, in 1933–35, he did study Hegel while working on his biography of Lenin. In preparation for his study of Lenin's *Philosophical Notebooks*, Trotsky studied Aristotle, Descartes, and, especially, Hegel. The notebooks and the notes that he continued to make until the time of the debate in the SWP contain some of the most incisive thinking about the dialectic since Marx, albeit in a fragmentary style. They form a remarkable unity with his earlier comments on the dialectic in the 1920s and his polemical defense of the dialectic in the debate with Burnham. Many of the formulations bear directly on the objections now frequently raised against the dialectic.

TROTSKY'S NOTEBOOKS ON DIALECTICS

Trotsky begins by making some important observations on the difference between the Hegelian and the marxist dialectic. Hegel had insisted on the identity between men's consciousness of the world and the real structure of the world itself, the identity of knowing and being. Hegel believed that the history of the world mirrored the unfolding of human consciousness. This is the root of his idealism. Marx, as we have seen, refused to accept the dialectic in this form, although he understood that Hegel had struck an important blow against Kantian dualism by asserting that thought and reality were part of one whole and could not be separated into two spheres. So how should a materialist theory interpret this relationship? Lenin, in an important aside in the *Philosophical Notebooks*, remarked that marxists should prefer the formulation "the unity of knowing and being" rather than the *"identity* of knowing and being." Trotsky elaborates this insight:

> According to Hegel *being* and *thinking* are identical (absolute idealism). Materialism does not adopt this *identity*—it premises being to thought. . . .
>   The identity of being and thinking according to H[egel] signifies the identity of objective and subjective logic, their ultimate congruence. Materialism accepts the correspondence of the subjective and objective, their unity, but not their identity, in other words it does not liberate matter from its materiality, in order to keep only the logical framework of regularity, of which scientific thought (consciousness) is the expression.[44]

Hegel's *Logic* is, of course, a massive example of a "logical framework" constructed by "liberating matter from materiality." However, this edifice can only be kept from collapsing by doing enormous violence to the facts, so that they fit into the construction *and also* by hammering the logical framework until it fits the facts.

Trotsky is arguing that a materialist dialectic must show both how dialectical logic can only arise from a dialectical reality and that the relationship between thought and reality cannot be as rigid and constricted as it is in Hegel's idealism. For marxists, the dialectic in history—the contradiction between the forces and relations of production, the clash of the class struggle—cannot have a structure *identical* to the intellectual process by which we come to understand history. The dialectical method involves analytically separating a chaotic social whole into its various constituent economic formations, classes, institutions, personalities, and so on. It then involves showing how these factors interrelate and contradict each other as part of a totality. Such an intellectual operation gives us a finished picture of the dialectic in history, but it is not itself the same as that dialectic. Trotsky goes on to spell out some of the implications that this distinction involves:

> What does logic express? The law of the external world or the law of consciousness? The question is posed dualistically, [and] therefore not correctly [for] the laws of logic express the laws (rules, methods) of consciousness in its active relationship to the external world. The relationship of consciousness to the external world is a relationship of the part (the particular, specialised) to the whole.[45]

Trotsky is allowing for interaction and contradiction to emerge between thought and reality in a way that was inadmissable for Hegel. Any materialist theory must develop a method capable of dealing with all history's lapses, leaps, inconsistencies, and unevenness. To meet this challenge the distinction between the Hegelian identity and the marxist unity of thought and material reality is vital. Trotsky calls this kind of distinction a "differentiated unity." Indeed, he uses this phrase to describe the term dialectical materialism itself.[46] Differentiated unity is a concept that Trotsky uses again and again to distinguish a dialectical materialist approach from a reductionist, deterministic approach. It is particularly useful in describing the relationship between the dialectic in nature and the dialectic in society.

Trotsky realized that natural scientists were less directly affected by the class nature of the dominant ideology than social scientists. He based this belief on the fact that although the bourgeoisie no longer needs to transform the social structure and so no longer has need of a critical social science, as it did in its revolutionary years, it still does need to transform the natural world. The competition between different capitals, the drive to accumulate, means that capitalism still needs the ability to transform nature and to develop new technology. Of course, the class nature of this process leaves its mark even on natural science—by compartmentalizing areas of study and subordinating research to the needs of economic and military competition. And the more science attempts to generalize, the more it attempts to overcome this compartmentalization and restriction, the more it has to confront philosophical issues. And the more it confronts these issues, the more it is liable to find itself in conflict with the ideological prejudices of the ruling class.

So, for nature to be fully understood, it had to be seen as a totality and in its full connection with society. Following Marx and Engels, Trotsky sees Darwin's theory of evolution as an important breakthrough for a materialist understanding of history but argues that it is "less concrete, with less content, than the dialectical conception." This is partly because Darwin's Christianity led him to refuse to generalize his findings, ultimately compromising the significance of his own theory. But also Darwin partly did not have a conscious dialectical method which would have enabled him to refine his findings, seeing them in the broader framework. Such a framework would have made it easier to see that there is no impenetrable barrier between "nature" and "human society." Human beings' battle for survival is, as Marx put it, the "everlasting, nature-imposed condition of human existence."

Nature had to be seen dialectically, not just in its connection to society, but in itself as well. Trotsky, again following Marx, saw that human beings are part of the natural world and that any attempt to break this unity would result in dualism:

> Dialectics is the logic of development. It examines the world—completely and without exception—not as the result of creation, of a sudden beginning, the realisation of a plan, but as a result of motion, of transformation. Everything that is *became* the way it is as a result of lawlike development . . . the organic world emerged from the inorganic, consciousness is a capacity of living organisms depending upon organs that originated through evolution.
> In other words "the soul" of evolution (of dialectics) leads in the last analysis to matter. The evolutionary point of view carried to a logical conclusion leaves no room for either idealism or dualism, or for the other species of eclecticism.[47]

In other words, the alternative to seeing both history and nature as dialectical in structure is to assume that nature has a series of laws totally separate from those governing human society. The result is either to reduce nature to an unknowable realm (a Kantian thing-in-itself) or to abandon the theory of evolution, because it assumes that humans did grow out of nature and are still part of nature.

Trotsky had already made some similar observations in his 1925 speech on "Dialectical Materialism and Science." Here he argued that each of the sciences were bound in a totality. Psychology "in the *final instance*" rests on physiology, which rests on chemistry, mechanics, and physics. Without such an approach "there is not and cannot be a finished philosophy linking all phenomena into a single system."[48] In his notebooks on dialectics, he put the same point even more strongly:

> All evolution is a transition from quantity into quality. . . . Whoever denies the dialectical law of the transition from quantity into quality must deny the genuine unity of plants and animal species, the chemical elements, etc. He must, in the last analysis, turn back to the biblical act of creation.[49]

Such phrases inevitably raise the objection that Trotsky is importing the blind, deterministic laws of the natural sciences into marxism and generally paving the way for a vulgar materialism in the manner of the Second International. Careful reading of "Dialectical Materialism and Science" alone should dispel these objections. For instance, Trotsky argues:

> Human society has not developed in accordance with a pre-arranged plan or system, but empirically, in the course of a long, complicated and contradictory struggle of the human species for existence, and, later for greater and greater mastery over nature itself. The ideology of human society took shape as a reflection of and an instrument in this process—belated, desultory, piecemeal, in the form, so to speak, of conditioned reflexes, which are in the final analysis reducible to the necessities of the struggle of collective man against nature.[50]

Without losing sight of its material base, Trotsky spells out that human ideology is not simply a "reflection" of the historical process but also "*an instrument in* this process." Elsewhere in the same speech, he uses the idea of a "differentiated unity" in his analysis of the sciences. We have seen that he argues that psychology rests on physiology which rests on chemistry and so on. But he goes on to say that "chemistry is no substitute for physiology." In fact, "chemistry *has its own keys*," which must be studied separately using "a special approach, special research technique, special hypotheses and methods." Trotsky concludes, "Each science rests on the laws of the other sciences only in the so-called *final instance.*"[51]

This understanding prevents Trotsky from crudely applying natural laws to society. He warns that it is a "fundamental mistake" when "the methods and achievements of chemistry or physiology, in violation of all scientific boundaries, are transplanted to human society." It is true, says Trotsky, that "human society is surrounded on all sides by chemical processes." Nevertheless, "public life is neither a chemical nor a psychological process, but a social process which is shaped by its own laws."[52]

What of the dialectic itself? It is one thing to say that the laws of natural science cannot be automatically transferred to the analysis of society, but where does this leave the claim that the writ of the dialectic runs in both the natural and the social world? Trotsky presents a startlingly clear restatement of the original marxist approach to these questions in his notebooks on dialectics. He continues to insist that human beings are part of nature, that the conscious grew out of the unconscious. "Our human reason is nature's youngest child," he argues. But the development of this consciousness marks a new historical phase that cannot simply be analyzed using the tools that are adequate for objective nature:

> Dialectical cognition is not *identical* with the dialectic of nature. Consciousness is a quite original *part* of nature, possessing peculiarities and regularities that are completely absent in the remaining part of nature. Subjective dialectics must by virtue of this be a distinctive part of objective dialectics—with its own special forms and regularities.[53]

Trotsky then goes on to argue, in an aside leveled at Hegel's attempt to transfer the dialectic of consciousness onto the dialectic of nature, that "the danger lies in the transference—under the guise of 'objectivism'—of the birth pangs, the spasm of consciousness, to objective nature." Actually, since Hegel, few have tried to claim that nature reproduces the patterns of human consciousness. The main danger, at least within the socialist movement, has been the opposite. It was a feature of both Stalinism and the marxism of the Second International that they tried to reduce the dialectic to a series of positive laws which rigidly determined the course of history. Trotsky's differentiation between the form of the dialectic appropriate in nature and that adequate for the study of society both preserves the unity of the dialectic (thus avoiding dualism) and also prevents a deterministic interpretation of marxism.

Trotsky sums up the relationship between theory and practice in words that strongly recall Marx's use of the term "practical-critical activity":

> The dialectic of consciousness (cognition) is not thereby a *reflection* of the dialectic of nature, but is a *result* of the lively interaction between consciousness and nature and—in addition—a method of cognition, issuing from this interaction.[54]

For Marx, "practical-critical activity," or practice, meant the unique capability of human beings to alter consciously the material world that determines their existence. Trotsky points to the same dialectical combination of subjective and objective factors in human action when he says that the "attempt to set up a hostile opposition" between determinism, "the philosophy of objective causality," and teleology, "the philosophy of subjective purposes," is "a product of philosophical ignorance."[55]

Such distinctions between the dialectic in nature and that in history inevitably mean a transformation of some key dialectical concepts. Trotsky, for instance, puts great stress on one particular dialectical law—the transition from quantity into quality. This emphasis differs from that given in many accounts of the dialectic that stress the negation of the negation. A distorted account of the negation of the negation can be used to accuse marxism of determinism. Crudely, the argument runs that the contradiction between capitalism and its antithesis, the working class, must inevitably be resolved in a synthesis, a socialist society in which classes disappear. The negation is negated. The marxists of the classical marxist tradition have long argued that the resolution of such contradictions is not automatic, but a question that can only be resolved in struggle. Marx and those who followed him have insisted only that the *struggle* between the classes is inevitable, but *not* its outcome. Trotsky's interpretation of the dialectic is wholly in this spirit. He says that the dialectic gives us the "forms of the transformation of one regime into another" but then continues:

> ... in such a general form it is only a matter of possibility. ... Thus, from the possibility of a bourgeois victory over the feudal classes until the victory itself there were various time lapses, and the victory itself frequently looked like a semi-victory. In order for the possibility to become a necessity there had to be a corresponding strengthening of some factors and the weakening of others, a definite relationship between these strengthenings and weakenings. In other words: it was necessary for several quantantive changes to prepare the way for a new constellation of forces.[56]

Trotsky is so committed to the view that the dialectic in history is a *tendency*, not a deterministic law, that he defines the negation of the negation, or triad (the thesis negated by the antithesis in turn negated by the synthesis), as "the 'mechanism' of the transformation of quantity into quality." Trotsky expresses his understanding of the dialectic particularly sharply in the notebooks, but he had been using the method for much longer. His analysis of the role of the individual in history shows just how brilliantly he wielded the marxist method.

THE INDIVIDUAL IN HISTORY

To account for the role of the individual in history is a serious test for any materialist theory of history. Today, when so much that passes for social theory— including that written by postmodernists, feminists, and analytical marxists— insists on the irreducible nature of individual experience, it is more important than ever that marxists approach this problem correctly. Trotsky gives a marvellous account of the formation of individuality in his *Literature and Revolution*:

> The truth is that even if individuality is unique, it does not mean that it cannot be analysed. Individuality is a welding together of tribal, national, class, temporary and institutional elements and, in fact, it is in the uniqueness

of this welding together, in the proportions of this psychochemical mixture, that individuality is expressed.[57]

In the *History of the Russian Revolution*, Trotsky expressed a similar thought: "The 'distinguishing traits' of a person are merely individual scratches made by a higher law of development."[58] Trotsky argues that it is only because each of us is a *unique fusion* of elements that are *common* that we can understand individual works of art. The work of art combines forces that are at work on all of us, but it does so in a unique way determined by each particular artist:

> So it can be seen that what forms a bridge from soul to soul is not the unique, but the common. Only through the common is the unique known; the common is determined in man by the most persistent conditions which make up his "soul," by the social conditions of education, of existence, of work, and of associations.[59]

This is why "a class standard is so fruitful in all fields of ideology." But, as should now be obvious, Trotsky did not mean that each individual could therefore be reduced to a simple stereotypical example of their class. He wrote:

> We do not at all pretend to deny the significance of the personal in the mechanics of historic process, nor the significance in the personal of the accidental. We only demand that a historic personality, with all its peculiarities, should not be taken as a bare list of psychological traits, but as the living reality grown out of definite social conditions and reacting on them. As a rose does not lose its fragrance because the natural scientist points out upon what ingredients of soil and atmosphere it is nourished, so an exposure of the social roots of a personality does not remove from it either its aroma or its foul smell.[60]

Of course, it is one thing to be able to develop a general formula with which to understand the problem of individuality, it is quite another, more difficult, problem to make it render an account of the specific role of particular individuals. Trotsky is the author of one such study: Lenin's role in the Russian revolution.

Trotsky examines Lenin's role in April 1917, when the Bolsheviks were failing to challenge the provisional government. Would the Bolsheviks have reoriented themselves and begun the fight for a second, socialist revolution without Lenin? Trotsky's argument is that they probably would have done so, but not in time, because: "the war and the revolution would not allow the party a long period for fulfilling its mission. Thus it is by no means excluded that a disoriented and split party might have let the revolutionary opportunity slip for many years."[61]

It was Lenin's "personal influence" that "shortened the crisis." Here, says Trotsky, "the role of the personality arises before us on a truly gigantic scale," but we should have no difficulty accepting this because "dialectical materialism . . . has nothing in common with fatalism."[62]

Trotsky's account is hotly contested by Isaac Deutscher in *The Prophet Outcast*. Deutscher claims that this analysis is one of Trotsky's "least success-ful." He accuses Trotsky of a "subjectivism" that "goes strongly against the grain of the Marxist intellectual tradition."[63] In opposition to Trotsky, Deutscher champions Plekhanov's essay *The Role of the Individual in History*. Deutscher paraphrases Plekhanov in insisting, "the leader is merely the organ of an historic need or necessity, and that necessity creates its organ when it needs it. No great man is therefore 'irreplacable.'" And he quotes Plekhanov favorably when he says that if Robespierre had been killed in January 1793, "his place would, of course, have been taken by someone else; and although that other person might have been inferior to him in every respect, events would have nevertheless taken the same course."[64]

On this analysis, "History's" carelessness in not replacing Rosa Luxemburg in 1919 is inexplicable. But, untroubled by such thoughts, Deutscher continues:

> Have not in our time the Chinese and the Yugoslav revolutions triumphed . . . under leaders of smaller, even much smaller, stature? In each case the revolutionary trend found or created its organs in such human material as was available.[65]

Deutscher has obviously lost sight of the fact that Mao and Tito were not representatives of the working class, did not head revolutionary parties, and were not leaders of working-class revolutions. It is, therefore, hardly surpris-ing to find that in these examples the role of the working class has been filled by a "revolutionary trend" that is "creating" what it requires without human intervention.

If we return to Trotsky's analysis of Lenin's role in the Russian revolution, we can see that rather than tearing the question of leadership free of its historical context, as both Deutscher and Plekhanov do, he roots it firmly in that context. Trotsky insists that "Lenin was not a demiurge of the revolutionary process," he "merely entered into a chain of objective historic forces." Lenin did not "oppose the party from the outside, but was himself its most complete expression. In educating it he had educated himself." Lenin guided the Bolsheviks, not because he was a solitary hero but because he had been *created* by the Bolshevik party. The endless struggle to build the party, the streams of letters stretching back over decades from Lenin to the workers and party members and from them to Lenin, the articles and speeches both given by Lenin and given by others to which Lenin had listened, these were what had formed Lenin. As Trotsky says:

> Lenin was not an accidental element in the historic development, but a product of the whole of Russian history. He was embedded in it with the

deepest roots. Along with the vanguard of the workers, he had lived through their struggle in the course of the preceding quarter century.[66]

It was precisely what Lenin had in *common* with his party that made him able to speak with it, from "soul to soul," thoughout 1917. His uniqueness was that he expressed this common tradition more accurately, more completely than his opponents. Trotsky spells this out most clearly in the notebooks on dialectics:

> Lenin, at times erred not only in minor but in major issues. . . . A whole row of persons can, with every justification, point to their correctness and Lenin's errors in given, sometimes very important, issues. The group Bor'ba [The Struggle] was correct in its criticism of Lenin's first agrarian programme . . . Plekhanov was right in his criticism of Lenin's theory of socialism "from the outside"; the author of these lines was correct in his general prognosis of the character of the Russian Revolution. But in the struggle of tendencies, groups, persons, by far no one was able to yield an account with a credit like Lenin's. In this lay the secret of his influence, his strength and . . . not in a fraudulent infallibility, of the sort portrayed in the historiography of the epigones.[67]

This fact would have been more obvious, and Lenin's individuality less striking, had it not been for the exceptional circumstance that he was a revolutionary leader returning from exile. This physical separation made for an easy, impressionistic counterposition of the "hero" and the "mass." Had Lenin not been in exile, the "inner continuity of the party's development" would have been more readily discernible.[68]

From this account, two things are clear. First, such a leader forged by an organization during decades of theoretical work and practical struggle cannot be simply "replaced" on the eve of revolution by the "forces of history." Second, the uniqueness of such a leader lies only in his or her ability to summarize the common experience of those with whom they have built such an organization and the facility with which they bend that common tradition to meet new tasks. Without a revolutionary organization, they would have neither the means to understand the struggle, nor the capacity to direct it.

Any collective working-class organization, whether a revolutionary party, a trade union, or even a reformist party, gives something of this power to change history to its members and its leaders. But how much power they have, and whether they use it effectively, depends on many things—the size of the organization, its politics, its history, the economic situation in which it operates, the strength and organization of the ruling class, and so on.

When most social theorists examine the situation of the individual, however, they do not look at this collective context. Many of the difficult issues with which some socialists and feminists have become most concerned in recent years—rape, pornography, crime, and drug abuse—are situations in which the individuals themselves are most cruelly separated from any collective power. To argue that such individuals, whether they are the victim or the perpetrator, exercise a choice in their individual destiny in the same way that the individual members and leaders of great social movements exercise power over their collective fate is wrong.

What gave Lenin or Cromwell or Robespierre the ability to make an individual contribution to history was the great power of the movements from which they rose. What crushes the element of real choice out of the lives of isolated individuals is their total separation from any such movement and their utter dependence, both economically and ideologically, on a system that is entirely hostile to their needs and aspirations. The more isolated and powerless the individual and the more brutal the circumstances he or she confronts the less chance he or she has of influencing their individual fate. As Trotsky put it:

> To a tickle, people react differently, but to a red hot iron, alike. As a steamhammer converts a sphere and cube alike into sheet metal, so under the blow of too great and inexorable events resistances are smashed and the boundaries of "individuality" are lost.[69]

THE DIALECTIC OF PERMANENT REVOLUTION

The theory of permanent revolution marked an important break with the determinism of the Second International. Later it became the cornerstone of Trotsky's fight against Stalin's fatalistic theory of "socialism in one country." In both cases, Trotsky argued that for a backward country to be ripe for socialist revolution it did not have to go through all the stages of capitalist development that characterized the history of the advanced capitalist powers. Trotsky's theory, the law of combined and uneven development, stressed that any analysis of the revolutionary potentiality of backward countries must start from the *totality* of capitalist development on a world scale. Here it was clear that the material conditions for a socialist society existed, even if they did not exist in each part of the world system taken in isolation. If a revolution was to be successful in a backward country, then it must spread to other parts of the system and so tap their material wealth. Thus seeing the *interconnectedness* of the different parts of the totality was also the key to Trotsky's analysis. To realize this potential, the working class would have to battle consciously for the leadership of the revolution.

Even from this thumbnail sketch, it is clear that Trotsky's theory was a brilliant application of the dialectical method to new historical circumstances.[70] He did not simply impose an abstract dialectical scheme on recalcitrant facts. From empirical research, he built up a picture of the totality of class relations and formulated the law of combined and uneven development to trace the relationship between the different parts of that totality. It is a picture accurately described by the phrase that he later used in the notebooks on dialectics—differentiated unity.

In answer to the Stalinists who accused him of "skipping over historical stages" he spelled out this conception:

> It is nonsense to say that stages cannot in general be skipped. The living historical process always leaps over isolated "stages" which derive from theoretical breakdown into its component parts of the process of development in its entirety, that is, taken in its fullest scope. . . . It may be said that the first distinction between a revolutionist and a vulgar evolutionist lies in the capacity to recognise and exploit such moments.[71]

Trotsky gave equally short shrift to his opponents talk of historical inevitability:

> One stage or another of the historical process can prove to be inevitable under certain conditions, although theoretically not inevitable. And conversely theoretically "inevitable" stages can be compressed to zero by the dynamic of development, especially during revolutions.[72]

Trotsky's theory of permanent revolution is an example of applied dialectics. It contains in a concrete analysis all the propositions that he later formulated as general principles in his writings on the dialectic.

We find the same principles at work when we look at Trotsky's writing on art. Here he ties culture to its material roots, insists that the "class criteria" is vital in art, but also argues that art must be "judged according to its own laws." This sounds like a contradiction until we understand it as another example of a "differentiated unity." In Literature and Revolution, Trotsky again shows that neither idealism nor vulgar materialism are sufficient to analyze the role of art. Art, he argues, is neither a mirror, which simply reflects society, nor a hammer, which can shape society according to its own desires.

Trotsky dismisses "pre-October art," which simply hankers nostalgically after the days of the tsar. But he is far from uncritical of the Futurists and the practitioners of proletcult. He says that the Futurists' call to break with the art of the past only "has a meaning insofar as the Futurists are cutting the cord which binds them to the priests of bourgeois literary tradition." But for the working class this call means nothing, because "the working class does not have to, and cannot break with literary tradition because the working class is not in the grip of such a tradition."[73]

Trotsky's argument is that the working class must master the old culture as well as forge the new. In the course of this, they will both create new artistic forms and revitalize old forms. This attitude is based on an appraisal of the development of culture as a whole, seeing both its continuity and discontinuity with the prerevolutionary society. It is an attitude that stresses that a transformation of art can only be based on an understanding of the relationship between revolution and art, which neither passively accepts art as an independent realm nor reduces art to an immediate expression of society's needs, to the level of propaganda:

> One cannot turn the concept of culture into the small change of the individual daily living and determine the success of a class culture by the proletarian passports of individual inventors or poets. Culture is the organic sum of knowledge which characterises the entire society, or at least its ruling class. It embraces and penetrates all fields of human work and unifies them into a system. Individual achievements rise above this level and elevate it gradually.[74]

Individual artists can help remake culture, but not in isolation and not in conditions of their own choosing.

CONCLUSION

Trotsky's philosophical writings are often short and their meaning compressed. Indeed, some were notes not intended for publication. Perhaps their full significance is only clear against the background of the tradition of dialectical thought which began with Hegel and which passes down through the writing of Marx and Engels, Luxemburg, Lenin, Lukacs, and Gramsci. Trotsky obviously thought this was the case, because his writings are partly a comment on Hegel's writings and partly a preparation for studying Lenin's *Philosophical Notebooks*. This conclusion simply spells out the positions to which this tradition commits us.

First, it binds us to a view of the natural and social world as a single totality developing over time as a result of its internal contradictions. Any other position reduces the natural world to an unknowable realm, separate from society and developing according to alien principles. Moreover, because the social world grows out of the natural world (and is still shaped by constant interaction with it), there is every reason to believe that if one has a dialectical structure, so will the other.

The reason why natural science seems to have less need of a dialectical method than the social sciences is because the compartmentalized and instrumental nature of much scientific research is sufficient for the purposes of capitalist society. Nevertheless, this scientific work, real though its fruits are, is necessarily limited in achievement and in method. The ends of science are partly predetermined by the bourgeois nature of society, and this closes off much discussion about the overall structure of the natural world and the purposes of science. The moment scientific research pushes beyond these boundaries—whether it be in the areas of evolution, relativity, or in chaos theory, or in the theories that deal with the nature of the universe—questions of dialectics often arise. In many cases (Darwin is the example which Trotsky cites), natural scientists develop quasi-dialectical theories. This is an indication both that the reality they study has a dialectical form of development and that they would find a dialectical framework the most useful in such study. This, of course, is an argument that can only be decisively proved by a detailed analysis of modern science.

There are, however, a number of general reasons for supposing that nature is dialectical. We can clearly say that nature is an interconnected system that developed for millions of years before human beings walked the earth. It continues to develop now and would do so whether or not humans labored upon it. It, therefore, has an internal dynamic. We can also confidently claim that nature did not develop randomly but rather according to certain rationally comprehensible principles. Neither did it develop smoothly and evenly. It evolved through great transformations which, although prepared by small molecular changes, once they occurred, were to leave the world qualitatively and fundamentally different from what went before. Trotsky points to the development of human consciousness as one such moment of transformation.

Second, this view lays the basis for an argument that avoids the accusation that any conception of the dialectic which embraces both nature and society must run the danger of importing the objective laws of natural development into the social sphere, thus reducing marxism to a determinism. Trotsky's notebooks provide a solution to this problem. Trotsky's point is not just that the "conscious rose out of the unconscious" and thereby opened a qualitively new phase in history. He also argues, following Engels, that the structure of the dialectic in society is different to that in nature—the former must take account of the development of consciousness in a way that the latter need not. The dialectic cannot remain some immutable substratum above which everything else changes but which is itself immune to change. The dialectic itself is transformed as the natural world and the social world develop. This is a fundamental feature of a materialist dialectic which is wholly missing from Hegel, who had no need of an articulated dialectic capable of molding its form to meet the contours of the material world from which it rises.

In this view, nature and society are "a unity," but they are not identical. They are a "differentiated unity" in which each particular sphere is still connected to every other, but in which each sphere also produces its own special processes, laws, and so on. Trotsky had long used a similar distinction in his theoretical work. It was a guiding principle in his theory of permanent revolution, in his historical writing, and in his analysis of art. Trotsky's conception of "differentiated unity," a philosophical equivalent of combined and uneven development, is an original formulation.

This is a marxist analysis which stands in no need of being refined by notions such as "relative autonomy," does not require that we relapse into dualism for the sake of maintaining that conscious human action plays a role in changing society, and does not demand that we fall into idealism to explain the role of the individual in history.

It is, however, a method that needs defending. Many socialists in the advanced capitalist economies have experienced ten years or more where the genuine marxist tradition has been in retreat. As Trotsky noted, "Reactionary periods . . . naturally become epochs of cheap evolutionism," and, he might of added, of its dialectical opposite, rampant idealism. We have had plenty of both. Now it looks as if that period may be coming to an end. There could be no better time to reassert the genuine marxist tradition and no better example than Trotsky's writings.

Notes

1. Quoted in I. Deutscher, *The Prophet Outcast* (Oxford: Oxford University Press, 1963), 220.
2. See, for instance, John Molyneux's *Leon Trotsky's Theory of Revolution* (Brighton: Harvester, 1981).
3. M. Merleau Ponty, *Adventures of the Dialectic* (London: Heinemann, 1974), 74.
4. K. Anderson, *Lenin, Hegel and Western Marxism* (Chicago: University of Illinois, 1995), see 271 n. 21, and 279, n. 3. Merleau Ponty at least had the excuse of not having seen Trotsky's notebooks on dialectics, but Anderson specifically makes these remarks about these same notebooks. This can only be taken as further evidence of the left Hegelian tradition's inability to come to terms with anything other than a straight transposition of Hegel's categories into revolutionary theory.

   For a alternative recent account, see R. Day, "Between Hegel and Habermas: The Political Theory of Leon Trotsky," in T. Brotherstone and P. Dukes, eds., *The Trotsky Reappraisal* (Edinburgh: Edinburgh University, 1992), which stresses that "addressing problems which Marx had never anticipated, Trotsky intuitively found his way, through Marx's dialectic, to Hegelian concerns" (124). Day also rightly insists that Lenin's study of Hegel came to "conclusions strikingly similar to Trotsky's" (122).
5. L. Trotsky, *My Life* (London: Penguin, 1975), 123.
6. Ibid.
7. Ibid.
8. A. Labriola, *Essays in the Materialist Conception of History* (Chicago: C.H. Kerr, 1904).
9. Ibid., 77.
10. Ibid., 17–18.
11. Ibid., 152.
12. See chap. 1 and similar discussions by Marx and Engels and by Plekhanov in chaps. 2 and 3, respectively.
13. Labriola, *Essays*, 85.
14. Ibid., 26.

15. Ibid., 145.
16. Ibid., 145.
17. Ibid., 152.
18. L. Trotsky, "Philosophical Tendencies of Bureaucratism," in *The Challenge of the Left Opposition 1928–1929* (New York: Pathfinder, 1981), 392.
19. Ibid., 393.
20. Ibid.
21. Ibid., 398.
22. Ibid., 395–96.
23. Ibid., 405.
24. The American Socialist Workers Party, which has now abandoned Trotsky's theory of permanent revolution, was in the 1930s one of the more promising sections of Trotsky's Fourth International.
25. G. Novack, *Polemics in Marxist Philosophy* (New York: Monad, 1978), 269–70.
26. See Steve Wright's article on Hal Draper, particularly the appendix. For a wider perspective, see Chris Harman's "From Trotsky to State Capitalism." Both are in *International Socialism* 47 (Summer 1990).
27. Deutscher, *The Prophet Outcast*, 430.
28. Ibid., 442–43.
29. L. Trotsky, *Their Morals and Ours* (New York: Pathfinder, 1973) 45.
30. J. Burnham, "Science and Style," reproduced in L. Trotsky, *In Defence of Marxism* (New York: Pathfinder, 1973), 190–91.
31. Ibid., 198.
32. Ibid., 196.
33. Ibid., 192.
34. Trotsky, ibid., 43–44.
35. Ibid., 45.
36. Ibid., 44–45. Although, of course, Trotsky realized that it would be "lifeless pedantry" to demand that "every party member occupy himself with the philosophy of dialectics."
37. Ibid., 49.
38. Ibid., 52.
39. See L. Trotsky, *Problems of Everyday Life* (New York: Monad, 1973), 233.
40. "Dialectics and the Immutability of the Syllogism," in *Writings of Leon Trotsky, 1939–40* (New York: Pathfinder, 1973), 400–401.
41. Trotsky, *In Defence of Marxism*, 49.
42. Ibid., 50.
43. Ibid., 51.
44. *Trotsky's Notebooks 1933–35: Writings on Lenin, Dialectics and Evolutionism*, trans. P. Pomper (New York: Columbia University Press, 1986), 77.
45. Ibid., 87.
46. Ibid., 97.
47. Ibid., 96–97.
48. L. Trotsky, "Dialectical Materialism and Science," in *Problems of Everyday Life*, 212–14.
49. *Notebooks 1933–35*, 113.
50. "Dialectical Materialism and Science," 215.
51. Ibid., 214.
52. Ibid., 216.
53. *Notebooks, 1933–35*, 102.

54. Ibid., 101–2.
55. Ibid., 113.
56. Ibid., 90.
57. L. Trotsky, *Literature and Revolution* (New York), 59–60.
58. L. Trotsky, *The History of the Russian Revolution* (London: Pluto Press, 1977), 73.
59. *Literature and Revolution*, 60.
60. L. Trotsky, *History of the Russian Revolution*, quoted in G. Novack, *Polemics in Marxist Philosophy*, 281–82.
61. L. Trotsky, *History of the Russian Revolution* (London, Pluto Press, 1977), 343.
62. Ibid.
63. Deutscher, *The Prophet Outcast*, 241, 242, 251.
64. Ibid., 243.
65. Ibid., 245–46.
66. L. Trotsky, *History of the Russian Revolution*, 344.
67. *Notebooks, 1933–35*, 84.
68. L. Trotsky, *History of the Russian Revolution*, 344.
69. L. Trotsky, *History of the Russian Revolution*, quoted in G. Novak, *Polemics in Marxist Philosophy*, 287.
70. For a more extensive account, see T. Cliff, *Trotsky*, Vol. 1, (London: Bookmarks, 1989), chap. 10, especially, 201–4. And for a brilliant extension of the theory to explain the fate of the Cuban and Chinese revolutions, see T. Cliff, "Deflected Permanent Revolution" (London: Bookmarks, 1990), originally published in *International Socialism*, first series no. 12 (London, 1963).
71. L. Trotsky, *The Permanent Revolution* (New York: Pathfinder, 1976), 240.
72. Ibid., 241.
73. L. Trotsky, *Literature and Revolution*, 130.
74. Ibid., 200.

Conclusion: Contradictions of Contemporary Theory

To appreciate fully the account of the dialectic given in this book, it is necessary to provide a brief resume of the territory into which it is launched. The inability of the contemporary left to come to terms with the development of capitalism in the late twentieth century has deep roots in its history, ultimately stretching back to the division between Stalinism and genuine revolutionary marxism in the late 1920s. But for our purposes the story can begin in 1956 with the first cracks in the Stalinist monolith.

In that year, two events dealt severe blows to Stalinism. Khrushchev's secret speech indicted Stalin's "cult of personality," and the Russian suppression of the Hungarian revolution precipitated a mass exodus from Communist Parties internationally. Some seven thousand left the relatively small British Communist Party. Most of them were workers, but they also included nearly all the luminaries of the Communist Party historians' group, among them Edward and Dorothy Thompson, John Saville, and Christopher Hill. A letter written by Thompson to Saville, before the suppression of the Hungarian rising, gives some sense of the mood of many Communist Party members at the time:

> Never have I known such a wet flatfish slapped in our face as our 24th [Congress of the CPGB].... Not one bloody concession as yet to our feelings and integrity: no apology to the rank and file, no self-criticism, no apology to the British people, no indication of the points of Marxist theory which now demand revaluation, no admission that our Party has undervalued intellectual and ideological work, no promise of a loosening of inner party democracy, and of the formation of even a discussion journal so that this can be fought out within our ranks.[1]

In July 1956, Thompson and Saville launched their own discussion journal, *The Reasoner.* In its editorial, they explained:

> Nothing in the events of past months has shaken our conviction that the methods and outlook of historical materialism, developed by the work of Marx and Engels, provide the key to our theoretical advance ... although it should be said that much of what has gone under the name of "Marxism" and "Marxism-Leninism" is itself in need of re-examination.
>
> History has provided a chance for this re-examination to take place; and for the scientific methods of Marxism to be integrated with the finest traditions of the human reason and spirit which we may best describe as Humanism.[2]

290

This was the birth of the New Left. After the split with the CP, there were short-lived, if sporadically revived, attempts to give the New Left some permanent organizational form. But the real home of the New Left was "the new social movements," as they would later become known. As Dorothy Thompson remembers, "The anti-nuclear movement was an essential part of the New Left from the beginning."[3] Later the anti-Vietnam War movement and the women's movement would be as important.

As the New Left developed, it began to search for new sources of theoretical inspiration on which it could draw in its battle against the old determinism of Stalinist orthodoxy. It found them in the recently published works of the young Marx, in the soon to be published translations of Lukacs, Korsch, and Gramsci's writings from the 1920s and, in minor part, in the orthodox Trotskyist tradition.[4] In all this, the New Left marked a renaissance in genuine marxism, at last creating a tradition of analysis and debate beyond the sterility of Stalinism. The struggles of the 1960s, culminating in 1968 in the May events in France and the Prague Spring, and rolling on into the industrial struggles of the early 1970s, most notably in Italy and Britain, provided a massive boost to this regeneration of marxism.[5] The founding figures of the New Left went on to produce a substantial body of marxist historical analysis—to Thompson's *The Making of the English Working Class*, we can add his *Whigs and Hunters*, Christopher Hill's prodigious body of work on the English Revolution; John Saville's writings on Chartism and the Labour Party; and Victor Kiernan's impressively catholic series of historical studies.

In the face of this ideological and practical revolt, Communist Party members launched a theoretical counterattack. This counterattack became associated above all with one theoretician: French Communist Party intellectual Louis Althusser.

Althusser's project was to resist the tide of the New Left, of marxist humanism, Hegelian marxism, and all that he associated with the erosion of orthodox historical materialism. In this he made use of two intellectual resources. In the early part of his career, until the mid-1960s, he relied on importing into marxism structuralist notions then popular in French academia. Later, he supplemented this approach with a political and intellectual reliance on the one institution seemingly untouched by any attempt to revise communist orthodoxy, the Communist Party of China.

In the first phase of his development, Althusser was simply borrowing from a then emerging intellectual fashion, structuralism. This trend opposed the French Hegelian tradition which, in the philosophy of Sartre and in some interpretations of marxism, was a constituent part of the intellectual scene after the Second World War. Michel Foucault, one of the key figures in this movement and himself a former member of the French Communist Party (PCF) recalls: "It was Hegelianism . . . that was the best the French

university could offer; it was the widest form of understanding possible for
the contemporary world which had just emerged from the tragedy of World
War II and the great upheavals that had preceded it: the Russian revolution,
Nazism, etc."[6]

The key point to which structuralism objected was the idea that history
was intelligible from the point of view of the human subject, understood
either as individuals or as a class, or that such a subject could shape the
historical process. As Foucault explains:

> There was one point in common among those who in the last fifteen
> years were called "structuralists." . . . It was a matter of calling this theme
> of the subject into question . . . [in psychology] Lacan concluded that it
> was precisely the philosophy of the subject which had to be abandoned. . . .
> In turn, Levi-Strauss also managed to call the theory of the subject into
> question through the structural analyses that could be conducted on the
> basis of the findings of linguistics; this also occurred as a result of literary
> experiences, as in the case of Blanchot and Bataille. Following another
> route, Althusser performed a similar task when he elaborated his criticism
> of French Marxism, which was imbued with phenomenology and human-
> ism and which made the theory of alienation, in a subjectivist key, into
> the theoretical basis for translating Marx's economic and political analyses
> into philosophical terms. Althusser reversed this point of view.[7]

It was not primarily the PCF, one of the most Stalinized of all communist
parties, that was "imbued with humanism." It was the critics of the PCF
who were using this interpretation of marxism as a platform. Most of the
anti-Stalinist left rejected structuralism. Foucault remembers that in 1968 it
was "those neo-Marxist intellectuals who were completing their theoretical
formation and who in general opposed the traditional intellectuals of the
French Communist Party . . . [who] did not forgive me for what I had written."[8] But Althusser had, long before 1968, embraced the structuralist fashion and now sought to give it a left-wing gloss by combining it with a
Maoist political orientation.

It was the Sino-Soviet split that enabled some credence to be attached to
Althusser's maneuver: "By 1963, posing as champions of Leninist orthodoxy, the Chinese were engaged in a neo-Stalinist defence of Stalin." Althusser
"saw the Chinese revolution as a 'concrete critique' of Stalinism and sought
to theorize it as such."[9] The radicalization of the 1960s was such that Althusser
had to present his theory as a left-wing critique of Stalinism. Indeed, in a
grand gesture that theoretically eradicated the Trotskyist tradition as completely as Stalin had eradicated its founder, Althusser asserted that his was
the "first *left wing* critique of Stalinism." However, when "Althusser's 'left
wing' critique was finally issued, it contained the major surprise of defending Stalin against critiques from the left."[10] In all this,

Althusser's treatment of other members of the Western Marxist tradition was crude and cavalier; his typology of Marxisms undiscriminating, and his own reconstruction of historical materialism defective. Moreover, he accepted elements of the Stalinist codification of Marxism . . . and . . . the travesty of Trotskyism.[11]

This unstable admixture of structuralism and the Maoist edition of Stalinism was not able to survive, any more than it was capable of foreseeing, the successive blows that historical development rained on its head after 1968. The events of 1968, which the PCF worked so hard to curtail, and continued repression in Eastern Europe and Russia diminished the appeal of Moscow-oriented Stalinism still further. Peking-oriented Stalinism was tarnished by the collapse of the Cultural Revolution and the crisis that followed it. And as the level of struggle declined in the 1970s, right-wing social thought in all its various shades—historical revisionism, monetarism, sociobiology, and poststructuralism—routed its opponents on the left, at least in academia. As Gregory Elliott reports:

> By 1977 historical materialism was generally regarded as theoretically and politically discredited in France. A fightback was long overdue. If one senior French Marxist could have been expected to shoulder the task, the obvious candidate was Althusser.[12]

Althusser was in no position to take on this project. He was doubly compromised. As practically the last Stalinist theoretician, he was compromised in trying to defend marxism. As the man who had attempted to fuse structuralism and marxism he was now the target of the post-structuralists emerging through the revolving door of intellectual fashion: "The alliance Althusser had sought in the early 1960s between Marxism and avant-garde French theory unravelled after 1968 as the philosophies of desire and power . . . drove high structuralism from the seminar room."[13] Thus it was that Althusser "came less to defeat his antagonists in a head on confrontation than to underwrite—albeit unwittingly, by demission and default—some of their pronouncements. . . . In the second half of the 1970s he proved powerless to meet the challenge of post-structuralism."[14]

One "socialist humanist" at least did rise to the challenge, both of providing a damning critique of Althusser and, by extension, of the post-structuralists who poured over the bridge that he had constructed. E. P. Thompson's *The Poverty of Theory* was not without its own weaknesses, but it was vastly superior to anything that Althusserianism had produced. Thompson insisted that Althusser's approach was "derivative from a limited kind of academic learning process," which left him "with no category (or way of handling) 'experience' (or social being's impingement upon social consciousness); hence he falsifies the 'dialogue' with empirical evidence inherent in knowledge-production, and Marx's own practice, and thereby falls continually into modes of thought designated in the marxist tradition as 'idealist.'" Furthermore, argued Thompson, "Althusser's structuralism is a structuralism of *stasis*," which "has no adequate categories to explain contradiction or change."[15]

And, just as accurately, Thompson outlined the most immediate social milieu of Althusserianism. Althusser's supporters were, Thompson argued,

> The bourgeois *lumpen-intellegensia*: aspirant intellectuals, whose amateurish intellectual preparation disarms them before manifest absurdities and elementary philosophical blunders . . . and *bourgeois*, because while many of them would *like* to be "revolutionaries," they are themselves products of a particular "conjuncture" which has broken the circuits between intellectuality and practical experience (both in real political movements, and in the actual segregation imposed by contemporary institutional structures), and hence they are able to perform *imaginary* revolutionary psycho-dramas (in which each outbids the other in adopting ferocious verbal postures) while in fact falling back upon a very old tradition of bourgeois elitism for which Althusserian theory is exactly tailored.[16]

Thompson clearly saw the objective effect of the Althusserian project: "Whereas their forebears were political interventionists, they tend more often to be diversionists . . . disorganising the constructive intellectual discourse of the Left, and . . . reproducing continually the elitist division between theory and practice."[17]

For all their obvious superiority to the Althusserians, the founders of the New Left and their later adherents had important weaknesses. As they recoiled from Stalinism, they were still marked by the experience. First, they tended to equate any party organization with the Stalinist form of party which they had rejected. In particular, they did not distinguish clearly between Lenin's conception of the party and the Stalinist corruption of that model.[18] Consequently, they rejected disciplined party organization in favor of loose discussion circles grouped around journals. Second, they remained influenced by what they took to be the non-sectarian element of the Stalinist experience—Popular Frontism. This policy stressed the supposedly common ground on which workers, some of the middle class and even some capitalists, could find in the fight against fascism. This then fitted well with the experience of the Campaign for Nuclear Disarmament (CND), but not with any consistent orientation on the working class as the key element in any such strategy.

Finally, at the level of theory they tended, to different degrees, to define class without any strong reference to its economic structure. Most famously Thompson's *The Making of the English Working Class* (1963) argued that class and class consciousness were the same thing. That is, a class could only be truly said to exist when it had developed the appropriate consciousness. Marx had argued that a class is defined by its objective place in the productive process, even if its consciousness does not yet, or fully, reflect this situation. Marx developed the distinction between a class "in itself" and a class "for itself" to account more clearly for the passage between class interests, which can be extrapolated from class position, and class consciousness. Thompson's retreat from this approach justified his ridicule of "hysterical and diabolical materialism," as he described it in *The Poverty of Theory*.

Neither were the original theorists of the New Left quite as immune to the "segregation imposed by institutional structures" which had "broken the circuits between intellectuality and experience" as Thompson liked to pretend. Thompson himself remained a political activist, but he increasingly became the exception, not the rule.

These problems made it possible for the professional historians to reduce the impact of the right-wing offensive in their chosen areas—Christopher Hill, in particular, fought an impressive rearguard action against the revisionist historians of the English Revolution—but, after *The Poverty of Theory*, there was no further general rebuttal at the philosophical level and no organizational structure through which such an understanding of marxism could be generalized.

These are the passes through which the postmodernist army filed before it occupied the broad intellectual plain in the 1980s. Its quick victory was predicated on the defeats suffered internationally by the working-class movement in the mid and late 1970s. Intellectually, it rested on ground secured by Althusserianism, even though it pushed these positions to such extremes that it eradicated its sponsor. Where Althusser had insisted on the "relative autonomy" of theory, the postmodernists went a step further and argued its complete autonomy. Althusser argued: "The *object* of knowledge . . . [is] in itself absolutely distinct from the *real object* . . . the *idea* of the circle, which is the *object* of knowledge must not be confused with the circle, which is the *real object*."[19] On what else but this kind of distinction can the postmodern insistence on a radical break between thought and the real world, to the point of insisting that there is no other world than that of thought, rest?

THE LONG RETREAT FROM 1968

The impasse that these developments have now reached can be judged by the pronouncements of some of postmodernisms leading representatives. For Jean-François Lyotard, there is no necessary connection between thought and reality. Moreover, the recurring danger in human history is that people should come to believe that their ideas can result in social progress:

> One can note a sort of decay in the confidence placed by the last two centuries in the idea of progress. This idea of progress as possible, probable or necessary was rooted in the certainty that the development of the arts,

technology, knowledge and liberty would be profitable to mankind as a whole. . . .

After two centuries we are more sensitive to signs that signify the contrary. Neither economic nor political liberalism, nor the various Marxisms, emerge from the sanguinary last two centuries free from the suspicion of crimes against humanity.[20]

This profound pessimism is founded on the absolute gulf said to exist between our knowledge of the world and the world itself. Any attempt to act as if such knowledge actually enabled us to transform the world is an error that can only lead to disaster:

> I use the name of Auschwitz to point out the irrelevance of empirical matter, the stuff of recent past history, in terms of the modern claim to help mankind to emancipate itself. . . . So there is a sort of sorrow in the Zeitgeist [the spirit of the age]. This can express itself by reactive or reactionary attitudes or by utopias, but never by a positive orientation offering a new perspective.[21]

Naturally such a perspective denies the self-emancipation of the working class. For Lyotard, the working class, understood as a class capable of liberating itself, is merely an idea put about by marxists. We cannot even be sure that such a class really exists.

> Nobody has ever seen a proletariat. . . . It's impossible to argue that this part of society is the incarnation of the proletariat, because an Idea in general has no presentation. . . . we must say that the question of the proletariat is the question of knowing whether this word is to be understood in terms of the Hegelian dialectic (that is to say, in the end, in terms of science), expecting to find something experiential to correspond to the concept, and maybe to be the concept itself; or is the term "proletariat" the name of an Idea of Reason. . . . In the second case we give up the pretension of presenting something in experience which corresponds to this term.[22]

For Michel Foucault, the difficulty is not just that of being sure about the relationship between thought and reality. For him the mere elaboration of a system of thought *is* a form of coercion, the exercise of power that oppresses others:

> I absolutely will not play the part of one who prescribes solutions. I hold that the role of the intellectual today is not that of establishing laws or proposing solutions or prophesying, since by doing that one can only contribute to the functioning of a determinate situation of power.[23]

In this topsy-turvy world, the speech of a socialist urging his workmates to strike against an imminent military coup is just as much the exercise of power, and just as "totalitarian" as the general whose order unleashes tanks and machine guns on an unarmed population. To avoid the danger of "contributing to the situation of power," Foucault limits himself to "determining problems, unleashing them, revealing them within the framework of such complexity as to shut the mouths of prophets and legislators: all those who speak *for* others and *above* others."[24] Foucault does not name even one legislator who has had his mouth shut by this torrent of critical criticism. The suspicion grows that his stance may simply be a revitalized excuse for proceeding "a little at a time, to introduce modifications that are capable of, if not finding solutions, then at least of changing the givens of a problem."[25] The familiar outline of reformism emerges from the mists of theory—and even that is only at the local level of the "microcosm of power."

Neither Lyotard nor Foucault, however, can lay claim to the title of "purveyor of some of the silliest ideas yet to gain a hearing among disciples of French intellectual fashion."[26] That honor goes to Jean Baudrillard and his argument that the Gulf War of 1991 did not take place. The "sense" of Baudrillard's argument is that all that most people know of the war is what they learned through the mass media. This media representation is then, for them, the only reality they know. There is no "reality" beyond the image that they can meaningfully compare with that image. The image *is* the truth.

"That this is sheer nonsense," as Christopher Norris notes, "should be obvious to anyone not wholly given over to the vagaries of current intellectual fashion."[27] It is particularly and obviously nonsense to those trained to look for the fault lines in ruling class ideology, a necessary result of the division between competing units of capital (including nation states) and for the contradictions in workers' experience that allows them to generalize views opposed to those of their rulers. This analysis, sustained in previous chapters, need not be restated here. The point here is to explain the causes and consequences of treating views like Baudrillard's seriously.

The social root of these ideas has been identified as the new middle class in retreat from the values of the 1960s.[28] But the narrower intellectual source of Baudrillard's views is the intellectual climate in which postmodernist notions such as the idea that "'reality' is a purely discursive phenomena, a product of various codes, conventions, language games or signifying systems which provide the only means of interpreting experience,"[29] have been circulating for more than a decade. What often results is "a half-baked mixture of ideas picked up from the latest sources, or a series of slogans to the general effect that 'truth' and 'reality' are obsolete ideas, that knowledge is always and everywhere a function of the epistemic will-to-power, and that history is nothing but a fictive construct out of the various 'discourses' that jostle for supremacy from one period to the next."[30]

The consequences of such an approach are to vitiate any possibility of understanding the contradictions of contemporary capitalism and, therefore, of any possibility of transforming society. It is with some justification that Habermas has described the postmodernists as "Young Conservatives."

But the postmodernists are not the only theorists to start out with claims to radicalism and end in the most abject conformism. More than fifteen years ago the analytical marxist tradition began its journey, like the structuralists, with a rejection of marxism's Hegelian heritage. Indeed, Althusser was as much a precursor of analytical marxism as he was of post-structuralism. Alex Callinicos has identified three ways in which Althusser paved the way for analytical marxism: "First, he established the incompatibility of historical materialism with Hegelian modes of thinking previously adhered to by Marxist philosophers." Second, Althusser inaugurated a fashion for "the systematic interrogation and clarification of basic concepts." Third, Althusser's ultimate failure "acted as a kind of negative proof" that encouraged these philosophers in the view that there was nothing distinctive in the marxist method.[31]

The upshot was an empiricist view in which the notion of the working class as the subject of history is replaced by "methodological individualism." Individuals, acting from rational calculation on the model of the consumer in free market economics, are the fundamental building blocks of social theory. But rather than investing the historical process with some kind of subjectivity, the analytical marxists, in spite of first appearances, end by denying any subjective element in the historical process. Their argument is that the intersecting goals of the variously motivated individuals produce a result quite different to that intended by any one, or any group, taken separately.

On this reading, one prominant analytical marxist, Jon Elster, explained that Marx's most significant finding was that history was the result of the unintended consequences of conflicting individual actions. Actually, this theory owes more to Adam Smith's hidden hand, Hegel's ruse of reason, and the determinism of the Second International than it does to Marx. Indeed, one of the founding texts of the analytical marxist tradition, G. A. Cohen's *Karl Marx's Theory of History: A Defence*, reproduced many of the characteristics of the reductionism of the Second International marxism.

The analytical marxists have little time for the dialectic conceived on any other model than this. In *An Introduction to Karl Marx*, Jon Elster discusses what is living and what is dead in the dialectic. What is living turns out to be no more than "the perverse mechanism whereby individually rational behaviour generates collectively disastrous outcomes." The destructive outcome of this process is the thing that distinguishes Marx's approach from that of Adam Smith: "Against Adam Smith's view that the self-interest of the individual and the collective interest of society need not conflict . . . Marx was more impressed by negative unintended consequences."[32] What is dead in the dialectic turns out to comprise a rather longer list. First, "there is no coherent and interesting sense in which any of the central views of Marxism are 'materialist,'" and "no Marxist philosopher has offered any useful insights on the problems of philosophical materialism."[33] Elsewhere Elster connects this analysis to the claim that "When Marx explicitly refers to dialectics, it is generally in such general, even vapid terms, that it is hard to see what implications they have for more specific analyses."[34]

Perhaps the argument in favor of a dialectical analysis will be more easily grasped if we pause for a moment to examine one "specific analysis" that Jon Elster has undertaken with the help of his own particular version of the marxist method. Shortly after the collapse of the Stalinist states in Eastern Europe, Elster wrote an essay in which he attempted to use the rigor of methodological individualism to explain this central event of the late 20th century. "When Communism dissolves" did not make a promising start:

> We shall probably never be able to understand the exact dynamics of the changes that have taken place in the Communist countries over the last year or two. The combination of motives—rational and irrational, selfish and selfless—that made for success in some cases and failure in others is almost certainly too complex to be fully unravelled.[35]

But, Elster continued, "we can at least point to some of the ingredients in the mixture, and identify some of the strategies open to the participants." Elster first examines the "four options" from which "totalitarian leaders of a country riddled with inefficiency and popular discontent" must choose a course of action: "reform, repression, inaction and pre-emption." The actions of the various rulers, from Ceausescu to Gorbachev, are then analyzed according to their place in this entirely artificial and ahistorical, scheme. In point of fact, the rulers of Eastern Europe used all these options, and others, to different degrees at different times according to the economic and social pressures on them. And, despite Elster, these pressures included the willingness of the working class and other oppositional strata to fight them.

But the inadequacy of Elster's approach does not become completely clear until he attempts to explain the rise of the popular movements that confronted the Stalinist regimes in 1989. He describes how "from Leipzig to Bucharest, we have observed the snowball effect by which crowds grow bigger from one demonstration to the next." The "internal dynamic" of this new, rigorously analytical concept—the snowball effect—is then spelled out by examining the motives of those who took part in the demonstrations:

> Some probably had nothing to lose; others may have acted on something like the categorical imperative; some may have perceived, shrewdly, that by participating in what was likely to be a small event they could have an impact on the size of future demonstrations; some may have joined for kicks: and some out of plain eccentricity.[36]

This insight is then generalized into an "explanation" of the East European revolutions:

> For each event that was announced, there was a general expectation that the number of participants would be at least as great as on the preceding occasion. For the reasons stated . . . the hesitation of some additional participants would be dissipated; and by joining, they created even higher expectations, thus inducing more people to participate in the next event, until eventually the numbers reached six figures and the regime fell.[37]

Elster makes no attempt to explain how the ideology of the popular movements might differ from the sum of the ideas of the individual participants, because his presuppositions rule out the existence of any such "collective subject." Neither can he account for the relationship between these subjective factors and the economic and social preconditions on which they rest, a task made all but impossible by his rejection of any notion of the relationship between the forces and the relations of production.[38]

Even Elster admits that "this cannot be the whole story." But his attempts to supplement it simply make his theoretical predicament even more untenable. We are told that "one factor in the explanation may be growing dissatisfaction with the economy." Another "the most important cause" is the Gorbachev doctrine of non-intervention in Eastern Europe.

Thus, Elster departs from his own "methodological individualism" only to invoke journalistic commonplaces in the most arbitrary manner. He does not seem to be aware that some explanation of the connection between economic crises and popular consciousness might be called for nor that there might be some link between the economic decline of Eastern Europe, the state of the Russian economy, and its rulers' sudden unwillingness to engage in any further police actions in Eastern Europe.

So, although they started from very different points of view, the postmodernists and the analytical marxists concur on a number of essential issues: The Hegelian marxist tradition is outmoded; the dialectic is of no, or very little, use; the working class is not the subject of history; and individual interpretation of events is the key to social theory. And because any talk of a contradiction between the forces and relations of production is illegitimate, large-scale social transformations are all but impossible to explain. Indeed, the task of social theory is to examine, with Foucault, "the microphysics of power," or, with Elster, the "microfoundations" of society. The amenability of such ideas to reformist politics, for all their apparent initial radicalism, has been increasingly obvious over the past decade.

Yet the more the complacency of these theorists has been shaken in the aftermath of the Reagan-Thatcher years—by the fall of Stalinism, by the Gulf War, by the collapse of apartheid, the civil wars in Yugoslavia and the former USSR, the rise of European neo-fascism, renewed economic crisis, and political instability—the more obvious the current impasse "radical" thought has become.

To break this impasse, a return to the classical marxist tradition will be necessary. And part of such a return, especially given the fact that so much debate in the last forty years has been fought on philosophical territory, will be a return to Marx and Engels's conception of the dialectic, later developed by Luxemburg, Lenin, Lukacs, Gramsci, and Trotsky.

FROM THEORY TO PRACTICE

Inseparable from this notion of the dialectic, in fact a constituent part of it, is an appreciation of the revolutionary potential of the working class. It is resistance to this political conclusion, as much as purely theoretical objections, that stands in the path of a renewal of marxism at every level. "The crisis," as Joseph McCarney has written, "is ultimately not one of Marxist philosophy but of Marxist social theory."[39] Yet, in spite of a valuable critique of anti-marxist theories, it is precisely on this question that McCarney, like many on the left, has the greatest doubts. In particular, many socialists doubt that the working class can any longer "meet the criteria for the revolutionary subject."[40]

Thus, even the critics of recent right-wing social theory seem to see the defeats of the 1980s as more than merely lost battles. They see in them the end of a class capable of ever mounting resistance again.[41] This is not the place to rehearse the arguments against this view. But what the existence of such pessimism does show is that any renewal in marxist philosophy can only come as part of a battle to reverse the defeats of the 1980s, rebuild the working-class movement, and so prove in practice that a revolutionary subject is still emerging in the countries at the heart of the world system.

For all the classical marxists, the question of the revolutionary potential of the working class was indissolubly linked with the need to build a revolutionary organization. Indeed, for Lenin, Luxemburg, Lukacs, Gramsci, and Trotsky, the revolutionary potential of the working class was bound not simply to the question of revolutionary organization in general, but to the need to build a "party of the new type" modeled on the Bolshevik experience. They did not win this insight lightly, and it would be wrong to discard it lightly. A revolutionary organization remains the indispensable tool for overcoming the unevenness in working-class consciousness, maximizing the effectivity of working-class struggle, recalling the lessons of past victories and defeats, and educating and leading workers in struggle. Formed from the working class by working-class people to help generalize and organize the struggle of the whole class, it is itself a dialectical organism. Without the struggle to build such an organization, the danger remains that the dialectic of capitalist development will remain blind and destructive; but if the struggle to build such an organization is successful, we have a chance—not more, not less—to make the leap from the realm of necessity to the realm of freedom.

Notes

1. Quoted in J. Saville, "Edward Thompson, the Communist Party and 1956," in *Socialist Register 1994* (London), 23.
2. Ibid., 28.
3. D. Thompson, "On the trail of the New Left," in *New Left Review* 215 (London, 1996), 98.
4. Although the former Communist Party members remained pretty much immune to Trotskyism and the later New Leftists were often as much influenced by Trotsky's interpreters, Issac Deutscher and Ernest Mandel, as by Trotsky's writings.
5. For a excellent account of this process, see C. Harman, *The Fire Last Time, 1968 and After* (London: Bookmarks, 1988).
6. M. Foucault, *Remarks on Marx* (New York: Semiotext(e), 1991), 44–45.
7. Ibid., 56–57.
8. Ibid., 106–7.
9. As Gregory Elliott's scrupulously researched study shows: *Althusser, The Detour of Theory* (London: Verso, 1988), 252–53.
10. Ibid., 274.
11. Ibid., 327.
12. Ibid., 282.
13. Ibid., 282.
14. Ibid., 282–83.
15. E. P. Thompson, *The Poverty of Theory* (London: Merlin, 1978), 196–97.
16. Ibid., 195.
17. Ibid. Thompson went on to point out that those who believed that "bits can be borrowed" from Althusser's system in the belief that "after all, we are all Marxists together" were wrong. "This is reprehensible because it is theoretically unprincipled. Althusser and his acolytes challenge, centrally, historical materialism itself. They do not offer to modify it but to displace it. In exchange they offer an a-historical theoreticism which, at the first examination, discloses itself as idealism. How then is it possible for these two to co-exist within one single tradition" (195–96).
18. See, for instance, ibid., 374–75 and 397 n. 177.
19. L. Althusser, and E. Balibar, *Reading Capital* (London: New Left Books, 1970), 40.
20. J. F. Lyotard, "Defining the Postmodern," in L. Appignanesi, *Postmodernism* (London: Free Association Books, 1989), 8–9.
21. Ibid., 9.
22. J. F. Lyotard, "Complexity and the Sublime," in L. Appignantsi, *Postmodernism*, 23–24.
23. Foucault, *Remarks on Marx*, 157.
24. Ibid., 159.
25. Ibid.
26. Christopher Norris's description of Jean Baudrillard in *Uncritical Theory* (London: Lawrence and Wishart, 1992), 11.

27. Ibid., 15.

28. See A. Callinicos, *Against Postmodernism* (Cambridge: Polity, 1989).

29. Norris, *Uncritical Theory*, 16.

30. Ibid., 31.

31. A Callinicos, "Introduction: Analytical Marxism," in A. Callinicos, ed., *Marxist Theory* (Oxford: Oxford University Press, 1989), 5.

32. J. Elster, *An Introduction to Karl Marx* (Cambridge: Cambridge University Press, 1986), 194.

33. Ibid., 190.

34. J. Elster, *Making Sense of Marx* (Cambridge: Cambridge University Press, 1985), 37.

35. J. Elster, "When Communism Dissolves," in *London Review of Books*, 25 (January 1990), 3.

36. Ibid., 4.

37. Ibid.

38. For instance, "The theory of productive forces and relations of production—perhaps the most important part of historical materialism—is dead. . . . The main objection to the view that property relations rise and fall according to their tendency to promote or hinder the development of the productive forces is that it has no microfoundations." Elster, *An Introduction to Karl Marx*, 193.

39. J. McCarney, *Social Theory and the Crisis of Marxism* (London: Verso, 1990), 189.

40. McCarney's preferred alternative is that we "look to the victims of the exploitative relationship; that is, the masses of the Third World." Ibid., 192. He is, however, careful to stress he means the exploited classes of the third world to distinguish his position from the failed third worldism of the postwar New Left.

41. There is some good work which stands against the stream. For instance, Alex Callinicos, *The Revenge of History* (Cambridge: Polity, 1991); John Molyneux, *What Is the Real Marxist Tradition?* (London: Bookmarks, 1985); Chris Harman, *The Economics of the Madhouse* (London: Bookmarks, 1995); Lindsey German, *A Question of Class* (London: Bookmarks, 1996); Stephen Perkins, *Marxism and the Proletariat, a Lukacsian perspective* (London: Pluto Press, 1993); and Paul Le Blanc, *From Marx to Gramsci* (New Jersey: Humanities Press, 1996).

Index

305

CPSIA information can be obtained at www.ICGtesting.com
Printed in the USA
BVOW041617110911

270965BV00002B/8/A